Beyond the Fence Rows

Beyond the Fence Rows

A History of Farmland Industries, Inc.
1929–1978

Gilbert C. Fite

University of Missouri Press
Columbia & London, 1978

Copyright © 1978 by Gilbert C. Fite
University of Missouri Press, Columbia, Missouri   65201
Library of Congress Catalog Card Number 78–62287
Printed and bound in the United States of America

Library of Congress Cataloging in Publication Data

Fite, Gilbert Courtland, 1918–
    Beyond the Fence Rows.

    A revised and updated edition of the author's
Farm to factory, published in 1965.
    Bibliography: p. 397
    Includes index.
    1.   Farmland Industries.   I.   Title.
HD1491.U5F57   1978   334'.5'09778411   78–62287

For
Dr. Roscoe E. Dean Jr.,
my lifelong friend,
whose roots sink deep
in the South Dakota soil

Preface

During the past century, agricultural cooperatives have shown steady and significant growth. Yet, the impact of farm supply and marketing associations on the national agricultural economy has been relatively small compared to the plans and hopes of cooperative leaders. Even in the 1970's, farmer cooperatives transacted only a modest percentage of the total farm supply and marketing business. Within the cooperative movement, however, there have been some conspicuous examples of growth and business success. The most important of these is Farmland Industries, Inc. of Kansas City, Missouri.

Established as the Union Oil Company in 1929, this small brokerage firm, which handled petroleum products on a cooperative basis, grew steadily throughout the great depression, a world war, and the economic uncertainties of the postwar years. During its first half-century this regional association expanded into a huge agribusiness conglomerate that produced and distributed petroleum products, fertilizer, agricultural chemicals, feed, and other farm supplies. The company processed and sold meat and in 1977 entered the grain-marketing business. Farmland Industries also provided a wide range of financial and management services to 2,260 member farmer cooperatives in its sixteen-state service territory. In 1977 Farmland had sales of more than $3 billion and was the nation's largest farmer cooperative. It was coming to have a substantial economic influence on the agricultural economy of the Midwest.

The business record alone warrants a study of Farmland Industries, Inc. More significant, however, is the fact that the company's history provides an important case study of the farmer cooperative movement in the United States. Here was an effort to help farmers solve the perennial cost-price squeeze. In the fight to reduce the cost of farm operations and to improve marketing conditions, this cooperative achieved a distinctive character because of its high degree of industrial and business integration. Through Farmland Industries farmers gained control of the processes of production and distribution, from the ownership of raw materials to the sale of finished products. In this respect Farmland applied the same kind of business organization, as used in a large-scale corporate business in America, to cooperative-controlled enterprise in the farm supply and marketing field. Why and how this was done are the themes of this book.

The first part of the history of Farmland Industries was published in 1965 under the title, *Farm to Factory: A History of the Consumers Cooperative Association.* That study, now out of print, carried the story to the early 1960's. However, as Farmland approached its semicentennial at the end of 1978 it seemed most appropriate to update the company history. With only minor revisions, this volume includes the same material found in the first thirteen chapters of *Farm to Factory.* Chapter 14 has been revised and reorganized. Five new chapters have been added, covering the period from 1961 to 1978.

As every historian knows, writing contemporary history is a risky undertaking. One must write without the desired perspective provided by time. But the advantages of being able to interview the main participants associated with Farmland's history offsets to a considerable extent the disadvantages of a brief historical perspective.

Neither this book nor *Farm to Factory* could have been written without the help and cooperation of everyone at Farmland Industries. The company opened its records and also provided me with a travel and research grant. Howard A. Cowden, the company's founder and guiding light until 1961 was of tremendous help in writing the initial study. He supplied many facts not found in the written record. Miss Betsy Phelan, Cowden's secretary for many years, was especially helpful in locating fugitive records that dealt with the early history of the company. Glenn S. Fox and F. R. Olmsted also assisted me with the original volume. W. Gordon Leith, Corporate Secretary, and D. E. Ewing, Treasurer, made materials available and extended lengthy interviews that were extremely useful as I wrote both the earlier work and the revision. Former President Homer Young took time out from a comfortable retirement to discuss many important issues with me, and President Ernest T. Lindsey was liberal with his time and the historical data in his office. Vice-President Robert L. Beasley and Bill Matteson, Executive Director, Communication Services, offered every assistance and opened up many doors. Harold Hamil, former Vice-President, Information and Public Relations, assisted in a number of ways with both *Farm to Factory* and with the sequel. Scores of others, including company executives, secretaries, and staff people were all generous with their time. Some of them spent hours researching our statistics and other records. Ms. Janelle Andrews was especially helpful.

I am most appreciative, however, for the assistance of Ms. Nellie Mae Crank who has done more than anyone else to develop and maintain the company's historical records. She guided me to unknown but rewarding sources, found fugitive materials, reproduced records, and helped in many other ways. I am greatly in her debt. My research assistants, David D. Potenziani and Edward C. Nagy, helped in many ways and without them the project would have taken much longer. The book could not have been completed, of course, without the work of my typist, Mrs. Edna Fisher. To her I am most grateful.

G. C. F.
Athens, Georgia
April, 1978

Contents

Original Farmland Industries, Inc. headquarters, the "two-car garage," 1721 Iron Street, North Kansas City, Missouri, 1929.

The expanded headquarters, 1933

Farmland Industries headquarters, 1500 Iron Street, 1935.
In the background is the bluff where the new headquarters
building was constructed in 1956.

Board of Directors of the Union Oil Company (Farmland Industries),
1931. They are, left to right: BACK ROW: Howard A. Cowden, Kansas
City, Mo.; R. A. Hedding, Burlington, Colo.; Joe E. Nicholl, Hitchcock,
S.D.; Thomas H. DeWitt, Green City, Mo.; J. E. Rise, Scranton, N.D.;
S. S. Ebbert, Quinter, Kans. FRONT ROW: W. A. (Bill) Kearns, Kahoka,
Mo.;E. A. Backus, Wray, Colo.; O. C. Servis, Winfield, Kans.; R. J. (Bob)
Ackley, Garden City, Kans.; H. E. (Harry) Witham, Kansas City, Mo.;
A. W. Gale, Chillicothe, Mo.

Farmland's "Co-op" building in downtown Kansas City, 1944

Phillipsburg oil refinery, Kansas, 1940

Farmland Industries' oil refinery at Coffeyville, Kansas

Dedication of Phillipsburg oil refinery, May 4, 1940.
(Cowden and Ralph Snyder)

A local co-op's equipment to serve farmer members, July, 1959

Crawford County Packing Company, Denison, Iowa, 1959.
Farmland's first entry into the red meat business.

The Cooperative Farm Chemicals Association's nitrogen plant at Lawrence, Kansas. Seventy-five per cent owned by Farmland Industries.

Farmland offshore oil-exploration rig off the Texas gulf coast

Ham-canning facility of Farmland Foods' plant in Carroll, Iowa

Farmland's grease-manufacturing facility, North Kansas City, Missouri

Activity at one of Farmland's swine-testing stations, Lisbon, Iowa

Modern cooperative farm and home service center

Local cooperative tank wagon delivery to farmer member

One of Farmland's modern feed mills

Far-Mar-Co's grain terminal in Hutchinson, Kansas

Local cooperative grain elevator with fertilizer, feed, and propane service for members

Farmland Training Center

Farmland Industries, Board of Directors, 1978. They are, left to right: FRONT
ROW: Keith M. Voigt, general manager, Boone Valley Co-op Processing Associa-
tion, Eagle Grove, Iowa; Ralph Ball, farmer-stockman, Sterling, Kans.; Doyle N.
Smith, general manager, Monte Vista Co-op Association, Monte Vista, Colo.;
Roy Chelf, chairman of the board, general manager, Panhandle Co-op Associa-
tion, Scottsbluff, Nebr.; William E. Rice, farmer, Baldwin, Kans.; Allen Schroe-
der, general manager, Farmers Co-op Mercantile Co., Leigh, Nebr.; Don T.
Kirby, farmer, Lamont, Okla.; Homer J. Norem, farmer, Newark, Ill.; and
Roger R. Clark, farmer, Brady, Nebr. BACK ROW: David L. Williams, farmer,
Villisca, Iowa; Philip Hand, farmer, Center Point, Iowa; Edgar N. Petty,
farmer, Kearney, Mo.; Francis B. Gwin, general manager, Farmway Coopera-
tive, Beloit, Kans.; James M. Moen, general manager, Kindred Oil Co., Kindred,
N.D.; Roland R. White, general manager, Aurora Co-op Elevator Co., Aurora,
Nebr.; Albert Schramm, general manager, Farmers Co-op Oil Association,
Winner, S.D.; Frank Lightner, farmer, Garden City, Kans.; Dan Quigley,
farmer, Olton, Tex.; Jere O. West, general manager, Crescent Co-op Association, Crescent, Okla.; Vaughn O. Sinclair, general manager, Watonwan Farm
Service Co., St. James, Minn.; Ted Sutter, vice-chairman, farmer, Eaton, Colo.;
and Ernest T. Lindsey, president and chief executive officer, Liberty, Mo.

Farmland Industries annual meeting, Kansas City, Missouri

Farmland Industries, Inc. headquarters building,
3315 North Oak Trafficway, North Kansas City, Missouri

Farmer cooperative member applying nitrogen fertilizer to a field in the
shadow of Farmland's Fort Dodge, Iowa, nitrogen plant.

Howard A. Cowden, founder and president of
Farmland Industries, Inc., 1929–1961

Homer Young, Farmland's president, 1961–1967

Ernest T. Lindsey, Farmland's president, 1967–

D. E. Ewing, financial vice-president and treasurer, 1933–

W. Gordon Leith, corporate vice-president and secretary, 1949–

Chapter 1

Farm Problems
and the Cooperative Movement,
1865-1920

I<small>T WAS NOVEMBER</small> 30, 1977. More than 20,000 farmers, farmer cooperative employees, company officials and visitors were gathered for the 49th annual meeting of Farmland Industries, Inc. in Kansas City. The earlier struggle of the farmer cooperative movement was only history to most of those in attendance. President Ernest T. Lindsey reported that Farmland Industries' total sales for the fiscal year ending August 31, 1977, had exceeded $3 billion and net savings before income taxes had reached $79 million. Some $38 million was paid in cash patronage refunds to member cooperatives. Farmland Industries had become the largest farmer cooperative in the United States and represented a growing role of supply and marketing cooperatives in American agriculture. For about a century farmers had been trying to improve their economic position by organizing cooperatives which they hoped would give them greater power in the market place. They had not fully achieved that objective, but the history of Farmland Industries demonstrates a degree of success never dreamed possible fifty years earlier.

Beginning in the late 1860's, American farmers entered a long period of depression which, with brief respites, lasted until near the end of the century. The basic difficulty was that farmers produced more than both domestic and foreign markets could absorb at prices profitable to the producers. Rapid expansion into the western prairies and Great Plains was responsible for an enormous expansion of both acreage and production between 1860 and 1910. For example, in that half century farm acreage more than doubled, increasing from 407 to 878 million acres. Production of basic crops more than kept pace with this growth of acreage. The output of wheat rose from 173 million bushels in 1859 to 657 million in 1909, while cotton production nearly doubled during those years. There were nearly two and a half times as many cattle on American farms in 1910 as there had been fifty years earlier.

Expansion of acreage was only one factor responsible for the greatly increased output of agricultural commodities after the Civil War. New and better machinery aided practically every phase of farm production. Improved planters, cultivators, harvesters, threshers, and other machines contributed to greater efficiency in agricultural production. The investment in machinery by United States farmers multiplied by five between 1860 and 1910. New crops, the use of fertilizers, and the application of science to agriculture, especially after 1900, also helped to expand the productive capacity of American farms.

The heavy production of farm commodities resulted in steadily declining prices, with only occasional profitable years between 1870 and 1897. In 1866 wheat brought farmers $1.52 a bushel, but by 1894 the average farm price had dropped to only 49 cents; cotton, which commanded 18 cents a pound in 1871, brought less than 5 cents in 1894; corn became so cheap in some western states in the late 1880's and early 1890's that farmers burned it for fuel. Producers often experienced the paradox of receiving less money for a good crop than for a poor one; for example, the bumper wheat crop of 515 million bushels in 1892 brought several million dollars less than the 399-million-bushel crop of 1890. In short, farmers suffered from the problems created by surplus products.

During years of hard times, farmers complained about high interest rates, excessive transportation charges, monopolistic control of livestock and grain-marketing facilities, and tight money. In many instances there were just and abundant reasons for these complaints. Interest rates ranged from 8 to 12 per cent on real estate mortgages in some of the western states, and mortgages on chattels carried interest charges as high as 20 and 25 per cent. Railroads lowered their freight rates in the late nineteenth century, but at points where no competition existed it was common to charge all that the traffic would bear. As a Nebraskan wrote in 1890, his state had three crops: "One is a crop of corn, one is a crop of freight rates, and one is a crop of interest." Processors like Armour and Swift determined the prices received for livestock, and grain-marketing facilities were mostly in the hands of the railroads or a relatively few grain merchants. Over all, the farmers were in an unfavorable position.[1]

Despite the specific grievances about which farmers grumbled, other more basic factors handicapped agriculture in the post-Civil War years. In the first place, farming was a highly competitive enterprise in an economy in which business and industry were stabilizing their positions through pools, trusts, holding companies, and other types of combination. By these means industrialists were able to reduce or eliminate the downward pressure on prices exerted by competition. Industrialists sought with some success to regulate the prices of their products either by agreement or by gaining control of a large share of the market. For example, by 1890 Standard Oil Company controlled about 90 per cent of the oil refining business and consequently could establish the price of the kerosene that was used by millions of consumers, including farmers. Labor also gained a measure of control over wages by combining in unions. Farmers, on the other hand, acted individually and competed with one another for the available markets.

In this connection, farmers were at a further disadvantage because they could not control production as could industrial producers. A manufacturer of farm machines would determine the market for reapers and then gear his output to meet that demand. He usually did not manufacture more than could be sold at a profitable price. But a farmer could not start and stop production like a manufacturer. Even if agricultural producers regulated their acreage, they could not rigidly control output. Total production varied because of weather conditions, damage from insects, and productivity of the soil. Thus, if millions of farmers should agree on the amount of a commodity to be produced and to be sold at profitable prices, there was no certainty that they could achieve their aim. Farmers, however, did not even try to set production goals. They took the position that so long as people were hungry anywhere in the world, no genuine surplus existed.

---

[1] For farm problems in the late nineteenth century, see Fred A. Shannon, *The Farmer's Last Frontier, Agriculture, 1860–1897* (New York, 1945), Chapters 8, 13, and 14; John D. Hicks, *The Populist Revolt* (Minneapolis, 1931), Chapter 3.

Farmers produced blindly, paying little or no attention to what other agriculturists were doing. As a result, agricultural output continued large between the Civil War and World War I, and unprofitable prices prevailed during much of the period.

The result of this situation was to place farmers in an unfair price relationship with other economic groups. The prices they received for agricultural commodities were low, compared to the prices they paid for industrial goods. The price of a farm product is not so important in itself; what matters most to the farmer is the exchange value of his commodities. Stated otherwise, how great a quantity of industrial goods will a bushel of wheat or a pound of cotton buy? If a harvester, for example, costs $250 and wheat sells for $2 a bushel, it takes 125 bushels to pay for the machine. But if wheat drops to $1 a bushel and the price of a harvester remains the same, 250 bushels are required to pay for it. An unfavorable exchange value between farm and nonfarm commodities was basic to many of the farmer's problems in the late nineteenth century. This condition was referred to by mid-twentieth-century farmers as "the cost-price squeeze."

So long as farmers operated on an individual, competitive basis, they were in no position to establish a favorable economic relationship with industry except during a few years that were certainly not typical. In the first place, the farmer had no control over the prices that he received for his commodities. When, for example, he took his wheat to the elevator, he had to accept the price set by someone else; when he went to buy groceries, machinery, lumber, and other supplies, he had to pay prices determined by others. With no control over the prices that he received for his products or over those that he paid for nonfarm goods, the farmer found himself in a most disadvantageous position. He was one of the few businessmen who suffered from such a situation.[2]

As farming became more commercialized, the price relationship between farm and nonfarm goods increased in significance. So long as a farmer ground his own wheat and made flour for his family, the price was not so important. Wheat which brought only 50 cents a bushel was as filling and nourishing as that which commanded $3. But when he sold the wheat and bought flour or any other commodity

[2] Theodore Saloutos, "The Agricultural Problem and Nineteenth-Century Industrialism," *Agricultural History*, XXII (July, 1948), 156–74; E. A. Allen, *Labor and Capital* (Cincinnati, 1891), 188–89; Gilbert C. Fite and Jim E. Reese, *An Economic History of the United States*, 2d ed. (Boston, 1965), 433–42.

produced off the farm, the amount of money that he received for wheat or whatever he sold was of utmost importance. In the late nineteenth century, commercialized and specialized farmers sold their products and bought more manufactured goods, such as machinery and lumber. In other words, what the economist calls nonfarm inputs were figuring more prominently in living and production expenses. Any reduction in the cost of these inputs would help the farmer by that much. It was here that consumers' cooperatives entered the picture.

What could farmers do about their basic economic problems? In the 1870's leaders of the Grange demanded government control and regulation of the railroads, and by the late 1880's many farmers were calling for government ownership of railroads and telephone and telegraph lines. Government control of industrial monopolies was advocated by Grangers, Populists, and other agrarian groups. It was argued, too, that inflation of the currency through the free and unlimited coinage of silver would raise prices and help depression-ridden farmers. The campaign for free silver became so strong among agrarians that William Jennings Bryan and the Democrats made it the principal issue in the presidential campaign of 1896. A large number of farmers came to believe that government action was necessary to help them achieve a better economic position in an economy that was becoming increasingly urban and industrial.

While many farmers clamored for some kind of governmental assistance for agriculture, others looked to self-help through cooperative effort. These farmers believed that they could increase their bargaining power by collective or group action. If producers would organize, it was argued, they could exert some influence on the prices that they received for their produce, and if farmers would cooperate as consumers they could buy their nonfarm commodities at cheaper prices. By cooperative action it was hoped that manufacturers would be forced to lower their prices and that the middleman's margin on the sale of agricultural produce might be reduced or eliminated. The cooperative ideal, then, was stimulated by farm grievances against the business community. These complaints included lack of competition among buyers of farm products, high prices for manufactured goods, poor service, dishonest grading, short weights, excessive commissions, and charges by middlemen.

Some attempts had been made at both producer and consumer cooperation, mostly by workingmen, in the pre-Civil War years. But it was the Grange, or Patrons of Husbandry, which first promoted the principles of agricultural cooperation on a national scale as a means of improving the business position of farmers. Founded in 1867 by Oliver H. Kelley, the Grange had as one of its major objectives the cutting of marketing costs and the price of supplies for the farmer.[3] When farmers inquired about the financial benefits that they might expect from their support of the Grange, organizers explained that cooperative plans of buying and selling would bring dollars-and-cents rewards.

In order to purchase supplies at better prices, members of the Grange banded together, combined their orders, and appointed a local agent to buy in volume from jobbers and manufacturers. For example, farmers in a community might buy a carload of lumber or a dozen or more reapers and get them at reduced prices because of the quantity. When the shipment arrived, farmers would take delivery on whatever they had ordered, thus bypassing the usual middlemen and commission agents.

Following the organization of local groups, state agencies were formed to buy and ship farm produce and to purchase supplies for patrons on a bulk basis. As early as May, 1872, Kelley addressed a letter to manufacturers of farm machinery, asking them to submit price lists for equipment and explaining that the Grange wanted to save the commissions usually paid to agents "and the profits of the long line of dealers standing between the manufacturers and the farmers."[4] The state Grange agent in Iowa bought thousands of dollars' worth of reapers directly from the manufacturers and sold them to patrons at a considerable saving on the usual retail price. It was estimated that in 1873 the Grangers saved 15 per cent on family supplies and 20 per cent on farm machinery by purchasing through their state agent and local associations. The Iowa Grange was so successful as a buying agent that in 1875 it embarked upon a program to manufacture farm machinery. If savings could be made through cooperative purchasing, Grange officials reasoned, even more benefits could be derived from manufacturing the products. However, this project failed because of

---

[3] On the cooperative activities of the Grange, see Solon J. Buck, *The Granger Movement* (Cambridge, 1913); O. H. Kelley, *The History of the Patrons of Husbandry* (Philadelphia, 1875); Edward W. Martin, *History of the Grange Movement* (Chicago, 1874); Carl C. Taylor, *The Farmers' Movement, 1620–1920* (New York, 1953), 149–71. George Cerny, "Cooperation in the Midwest in the Granger Era, 1869–1875," *Agricultural History*, XXXVII (October, 1963), 187–205.

[4] Kelley, *The History of the Patrons of Husbandry*, 385.

lack of capital, patent infringement suits, and other factors, and failure in this business enterprise hastened the decline of the Grange in Iowa. Meanwhile, in many parts of the country producer cooperatives were organized to market grain, livestock, and fruit. In some cases the cost of selling farm products was measurably reduced through cooperation.

Despite some temporary success, most of the agency systems ultimately failed, and many Grange members lost faith in this means of solving their purchasing problems. After all, the agency was a flimsy organization that did not provide for an efficient system of distribution. The national Grange then began encouraging the establishment of cooperative stores. At first these Grange stores sold goods at reduced prices and consequently aroused the enmity and opposition of local merchants. However, in a short while many of these stores were organized around the Rochdale ideas of cooperation as inaugurated by the workingmen of Rochdale, England, in 1844.

The main principles of the Rochdale cooperators were: (1) membership was open for all; (2) each member was entitled to only one vote regardless of how many shares of stock he held in the cooperative corporation; (3) stock or share capital carried a limited, but fixed, return; (4) the profits, or what cooperators called net savings, were returned to the patrons in refunds on the basis of the volume of business done with the cooperative. The Rochdale cooperatives did not cut prices below the established level, thereby hoping to reduce the opposition of business interests. Since patronage refunds were distributed according to the amount of business done by each patron, members received what amounted to a reduction of prices when they got their share of the savings at the end of the year. The refunds to members also encouraged patrons to deal with their own cooperative.[5]

Hundreds of cooperative stores were established by local granges in the middle 1870's. The Grange also extended its business ventures to insurance companies and banks. In Ohio the Cincinnati Grange Supply House was set up to supply goods to local granges and cooperatives in Ohio and surrounding states. This was one of the earliest antecedents of the modern regional cooperative wholesale. Many of the Grange cooperatives were not organized entirely on Rochdale principles, but farmers gained valuable experience in cooperative effort from these enterprises.

---

[5] Florence E. Parker, *The First 125 Years* (Superior, Wisconsin, 1956), xv.

Unfortunately, however, within a few years most of the cooperatives sponsored by the Grange failed. The attempts of farmers to achieve economic independence and prosperity by trying to eliminate the charges of middlemen and even by manufacturing needed supplies through cooperative effort had a dreary history of failure. The principle of increasing their bargaining power with other elements in the economy was sound, but the means to achieve this objective were poorly developed and clearly inadequate.

The cooperatives sponsored by the Grange did not succeed for a variety of reasons. In the first place, most of the enterprises lacked sufficient capital, and this lack was especially damaging when they attempted to operate on a larger scale. In many instances, too, farmers entered business schemes about which they knew very little or which did not lend themselves to cooperative operation. Management of the cooperatives was often poor; it was not uncommon for a farmer who had little business experience to be placed in charge of a local cooperative. Bad business decisions ruined many cooperative enterprises. Even though the Grange encouraged farmers to operate on a cash basis, one of the most damaging weaknesses in the management of cooperatives was the excessive extension of credit, which often resulted in bankruptcy.

But an even greater problem was the lack of genuine cooperative spirit among the individualistic American farmers. This is a difficult factor to analyze quantitatively, but evidence is found everywhere that farmers did not believe strongly in the cooperative ideal. Unwilling to forego immediate gains for long-range benefits, farmers often would purchase commodities from a competitor of their own cooperative if the price were a few cents lower.

Nonetheless, the Grange cooperatives contributed positive, if somewhat limited, results to the infant agricultural cooperative movement in the United States. Some farmers were educated in cooperative principles, and they came to accept the cooperative philosophy and methods of doing business. The activities of the Grange had shown the economic values that farmers could achieve if they worked together. Moreover, a few of the cooperatives were successful; they saved patrons money in buying and selling, demonstrating that farmers need not be helpless in their dealings with businessmen.

The failure of most of the Grange cooperatives did not kill the desire of farmers to improve their economic position by gaining control of buying and selling their products. The Farmers Alliance, which started in Texas in 1874 and in Illinois in 1880, included cooperative business enterprises as a vital part of its program. Like the Grangers, Farmers Alliance members suffered from the gross exactions of middlemen and from the manipulation of agricultural markets. Alliance groups developed cooperative stores, insurance companies, and other businesses, all designed to save money for rural consumers. The agent system was also tried, and there were a few attempts to enter manufacturing. The Dakota Farmers' Alliance Company, set up in July, 1887, sought to save farmers money by purchasing supplies in wholesale lots. It bought coal, binder twine, and other commodities that were in turn sold to consumers through local cooperatives and Alliance agents. The Texas Farmers Alliance developed a program of group selling, and the Texas Exchange was set up to handle a large variety of goods required by farmers.[6]

By the late 1880's Alliance men in both the North and South were carrying on many cooperative business activities. However, as the Farmers Alliance became more concerned with political objectives in the early 1890's, interest in cooperative enterprises declined, and many of the cooperatives failed for much the same reasons as had those of the Grange. But, despite these failures, farmers gained further experience in cooperative economic activities. Only a small number of the purchasing cooperatives were based on Rochdale principles, but this type of organization was gaining favor with farmers by the end of the nineteenth century.

In 1902 James A. Everitt established the American Society of Equity at Indianapolis. Everitt's main idea was to regulate the production and marketing of agricultural products in order to achieve "equitable prices" for farmers. He saw the crux of the farmer's problem as control of production and sales. But farmers did not readily respond to plans for restriction of production, so a sharp split developed in the Equity between Everitt's followers and those who wanted the organization to sponsor business cooperatives. In 1907 C. M. Barrett of Kentucky was elected president of the group, and within a short time local and state units of the loosely knit Equity began forming both marketing and consumer cooperative associations. Hundreds of cooperative stores were established in the north central states. By 1913 there were about fifty cooperative stores in

---

[6] Hicks, *The Populist Revolt*, pp. 96–152; Taylor, *The Farmers' Movement*, 226–43; Martin A. Abrahamsen and Claud L. Scroggs, eds., *Agricultural Cooperation* (Minneapolis, 1957), 16–21.

Wisconsin alone, and most of these businesses were organized on Rochdale cooperative principles. The Equity Cooperative Exchange, a buying and selling agency, was set up in 1908, and in 1916 a terminal elevator in St. Paul began to serve the many cooperative elevators established by the Equity in the north central states. At about the same time the Equity started to market livestock and wool. The Equity Cooperative Exchange ultimately failed, and many of the local cooperative stores also went out of business.[7]

Despite poor business leadership and internal conflicts, the Equity left its mark on both the producer and consumer phases of the farm cooperative movement. Additional cooperative experience had helped to educate farmers about the needs and methods of more efficient buying and selling. The Equity was important in the history of cooperatives because it served as a training ground for many of the leaders who later established successful cooperative marketing and purchasing associations, and two of the earliest cooperatives to affiliate with the Consumers Cooperative Association had been established by the Equity. They were the Garden City Co-op Equity Exchange of Garden City, Kansas, and the Equity Cooperative Exchange at Burlington, Colorado.

Meanwhile, the Grange, the newly organized Farmers Educational and Cooperative Union of America, and the budding farm bureaus were promoting business cooperation among farmers. By 1913 the Farmers Union, which had been established in 1902, had 125 cooperative stores in Missouri and a substantial number in Kansas, Nebraska, and other states. In order to supply the growing number of local cooperatives, state and regional wholesales were formed. The Farmers Union State Exchange was organized in Omaha in 1914, and the Cooperative Central Exchange was set up at Superior, Wisconsin, three years later. These wholesales, along with numerous others, were soon supplying their local members with hundreds of thousands of dollars' worth of goods annually. They handled groceries, fencing, lumber, binder twine, and many other commodities used by farmers. One of the most successful wholesales was the Cooperative Grange League Federation, incorporated in New York during June, 1920. Organized with the joint support of the Grange, the Dairymen's League, and the New York State Federation of Farm

---

[7] Theodore Saloutos and John D. Hicks, *Agricultural Discontent in the Middle West, 1900–1939* (Madison, Wisconsin, 1951), 56–86, 111–48; Taylor, *The Farmers' Movement*, 391–410.

Bureau Associations, the Cooperative Grange League Federation planned to supply high-quality feeds to New York dairymen.[8] At the same time that the cooperative movement was advancing in the Midwest and Northeast, associations were being formed in California and the Pacific Northwest.

S. J. Lowell, Master of the New York State Grange, declared in January, 1917, that "no one thing receives so much discussion and in no one thing has there been less accomplished than in rural cooperation."[9] Lowell may have been right. But in the generation before World War I, farmers in many sections of the United States had participated in cooperative business ventures. These years of cooperative experience, many of them filled with failure, did much to educate farmers in the problems as well as the values of group economic action. A foundation, somewhat weak to be sure, had been laid by 1920 on which to build both producer and consumer cooperation. Some farmers were disillusioned at the cooperatives' failures, but there was a substantial core of local, state, and national leaders who kept presenting economic cooperation as the best way to solve the farmers' chief problems.

In 1923 the Bureau of Labor Statistics published a survey, *Consumers' Cooperative Societies in the United States in 1920*. This study differentiated between strictly consumer cooperatives, which served both rural and urban patrons, and so-called "agricultural societies," which did both a cooperative marketing and purchasing business, primarily for farmers. There were, according to the survey, 696 consumers' cooperatives and 270 agricultural societies, and they reported a membership of 260,000. About two-thirds of the cooperative societies and three-fifths of the total membership were in middle western states. In 1920 the cooperatives which reported on their transactions did $80 million worth of business, operating mostly on Rochdale principles.[10] A clearer idea can be gained of the cooperative movement in the Midwest by looking at Kansas, which had the largest number of cooperatively operated businesses in the nation. In that state the local co-

[8] Joseph G. Knapp, *Seeds That Grew, A History of the Cooperative Grange League Federation Exchange* (Hinsdale, New York, 1960), Chapters 5 and 6.

[9] *Ibid.*, 20.

[10] Florence E. Parker, *Consumers' Cooperative Societies in the United States in 1920*, Bureau of Labor Statistics, Bulletin No. 313 (Washington, 1923). Hundreds of known cooperative societies did not report to the Bureau of Labor Statistics in 1920. It was estimated that all cooperatives in the United States may have done as much as $285 million worth of business that year. See page 81.

operatives averaged about $93,000 worth of business annually, or $469 per member. Strong cooperative societies also operated in Nebraska, Wisconsin, and Minnesota. In considering the subsequent establishment of the Consumers Cooperative Association in Kansas City, it is important to keep in mind that by World War I the cooperative movement had achieved its greatest strength in the Midwest.

The national cooperative movement received momentum in 1908 when President Theodore Roosevelt's Country Life Commission recommended expansion of farm cooperative enterprises. Furthermore, the Cooperative League of the United States of America, established in March, 1916, to promote cooperative principles on a nationwide basis, did much to publicize cooperative effort and activity. James P. Warbasse, a medical doctor, became head of the League, and for many years he was one of the country's leading propagandists for consumer cooperation. Although consumer cooperatives made some headway in the cities, by 1920 about two-thirds of them were established in small towns for the benefit of farm patrons.

By 1920 cooperative business associations had begun to gain special recognition by both state and national lawmakers. Although states had earlier passed laws relating to cooperatives, it was not until 1911 that Nebraska and Wisconsin took the lead in enacting legislation especially benefiting cooperatives. These measures, together with laws subsequently passed by other states, defined a cooperative corporation and outlined rules for its operation. For example, the Wisconsin law stated that, in order for a corporation to use the name "cooperative," it had to be organized by not less than five members, no member could own more than $1,000 of the capital stock, each member had only one vote, and distribution of the dividends and net earnings must be made according to law.[11] Moreover, cooperatives were given special recognition in the Clayton Antitrust Act of 1914, which exempted farm organizations from the federal antitrust statutes. But it was the Capper-Volstead Act of 1922 that assured cooperatives freedom from antitrust action.

Following World War I new elements appeared in the expense accounts of many farmers — gasoline, oil, and grease for the rapidly increasing number of tractors, trucks, and automobiles. In 1920 there were 246,083 tractors on American farms, but by 1925 this number had risen to 505,933 and by 1930 to 920,021. There were also about

[11] *Ibid.*, Appendix A, "General Features of State Laws," 88 ff.

900,000 trucks on farms in 1930. In the west north central states 13.6 per cent of the farms had tractors by 1925. The oats and hay that farmers customarily raised to feed their work animals were of no use in powering the iron horse. The need for gasoline and oil increased the farmers' dependence on nonfarm inputs in their production, and this in turn increased the cash cost of agricultural operations. While many farmers were demanding federal relief in the 1920's, and others supported large-scale marketing cooperatives, a small minority began to attack at least one aspect of their immediate problems by establishing cooperative oil companies.

The Farmers Union Cooperative Association of Mitchell County, Kansas, was the earliest known attempt by farmers to handle petroleum products cooperatively. In 1913 the Mitchell County association operated elevators, stores, cream stations, and a service station that handled "coal oil [kerosene] and gasoline."[12] The few cooperatives that originally dealt in gasoline and oil did so in conjunction with an elevator or some other business. For example, the Farmers Union Elevator Company, which opened in 1920 at Hazelton, North Dakota, established an oil department that continued operating even after the elevator closed.

The first cooperative association formed to handle petroleum products exclusively was the Cottonwood Oil Company of Cottonwood, Minnesota. It was organized on July 7, 1921.[13] Before the end of the year several other cooperative oil companies were established, and within four or five years Minnesota, Wisconsin, Nebraska, Kansas, Colorado, and other states were dotted with cooperative oil associations. Most of these companies were organized on Rochdale principles and enjoyed success from the beginning. They distributed quality products at regular market prices and saved money for their patrons. In 1926 several of the local cooperative associations joined forces to form the Minnesota CO-OP Oil Company, with an office in Minneapolis. This was essentially a wholesale firm that supplied products to individual cooperatives throughout the state and also provided advisory and bookkeeping services to the locals. By 1928 the Minnesota CO-OP Oil Company did about $400,000 worth of business.[14]

The oil cooperatives achieved unusual results, especially when com-

---

[12] Parker, *The First 125 Years*, 44.
[13] Minnesota CO-OP Oil Company, *The Co-operative Oil Movement in the Northwest* (n.d., n.p.,), 1, pamphlet, Howard A. Cowden Papers.
[14] *Ibid.*, 2–4.

pared to some other kinds of cooperative businesses. Several factors contributed to this record of success. In the first place, practically all farmers used some kind of petroleum products. Even those who did not operate a tractor purchased grease for their horse-drawn machinery and kerosene for lamps. More important in the success of the oil cooperatives, however, was the fact that distributing oil, gasoline, kerosene, and grease was a fairly simple business operation. Management had to deal with only a few products, and capital requirements were relatively small. A study made of nineteen cooperative oil companies in Minnesota and Wisconsin in 1927 showed that the average investment in equipment was only $10,500.[15] Many oil associations began business with much less. Capital was raised by selling stock, usually in shares valued at $10 or $25, and by reinvesting part of the annual savings. Cooperative stock bore a fixed rate of return, commonly 6 to 8 per cent.

Equipment for the average bulk plant included tanks for gasoline and kerosene, a cheap, warehouse-type building for oil and grease, a tank truck to deliver products to farmers, pumps to unload gasoline from the tank cars, and office space. Once established, the cooperative simply contracted for petroleum products in bulk quantities and resold them to local customers. If the cooperative had efficient management and controlled credit sales, chances for success were high.

From the outset, oil cooperatives maintained regular prices set by the major companies and then refunded the profits or savings to patrons on the basis of the volume of business each had done with the cooperative. Stockholders received patronage refunds in cash, but nonmembers got their refunds in the form of credit on a share of stock. When the credits built up to the value of a share of stock, the nonmember became a shareholder eligible for cash refunds.

Not only were the business operations of cooperative oil companies fairly simple, but the wide margins between wholesale and retail prices of gasoline and oil helped petroleum cooperatives to prosper. It was this wide margin of profit, sometimes as high as 8 to 10 cents a gallon on gasoline, that prompted farmers to establish cooperative oil businesses. They rightly believed that large savings could be made. Even when the major oil companies cut retail prices in an attempt to destroy the cooperatives, the local associations were usually able to meet the competition and still pay patronage dividends. The study

---

[15] D. E. Montgomery, *Co-operative Oil Marketing in Wisconsin and Minnesota*, Wisconsin Department of Markets Bulletin, Vol. 8 (Madison, August 15, 1927).

of Minnesota and Wisconsin cooperative oil companies showed that they did well from the beginning of operations.[16] Experience of the oil associations in the 1920's proved that farmer-owned purchasing cooperatives could successfully provide many of the most important services and products needed in agricultural production.

The consumers' cooperative movement that developed in the United States was antimonopolistic in philosophy and outlook. By the 1920's cooperators had not completely abandoned their earlier trust-busting attitudes, but practical experience had shown them that this kind of campaign did not reduce the powers of large-scale, corporate business. Consequently, while still repeating the Granger and Populist antimonopoly rhetoric, cooperative supporters argued that farmers could best protect their interests by joining together. In this action they tacitly accepted the growing collectivist tendencies in American economic life and planned to use the united power of farmers to gain specific buying and marketing benefits for individual producers.

The cooperative movement was not anticapitalistic, however. From the outset, farmers organized and joined their cooperatives as a means of reducing the economic toll exacted by monopolies and middlemen. They were primarily interested in immediate dollars-and-cents benefits. Farmers did not view the formation of cooperatives as an aspect of reform. The idea of establishing a so-called cooperative commonwealth was foreign to the desires of most cooperators. In other words, supporters of the cooperative movement did not anticipate, or work toward, changes in the nation's fundamental social and economic structure. When farmers were asked why they joined a cooperative, they usually replied that they expected cheaper prices, patronage refunds, better service, or higher quality products. These were immediate and practical advantages. Most cooperative leaders were committed to farming as a way of life, but they believed that this way of life could be made more prosperous and satisfying through the organization and operation of cooperatives. Members viewed their cooperatives as a special type of business organization which would be more efficient and provide greater financial rewards than a noncooperative business, and the cooperative that could not meet these standards seldom had a long history. The success with which the Consumers Cooperative Association met the tests of service and fair prices is largely responsible for its achievements as a regional wholesale cooperative.

---

[16] *Ibid.*

Chapter 2

Howard A. Cowden:
The Beginning of a Career
in Agricultural Cooperation

BY THE 1920's conditions seemed favorable for the organization of a regional cooperative wholesale in the Kansas City trade area. Many local cooperative associations had been established by farmers in nearby Kansas and Nebraska, and the movement was growing in Missouri. Too, farmers had experienced at least a limited education in the principles of cooperative economic effort. Among the strong believers in cooperatives was Howard A. Cowden. He envisioned a future in which cooperatives would be supplying a large percentage of the things farmers used in the home and in production. By 1929 he decided to commit all of his time and energy to this cause.

Howard A. Cowden, the sixth son in a family of eight boys and one girl, was born at Pleasant Hope in southwestern Missouri on May 18, 1893. His parents, John Porter and Margaret Burns Cowden, were both of Scotch descent; their ancestors had reached Missouri through North Carolina and Tennessee. The Cowdens lived on the farm that had been settled by Howard's grandfather. Young Cowden spent all of his early life there, except for two years when the family resided in Bolivar where his father served as tax collector.

Howard's early life was not unlike that of many other rural youths at the turn of the century — hard work from early morning until late at night. He milked cows, fed hogs, and toiled in the fields. When he was not helping at home, Cowden attended the Pleasant Hope grade school. John Porter Cowden believed in the values of education. All of his sons completed high school, and some of them attended college. In September, 1909, Howard enrolled in classes in civics, history, English, algebra, and agriculture at the local high school. His record reveals that he was a capable and conscientious student. All of his grades were good, but his highest marks were in civics and history.[1]

But not all of his education was gained in the classroom. Work on the farm provided practical knowledge and skills, and the Cowden home supplied books, periodicals, and newspapers to broaden the interests and outlook of the growing family. Howard spent long winter evenings poring over William Jennings Bryan's *Commoner, Colman's Rural World,* and other publications that arrived regularly in the mail. The religious training that was stressed in the Cowdens' home was strengthened by the formal instruction in the local Cumberland Presbyterian church. To round out these early experiences, young Cowden was able to indulge his fondness for sports; he won several prizes in local track meets, and during his high school years he achieved some fame around Bolivar as a baseball pitcher.

General farming predominated on the gently rolling prairies of Polk County. Corn, oats, and wheat were the principal crops, and farmers raised hogs, cattle, poultry, and some sheep. In 1900 the average size of farms in the county was small — only 98 acres — but the Cowden holdings were far greater. Their 500-acre farm, part of which lay in the Pomme de Terre River bottom, was among the dozen largest in the county.[2] Howard's father was a progressive farmer who believed that brains were as important as brawn in agricultural operations. The new ideas that were coming out of the United States Department of Agriculture under the administration of Secretary James Wilson excited him. He read about improved crops, fertilizers, livestock breeding, and other developments that seemed to promise increased earnings for farmers, and he put these ideas into practice. John Porter Cowden introduced purebred shorthorn cattle into the community;

---

[1] Howard A. Cowden, Transcript of Record, High School, Pleasant Hope, Missouri.
[2] U.S., Department of Commerce, Bureau of the Census, *Twelfth Census of the United States*, Agriculture, V (1900), 98.

he built the first silo in the area in order to improve his feed supplies; and he was among the earliest of the farmers in the neighborhood to grow alfalfa. He selected his seed corn carefully and strove to improve the quantity and quality of his crops.

Howard's first opportunity to get away from Polk County and to see some of the outside world came as a result of the family's progressive farming. In the spring that Howard was seventeen, he noticed an announcement in the newspaper that the Frisco Railroad was offering a $100 scholarship to the University of Missouri's College of Agriculture for the best ears of corn exhibited in the county. "My first impulse was to get into the contest," Cowden recalled in 1922, but then he wondered if he had any chance to win. However, his father urged him to enter the contest, and during the summer of 1910 Cowden worked harder than ever with his corn crop. He dreamed of corn shows, blue ribbons, and the agricultural college.

When fall came, he selected his ten best ears of Reid's Yellow Dent and spread them in display on a table in the basement of the courthouse in Bolivar. "I still remember how my heart throbbed as Sam Jordan 'nosed' around over the corn and finally placed the blue ribbon on mine," Cowden wrote later. He won the contest. As he left the courthouse with the prize ears of corn firmly in his hands, he realized that at least some of his dreams had come true. In this instance scientific or progressive farming had paid practical dividends. With the $100 scholarship, he was soon on his way to Columbia, where, on November 1, 1910, he enrolled in the four-month winter course in agriculture.[3]

During the first two-month session, Cowden studied grain and livestock judging, dairying, feeding, and shop work. In the second term he added veterinary science, tillage methods, agricultural botany, and farm management. Returning home about the first of March, 1911, Cowden finished a short sophomore year of only sixty-four days at the Pleasant Hope High School, and throughout the summer he worked on the farm. By November 1, however, he was back in Columbia, attending his second agricultural short course. He took more work in some of the subjects he had studied the year before, and to them he added courses in orchards and small fruits, soil management, farm building and machinery, milk production, farm accounts, poultry

---

[3] Cowden recalled these events a dozen years later in *The Missouri Farmer*, XIV (July 1, 1922), 7. For the record of his work at the College of Agriculture, see Howard A. Cowden, Enrollment Records, University of Missouri, Columbia.

husbandry, and advanced corn judging.[4] Apparently, Cowden was already a competent judge of corn. There were no frills about this program. It was a practical curriculum designed to help farm boys increase their agricultural production and improve farm management. After all, wasn't this the road to agricultural prosperity?

But even though young Cowden had absorbed some of the accumulated wisdom available at Missouri's great College of Agriculture, questions that were not answered in the short-course curriculum still bothered him. There seemed to be no certain solutions to the problems of farmers about which Howard had often heard his father talk. John Cowden had been an organizer for the Grange and had seen Grangers and Populists defeated in their efforts to right the wrongs of agriculture. In 1896 he had helped carry Polk County, which usually went Republican, for the Democratic candidate William Jennings Bryan. The years between the Spanish-American War and the first World War were indeed much more prosperous than the depression-filled 1890's, but even this so-called Golden Era of American Agriculture did not put farmers' income on a parity with that of other major but better-organized economic groups. It might be expected that ignorant farmers working on unproductive and worn-out soil could not make a decent living, but what was the matter when hard-working, efficient producers like the Cowdens failed to enjoy prosperity?

Years later, Howard Cowden recalled how deeply he resented the conditions against which farmers struggled. High interest rates on mortgages, lack of competition in the purchase of agricultural commodities, and excessive transportation costs all spelled hard times for the farmer. His bitter comment was:

> Well I can remember how we used to ship our livestock to Kansas City after growing the steers for two years and feeding them all winter in the cold slush the corn we ourselves had grown. When they were shipped to the Kansas City market my father would come back and say to the boys, "Well, the market was off 75 cents or $1 per hundred." [5]

Time after time the elder Cowden explained that farmers had no influence at the Kansas City market and that they had to take whatever was offered, regardless of profit or loss. Howard also recalled that the price for eggs was always lowest when hens were laying most heavi-

[4] *Ibid.*
[5] Statement dictated by Howard A. Cowden, May 11, 1951, Cowden Papers.

ly, wool prices were down at shearing time, and the price for wheat was lowest during threshing. Something was wrong. Cowden concluded that there was "a great injustice in the market system." The more intently young Cowden considered the unfavorable position of farmers, the more strongly he resented their helplessness in their dealings with urban packers and the other processors who handled agricultural commodities. He began to see that farmers were at the mercy of other economic groups, both in buying and selling. Moreover, questions arose in his mind about the validity of certain standard and widely accepted economic principles. He saw evidence everywhere that the price and money systems did not operate as automatically and impersonally as he had heard and read.

John Porter Cowden was an intelligent and articulate man who recognized some of these basic problems, and he frequently discussed the economics of farm life with his sons. Thus, through study, discussion, and practical experience, Howard had ample motivation to consider devoting his life to helping farmers. Yet, after he came home from his second term at the University of Missouri, such a plan did not enter his mind; in fact, he strongly considered leaving the farm. He was not trying to run away from problems; he was simply like hundreds of thousands of other rural youths in their belief that a better life could be found off the farm. After taking the teachers' examination at Bolivar, Cowden was granted a certificate, and in the fall of 1914 he began to teach in a one-room country school known as "Providence." [6] He rode horseback to and from school and received a salary of $40 a month, plus $2.50 for doing the janitor work.

In 1915–1916 Cowden moved from the one-room country school to the school at Pleasant Hope where he had received most of his education. There he taught the intermediate grades.[7] It was during this school year that Cowden read the novel, *The Brown Mouse*, which he later declared had a tremendous influence upon his life. Written by Herbert Quick and published in 1915, this book was the story of Jim Erwin, a young farmer turned teacher who devoted himself to teaching farmers better agricultural methods and techniques. As confidence in himself and his ideas developed, Erwin made speeches on progressive agriculture, and from his knowledge of agricultural cooperatives he saved his community from falling prey to a sharper who tried to

---

[6] Records of the County Clerk, Polk County, Missouri.
[7] Records of Pleasant Hope School.

organize a cooperative creamery on a questionable basis. A neighbor said: "Jim Erwin stood for more upward growth of the average American."

Howard Cowden saw himself reflected in the story and in the activities of the central character in Quick's novel. Ideas were turning over in his mind as to how the economic position of farmers might be improved and what he might do to help the situation. He would do for Polk County what Jim Erwin had done for his community. The farm world could be made better through imaginative leadership and systematic and intelligent effort. As an expression of this belief, Cowden was, at the moment, supervising a "pig club" that some of his students had organized in the Pleasant Hope school. The boys sold magazine subscriptions and won a young sow as the prize, and eventually each boy raised a pig. Two of the contestants won prizes offered by William Hirth, publisher of *The Missouri Farmer*, in a state pig-feeding contest.

Shortly after the beginning of his third year of teaching at Pleasant Hope, Cowden, on November 1, 1917, married Thelma Lundy, and within the next few years, two sons, Keith L. and John Henry, were born. Several years later Cowden and Thelma Lundy Cowden were divorced. Meanwhile, the United States had entered World War I. Howard was not drafted, but on September 30, 1918, he enrolled at Missouri State Normal School in Springfield and joined the Student Army Training Corps.[8] Along with his military training, Cowden finished the high school requirements he had not completed at Pleasant Hope.[9] He also took seven and one-half semester hours of regular college courses, including French. Within a few weeks after Cowden enrolled at Springfield, the Armistice was signed. The SATC was disbanded, and at the end of the semester he quit college.

While he looked around for a permanent job early in 1919, Cowden worked in his brother's abstract office in Springfield. A career as a schoolteacher did not appeal to him, and he had no desire to return to farming, although he was interested in work connected with agriculture. Consequently, when he was offered the position of secretary of the Polk County Farmers Association, he quickly accepted it and went to work on March 10. This was one of the most important deci-

---

[8] Records of the Registrar, Southwest Missouri State College, Springfield.
[9] Not all of Cowden's high school records are extant, but the transcript of his work at Springfield shows that he entered the college without a high school diploma.

sions in Cowden's life, for it started him on his career as a farmer cooperative leader that spanned more than forty years.

The organized cooperative movement, as it then existed in Missouri, was largely the work of William Hirth. In October, 1908, Hirth began publishing *The Missouri Farmer and Breeder* at Columbia to provide farmers with a good agricultural journal and to serve as a publicity organ for a yet unborn farm organization. Hirth shortened the title to *The Missouri Farmer* in 1912 and under the new title urged farmers to attack their economic problems through cooperative buying and selling. Practically every issue of his paper explained the benefits of united cooperative action among farmers and pressed them to form local Farm Clubs. The first Farm Club was organized in Chariton County in March, 1914, and during succeeding months many others were formed. By the end of 1915 the local Farm Clubs were beginning to set up county associations, and Hirth was calling for a state-wide organization. In January, 1917, Farm Club representatives met in Columbia and established the Missouri Farmers Association.

The MFA was organized primarily for economic purposes. The Farm Clubs had, through their secretaries, bought feed, seed, and other farm supplies in bulk and had sold them to members at lower than prevailing prices. When the county associations came into existence, the Farm Club secretaries pooled their orders, and the county secretary purchased supplies in carload lots for resale to members at even greater savings. Hirth now urged farmers to build elevators and to establish livestock markets to be operated on a cooperative basis. In order to promote the organization and to systematize the business activities of Farm Clubs, Hirth strongly recommended that each county association employ a paid secretary. He argued that a good man in this position could earn his salary many times over.[10]

Hirth was largely responsible for getting Cowden into the Farm Club movement. Influenced by the vigorous and cogent arguments in the columns of *The Missouri Farmer*, Cowden organized several Farm Clubs in Polk County during 1915 and 1916, and although he had then turned to other things, he had impressed Hirth. "I have had my eye on Cowden for two years and only recently wrote him at Springfield . . . pleading with him to get into the Farm Club fight," Hirth

---

[10] Ray Derr, *Missouri Farmers in Action* (Columbia, 1953), 36–53.

declared in 1919.[11] Commenting on Cowden's appointment as secretary of the Polk County Farmers Association, Hirth called it "great news." He described Cowden as "a very bright and strong man" who would finish the job of organizing Farm Clubs in every school district in the county, and he predicted that "he will make one of the strongest county secretaries in the state."[12] And Cowden soon earned the confidence of his friend and backer in Columbia.

When Cowden undertook his work as secretary of the Polk County Farmers Association, he was twenty-six years old — a tall, ruggedly built, handsome man. Aggressive and possessed of tremendous energies, Cowden worked most effectively when there were problems to solve and opposition to overcome. He could never be a mere caretaker in any position; he was driven by a strong desire to achieve. Positive and self-confident, neither difficult jobs nor long odds frightened or deterred him. If Cowden ever felt unsure about anything, he covered his feelings with outward firmness. Whatever he believed, he believed intensely and completely. For example, once Cowden became convinced of the value of consumer cooperation to farmers, he never wavered from the principle. A friend once wrote: "I wish to God I had a cause to believe in as you believe in the cooperative movement."[13]

Cowden inspired loyalty and confidence in his associates, partly through his own self-assurance, but also through his practice of never asking others to do what he himself was unwilling or unable to do. His force was not the result of outward bluster or noisy enthusiasm; rather, it came from the controlled powers of a quiet, thoughtful, and soft-spoken man. He commanded respect through an inner strength of character; he stood firm in his convictions. Anyone who tried to run over Howard Cowden was certain to encounter a strong obstacle.

When the Polk County Farmers Exchange began to sell twine, it cut heavily into the business of the local hardware merchant in Bolivar. Smarting under this new competition, the dealer told his customers that twine sold by the exchange was short and too fuzzy to work well in the knotter of a binder. Cowden did not explode in anger; he merely picked up a ball of his twine and walked over to the merchant's store and asked him if he had run down the exchange's twine. The

[11] *The Missouri Farmer*, XI (March 15, 1919), 147.
[12] *Ibid.*
[13] G. Phil Scott to Cowden, May 2, 1948, Cowden Papers.

storekeeper admitted that he had made such statements to local farmers. In a friendly manner Cowden suggested that they each take a ball of his twine and unroll it along the road so that farmers could judge for themselves. Flustered by this challenge to compare length and quality of the two products, the hardware dealer said he did not care to make the test. Word of this encounter soon spread throughout the community, and before long the exchange had most of the twine business in Bolivar.

Howard Cowden had a warm, friendly personality and gave the impression of being kind and fatherly. But he had presence and a dignity that commanded respect and discouraged familiarity except from a few very close friends. Even employees and associates who had worked with him for many years called him "Mr." Cowden. When one man who had known Cowden for some time went to work for the Consumers Cooperative Association in the 1940's, he discussed with a long-time employee and department head the matter of how to address his new boss. The newcomer mentioned that he had known Cowden on a first-name basis and wondered if he should refer to him as "Howard." This was a shocking thought to the old-timer, who threw up his hands and could only exclaim: "Oh, my God!" It was not that Cowden demanded this kind of respect or deference; employees just did not feel familiar with him.

To Cowden the Midwest was the best part of America; the nation's great central region was not only the economic but the spiritual heartland as well. This view did not stem from provincialism, but from a deep-rooted love of the land and its products. While he did not want to make his living by operating a farm, Cowden had a strong emotional attachment to the purported virtues of agricultural life. His roots were deep in the Missouri soil, and his strong agrarianism placed him among the most devoted spiritual heirs of Thomas Jefferson.

Howard Cowden quickly became fully absorbed in his new job. Besides acting as secretary of the Polk County Farmers Association, he managed the Polk County Farmers Exchange, a cooperative enterprise organized and controlled by farmers. A law passed by the Missouri legislature early in 1919 made possible the incorporation of genuine cooperative business organizations. Local Farm Clubs then combined, as they had in Polk County, to buy stock in exchanges that were established to meet the special purchasing and marketing needs of farmers. Under Cowden's management the Bolivar exchange was doing a thriving business among farmers in the community by the summer of 1919. In order to save money on purchases of supplies, the secretaries of local Farm Clubs would send their orders to Cowden, who would combine them and buy in Kansas City or elsewhere, usually in carload lots. Feed, seed, twine, flour, fertilizer, and other commodities were purchased in this fashion, with substantial savings to farmers.

Besides trying to help producers by lowering the cost of items required for production, the exchange sought to better the marketing of agricultural commodities. Cowden began shipping eggs directly to the Kansas City market, and farmers realized seven or eight cents more per dozen than they had received from local produce dealers. This venture was successful until hot weather arrived, and the eggs began to spoil in transit. Cowden called a meeting at Springfield of farmers interested in cooperative marketing, and subsequently the Producers' Produce Company was organized. This new cooperative bought out a firm that had facilities for cold storage, thus giving the farmers in that vicinity their own market outlet for eggs and cream.

Meanwhile, Cowden was organizing additional Farm Clubs. From morning until night, he traveled over the dirt roads in his Model-T Ford to reach rural schoolhouses where he explained to the assembled farmers the need for cooperative action. The farmers responded to his enthusiasm and sincerity. What Cowden said about the weakness of unorganized producers made sense to men who found their costs of operation going up faster than the prices for their commodities. Cowden offered them a positive, practical kind of help that was achievable, providing farmers were willing to work together in their business arrangements. M. R. Miller, a member of the Board of Directors of the Polk County Farmers Association, later recalled Cowden's effectiveness as an organizer.

Cowden's success both as a business manager and a Farm Club organizer soon brought him state-wide attention, and Hirth began giving space to his views in the pages of *The Missouri Farmer*. In his first article, published on January 15, 1920, Cowden explained what he considered some of the basic principles of successful cooperatives. He emphasized the importance of incorporating business cooperatives, but warned against permitting any stockholder to buy more than one-twentieth of the paid-up capital. Every precaution should be taken, he argued, to keep any single individual from gaining control of the cooperative. He emphasized also the importance of effective management. A good cooperative exchange manager, he said, should be interested in the Farm Club movement, he should have some book-keeping experience, and he should possess horse sense. He concluded: "One of the most important things in the management of an exchange is to keep in touch with, and follow the leadership of your county and state association — for remember that singly your exchange is hopeless in the fight we have undertaken. But collectively, we are coming to be a power in the market place."[14]

William Hirth realized that Cowden's energies and talents were not being fully utilized in Polk County. When it was decided, early in 1920, to expand the organizational activities of the Missouri Farmers Association, Cowden was named fieldman.[15] Cowden now began traveling to all parts of the state, where he held scores of organizational meetings. Late in 1920 Hirth referred to him as "one of the most effective and well-known fieldmen of our state association."[16] Cowden also continued to write for *The Missouri Farmer*. One of his main themes was loyalty to the cooperative. In an article entitled "Mr. Cowden Talks Sense," he argued that farmers should stick to their cooperative exchanges even when they were offered slightly more for produce by private dealers. The cooperative way of doing business, he insisted, would ultimately pay off in dollars and cents. While some farmers were beguiled by opponents of cooperatives, Cowden optimistically declared that "there are always a lot more farmers in a community that can look over a dime and see a dollar bill a little farther down the road."[17] Cowden did not mince words. Answering his own question as to why farmers did not show greater loyalty to their cooperative exchanges, he declared: "I believe it is because a lot of fellows have become so entrapped in the old system that they are not 'he-men' enough to help us change it. Some of them are so 'hen-pecked' by the old crowd, they cackle when they try to talk."[18] Both as an organizer and as a propagator of the cooperative philosophy, Cowden was now playing an increasingly important part in the Missouri Farmers Association. His growing stature was reflected in his being chosen to serve as secretary at the annual state convention in 1920.

Shortly after Cowden assumed his duties as a fieldman for MFA, the agricultural depression struck the farmers of the country. Prices began

---

[14] *The Missouri Farmer*, XII (January 15, 1920), 21.
[15] *Ibid.* (June 1, 1920), 6.
[16] *Ibid.* (November 15, 1920), 7.
[17] *Ibid.* (June 1, 1920), 6.
[18] *Ibid.* (December 15, 1920), 10.

tumbling in June of 1920, and within eighteen months such commodities as wheat and hogs were bringing less than half as much as they had in 1919. To make matters worse, nonfarm prices did not drop proportionately, and farmers suffered from a burdensome inequality. Considering 1913 as equaling 100, the purchasing power of several basic farm products dropped to 67 in 1921. These conditions, however unfortunate, offered Cowden an ideal opportunity to demonstrate the values of cooperatives, since the pocket nerve of practically every farmer in Missouri was being pinched. Not content to sit behind his desk and wait for events, Cowden took the message of cooperation to every corner of the state. During 1920 and 1921 he added thousands of new members to the Missouri Farmers Association and organized scores of new cooperatives.

Advancement in the organization on the basis of this record was not long in coming. On January 1, 1922, Cowden began serving as the first full-time paid secretary of the MFA. He moved to Columbia, rented an office, bought some secondhand office furniture, and established a state headquarters. Up to this time, most of the association's business had been carried on by Hirth in the offices of *The Missouri Farmer.* Since Hirth was interested in many activities, there was little order in the affairs of MFA and little of anything that resembled a business system. Cowden introduced new business methods in the office at Columbia and assumed responsibility for most of the organizational work.[19]

Cowden and Hirth worked closely together; Hirth often flattered Cowden and praised his work in the columns of *The Missouri Farmer.* On September 15, 1922, Hirth published an editorial entitled, "Everybody Likes Howard Cowden":

> there is no more popular man in the ranks of the MFA than Howard A. Cowden, Secretary of the State Association — a young man who was a country schoolmaster down in the hills of Polk County only three or four years back and who has thus "spelled up from the foot of the class." To begin with, he is a young man of far more than ordinary ability and with him love of the Farm Clubs overshadows all else, for it would not be difficult for him to get twice the salary he is now receiving in other quarters. A natural born diplomat, he has no superior and few equals in the farm organization circles of the Corn Belt. Courteous, soft spoken and modest, he never-

[19] Derr, *Missouri Farmers in Action,* 70.

theless isn't afraid of the Devil — this quiet, long legged school master from Polk who numbers his friends by the thousands and who toils and plans almost day and night for the advancement of the Farm Clubs.[20]

As secretary of the MFA, Cowden wrote a regular column for *The Missouri Farmer*. He expounded the cooperative philosophy, emphasized the need for alert and educated leaders, and insisted on good business methods for the cooperative exchanges. But he never hesitated to criticize if he thought criticism was needed and deserved. In one of his articles he took cooperative managers to task for being unaware that they could buy salt, tankage, feeds, and other products through the MFA at substantial savings. He urged farmers to deal exclusively with their cooperatives and not to contribute profits to old-line business and commission firms.[21] Cowden was both a moving force and a prophetic voice in the MFA.

Since farmers were beginning to use tractors and trucks increasingly, Cowden became interested in establishing cooperative outlets to provide operators with kerosene, gasoline, oils, and greases. In 1922 he made a trip to Cottonwood, Minnesota, to visit the Cottonwood Oil Company, which had been organized by a few cooperative-minded farmers the year before. He returned to Missouri fully convinced that consumer cooperatives could make one of their greatest contributions by providing farmers with high-quality petroleum products at reasonable prices. Cowden found farmers and MFA leaders interested, and by the middle 1920's scores of bulk stations were being operated throughout Missouri by MFA cooperatives. The business arrangements were simple: The association contracted with Standard Oil Company or some other major company to furnish needed petroleum supplies for MFA exchanges; the savings on large orders were passed on to local patrons in the form of patronage refunds.

Although the Missouri Farmers Association grew in size and expanded its services to members, the organization came to be plagued by internal dissension. After 1922 Cowden had been given increasing responsibility for the association's policies, but by 1927 difficulties had arisen between him and Hirth that could be resolved only by one of them leaving the association; the MFA was not big enough to hold two such strong, dominating personalities. The differences that de-

[20] *The Missouri Farmer*, XIV (September 15, 1922), 10.
[21] *Ibid.* (June 15, 1922), 5; and XIX (January 15, 1927), 10.

veloped between the two men centered mainly around the means by which farmers should be signed up under the Producer's Contract and the distribution of the savings made by the state office on wholesale contracts. The Producer's Contract was an agreement by which farmers bound themselves to sell exclusively through MFA outlets. This program was started in 1923, and an intensive campaign was carried on to sign up every Farm Club member. Hirth believed the contract campaign should be handled by local county leaders, while Cowden thought paid fieldmen were necessary. Moreover, Hirth insisted that a larger percentage of the brokerage earned by the state office in handling produce at wholesale should be returned to the local elevators and exchanges rather than retained by the state association.[22] In other words, while there were policy differences between Hirth and Cowden, the crux of their conflict was Hirth's fear of losing influence and power in the organization that he had created.

Early in 1927 Hirth wrote to members of the Executive Committee that Cowden was not doing a competent job. He accused the Secretary of poor organizational techniques, of failure to hold the respect and support of "erstwhile loyal members," and of spending excessive amounts of money in the state office. He charged that Cowden had spent little time in the field during the past two years, despite the fact that he had plenty of office help, including "an exceptionally capable woman secretary."[23] For a salary of $5,000 a year plus expenses, "the association is entitled to something more than a mere perfunctory service," Hirth argued.

These charges of inefficiency were only a smoke screen for Hirth's real objection to Cowden. He explained that, despite Cowden's denials, "it has been Mr. Cowden's deliberate purpose to obtain control of the state association." Then Hirth added that most of the fieldmen were an organized "cabal against me from one end of the state to the other." Feeling that he was being pushed out of his position of leadership and power, Hirth concluded that "in plain words, the time is come when the board [of directors] must choose between Mr. Cowden and myself."[24]

Distressed by the differences boiling up within MFA, the Board of

[22] Derr, *Missouri Farmers in Action*, 85.
[23] Hirth's letter to R. T. Pence March 14, 1927, is reprinted in *A Statement of the Missouri Farmers Association by the Executive Committee Answering Mr. Hirth's Statement of January 12, 1928*, pamphlet, Cowden Papers.
[24] *Ibid.*

Directors asked Cowden to answer Hirth's charges. Cowden explained that Hirth had been making similar accusations for about eighteen months and that *The Missouri Farmer* had not supported his efforts for three years. In this situation Cowden felt that he must submit his resignation. He could not carry out his responsibilities and at the same time "defend myself against those from whom I have a right to expect support." Cowden denied Hirth's charges, citing the steady growth of MFA membership as evidence of his administrative and organizational efficiency. He insisted that he had no desire to gain control of MFA and added that "for the past six years every hope I have had has been in connection with the M.F.A. and cooperative marketing." Despite the fact that he had every right to be proud of his record, Cowden said he was willing to sacrifice whatever future he might have with MFA for the sake of harmony.[25]

Up to this point, details of the conflict had been confined within the official MFA family. The simple statement on the editorial page of *The Missouri Farmer* of April 1, 1927, headed "Secretary Cowden Resigns," gave no indication of the strife between Hirth and Cowden. Readers recognized some policy conflicts, but they had no way of knowing how deep the rift between the two men had become. Cowden explained that "for several years there had been a decided difference of opinion between Mr. Hirth and myself regarding various policies of the Association" and that these differences were not conducive to harmony. Consequently, he told his readers, for the good of MFA he had resigned.[26] Cowden expressed his continuing vital interest in the association and his conviction that "the cooperative movement is the only hope of the farmer." The tone of his announcement was calm. At the end of Cowden's statement, Hirth added a publisher's note that he would explain in a subsequent issue the differences which had developed between himself and Cowden. On May 1, however, Hirth wrote that he had decided not to air his differences with Cowden because any open conflict would be seized upon by the enemies of MFA to divide and destroy it. But he did explain his opposition to the use of fieldmen in the Producer's Contract campaign. Regardless of how conscientious fieldmen might be, he said, they did not justify their cost.[27]

---

[25] Cowden to Board of Directors, Missouri Farmers Association, March 26, 1927, *ibid.*
[26] *The Missouri Farmer*, XIX (April 1, 1927), 13.
[27] *Ibid.* (May 1, 1927), 10.

The Board of Directors was anxious to keep the internal problems as quiet as possible, but they were unable to muzzle Hirth. When it was learned that Hirth planned to present his side of the controversy in a public announcement, the Board of Directors passed a resolution protesting the release of any statement on questions of association policies by a member of the board or by any employee unless it had been approved by the board or the Resolutions Committee.[28] Completely ignoring the board, Hirth loosed a blast against the association's management and policies on August 17, just prior to the state convention, and sent it to all Farm Clubs and exchanges in the state. Four days later the Executive Committee met in Columbia and prepared to answer Hirth. Even though Cowden had resigned as secretary, the Executive Committee defended his work and declared that Hirth's charges were unfair and unjust. At this point Cowden had the support of the Executive Committee, but he had no desire to engage in a head-on fight with Hirth over matters of policy and of control of MFA. His chances of coming out on top in any such struggle were not good, because he did not have the backing of the full board, and Hirth controlled *The Missouri Farmer*, the principal means of communicating with farmers throughout the state.

An open fight was avoided at the state convention in August, 1927, at which Tom DeWitt, a Cowden supporter, was elected president. Cowden's resignation became effective at the same time, but he continued for a time to write his column in *The Missouri Farmer*, the last one appearing on November 15. However, the Hirth forces rapidly gained control of the association, and at the annual convention in August, 1928, Hirth was elected president, and the Executive Committee friendly to Cowden was replaced by a group of Hirth's friends.[29] Cowden had made no effort to maintain his position in the MFA, but it no doubt hurt him to see his loyal backers pushed out of places of influence in the association.

Meanwhile, Cowden had decided to enter the wholesale oil business. Before his resignation became effective, he explained to the friendly Executive Committee that he would like to have the MFA oil contract that had been held by Standard Oil.[30] On October 14, 1927, the

---

[28] Minutes of the Board of Directors, MFA, August 5, 1927, Cowden Papers.
[29] *Sedalia* (Missouri) *Democrat*, August 28, 1928.
[30] Minutes of the Executive Committee, MFA, July 29, 1927, Cowden Papers.

Executive Committee awarded the contract to Cowden. Although Hirth charged that this was favoritism, the committee defended its action by pointing to the lower prices on oil that Cowden provided to MFA exchanges. The committee declared that the MFA was "buying a better oil for less money" from Cowden than it had from Standard Oil.

To handle this new business, the Cowden Oil Company was incorporated on January 27, 1928.[31] It had an authorized capitalization of $50,000, of which only $5,000 was paid in. Cowden owned 48 of the $100 shares, and single shares were held by his brother W. L. Cowden and Harry E. Files. Cowden opened offices in Columbia and sought contracts to supply petroleum products to local bulk plants. This small company was little more than a commission agent between the large suppliers and the retail outlets.

The future of Cowden's business was not encouraging; once Hirth won control of MFA, Cowden's contract to supply petroleum products to the association's exchanges surely would not be renewed. Furthermore, he could expect a certain amount of outright opposition from Hirth's friends throughout Missouri. Cowden was not, however, primarily interested in developing a private business for his own profit; he had never shown any desire to spend his time and energy merely to make money. In the cooperative movement he saw a worth-while cause, and to Cowden, worthy causes demanded a man's first allegiance. At this time, Cowden saw the establishment of a wholesale cooperative that would deal in gasoline and oils as the best way to foster consumer cooperation. Moreover, this type of business had a good chance for success. In view of the growing number of cooperatives in the Midwest, location at Kansas City, Missouri, seemed to be the most suitable for a new venture of this type. Late in 1928 he moved the offices of the Cowden Oil Company to Kansas City and began making plans to establish a regional wholesale cooperative.[32]

---

[31] Cowden Oil Company, Articles of Incorporation, Cowden Papers.

[32] After 1928, under the leadership of Hirth and F. V. Heinkel, the Missouri Farmers Association greatly expanded its business activities. It eventually engaged in fertilizer production, oil refining, milk processing, feed manufacturing, insurance, and many other enterprises. As MFA grew and expanded, it made an important contribution to the cooperative movement in the Midwest. Part of the history of MFA can be found in Derr, *Missouri Farmers in Action.*

Throughout the 1920's Cowden had shown only casual interest in federal farm relief schemes like the McNary-Haugen bills. Hirth became prominent in the fight for federal legislation for agriculture, but Cowden confined his efforts to securing help of a different kind. He favored, in principle, legislation that would provide control of surpluses, but his real commitment was to cooperation.

Chapter 3

Founding the Union
Oil Company (Cooperative)

T HE IDEA OF ESTABLISHING a regional wholesale cooperative to distribute petroleum products to farmers throughout the Midwest had been considered for several months by Cowden. Although he had not been directly connected with the cooperative movement since his resignation as secretary of the Missouri Farmers Association in August, 1927, his enthusiasm for cooperative business principles had remained strong. Cowden firmly believed that farmers were profiting from their local associations sponsored by the MFA and other farm organizations, but he envisioned far greater benefits from a large wholesale operated on true cooperative principles. The wholesale could obtain better prices through volume purchases, he argued, and these savings could be passed on to the local cooperatives and, finally, to the ultimate consumer, the farmer.

Extending the cooperative method of doing business to the wholesale level seemed not only desirable to Cowden but absolutely necessary if farmers were to enjoy the full benefits of consumer cooperation. By 1928 there were twelve fairly large cooperative wholesale associations, but most of them were operated by one of the major farm organizations, and usually their business was confined to cooperatives within a single state. But Cowden was thinking in regional terms, with Kansas City as the hub. He envisioned an extensive chain of petroleum cooperatives to be supplied by a regional wholesale owned and controlled by the affiliated locals. Because of jealousy and competition among the major farm organizations, Cowden did not want his cooperative wholesale to become identified with any single farm group. He hoped to build a cooperative supply company that would win the support of consumer cooperatives, regardless of their connection with the Missouri Farmers Association, the Farmers Educational and Cooperative Union, Equity, or any other agricultural organization.

Ideas are one thing, implementation of them is another. Cowden had discussed his plans with friends and supporters in the MFA and with other cooperative leaders. When the National Farmers Equity Union held its annual meeting in Kansas City on January 16 and 17, 1929, Cowden talked over his ideas with several of his friends and acquaintances among officials of the group. On the afternoon of January 17, Cowden addressed the convention and outlined for the delegates some of his views on the need for a cooperative petroleum wholesale in that region.[1] Before the convention adjourned, Cowden had promises from a number of Equity men to back him in establishing a wholesale cooperative.

The support he received from leaders of Equity convinced Cowden that he was on the right track. On January 5, nearly two weeks before, Cowden, as the principal stockholder, had voted to dissolve the Cowden Oil Company and to incorporate a new firm to be operated strictly on cooperative principles as provided in the Missouri statutes. The purpose of reincorporating was to organize the company according to the business plan of the cooperatives. All assets of the Cowden Oil Company, which had never been a very profitable venture, were to be transferred to the new corporation.

The general purpose of the new company, named the Union Oil Company (Cooperative), was to "deal in, handle, and distribute petroleum and various products and by-products" and "to purchase, lease, build, construct, maintain and operate warehouses, filling stations, pumping plants, compounding plants, refineries, and all other appliances and conveniences for use in connection with the manufacturing purchase and sale of gasoline, petroleum, lubricating oils

---

[1] The announcement of Cowden's part in the program was made in the *Weekly Kansas City Star*, January 9, 1929.

and all other petroleum and oil products." It is clear from the charter that Cowden intended to do much more than simply buy and distribute oil and gasoline to local cooperatives as he had been doing since 1927. The specific mention of refineries indicates that he was already thinking of a system of manufacture and distribution of petroleum products, on a cooperative basis, that would reach all the way from original producer to ultimate consumer. Cowden was dreaming of complete integration, through which the users themselves, mainly farmers, would own and control petroleum commodities through all phases of production and distribution.

The articles of association of the new company provided for the customary distribution of profits under the Missouri law concerning cooperatives. Not less than 10 per cent of the firm's net profits were to be set aside in a reserve fund until the amount reached 50 per cent of the paid-up capital. A dividend of not more than 10 per cent was to be declared on the stock, and any balance could be divided among the member or affiliated cooperatives who did business with the wholesale. The distribution of profits was to be made on the basis of the amount of business that each cooperative did with the Union Oil Company. The certificate of incorporation was issued by the Secretary of State of Missouri on February 16, 1929.[2]

The Union Oil Company was capitalized at $100,000, divided into 4,000 shares with a par value of $25 each. Twelve shareholders subscribed for 461 shares, but 396 of these were taken by P. C. Floyd of St. Louis, Cowden, and B. E. Musgrave, who held 160, 120, and 116 shares, respectively. The subscription of 461 shares, each having a book value of $25, did not mean that the company had $11,525 with which to begin business; in fact, the corporation began operation with practically no capital. The only cash in Cowden's hands was $3,000 invested by the six original cooperatives that became affiliated with the Union Oil Company by contracting to purchase their petroleum products from the new regional wholesale. The assets of the Cowden Oil Company that were transferred to the new company included office furniture and some equipment that had been loaned by firms to which Cowden had sold oil and gasoline; the value of these assets was nominal.

Control of the Union Oil Company was placed in a six-man board

2 Certificate of Incorporation, Union Oil Company (Cooperative), Cowden Papers.

of directors selected by the incorporators. Cowden was elected president, and the other directors were W. J. Solter, B. E. Musgrave, Emmett Sallee, W. R. Detmer, and T. H. DeWitt.[3] Changes were soon made to provide unofficial representation for some of the farm organizations and strong local cooperatives and to conform to Cowden's wish that the Board of Directors represent a wide geographic area. Musgrave, Detmer, Sallee, and Solter all submitted their resignations from the Board on March 4. Although he continued on the Board, Solter was replaced as secretary in May by R. A. Hedding, manager of the Equity Exchange at Burlington, Colorado, which had a successful oil department and was one of the original six to become affiliated with the Union Oil Company.[4] W. A. Kearns of Kahoka, Missouri, was elected to the Board in the spring of 1929 and became vice-president. He was vice-president of the Farmers Union Livestock Commission of Chicago, a successful farmer, and had done extensive organizational work for the Farmers Union. He had also served on the board of directors of the Missouri Farmers Association. DeWitt was one of the best-known cooperative leaders in Missouri. A native of Green City, he had served both as vice-president and president of the Missouri Farmers Association and had been a strong supporter of Cowden during his difficulties with Hirth. DeWitt had an outstanding record of organizing local cooperatives throughout Missouri. A. W. Gale, who was connected with the Producers Produce Company at Chillicothe, also became a member of the Board in late 1929.[5]

Cowden maintained absolute control over the company he created, and he managed to strengthen the position of the Union Oil Company among farmers and local cooperatives by seeing that devoted and successful cooperators were elected to the Board of Directors. From the beginning, the Union Oil Company was controlled by a group of men who were congenial to each other personally and who believed fervently in cooperation as a means of helping farmers. All of the founders had been reared on farms, and several of them were still active farmers. They were imbued with a deep agrarian bias, and

---

[3] *Ibid.*

[4] The other five were the Consumers Oil Company, Maryville, Missouri; Consumers Oil and Supply Company, Braymer, Missouri; Peetz Consumers Oil Company, Peetz, Colorado; Producers Produce Exchange, Chillicothe, Missouri; Garden City Equity Exchange, Garden City, Kansas.

[5] Board of Directors, Minutes, May 13 and October 1, 1929, Consumers Cooperative Association Files. All minutes hereafter cited are in the CCA Files in Kansas City.

they knew the problems and frustrations of farming from first-hand experience. They distrusted any novel or utopian solution to farm grievances and based their support of the company on the prospect of actual savings in purchasing goods and supplies through cooperative action.

Nothing in the records indicates that the founders of the Union Oil Company placed any special reliance upon the Agricultural Marketing Act or the Domestic Allotment plan of farm relief. Cowden favored the Agricultural Marketing Act and its emphasis upon promoting marketing cooperatives, but his support was casual rather than active. It was not that Cowden opposed government programs of farm relief; he was concentrating on establishing his own cooperative business, to the exclusion of everything else. Certainly, he could not give this new business the attention it required if he were away at Washington or working locally for specific legislation. Perhaps more important was the fact that from the outset Cowden, as a matter of policy, did not want to become identified with any particular farm organization or legislative program. To do so would almost certainly alienate some farm and cooperative leaders who might join his wholesale cooperative if he remained neutral on matters of broad agricultural policy. For instance, if Cowden had worked hard and publicly in support of the Federal Farm Board, he surely would have been unable to gain support from farmers who bitterly opposed the Board and its program.

Even while the incorporation papers were being processed, Cowden began an intensive advertising and organizational campaign. His task was twofold. First, he had to inform local cooperatives that they could purchase their petroleum supplies from a cooperative corporation; second, he needed to convince these associations that they would profit by doing business with a regional cooperative wholesale rather than with what he called an "old-line" company. By "old-line" company Cowden meant any private, noncooperative firm. Pitching his propaganda to the idea of members' owning their own wholesale, Cowden explained in his original printed announcement that the Union Oil Company had been organized as a cooperative "to permit you to become the *real owners* of the business." Individuals and cooperatives should become members of the Union Oil Company, he argued, so they could share in the profits. At last, Cowden wrote, a company had been formed to give cooperatives "their first chance to handle their own National Brand." The brand name adopted for gasoline and motor oils was "Union Certified," and Cowden chose the enticing slogan: "Our Profits Are Your Dividends." [6]

Cowden recognized that it was essential to establish and to get public acceptance and recognition of a cooperative brand. Otherwise, it would be difficult to meet the charges made by major oil companies that the Union Oil Company had no standing and could not compete with nationally known and advertised products like Standard or Sinclair. A popular brand name could be an important selling point for fieldmen to use when they approached local cooperatives for their business. In January, 1929, Cowden mailed out leaflets advertising a forthcoming series of radio programs in which he was to describe the objectives and advantages to customers of the new cooperative wholesale. On February 13, three days before the charter was issued, he addressed listeners on the subject, "A National Oil and Gasoline Movement," over Station WOS in Jefferson City. This is one of the most important documents dealing with the early history of the Union Oil Company because it expresses so clearly Cowden's ideas and ambitions at the time the company was formed.

Speaking to "everyone interested in saving money on gasoline and oil," Cowden gave the background of handling gasoline, oils, and grease through cooperative outlets. Several local cooperative oil companies were operating successfully, he said, but "the time has come when these companies, as well as the small independent oil companies, must cooperate in order to compete with the major companies." This was why the Union Oil Company (Cooperative) had been formed. "It was organized for the sole purpose of combining local effort and resources and establishing throughout the United States standardized grades of gasoline, kerosene, and motor oils for cooperatives; for cooperative buying and cooperative advertising, and merchandising." The Union Oil Company, he said, "seeks to promote the new day spirit of cooperation in business." The goal of the new company was to "serve cooperatives from coast-to-coast. Thus is unfolded one of the most interesting and quite likely one of the most magnificent developments in the history of cooperative purchasing." Cowden predicted that through the use of newspapers, road signs, and posters, the name "Union Certified" and the slogan "Our Profits Are Your Dividends" would be memorized by the motoring public. No longer would it be necessary for the local cooperatives to advertise

[6] "Announcement," an undated leaflet, Cowden Papers.

some other company's products. Cooperatives would now have their own national cooperative brand.

In order to attract the cooperatives to the Union Oil Company, Cowden explained that since Union Certified was sold exclusively through cooperatives, the tourist business of cooperators would be drawn to stations displaying a Union Certified sign. This, he said, would represent new business. Furthermore, when a cooperative station displayed the Union Certified sign, it would gain prestige that "comes to a business that is more than just local. It will be looked upon as a progressive business concern — a part of a national chain of cooperatives." Cowden went on to explain that, by affiliating with the Union Oil Company, local cooperatives would become a part of an organization that was conducting a "wide campaign of publicity and advertising." Finally, he described the savings that could be made by combining gasoline and oil purchases. In addition, the Union Oil Company helped local cooperatives by purchasing tanks, pumps, and other equipment at substantial savings. But these advantages were only the beginning, he declared. "It is the plan of the members of the Union Oil Company to, at the earliest possible moment, own a cooperative refinery."[7]

Cowden based his appeal for additional members on several basic motives: He pictured immediate profits for those cooperatives that joined the Union Oil Company in bulk purchasing; he appealed to pride by showing how cooperatives could have their own nationally recognized products and services; finally, he promised a future in which the cooperatives, working through the Union Oil Company, would operate their own refinery. Here was the outline of Cowden's dream of an integrated system manufacturing and marketing petroleum products on a cooperative basis.

This same message was circulated through other media. Early in 1929 Cowden began advertising in the *Kernel*, a paper published by the Equity Union. He emphasized the cooperative organization of the Union Oil Company and publicized the Union Certified insignia. In July, 1929, M. R. Miller, an old friend from Polk County days, began publishing the *Cooperative Farmer* in Chillicothe, Cowden used this paper as another means to take the Union Oil Company message to farmers and local cooperatives.[8] The Union Oil Company provided

---

[7] "A National Oil and Gasoline Movement," Cowden Speech File.

[8] See samples of this advertising for the months of February, March, and June, 1929, in Union Oil Company Scrapbook No. 2.

material for two pages in each issue and then took bulk subscriptions for distribution through cooperatives.

But Cowden did not confine his efforts to the usual publicity outlets. He depended heavily upon face-to-face contact, and during the early weeks of 1929 he traveled widely, visiting with cooperative leaders and attending farm organization meetings. The extent of Cowden's travels is reflected in his expense accounts. In April his expenses reached a high for the first six months of 1929 with the total of $226.10; most of the time, Cowden spent between $100 and $200 a month on travel.[9] Members of the Board of Directors were also busy soliciting business among cooperatives. In the middle of February Solter made oil and gasoline contracts with the Garden City Equity Exchange, one of the largest cooperatives in Kansas. Moreover, he sold the cooperative a substantial amount of Union Oil Company stock.[10] On February 25, Cowden wrote that during the past two weeks six "new cooperative companies have signed working agreements with us." And, writing to all MFA managers on March 18, Cowden reported that "during the past three weeks we have started nine new cooperative companies, three of them in Missouri, three in Nebraska, one in Kansas, and two in Colorado."

The broad acquaintance of Cowden and members of the Board with farm and cooperative officials paid off handsomely. On March 8 a resolution was passed at the annual meeting of the Farmers Cooperative Grain Dealers Association and the Farmers Cooperative Commission Company of Hutchinson, Kansas, endorsing "the principles and policies of the Union Oil Company." This was important support because many of the elevators handled gasoline and motor oils as a side line. Cowden immediately began to use this endorsement to help solicit business from cooperatives in Kansas. Although W. O. Sand, Secretary of the Farmers Cooperative Grain Dealers Association, complained that the resolution had been "railroaded through without time for reflection" and endorsed only the principle of cooperation, it was of considerable value as publicity to Cowden and the Union Oil Company.[11]

On June 17, 1929, Cowden made a contract with the Farmers Union Jobbing Association that called for the Kansas firm to handle and

[9] Cowden salary and expense statements, 1929, Cowden Papers.

[10] Cowden to C. E. Adams, February 25, 1929, CCA Files.

[11] Resolution dated March 8, 1929; Cowden to "Dear Sir" (form letter), March 13, 1929; Sand to Elevator Managers, March 19, 1929, Union Oil Company Scrapbook No. 1.

recommend only Union Certified petroleum products. In addition, the organizations agreed to employ a representative to organize cooperative oil companies within Farmers Union territory in Kansas. The Union Oil Company was to pay the Farmers Union Jobbing Association a brokerage fee, but $50 of this amount could be deducted each month and spent for advertising in the *Kansas Union Farmer*. It was also agreed that the Farmers Union would be represented on the Union Oil Company's Board of Directors at an early date.

Despite an intensive effort to get the new company operating, the Union Oil Company was initially little different from its predecessor, the Cowden Oil Company, except that it was organized on a cooperative basis. Cowden continued to do business from his office in Rooms 509 and 510 of the American Bank Building. His staff consisted of himself and his assistant, Edna May Reno. Miss Reno had worked for Cowden when he was secretary of the Missouri Farmers Association, and she continued to serve as his secretary after he formed his own oil company. As had been true earlier, Cowden did a commission or brokerage business, essentially, buying gasoline, oils, and greases from independents or major companies at wholesale prices and reselling them to the cooperatives affiliated with the Union Oil Company.

The first step in the business arrangements between the Union Oil Company and the local cooperatives was to make a contract. These agreements stipulated the quantity of gasoline, oil, and grease to be purchased by the association and the quality, price, terms of delivery, and payment. The early contracts required the local cooperative to invest 5 per cent of the capital of its oil and gasoline enterprise in Union Oil Company stock in order to qualify for representation in "the management and earnings of said company and to aid in building a national chain of cooperative companies." The local cooperative was then permitted to use the trademark and slogan of the Union Oil Company.[12] With this type of organization Cowden began to build a cooperative federation.

Except for the shares bought by the original promoters, Union Oil Company stock was purchased by local cooperatives as they became affiliated with the regional wholesale. The savings made by local cooperatives that purchased petroleum products from the Union Oil Company were then passed on to individual consumers in the form of patronage refunds. The amount refunded to cooperative associa-

---

[12] See copies of early contracts in the CCA Files.

tions depended on the percentage of business the local had done with the Union Oil Company, and the individual farmer's savings were determined by the amount of his purchases from his local cooperative. As mentioned earlier, the Missouri law concerning cooperatives required that after a reserve fund amounting to 10 per cent of the net profits had been set aside, an interest rate not to exceed 10 per cent was to be paid on capital stock. The rest of the profits or savings of the cooperative could then be distributed in dividends to participating members.

Cowden made his first contract for gasoline with the Kanotex Corporation. His procedure for filling an order for gasoline was to have the gasoline shipped on a bill of lading with sight draft attached. Orders were filled usually in carload lots shipped directly from the refinery to the cooperative that had placed the order.

This business arrangement usually worked smoothly, but any financial irregularity presented a threat to a company operating on meager capital. On one occasion Cowden was in McCook, Nebraska, soliciting business when he got word that two sight drafts accompanying shipments of gasoline had been turned down by the purchaser. The Union Oil Company's bookkeeper explained that there were insufficient funds to cover the drafts. What could he do? Somewhat desperately Cowden placed a telephone call to P. C. Floyd in St. Louis. Floyd had subscribed for some of the original Union Oil Company stock, and his friendship with Cowden was of several years' standing. Floyd had been in the fertilizer business and would have failed at one time except for some MFA business Cowden had given him when Cowden was secretary of the MFA. Now, when Cowden needed help, Floyd loaned him enough money to cover the sight drafts, and the crisis was passed.

The savings that the Union Oil Company could make by wholesaling gasoline and kerosene were modest. By the time Cowden began business, the wholesale markup on gasoline was only about $\frac{1}{4}$ of a cent a gallon.[13] There could never be substantial dividends to distribute out of this narrow margin unless he could develop a tremendous volume. The big profits were in oil and grease. Large savings would be provided to purchasers if the Union Oil Company could compound its own motor oils. The process, however, required a certain amount of technical knowledge and enough capital to establish

---

[13] Interview with E. O. Gillespie, August 15, 1961.

a compounding plant. These were big problems for a small, struggling company, but it was this kind of situation that found Cowden at his best.

The first major step toward expanding operations and achieving the integration that Cowden so much desired was taken by the Board of Directors on May 13, 1929, when it voted to buy property at 1721 Iron Street in North Kansas City. Cowden was authorized to pay as much as $11,750 for the property, but only $2,000 could be paid in cash.[14] Not even this small down payment was immediately available, so on May 29 Kearns, a member of the Board, loaned the Union Oil Company $1,500 on an unsecured demand note.[15] The deal was now closed; the cooperative owned its first property, consisting of land and a small garage-type building that was later referred to in CCA's publicity as "the two-car garage." A stucco building almost double the size of the two-car garage was attached to the original structure, and the Union Oil Company office moved to its new home. The south part of this building later became the office of a retail filling station. Meanwhile, plans were being made to construct a separate building east of the two-car garage to house the oil-compounding plant. Again Cowden was faced with the problem of securing funds. He approached the Jackson County Savings and Loan Association and on June 6 negotiated a $6,000 loan, to run for five years at 6 per cent interest. At the same time he borrowed an additional $975, to be repaid at $80 a month.[16]

Although the new building, a two-story structure approximately 60 by 40 feet, was not completed until August, the compounding of oil began on July 22. A writer for the *Kansas Citian* described it as "probably the best arranged plant in this section of the United States. So compact and complete is it that one man can make a carload of lubricating oil per hour." [17] This was the first cooperative oil-compounding plant in the United States.

The original equipment was simple and, luckily, inexpensive. It happened, quite by chance, that the Continental Oil Company was dismantling an oil and grease plant in North Kansas City. Also, Leonard Cowden, Howard's youngest brother, was assistant division manager of Continental for the states of Missouri and Kansas. Con-

---

[14] Board of Directors, Minutes, May 13, 1929.
[15] Audit of the Union Oil Company, 1931, CCA Files.
[16] *Ibid.*
[17] *Kansas Citian*, August 20, 1929.

tinental had built a new modern plant at Ponca City, Oklahoma, and the company's officials instructed Leonard to sell or junk the Kansas City factory. Leonard informed Howard that these facilities were available, but Howard replied that the Union Oil Company could not afford this class of equipment. Leonard assured him, "You don't need much money." Consequently, Cowden bought an oil tank for $25, an old delivery truck for the same price, and some laboratory supplies for a fraction of their real worth.[18]

The compounding of oil was, at that time, a cheap and simple process. It amounted to nothing more than buying what were known as neutrals and bright stocks and blending them into the desired weight of oil. The neutral was light-weight oil, and the bright stock was heavy. The company purchased these oils and had them shipped to North Kansas City in tank cars and unloaded into outside storage tanks. Inside the new compounding plant were five 1,000-gallon tanks into which varying quantities of neutral and bright stock were pumped, depending on the weight of the oil desired. To warm the oil and to promote blending, there were coils near the bottom of the tanks to which an old steam engine supplied steam. At first the oil was stirred with wooden paddles, but shortly it was stirred by air. Through an air line across the top of the tanks, the air flowed into a pipe that extended to near the bottom of each compounding tank. The air, forced to the bottom of the tanks, mixed the oil as it bubbled to the surface. While the oil was being blended and mixed, samples were drawn off frequently for testing. Hugo Solberg, commonly referred to as "Doc," did most of the testing during the initial operations. Later, a trained chemist was employed. When the oil had been blended to the proper weight, it was drawn off into 55-gallon steel barrels that had been painted with the orange-and-blue Union Oil Company colors and stamped with the Union Certified insignia. The filled barrels were then loaded on the old delivery truck and hauled to the railway station for shipment to the local cooperatives. All of this work was done by man power.[19]

Originally, the Union Oil Company compounded only three basic grades of oil — light, medium, and heavy. The company bought its premium oil from the Pennsylvania Motor Oil Company three blocks down the street, at 1500 Iron Street. One of the employees would drive

---

[18] Interview with Leonard Cowden, August 15, 1961.
[19] Interviews with Miles Cowden, Urban Eastburn, Leonard Cowden, and Howard A. Cowden, August 15, 1961.

the truck down the street and get 10 or 15 barrels of Penn oil; it was then trucked back to the Union plant and labeled "Penn Coop." However, after a year or so the manager of the Pennsylvania firm told the Union Oil Company that it was buying so little oil his company could not afford to bother with such small orders. The cooperative then began to blend its own premium oil. Ironically, within less than five years the Pennsylvania Motor Oil Company failed, and its property was purchased by the Consumers Cooperative Association.

Cowden later explained that the Union Oil Company began compounding oil because it could not depend upon the quality of the purchased product. The desire to provide a top-quality oil was no doubt a factor in Cowden's decision to blend oil in his own plant, but the fundamental reason was to reduce costs and to provide greater savings to consumers. He resented paying the major companies what he called a "manufacturing profit." Cooperators themselves should have this profit, which could be distributed in the form of patronage dividends. He used similar reasoning in justifying his demand for a cooperative-owned refinery.

Completion of the oil-compounding plant was only the initial phase of what Cowden envisioned as a completely integrated petroleum cooperative. The original organizational chart that he developed showed the Union Oil Company as the central directing agency for a cooperative-owned refinery, tank cars, and compounding plant, along with organization, advertising, and service departments. The Union Oil Company was to connect these businesses and services with the local cooperatives.

To solicit business, Cowden carried on an intensive letter-writing campaign among farmers and cooperative leaders during the first weeks after organizing the Union Oil Company. His strategy was to blanket particular local areas with letters and announcements. For example, on May 6 he sent a mailing to 174 leaders in the Chillicothe trade territory. At about the same time he mailed the same letter to 618 farmers in Macon County, Missouri. In July, 981 individuals received a letter from Cowden that began: "Here's a brand of farm relief at our 'very door.'" Literally thousands of these mimeographed communications, as well as hundreds of letters sent by first-class mail, were dispatched during the spring and summer of 1929.[20] This was

---

[20] See samples of these letters in Union Oil Company Scrapbook No. 2. The number of persons to whom each letter was sent is recorded on the letter.

Cowden's approach to solution of the farm problem at the very time Congress was passing the Agricultural Marketing Act in Washington.

In some letters Cowden boasted about the quality of his oil; in others he emphasized how much a patron could save by purchasing gasoline from a cooperative station; in others he asked for orders of gasoline and oil on a trial basis. In all he stressed the need for local cooperatives to buy cooperative products. "Why build up a business for an old-line company's private brand?" he asked in one letter. As Cowden put it, cooperatives ought to cooperate. Managers of cooperatives appreciated Cowden's emphasis upon the importance of buying cooperative products because it helped them in their educational work among local farmers.

Cowden also promoted various advertising schemes to attract the general public to his company and to the desirability of buying Union Certified commodities. At Braymer, Missouri, on October 26, for example, the local cooperative put on a free-oil day. Every customer who got an oil change for his car was given a half gallon of Union Certified oil. At about the same time, a coupon was included in advertising carried by the *Kansas Union Farmer*, entitling everyone who attended the Farmers Union Convention in Parsons to two quarts of oil, without cost. Cowden also publicized Union Oil Company products and the cooperative philosophy over the radio.

But throughout 1929, Cowden's main promotion efforts continued to be personal. He attended the annual convention of the Kansas Farmers Union and visited with cooperative leaders. In September he met with the Board of Directors of the South Dakota Farmers Union and explained his program to them.[21] Following correspondence and conferences with its secretary, Thomas M. Morrison, the Missouri Farmers Union endorsed the Union Oil Company's program at its 1929 convention. Morrison told those who inquired about the Union Oil Company that he knew Cowden personally and considered him "a good businessman and a real cooperator."[22] At a meeting on August 29, the Board of Directors of the National Farmers Equity Union endorsed the efforts of the Union Oil Company to develop a cooperative wholesale oil company.[23]

---

[21] Cowden to Thomas M. Morrison, September 13, 1929, Cowden Papers.

[22] See Cowden to R. W. Brown, August 1, 1929; Cowden to D. D. Kendell, August 16, 1929; Cowden to Thomas M. Morrison, September 13, 1929; and Morrison to Cowden, October 15, 1929, Union Oil Company Scrapbook No. 1.

[23] Board of Directors, Minutes, October 1, 1929.

Cowden was never far removed from serious problems. During the summer of 1929, for instance, he waged a running battle with the Missouri Farmers Association. Partly in order to thwart Cowden's efforts to sign contracts with MFA cooperatives, the Missouri Farmers Association Oil Company was incorporated on July 16 for the purpose of supplying MFA exchanges. Immediately, the secretary of the MFA sent out a questionnaire to all the exchanges, asking them about their use of Union Oil Company products.[24] Despite this additional competition, Cowden won the business of several MFA cooperatives.

Although Cowden was primarily interested in spreading consumer cooperation among farmers, he hoped that laborers might also be brought into the movement. He believed that farmers and workers had similar problems and interests as consumers, and that if they would join forces they could make large savings through cooperatives. On April 13, 1929, Cowden wrote to employees of the Chicago, Rock Island, and Pacific Railroad Company at Trenton, Missouri, suggesting that a closer bond of friendship and brotherhood should exist between workers and farmers. He pointed out that a cooperative had been formed at Trenton, and he invited the railroad employees to join the company. Cowden argued that this cooperative could save money on petroleum products for both farmers and laborers.[25] The true consumer cooperatives had sought to win the support of workers, but it was somewhat unusual at this time for the farm supply cooperatives like that set up by Cowden to appeal for business from labor.

At the meeting of the Board of Directors on October 1, a resolution was passed that declared: "The laboring man and the farmer are both consumers of these products, and cooperative oil associations composed of farmers and laboring men offer a splendid opportunity for the laboring men and farmers to cooperate." The Board commended efforts of local labor and farm groups to cooperate and expressed the belief that such cooperation should be extended to the national level. "To this end, we invite the American Federation of Labor to appoint three representatives to serve on our Board of Directors and cooperate with Agriculture in developing a cooperative oil association which

---

[24] R. F. Rosier to Farmers Exchange, Callao, Missouri, September 14, 1929, Cowden Papers.

[25] Cowden to Rock Island Employees, April 13, 1929, Union Oil Company Scrapbook No. 2.

would serve consumers throughout the Country." [26] But Cowden's attempt to enlist labor's support in the cooperative movement was no more successful than earlier efforts to get farmers and laborers to achieve political and economic unity. After 1929 he seldom spoke of cooperation between farmers and laborers, although at its meeting on January 14, 1930, the Board of Directors again invited organized labor to select a representative to serve on the Board.[27]

Signing up established associations was only part of the effort to build a national chain of cooperative gasoline and oil outlets. A bigger and more difficult task was to help form new cooperatives. This entailed a continuing and expanded program of education in the ideals and methods of the cooperative movement and actual organizational work. From the very outset, Cowden appreciated the necessity of providing advice and help to those farmers who were interested in forming new cooperatives as well as of assisting in solving the problems that confronted companies already in operation. This meant that the work of the Union Oil Company's fieldmen was extremely important, and that Cowden and members of the Board of Directors had to devote considerable time and effort to organizing new associations and strengthening old ones.

Walter Detmer and Robert Brown were the first regularly employed fieldmen. The Board of Directors, without explanation, dismissed Brown in January, 1930, but Detmer continued as a successful fieldman for the association for many years. As had a number of others who became affiliated with the Union Oil Company, Detmer got his early cooperative experience in MFA. He had been secretary of the Pettis County Farmers Association in the early 1920's.

However, the man who signed up more Union Certified memberships and helped to organize more new associations than anyone else was a member of the Board, Tom DeWitt. DeWitt was well known and highly respected by individual farmers and organized agriculture, and his friends were almost as numerous as his acquaintances. In his early days as a fieldman for MFA he visited hundreds of farmers in house-to-house campaigns to get members for local cooperatives. When he met with farm groups he often sang his "Fieldman's Song" to the tune of "Marching through Georgia." This ditty was a take-off on the farmer who wanted to wait a while before joining a coopera-

---

[26] Board of Directors, Minutes, October 1, 1929.
[27] Board of Directors, Minutes, January 14, 1930.

tive. Farm audiences responded to DeWitt's earnestness and sincerity, and his methods of recruiting succeeded. W. J. Solter, a member of the original Board, also did excellent organizational work. As had a number of other founders of the Union Oil Company, Solter had gained wide experience in cooperative work as a fieldman for MFA in the 1920's.

Cowden availed himself of every opportunity to spread his ideas beyond the Union Oil Company's trade territory. On August 8, 1929, he spoke on the subject, "Cooperative Oil Stations," before a meeting of the American Institute of Cooperation at Baton Rouge, Louisiana. After discussing the early development of cooperative bulk and retail stations, he told about organizing the Union Oil Company. By pooling their volume, he said, the affiliated local companies had created "an enormous buying power." Then Cowden added: "As soon as the volume will justify it, we hope to contract for the output of a refinery or to finance a refinery on a cooperative basis." He pictured a fully integrated cooperative oil business as his ultimate objective, a theme which he preached wherever men would listen.[28]

At its meeting on October 1, 1929, the Board of Directors moved to expand the Union Oil Company's services and activities. It was decided to add a line of dips, disinfectants, and roof coatings to the Union Certified line, which so far had been confined to oil, grease, kerosene, and gasoline. The Board voted also to install a bulk plant and retail service station at the company's headquarters, with offices in the original two-car garage. A bulk and retail outlet could serve the North Kansas City area, but, more important, its operation could provide managerial and business experience for cooperative gasoline and oil stations throughout Union Oil Company's territory. At this same meeting, the Board of Directors set Cowden's salary at $5,000 a year, the same amount he had drawn from the Cowden Oil Company.[29]

The audit made at the end of 1929 revealed the progress as well as the problems of Cowden's new cooperative venture. Total assets amounted to $50,226.18, but the current assets of $17,215.35 were less than the current liabilities of $17,676.67. The auditor called the Board's attention to the unhealthy relationship between current as-

---

[28] American Institute of Cooperation, *American Cooperation, 1929* (Washington, D. C., 1930), 457–67.
[29] Board of Directors, Minutes, October 1, 1929.

sets and current liabilities. Much of the Union Oil Company's financial problem, he said, was due to undercapitalization. Of the authorized $100,000 in capital stock only $18,470 had been subscribed and paid for. The auditor believed that the company was undercapitalized by at least $15,000 to $20,000. He pointed out that expenditures for development work "in establishing or securing members for the cooperatives" had been a heavy drain on the company. During the year $4,943.51 had been spent for travel and $1,566.20 for advertising. Salaries amounted to $12,104.55 for the six employees on the payroll at the end of the year. All together, operating expenses had been $30,035.76.[30]

To an outsider the expenditures for promotion may have seemed excessive, yet Cowden had no practical alternative to spending rather large sums on personal solicitation and advertising. Unless the services of the Union Oil Company were made known, and unless the cooperative principle was sold to farmers and local associations, failure could hardly be avoided. The founders of the Union Oil Company knew they had a principle to sell, an educational effort to accomplish, before a cooperative wholesale could succeed. Looking at the business from this angle, it is clear that whatever they spent on promotion was not only good business but an essential for continued existence.

Other parts of the audit revealed other aspects of the firm's financial position. There was only $529 in cash on hand on December 31, 1929. Additional assets included an old, secondhand Chevrolet truck, furniture and fixtures valued at $717, plant equipment worth $3,484, and buildings valued at $7,665; the company's land holding was listed at $6,000. So far as liabilities were concerned, nothing had been paid on the $6,000 first mortgage held by the Jackson County Savings and Loan Association, but monthly payments of $80 were being made on a second mortgage for $2,895. The problem of credit, which had plagued cooperatives for years, also showed up in the first audit of the Union Oil Company. Of the $12,214.96 in accounts receivable, 65.6 per cent were current, 17.4 per cent were over 30 days, and 17 per cent were delinquent between 60 days and one year. On October 1 the Board of Directors authorized Cowden to bring suit against one customer if he did not pay his account promptly.

[30] Audit of the Union Oil Company, 1929, CCA Files.

Net profits for the year, actually about ten months, amounted to only $4,921.51. This was a 26 per cent return on the actual capital invested, which appears very good until it is remembered that the Union Oil Company was greatly undercapitalized. The return on total business was only 1.2 per cent. The biggest profits were on oil; the company purchased oil for $17,372 and sold it for $25,310. The margin on gasoline was small, however, and $80,786 worth of gasoline had been sold for only $83,823. The profit on kerosene was equally meager.[31] The Board of Directors voted a 15 per cent patronage refund to affiliated cooperatives on gross earnings, which totaled $3,-048.61.

By the end of 1929 the Union Oil Company was operating successfully, although its future was by no means assured. During about ten months of operation, it had made contracts with twenty-two local cooperatives to supply their petroleum products. This was indeed a small start toward realizing Cowden's dream of a national chain of petroleum bulk plants and service stations, but it was a start. The company had sold 372 carloads of gasoline and kerosene, 135,362 gallons of lubricating oil, and 73,871 pounds of grease.[32]

In addition, the company had acquired property for office space, had established a bulk and retail station, and had begun operating the first cooperative oil-compounding plant in the nation. Less tangible, but perhaps even more important, was the fact that Cowden had begun to build a loyal and cohesive business organization. Furthermore, cooperative associations and their members and leaders in the Kansas City trade area were gaining confidence that the Union Oil Company's customers could save money on petroleum products. Cowden's vision of farmers joining together as consumers was taking on reality.

The Union Oil Company was a going concern. But what of the future? Before the company was even one year old, the stock market crash signaled a devastating depression. Could a small cooperative wholesale withstand the great economic forces that were sweeping the nation?

---

[31] *Ibid.*

[32] See Summary in Manager's Report, Seventh Annual Meeting, February 3–4, 1936, CCA Files.

Chapter 4

Expansion and Growth, 1930–1931

S HARPLY DECLINING farm prices were among the major indications that the stock market crash in October, 1929, was more than a financial panic and that the country was entering a full-fledged depression. Producing blindly and without regard to market demands, farmers kept their output high after 1929, and by 1932 prices had dropped to disastrous levels. Wheat that had brought midwestern farmers an average of $1.03 per bushel in 1929 commanded only 38 cents three years later. Livestock producers received more than $40 a head for cattle in 1929 but only $18 in 1932, and the price of hogs dropped more than 50 per cent in the same period. Gross income from farm production in the states of Missouri, Iowa, Kansas, Colorado, Nebraska, and the Dakotas, where the Union Oil Company did business, decreased from about $2.1 billion to less than $1 billion between 1930 and 1932.[1]

The depression directly affected merchants and businessmen who served agricultural communities. As hard times enveloped the heartland of America, an increasing number of vacant stores stared out upon hundreds of main streets, reflecting the exhausted purchasing

---

[1] U.S., Department of Agriculture, *Yearbook of Agriculture,* 1934 (Washington, 1935), 695.

power of farmers. Would these conditions wipe out the Union Oil Company before it was firmly established?

On first thought, it might seem that the depression would create insurmountable obstacles to the growth of the company. How could the company obtain the necessary volume, how could it avoid the pitfalls of credit business, and how could depression-ridden farmers be expected to respond to the cooperative method of doing business? These were indeed difficult questions that Cowden and his associates faced. But, contrary to the general trend, hard times turned out to be more a blessing than a curse. If farmers had been prosperous it might have been harder to sell them on the idea of consumer cooperation. The few cents or few dollars saved through patronage dividends would not have been so important to farmers who were selling wheat for $1 a bushel and hogs for $10 to $12 a hundred pounds. But, with some agricultural prices falling to an all-time low, farmers were searching frantically for ways and means to cut costs and to keep their heads above the swirling waters of bankruptcy. A cooperative wholesale oil company promised direct and practical help. While politicians and farm leaders explored and demanded various kinds of government aid, Cowden declared that farmers could help themselves by cutting their costs of operation through cooperative purchasing.

The depression stimulated an antibusiness attitude among farmers that Cowden quickly seized upon in his appeals for support. In his speeches and in his advertisements Cowden attacked the selfish attitudes and actions of big business and contrasted their motive of profit with the cooperatives' motive of service. Cowden eventually even tried to drop the word "profit" from his vocabulary. The original slogan, "Our Profits Are Your Dividends," appeared regularly on Cowden's printed report to members through the 1933 issue, but it was then dropped, and emphasis was placed on the concepts of service, utility, dividends, and savings. In his report to the Board of Directors in 1930, Cowden declared: "The Old Line system is on trial. I doubt if the leaders of the great industries of this country will be able to permanently solve the present economic situation which has been brought on by their greed for more business, and which resulted in over production."[2]

The depression also put farmers in a mood to try different ways and methods of doing business. Not only did Cowden attack big business,

---

[2] *President's 1930 Report*, pamphlet, CCA Files.

but he associated the great corporations with the East's exploitation of the West, a familiar theme of Grangers, Populists, and other farm groups. He wrote in 1930 that the Union Oil Company was owned by the people who used the products and "who are more interested in saving money for themselves than they are in making money for Old Line Companies, which for the most part are owned by eastern stockholders."[3] On another occasion Cowden wrote that profits from the "old-line" system went to a few who were probably already wealthy, while "the cooperative system makes it possible for the consumer to save the profits on the goods he consumes."[4] Cowden was extremely skillful in playing on the antimonopolistic, antieastern sentiment that had been so strong among western farmers ever since the Civil War.

Cowden was always careful to explain the anticipated results of the cooperative way. It meant, he said, the production and distribution of goods for use. Late in 1932, Cowden wrote: "All the farmer is fighting for . . . is just a little more of the good things of life to make it more pleasant for himself and his loved ones." Farmers deserved the saving derived from cooperative purchasing, he said, rather than "letting it flow back into the hands of wealthy stockholders of 'old-line' companies."[5]

Carrying his reasoning further, Cowden expressed the novel view that crude oil was actually a farm product. "Although practically all of it is originally owned by farmers," he wrote in his annual report for 1930, "comparatively few of these farmers have financially benefited by it." Then he explained that oil had probably produced more wealth than any other resource in the United States, "yet the streams of black gold, originating under farm lands, have, for the most part, flowed into the pockets of stockholders of eastern corporations."[6] Cowden wanted to keep the profits from oil production in the rural communities rather than to allow them to be siphoned off by outside interests. The best and perhaps the only way farmers could benefit from this wealth, he argued, was through cooperative action.

But Cowden's approach was not purely pragmatic, and he did not attack big business simply to arouse farmer support for cooperatives. Cowden was sincere in his belief that traditional capitalism had basic weaknesses as a method of conducting business and that people's

[3] *Another Melon Cut*, leaflet, CCA Files.
[4] *A Heart-to-Heart Talk*, November 1, 1932, leaflet, Cowden Papers.
[5] *Ibid.*
[6] *President's 1930 Report*. See also *A Heart-to-Heart Talk*, November 1, 1932.

economic needs could be supplied better through cooperatives. In one of his "heart-to-heart" talks he included a section on why capitalism had failed. Not only had capitalistic enterprise placed profit above service, but "the 'old' system has failed to properly distribute the earnings made possible by the 'rank and file' of our people." In other words, an intelligent people should not support a system that gave most of the fruits to a few. In developing a big network of cooperatives to serve farmer members, Cowden insisted, the Union Oil Company was building toward freedom from the capitalistic system which "through its operation for selfish gain, has wrought such great havoc throughout our great country."[7]

Writing in the same vein in later years, Cowden explained:

> What we are building here is not an institution to make richer a handful of men already too rich and too powerful, but an institution that will help lift living standards for the people of a great area; . . . an institution that may help correct some of the inequalities in our economic and social system and thus create a better nation and a better world in which this and other nations can live in peace and security.[8]

Cowden recommended a course between capitalism and socialism, the cooperative or "middle way." Cowden's earlier work with cooperatives had not included a direct attack on capitalism. As with many others in America after 1929, his ideas and attitudes were greatly modified toward the private system and its leadership by the depression.

Not only did cooperatives represent the "middle way" economically, but they had the additional virtue of being democratic. Discussing "A Cooperative Philosophy" in 1950, Cowden said that a cooperative was not *like* democracy, it *was* democracy itself. "That is one of the reasons," Cowden continued, "I have been so devoted to this movement. Perhaps the little people of this country can demonstrate to the little people of other countries that there is a way for us to work together without one exploiting the other." Cowden believed that cooperatives contributed to economic democracy "and thus make political democracy a continuing possibility."[9] He envisioned a society

---

[7] *A Face-to-Face Talk with Cooperators*, December 8, 1932, brochure, CCA Files.
[8] *A Middle Way for the Middle West*, speech delivered January 17, 1949, and published as a pamphlet, CCA Files.
[9] *Ibid.*

where Christian brotherhood would prevail over the dog-eat-dog actions of greedy men who tried to exploit other people for their own selfish purposes. Cooperatives, then, were to be the means to a richer and fuller life for millions.

In spite of Cowden's intense beliefs and promotional claims, the Union Oil Company did not actually have a great deal to offer farmers in 1929 or 1930. When the fieldmen approached officers and members of local cooperatives and asked them to buy their petroleum products from the Union Oil Company and to join in the effort to build a national chain of cooperative oil companies, they could not promise much by way of quick dividends or patronage refunds. The company's margin was too small to provide large initial savings, and, besides, patronage refunds were usually paid in stock or trade credit, rather than in cash — a situation that local cooperators fully understood. But Cowden kept hammering away at what farmers could have in the future. Always speaking with conviction and always announcing his conclusions as ultimate truth, he pictured the day when farmers would not only control and operate their own bulk and retail stations, but would also own a refinery, grease plant, feed mill, and other productive facilities. Cowden liked to tell the story of the old man who was planting an apple tree. As he worked, a youngster came along and said: "Grandpa, why are you planting an apple tree? You will never live long enough to enjoy any of the fruit." The old man replied that he was planting a tree because he had apples to eat when *he* was a boy. "We of the cooperative movement are planting apple trees," Cowden explained years later. "We're working for today and for tomorrow also, and for the days when, to us, there shall be no tomorrow."[10]

The founders of the Union Oil Company, especially Cowden, were imbued with a strong sense of idealism and optimism. Many people shook their heads in disbelief when Cowden talked about forming a centralized national cooperative organization that could supply petroleum products to every farm in America. "This may seem like a far-fetched dream," he told a group of cooperative leaders in 1931, "but I believe in time it will be realized."[11]

The main problem in the early days of the Union Oil Company was to sell an idea. The reason for this was well expressed by Homer

---

[10] *Ibid.*
[11] Address delivered at the Seventh Annual Session of the American Institute of Cooperation, Manhattan, Kansas, June 8, 1931, Cowden Speech Files.

Young, who spent more than thirty years selling cooperative products for CCA. "In the building of farmer cooperatives," he wrote, "the sale of ideas must precede the sale of the products the cooperatives handle."[12] Thus Cowden and his associates first had to get people to accept the cooperative principles of doing business. This meant *education* in the term's broadest meaning. Somehow people must be made to catch the vision which was so clear in Cowden's mind; they must view a future where business cooperation, quality, and service were emphasized rather than competition and private profits. One of the reasons so many marketing and consumer cooperatives had failed was the lack of this cooperative spirit and philosophy among farmers. During nearly a decade of work with the Missouri Farmers Association, Cowden had seen scores of budding cooperative enterprises fail when the patrons' loyalty waned and disappeared. Confidence in, and loyalty to, cooperative business principles were absolutely necessary if the Union Oil Company was ever to make any impact upon its trade area.

The depression undoubtedly made it easier to propagandize and advertise the advantages of consumer cooperation, but a vast amount of personal contact and hard work were necessary to help farmers catch sight of a future in which cooperatives would be a major element in the production and marketing of supplies needed in agricultural operations. It was not easy for individualistic farmers who had been doing business with Standard, Sinclair, and other petroleum giants to conceive of a time and circumstances when they could meet such competition with their own cooperatively organized and operated business corporation. But Cowden believed that farmers would accept the cooperative gospel if only it were preached with sufficient zeal. Thus from its very beginning, the Union Oil Company and its successor the Consumers Cooperative Association faced a major educational challenge. Fortunately, other cooperative groups were trying to spread the same message.

Cowden knew how to approach farmers, and his addresses and printed publicity were presented in terms they understood. In 1932 he started publishing and distributing what he called "Heart-to-Heart" talks. These leaflets or pamphlets were widely distributed to cooperative leaders and helped to develop support for Cowden's cooperative oil program. He wrote and spoke in a personal, folksy man-

---

[12] Quoted in *The CCA School of Cooperation* (1962), pamphlet prepared by CCA.

ner. Expressions like "sawing wood," "getting down to brass tacks," and "talking turkey" were the language every farmer knew. Cowden developed a close unity with his listeners when he played up his own early experiences and hardships on the farm. His attacks on monopoly, eastern investors, and the "old-line" crowd struck a warm response in the minds and hearts of bankrupt farmers.

A large part of Cowden's educational work was directed toward getting local cooperatives to buy only cooperative-distributed products. Before cooperative wholesales were established, local associations had no choice but to buy their supplies from private firms. The cooperative oil businesses, for example, purchased their gasoline and oil from Standard, Sinclair, or some other major firm. But Cowden argued that such an arrangement was no longer necessary, since retail and bulk cooperative outlets could now buy from the Union Oil Company and benefit from the savings or dividends. Local associations, he said, weakened the entire cooperative movement when they gave their business to an "old-line" firm. Such a practice was self-defeating for the cooperatives, Cowden warned. Every time a farmer bought a gallon of gasoline distributed by a regular oil company he contributed to the profits of the "old-line" company, profits that should be kept by the farmers. He wrote:

> During the past half century, more millions of dollars have been made out of the petroleum industry by eastern stockholders than perhaps any other one great industry of our country. The farmers have furnished a very large volume to the "old-line" companies making a large part of these millions of profit possible. Isn't it time we stopped this drain on American agriculture? [13]

In his annual report for 1930, Cowden wrote:

> We appeal to the directors and managers of Cooperative Oil Companies which are handling an Old Line Company's brand to affiliate with us. By doing so they too can receive the benefits of cooperation. [More patronage] will enable us to increase our volume and thereby increase our refunds.[14]

This in turn would be of mutual benefit to the local associations and the Union Oil Company.

---

[13] *A Heart-to-Heart Talk*, November 1, 1932.
[14] *President's 1930 Report*.

Cooperatives may have had a growing appeal for hard-pressed farmers, but they were bitterly opposed by private business interests. The major oil companies did everything possible to hold and expand their accounts with local cooperative associations and to meet the threat of the Union Oil Company. This new competition was not welcomed by the major firms that had controlled most of the wholesale petroleum business from the beginning. Cowden was fully aware that he would meet stiff resistance in the field, and part of his attack on monopolies and big business was designed to create an unfavorable public image of the major companies that opposed cooperatives. He already had evidence in his files which revealed the attitudes and actions of private oil firms toward cooperative business associations.

On September 20, 1928, the sales manager of the Mid-Continent Petroleum Corporation at Waterloo, Iowa, refused to permit gasoline and kerosene to be sold under its trade name to the Farmers Union Cooperative Oil Company at Albert City, Iowa. Mid-Continent's manager, F. B. Brocksus, wrote that when a cooperative granted patronage refunds on the basis of the quantity of merchandise purchased, "such a rebate has been interpreted by the leading oil companies as in reality a price cut," and "contrary to ethical marketing practices." Then Brocksus explained that the Farmers Union Oil Company would

> get into untold difficulties, because as soon as you start to taking customers away from the Standard Oil Company, they are going to make a rigid investigation of your methods of doing business, with the result that they will immediately class this as a price cut and reduce the tank wagon market, which will not only reduce your profits, but place you in a position where you will be unable to make any profit whatsover.

Brocksus urged the Farmers Union Oil Company to reorganize on a regular stock company basis, after which "we then would be at liberty to permit you to sell gasoline and kerosene under the Diamond Trade Brand, but we cannot do so at the present time as we would be criticized by many of our large jobbers in the state of Iowa." [15]

The Union Oil Company soon felt the pinch produced by the pressures from big business. Cowden explained to the Board of Directors early in 1930 that he had been unable to obtain a license to sell Ethyl

---

[15] F. B. Brocksus to Farmers Union Oil Company, September 20, 1928, copy in Cowden Papers.

gasoline. The Ethyl Gasoline Corporation, which was owned by Standard Oil and General Motors, he said, "has steadfastly refused to permit cooperatives to handle Ethyl, on the theory that we are unethical." [16] Faced with this problem, the Union Oil Company put its own antiknock gasoline, Ful-O-Pep, on the market. But Cowden admitted that this was not a very good alternative because extensive advertising of Ethyl had created a demand for this particular product.

Cowden also found that some major oil companies would not do business with the Union Oil Company because it paid patronage dividends to its members. As early as October 1, 1929, the Board of Directors took official notice that "certain Old Line Oil Companies are spreading misleading propaganda about the cooperative oil companies," and they urged local associations to work toward perfecting a national cooperative chain.[17] Union Oil Company stockholders passed a resolution in January, 1930, denouncing misleading and false propaganda "spread against our cooperative work by certain 'old-line' interests," and all cooperatives were asked to discontinue supporting companies which were "our competitors." [18]

In January, 1931, Cowden asked the Federal Trade Commission to rule on the legality of certain oil companies' refusal to do business with cooperatives. The chairman of FTC turned the letter over to the commission's chief law examiner, but Cowden never received any satisfaction on this point.[19] He was forced to continue meeting discrimination in the best way he could. Actually, the Union Oil Company was probably aided by the depression and the resulting surplus of oil and gasoline. Companies that might have refused to deal with a cooperative under more favorable economic conditions were anxious to get markets even if it meant doing business with the detested cooperatives. At its meeting on January 12, 1930, the Board of Directors considered bids from both Kanotex and the Continental Oil Company and unanimously agreed to accept Continental's offer.[20] This arrangement to buy Conoco gasoline may have been facilitated by Leonard Cowden, Continental's representative at Kansas City.

The first annual meeting of Union Oil Company stockholders was held at the Eagles Hotel in Kansas City on January 14, 1930. Sixteen

---

[16] *President's 1930 Report.*
[17] Board of Directors, Minutes, October 1, 1929.
[18] Stockholders' meeting, Minutes, January 14, 1930.
[19] C. W. Hunt to Cowden, January 14, 1931, Cowden Papers.
[20] Board of Directors, Minutes, January 12, 1930.

stockholders heard Cowden report on the company's progress during its first year. The President had also arranged to have a number of cooperative leaders present to discuss various aspects of consumer cooperation. These included D. D. Kendell, president of the Missouri Farmers Union, Cal A. Ward, president of the Kansas Farmers Union, and R. J. Ackley, president of the Garden City Kansas Equity Exchange. The most important resolution passed was the demand to develop a national chain of cooperative oil companies. Observing the narrowing margin between the refinery and retail price of gasoline, the Committee on Resolutions warned that it would be impossible for a single cooperative to show as great savings in the future as in the past. Therefore, "only by working together and developing our own company to the point where we will operate our own refinery, and in time develop our own tank farms and pipe lines, will we be able to meet this new condition." [21]

All members of the Board of Directors were re-elected, except W. J. Solter. He was replaced by Harry E. Witham, manager of the Kansas Farmer's Union Jobbing Association. Witham's election to the Board was part of the understanding made about six months earlier, when the Farmer's Union Jobbing Association had contracted to handle Union Oil Company products. Cowden wanted a representative from Kansas on the Board in order to draw more support from cooperatives in that state. The Board now had, in addition to Witham from Kansas, four members from Missouri, and one from Colorado. This was the beginning of a policy to provide representation from more farm organizations and from wider geographical areas on the Board of Directors. Cowden was re-elected president without opposition.

By early 1930 the management and operation of the Union Oil Company required additional personnel. On February 24, Urban Eastburn was hired to run the retail filling station that was located next to the company's office. E. O. Gillespie was employed as an accountant on July 4, and a chemist was hired to replace the untrained "Doc" Solberg in the laboratory. Miles Cowden, Howard's nephew who had come to work with the company in November, 1929, managed the warehouse and oil-compounding operations.[22] In August,

---

[21] *President's 1930 Report* and Minutes of the first annual stockholders' meeting, January 14, 1930.

[22] Interviews with Urban Eastburn, E. O. Gillespie, and Miles Cowden, August 15, 1961.

Bruce H. McCully, a son-in-law of fieldman Tom DeWitt, was employed as a salesman and organizer. As orders and correspondence increased, the secretarial staff had to be enlarged. Although Cowden was always in charge, his assistant Miss Reno managed the routine office chores. In 1932 she and Cowden were married, and she continued to work in the company's office. By the end of 1930 the Union Oil Company was employing thirteen persons, with an annual payroll of $38,270.[23]

Despite the deepening depression, Union Oil Company officials showed no signs of discouragement. They thought only in terms of growth and expansion. At its meeting on January 12, 1930, the Board of Directors instructed Cowden to contract with the Lee Tire Company for a supply of tires, tubes, and auto accessories as the next step in expanding the list of Union Certified products. At the same time, however, management was careful about cash outlays. The questions of cutting expenses to a minimum and of reducing the number of fieldmen during the winter months were discussed by the Board.[24]

But with the coming of spring there was a new burst of organizational activity. Cowden suggested that meetings be arranged at important towns and communities west of Kansas City. The Board of Directors thought such a series of meetings would gain greater prestige and publicity for the Union Oil Company if made by airplane, so they authorized Cowden to arrange for a plane. Cowden also emphasized the importance of working more closely with directors and managers of local cooperatives as a means of building Union Oil Company business. He favored holding special meetings for local cooperative officials at which the advantages of affiliating with the Union Oil Company could be explained.[25]

Meanwhile, consideration was being given to changing the bylaws and articles of incorporation. This question was discussed at the first annual meeting in January, 1930, but the decision was left in the hands of the Board of Directors. To conform to Missouri law, the original bylaws provided that each stockholder would cast one vote in all matters except in the election of directors. This provision was contrary to a basic Rochdale principle which held that in all questions of business each stockholder should have only one vote, regardless of his investment. Actually, at the first stockholders' meeting it

[23] Personnel records, CCA Files.
[24] Board of Directors, Minutes, January 12, 1930.
[25] Board of Directors, Minutes, May 28, 1930.

was unanimously agreed that each Union Oil Company stockholder could cast only one vote for directors, but this could not have been done if any stockholder had objected. In order to obtain a charter that would permit this important Rochdale one-vote principle, Cowden made arrangements to reincorporate under Kansas law. Cowden and the Directors also wanted to increase the number of Board members from six to thirteen in order to provide stronger and more widespread representation.

These changes, however, could not be approved until the second annual meeting of the stockholders in January, 1931. On January 13 a motion was made to incorporate in Kansas, but not enough of the outstanding stock was represented to constitute a legal vote. The votes were canvassed again the next day, but still less than 75 per cent of the company stock was available. Finally, on January 31, an adjourned meeting was resumed, and an almost unanimous vote was cast to change the company from a Missouri to a Kansas corporation.[26] The Secretary was instructed to draw up the legal papers on April 27, and exactly three months later the Board voted to dissolve the Missouri corporation and incorporate under the Kansas law on cooperatives.[27]

One of the strongest supporters for incorporating in Kansas was R. J. (Bob) Ackley of Garden City, who became a member of the Board in January, 1931. In 1915 Ackley had helped to form the Garden City Farmers Equity Exchange, which became one of the most successful cooperatives in western Kansas. He served as chairman of this cooperative's board of directors for many years, and by the time the Union Oil Company was organized Ackley was recognized as one of the outstanding leaders of cooperatives in Kansas. It was fortunate that Ackley decided to sign with the Union Oil Company as one of the six original cooperatives that affiliated with the infant wholesale. A farmer and stock raiser, Ackley lent strength and good judgment to the Union Oil Company's Board of Directors and, later, to CCA's Board until his retirement in 1956.

Revised bylaws were also adopted by the second annual convention. Among the most important changes were provisions for electing directors and for dividing the Union Oil Company territory into districts. Six districts were established; the number of directors to which each district was entitled depended on the amount of business it did

---

[26] Stockholders' meeting, Minutes, January 13, 1931.
[27] Stockholders' meeting, Minutes, July 27, 1931.

with the Union Oil Company. Missouri had four directors; Kansas, four; Colorado, two; Nebraska, one; South Dakota, one; and North Dakota, one. The Board of Directors was empowered to create two additional districts, consisting of Iowa and Montana, respectively, when the business in those states warranted representation in management.

Directors were elected in caucus by delegates from each district at the annual stockholders' convention. For example, if twenty delegates representing Missouri cooperatives attended the annual meeting, they would caucus and nominate four members for the Board. These names would then be presented to the entire convention for ratification and election. This was a somewhat unusual method of electing directors, but it worked well, and delegates from each district felt that they were participating directly in the election process. Here was democracy in action. Moreover, the system allowed little chance for any group or clique to get control of the organization against the wishes of member cooperatives. In the entire history of the Union Oil Company and CCA, the annual convention never rejected a nominee presented by any district caucus. Directors were to serve for two years and to receive $5 a day and expenses when engaged in company business. Although the directors were elected in open convention, the president, vice-president, and secretary-treasurer were chosen by the Board of Directors at a meeting to be held within ten days after the annual meeting.[28]

The organization of geographical districts and the enlargement of the Board of Directors reflected Cowden's basic optimism about the Union Oil Company's future. By the end of 1930 he had every reason to be confident. Despite the general business decline, the cooperative wholesale had shown a marked growth in both membership and volume. During 1930 the company had sold 1,196 carloads of refined products — mostly gasoline — compared to only 372 in 1929; more than twice as much lubricating oil and grease was handled during the second year of operation.[29] Total sales of all products reached $890,-437.06, which was 261 per cent above the figure for 1929. The largest profits continued to be from oil, as nearly 42 per cent of the gross gain stemmed from this source. Although gross profits amounted to $122,940.10, net gain for 1930 was only $24,977.70, of which $20,309.-

[28] Union Oil Company, Bylaws, 1931, CCA Files.
[29] These figures are summarized in Manager's Report, Consumers Cooperative Association, 1935, 5.

57 was made by the Wholesale Department and $4,668.13 by the Retail Department.[30] Patronage refunds to member cooperatives were $14,804.76. Considering that corporation profits as a whole were dropping sharply, this was a good record.

Expenses of operation continued heavy as Cowden vigorously pushed the firm's organizational activities. The cost of maintaining a field force was a large item of operational expense, second only to the salary budget. While there was always a hard core of fieldmen like Tom DeWitt, the total number who devoted full time to soliciting the business of established cooperatives and organizing new associations rose and declined with the company's needs and financial ability. In order to cut expenses, several fieldmen were usually laid off during the winter months when travel was difficult and people did not turn out for local meetings. For example, on October 16, 1930, the Board of Directors considered the question of reducing overhead expenditures, and Cowden announced that the services of several salesmen had been discontinued.

Although there were some attempts at economy, expenses totaled $79,745 in 1930. Among these outlays were $37,449.98 for wages and salaries, $16,342.49 for the expenses of fieldmen, sometimes called salesmen, $2,930 for advertising, $2,369 for telephone and telegraph, and $1,254.50 for postage.[31] Promotional efforts obviously paid off because by the end of 1930 forty additional cooperatives were affiliated with the Union Oil Company, nearly twice as many as had been added during the first business year.[32] Not only had more local associations signed with the cooperative wholesale, but each was doing more business. The Retail Department, established late in 1929, had been expanded, and this furnished additional outlets for Union Oil Company products. The company operated bulk plants at seven towns in Missouri, including North Kansas City, and at Parsons, Kansas. Six retail service stations were also in operation. The Retail Department showed a profit of only $4,668.13 in 1930, but most of the stations had been operating for less than a year.[33]

Lack of adequate capital was still a basic problem. During 1930 only $13,082 was added to the capital structure, making a total paid-

---

[30] Auditor's Report, 1930, CCA Files.

[31] *Ibid.*

[32] The list of cooperatives added to the Union Oil Company chain each year is given in the annual report, beginning in 1935.

[33] Auditor's Report, 1930.

in capital of $31,825. The auditor mentioned this matter for a second time in his report and remarked that "the amounts spent in stations and field work have cut your working capital to a minimum." [34] The seriousness of this problem was stressed by Cowden in his annual report. He pointed out that during the year the Board of Directors had considered the purchase of a refinery in Kansas "and a hook-up with the independent producers, which would have enabled us to have taken their oil, refined it in our own plant, and marketing it through our own Cooperative organization." But, Cowden explained, "we found . . . that we were not in financial position to make this forward step." Using this experience to appeal for more cooperative support, he said that if all of the cooperative oil companies in the country had been buying from the Union Oil Company during the past two years, "we could have saved enough on the wholesale profit with which to have purchased a refinery. . . . This should emphasize the necessity for greater cooperation among cooperatives." [35]

Undercapitalization had forced the Union Oil Company to delay reaching one of its major goals and was an obvious obstacle in preventing Cowden from achieving the integration he desired. Inability to grasp one good opportunity, however, only caused him to work harder than ever to increase the number of member companies and to enlarge the volume and the capital stock "so that ultimately we can own our own refinery and possibly producing wells." This was one of Cowden's first references to owning oil wells along with a refinery. Some capital was being raised by selling certificates of indebtedness that were first authorized by the Board of Directors on October 2, 1929. By the end of 1930, $5,500 of these securities had been sold, but neither the sale of stock nor of certificates of indebtedness could put the Union Oil Company in a favorable capital position.[36]

The best prospect of strengthening the capital structure was to expand the business, increase profits, and retain most or all of the patronage refunds for expansion of facilities and services. Cowden explained his position to the stockholders at the first annual meeting when he said: "Does it not behoove all Cooperative companies to work together and to keep within their control the wholesale profit, for this profit alone, in the space of a few years, will be sufficient for us to

[34] *Ibid.*
[35] *President's 1930 Report.*
[36] Auditor's Report, 1930.

develop all the facilities needed to serve cooperatives throughout the country." In keeping with Cowden's view, the Board of Directors urged member associations to take their patronage refunds in capital stock. At the end of 1931 about one-third of the working capital had been paid in cash; most of the remainder was accumulated savings. Cowden explained to the membership, "Your patronage has financed the company you are building." The idea of obtaining needed capital by reinvesting the profits may have been sound in principle, but these profits were too small in the early years to add much operating capital.

Besides heavy expenses for organizational work, additional outlays were made in 1930 to double the capacity of the oil-compounding facilities and to make other improvements in the plant and office. Additional outside storage tanks were set up, and plans were made to install new barrel-cleaning equipment, an elevator, and six more inside storage tanks. When these changes were made, the plant had a blending capacity of two carloads of oil per hour. New laboratory facilities also were added to permit tests not only of oils, but of gasoline, kerosene, and distillate, supporting Cowden's continuing emphasis on the Union Oil Company's aim to market quality products. To take care of expanding business, bookkeeping and billing machines were purchased for the office.[37] The total value of equipment on December 31, 1930, was $32,952, or more than eight times that of a year earlier. The Union Oil Company was now adequately organized and had facilities for substantial expansion.

Lack of office space tended to reduce administrative efficiency. Cowden announced at the stockholders' meeting in January, 1931, that the Directors were considering adding to the present office. The Board approved the proposal on April 27, and construction commenced late in May. By early July a second story had been built over the original two-car garage, and a new structure had been added on the ground floor, doubling the firm's office space. The entire structure was stuccoed, the company's name was painted on three sides, and the building was trimmed in blue and orange, the company colors. Some signs of affluence were evident in the decision to finish one office in oak wainscotting.

These changes represented the third major addition to the original two-car garage. First, there had been enlargement of the garage to provide space for offices in March, 1929; then, the compounding plant

---

[37] *President's 1930 Report.*

had been completed in July, 1929; and now, in July, 1931, a second-story addition was finished above the original property.[38] The company also rented warehouses in Aberdeen and Sioux Falls, South Dakota, in 1931, in order to provide quicker and more efficient service to cooperatives in the Dakotas.

Throughout the first year of the depression, Cowden seldom referred to the increasing hard times and their effect on business. The depression might even be beneficial, he told the annual meeting in January, 1931, because "it will make us more careful and cautious in conducting our respective businesses, which will make them more sound than ever before." [39] He strongly disapproved price-cutting by both major and independent companies and argued that cooperatives were a stabilizing influence in the market. Cowden criticized the old-line companies for overbuilding their distributing facilities, a practice that he believed required unduly large margins in order for the investments to pay out. He also attacked cut-rate stations. At their second meeting the stockholders passed a resolution declaring that such practices demoralized the market and were a confession of inadequate business methods. "Enduring prosperity is built upon sound economics, not upon temporary makeshift," read the resolution.[40] Cowden and the affiliated cooperatives had every reason to oppose cut-rate operations and extremely narrow margins. In some instances these practices were aimed at driving the cooperatives out of business; unless the cooperatives could show a saving and could pay patronage dividends or refunds the members might desert their local associations, and any weakening of the local cooperatives was bound to be felt in turn by the Union Oil Company. Therefore, it was to the cooperatives' advantage to work for market stability and reasonable margins of profit.

There was seldom a time when Cowden and the Union Oil Company were not confronted with challenging and difficult problems. This point is well illustrated by the plans to add tires to the Union Certified line. Although the Board of Directors had authorized adding tires, tubes, and auto accessories to the line in January, 1930, no definite arrangements had been worked out by the end of the year. In January, 1931, Cowden announced that he had contracted with the

---

[38] Board of Directors, Minutes, April 27, 1931; *President's 1931 Report*; and *North Kansas City News*, undated clipping, May, 1931, and July 7, 1931, Scrapbook No. 1.

[39] *President's 1930 Report.*

[40] Stockholders' meeting, Minutes, January 13, 1931.

Lee Tire and Rubber Company to purchase these products, but shortly after the Union Oil Company began handling tires the Lee firm sold out to the Phillips Petroleum Company and informed Cowden that henceforth orders must be processed through Phillips. Cowden did not like the new management, and the agreement was cancelled. He learned the lesson, however, that a cooperative should not rely on another company's product if it could possibly be avoided.

In its contract with Lee, the Union Oil Company was about to do what it had been urging its affiliated members not to do, namely, handle an old-line brand. It would be hard to justify distributing the Lee tire after trying to convince local associations that they should sell only Union Certified petroleum products. In any event, the experience forced Cowden and the Directors to rethink the tire program. A few Lee tires were distributed by the Union Oil Company in 1931, but the records do not reveal the number. There is no mention of a tire business in the annual report.

Meanwhile, in the summer of 1931, Cowden sent out questionnaires to scores of cooperative associations, asking for their opinions about the tire program. Most managers replied that they wanted to sell a tire with a distinctive cooperative brand, and most of them favored the trade name, "CO-OP." On the basis of this information, the Union Oil Company bought its own molds and contracted with the Mohawk Rubber Company to manufacture CO-OP tires. The Western Battery Company agreed to produce batteries under a CO-OP label. These arrangements were approved late in 1931, and the first CO-OP tires arrived in Kansas City about the first of January, 1932, just before the third annual stockholders meeting.

On February 2, a representative of the Mohawk Rubber Company announced to the convention that this was the first time his firm had ever put another name on a Mohawk product. He promised that the highest quality tires would be manufactured for the Union Oil Company and expressed approval of the firm's cooperative principles. When a committee urged that all cooperative associations handle CO-OP tires and batteries, delegates approved the resolution "unanimously and with great enthusiasm." [41] J. H. Appleby became manager of the Tire and Battery Department. Harry Appleby was a colorful, intense individual who brought a great deal of practical experience to

[41] Board of Directors, Minutes, January 12, 1930, and February 1–3, 1932; Stockholders' meeting, Minutes, February 2, 1932; and *President's 1931 Report*.

the tire business. Besides this, he was a master salesman. During the next twenty years he became something of a legend in CCA territory as he led hundreds of meetings in "The Tire Song" in his peculiar off-key singing.

The question of obtaining a refinery was never far from Cowden's mind, and in 1931 both he and the Board of Directors devoted a great deal of attention to this matter. Cowden announced at a special stockholders' meeting on July 27 that a small refinery in Oklahoma had gone into the hands of receivers and might be purchased at a favorable figure. After a thorough discussion the Executive Committee was authorized to investigate the possibility and advisability of purchasing the Crump Refinery.[42] When purchase of the Oklahoma City property did not prove feasible, Cowden investigated a refinery at Chanute, Kansas. He reported early in 1932 that a half interest in the refinery could be purchased for $50,000. Again, the Executive Committee was instructed to study the matter. Nothing came of this effort, however, but Cowden explained to members at the annual convention on February 2, 1932, that "we are looking toward the time when cooperative oil companies throughout the United States and Canada will be merged into one large unit which will own and operate oil wells and refineries as well as compounding plants and distributing agencies."[43]

Based on the volume of business, 1931 was an excellent year for the Union Oil Company. It shipped 1,766 carloads of refined products, an increase of 570 cars. About 510,881 gallons of lubricating oil were sold, exceeding 1930's sales by 190,297 gallons.[44] Sales of grease were up nearly 100 per cent. But dollar business increased less than $100,-000, rising from $890,437 to $981,490. This condition reflected the strong downward price trend caused by the worsening depression, yet, with modest increase in dollar sales, profits for the year were $45,899.-51, nearly double the figure for 1930. Actually, the net gain was more than this, as $10,371 of deferred expenses from previous years was charged against 1931 income.

The brighter situation was due to a great increase in the volume of wholesale business and retail sales rather than to a reduction of expenses. In fact, salaries and general operational outlays were $147,-157 for both the wholesale and retail departments, compared to only $79,745 a year earlier. A substantial amount of this increase was paid

---

[42] Stockholders' meeting, Minutes, July 27, 1931.
[42] *President's 1931 Report*; Stockholders' meeting, Minutes, February 2, 1932.
[44] Manager's Report, Consumers Cooperative Association, 1935.

to truck drivers in the Retail Department, who worked on a commission basis. However, the expense statements showed that the cost of doing business was fairly high. Travel and sales expense amounted to $26,646.23, and the bill for advertising reached $6,015.35. Salaries for fieldmen were down in 1931, as more emphasis was placed on general meetings and printed publicity to spread the Union Oil Company's message.[45]

By the end of 1931, the Union Oil Company balance sheet showed the following condition: [46]

CONDENSED BALANCE SHEET AS OF DECEMBER 31, 1931
ASSETS

Current Assets, Net	$ 33,734.52
Inventories	37,660.10
Deferred Charges	12,045.98
Fixed Assets, Net	59,450.29
	$142,890.89

LIABILITIES

Current Liabilities	$ 21,850.58
Notes and Mortgages	17,175.00
Accrued Liabilities	587.96
Members Prorate	430.67
Employees Insurance	283.02
Capital Stock	48,965.00
Surplus and Profits	53,598.66
	$142,890.89

COMBINED OPERATIONS, WHOLESALE AND RETAIL DEPARTMENTS, FOR THE YEAR OF 1931

Total Sales		$981,490.96
Inventory at beginning	21,225.63	
Purchases for the year	808,020.34	
Total	829,245.97	
Less Inventory at close	35,784.16	
Cost of Goods Sold		793,461.81
Gross Gain on Sales		188,029.15
Other Income items		14,558.81
Total Gross Income		202,587.96
Deduct—Expenses, Interest, Insurance and Taxes		147,157.92
Operating Gain for the year		55,430.04
Less-Depreciation taken	6,530.53	
Reserve for Bad Debts	3,000.00	9,530.53
Net Gain for the Year		$ 45,899.51

---

[45] Auditor's Report, 1931.
[46] *Ibid.*

This was a rather favorable financial picture, yet only twenty-nine new cooperatives affiliated with the Union Oil Company during 1931, compared to forty the year before. This was probably due to a slightly less intensive effort in the field as well as to the depression. On the other hand, patronage refunds granted by the Wholesale Department amounted to 25 per cent of the gross profits, or $26,134.61. This figure was nearly double that of 1930. The Wholesale Department paid its dividends in capital stock or in trade credit. A smaller patronage refund of only 12 per cent was paid by the Retail Department.

There were two kinds of membership in the Retail Department. One was held by the regular shareholder member who purchased a $25 share of Union Oil Company stock. This entitled the person to regular cash patronage refunds, governed by the profits of the Retail Department. However, since times were hard and money was scarce, it was clear that not many farmers were in a position to invest $25 in a share of stock, so a participating membership was provided that did not require any cash outlay. The participating member signed an application and began buying from a Union Certified bulk plant or service station. He then received dividends based on the purchases he made, but the Union Oil Company retained all refunds until $10, the value of a participating share, had been withheld. A participating member received only 75 per cent as much patronage refund as a regular shareholder. Without this method for permitting members to pay for a share of stock with their dividends, the Retail Department would not have made much headway. For example, at the beginning of 1931 the department had 1,300 members, of whom more than 1,000 were participating members. Although Cowden and the Board of Directors were vitally interested in expanding the Retail Department, it gradually became less important in relation to total business. The associations owned and operated by the Union Oil Company did provide valuable educational and business experience in the management of local cooperatives — experience which could be passed on to the affiliated local associations — but the company-owned retail outlets never became a major market for the cooperative wholesale.

Management of the Union Oil Company during its early years was highly personal and, to a considerable extent, informal. Cowden was general manager as well as president, and he kept a watchful eye on the entire operation; he found it hard to delegate any real authority to other employees. Yet, he never became so involved in day-to-day details that he neglected broad policy. One of the unusual things about

Cowden was his ability to keep in close touch with all operations without losing sight of the broad and fundamental questions of policy and administration that required thought and planning as well as action. Cowden worked closely with the Board of Directors, but he made most of the basic decisions, and there was never any question as to who was in control. He won this position of leadership by gaining the confidence of the employees and cooperative leaders and then employing his power with tact, responsibility, and good judgment.

The Board of Directors nearly always backed Cowden unanimously. He kept the Board fully informed at their quarterly and annual meetings, and a strong mutual confidence and personal friendship developed between Cowden and the Board members. This kind of association was not only desirable but absolutely necessary, since Cowden and the Board were dependent upon one another. Cowden probably could not have developed a large cooperative wholesale without the backing of strong cooperative leaders in the field like the men who served on his Board of Directors. On the other hand, these cooperators could not have built a wholesale without the vision, dedication, and abilities of a man like Cowden.

The close relationship between Cowden and his Directors is indicated by the praise that flowed back and forth constantly and by Cowden's unanimous re-election as president year after year. In his first annual report Cowden wrote that the Directors had "worked in perfect harmony during the year," and that almost every action had been taken by unanimous consent. He said that there were two classes of leaders in the cooperative movement, those "who can think through a thing, and the other those who are able to think a thing through." The Union Oil Company's Directors, he continued, were the type of men who could think a thing through.[47] At the same time, the Directors expressed confidence in Cowden and in his administration of company affairs. The Board frequently passed motions or resolutions praising him for his "conscientious service and capable management," as it did on April 27, 1931; at a meeting three months later, the Directors voted to raise his annual salary from $5,000 to $6,000, despite the bleak economic prospects.

There was not only a friendly working relation between Cowden and the Board of Directors, but also, management worked closely with representatives of the affiliated cooperatives throughout the Union

---

[47] *President's 1930 Report.*

Oil Company's territory. The annual meeting of the stockholders was started as a regular affair in January, 1930, and, beginning in 1932, it was held in the North Kansas City High School auditorium. It was found that a one-day convention did not provide enough time to transact all business, so in 1933 the company sponsored two-day sessions. Cowden usually opened the meeting by reviewing the previous year's accomplishments and by appealing for greater cooperative effort in the future. At the first two annual meetings he also read a formal printed report, but, starting in 1932, this report was simply distributed to the delegates.

The proceedings were quite informal. In the early years, when only 100 to 150 delegates attended — there were 124 present in 1932 — Cowden would ask each person to stand, introduce himself, and tell something about his work. Then members of the Board of Directors and, possibly, other cooperative leaders were called on to recount their experiences in handling Union Certified products. This part of the program had all the earmarks of an old-fashioned religious testimonial meeting, and it was designed partially to win the support of visitors who were considering affiliation with the Union Oil Company. It was not uncommon for ten or fifteen short speeches of this kind to be part of the program. A banquet, served in one of the local churches and paid for by the company, was a fitting climax of the early annual meetings.

Cowden intended that the yearly stockholders' meeting should provide an opportunity not only to review the company's business but also to educate cooperative officials — managers, local boards of directors, and others. The talks were geared to impart the cooperative philosophy and to picture the practical advantages that were being realized currently and that could be expected in the future. Later in CCA history delegates at the annual meeting were treated to the wit and wisdom of national commentators or to the pleasures of a symphony orchestra. But even if the Union Oil Company could have afforded such programs in the early 1930's, they would have been considered foolish and a waste of time. So much building was required on the cooperative structure that time and energy had to be concentrated on the immediate tasks. Delegates were informed not only through speeches, reports, audits, and pamphlets, but in 1932 a movie depicting the Union Oil Company's personnel and operations was shown to stockholders. The whole federated structure of the Union Oil Company was a closely knit organization, held together largely through the work and personality of Howard A. Cowden. Friendly and modest, Cowden drew recognition to the contributions of others and was careful not to take personal credit for the company's achievements.

Cowden was often the subject of gossip and criticism, some of which was no doubt started by competitors. Early in the company's history rumors circulated that Cowden held a large amount of capital stock and operated the firm for his own benefit. At the annual meeting in 1932 a stockholder asked about Cowden's stock ownership in a question from the floor and also inquired about the company's management and control. Cowden replied that he had nothing to hide, but the minutes do not reveal whether he publicly announced the amount of his stockholdings. In any event, within the year Cowden began selling his common stock to the company. On January 30, 1933, the Board of Directors voted to buy forty shares of Cowden's stock for transfer to the local cooperative associations.[48] Their action was in line with the general policy of getting the stock out of the hands of individuals, except for one share for each director, and placing it with the affiliated cooperatives.

Despite the depression, by the end of 1931 the Union Oil Company was firmly established. Now incorporated in Kansas and operating under true Rochdale principles, it had enlarged its physical facilities, added member associations, and greatly expanded the volume of business. Moreover, the company was emphasizing a broad program of cooperative education that was helping to build unity between local cooperators and the wholesale. This was indeed an encouraging beginning.

---

[48] Stockholders' meeting, Minutes, February 2, 1932; and Board of Directors, Minutes, January 30, 1933.

Chapter 5

Broadening Horizons

COWDEN WAS NOW SO INVOLVED in the cooperative movement that he gave very little attention to the broad matters of national agricultural policy that were being developed in 1932 and 1933. He virtually ignored the questions of acreage restriction, benefit payments, processing taxes, and the other economic principles that were being hammered out by agricultural economists and other social scientists in farm organization meetings and in the halls of Congress. Although Cowden never claimed that consumer cooperation was the full answer to the difficulties facing American agriculture, he was committed almost exclusively to this aspect of helping farmers. "We do not contend that the cooperative handling of petroleum products is going to solve all of the economic problems of the farmer," he told a radio audience in 1931, "but it will help to the extent that it lowers his cost of production." [1] Since the benefits that farmers could realize through cooperatives depended to a considerable extent upon the efficiency and extent of their operation, Cowden was constantly striving to expand and improve the services of the Union Oil Company.

---

[1] Speech delivered over radio station WIBW, Topeka, Kansas, March 20, 1931, Cowden Speech File.

But more than this, Cowden was among those leaders who wanted to bring cooperative wholesales together into a great national organization. He reasoned that if local cooperatives could achieve economic advantages by working through a cooperative wholesale, even greater savings could be made in buying such products as gasoline, should the regional cooperatives combine their purchases. In other words, because of the greater volume, a national buying agency would be able to get better prices than a regional. Cowden argued that if consumer cooperatives were to achieve their maximum economic power they must unite on a national, and eventually on an international, basis.

Cowden had first discussed the idea of combining state and regional purchasing cooperatives into a large national organization at the meeting of the American Institute of Cooperation at Baton Rouge, Louisiana, in August, 1929. A number of cooperative leaders, including Cowden, I. H. Hull, head of the Farm Bureau Oil Company of Indianapolis, and others, considered the advantages of unifying these cooperative buying agencies. Actually, more was at stake than economic advantage. Consumer cooperatives wanted a bigger voice in the whole cooperative movement; they resented operating in the shadow of the great producer cooperatives, like those in wheat and cotton, which got most of the attention and publicity. Suggestive of this resentment was Cowden's complaint that the program of the purchasing groups was scheduled on the last day of the meeting, indicating their secondary status! In any event, during the following two years Cowden and a few other officials of consumer cooperatives talked and planned about a national organization.[2]

On November 21 and 22, 1932, Cowden and Tom DeWitt met in the Sherman Hotel in Chicago with representatives of the Central Cooperative Wholesale of Superior, Wisconsin, the Farmers Union Central Exchange of St. Paul, the Farm Bureau Oil Company, Inc., of Indianapolis, and the Midland Cooperative Wholesale of Minneapolis. The outcome of this meeting was the formation of National Cooperatives, Inc. Hull was elected president and Cowden secretary-treasurer. Cowden wrote, later in the year, that he considered the part played by the Union Oil Company in setting up this organization as "outstanding among our accomplishments for the year."[3] On Decem-

---

[2] Speech delivered before the Indiana Farm Bureau Cooperative Association, March 9, 1933, Cowden Speech File.
[3] *President's 1932 Report.*

ber 12 the Board of Directors of the Union Oil Company subscribed for $250 in stock of National Cooperatives, Inc., and at the same time elected Cowden to serve on National's board of directors to represent the Union Oil Company.[4]

Immediately, the Union Oil Company began to place orders for some products through National Cooperatives, and Cowden reported that on oils, for example, a much better price was obtained than "we could have gotten by working alone." [5] At first National Cooperatives had no personnel or central office, and the purchasing was done by a committee consisting of regional managers.

Cowden worked hard to expand the membership and business of National Cooperatives because he believed that forming the national group was a significant step toward the national and international cooperation that he thought was so important. Addressing the Indiana Farm Bureau Cooperative Association on March 9, 1933, Cowden declared,

> It is not hard for me to visualize the time when our organiza-
> tion will reach out across the broad Atlantic and cooperate
> with the consumers of Europe. . . . Here is the picture as I
> see it: 100 to 500 farmers in a local community cooperate
> through their local companies in turn cooperate through their
> regional groups serving some 75,000 to 100,000 consumers; the
> regionals form the national representing nearly half-million
> farmers — and then reaching across the ocean and pooling our
> buying power with those consumers in Europe who have al-
> ready organized.[6]

He envisioned the Union Oil Company as a vital element in the substructure for this international cooperative organization.

An extremely important part of Cowden's program was to increase and strengthen the loyalty and efficiency of Union Oil Company employees. Early in January, 1930, Cowden and the Board of Directors considered a group life insurance program for every employee of the company and for those of cooperatives with 100 per cent memberships. It was especially important, Cowden felt, to win and hold the loyalty of the efficient managers of local cooperatives throughout Union Oil

---

[4] Board of Directors, Minutes, December 12, 1932.

[5] *President's 1932 Report.*

[6] Speech delivered before the Indiana Farm Bureau Cooperative Association, March 9, 1933, Cowden Speech File.

Company territory. He explained to the stockholders in January, 1931, "The greatest problem of the cooperatives is to keep in their ranks managers and operating men." Too often, he said, officials of the cooperatives were lured away by the higher salaries offered by private firms. In order to maintain personnel, Cowden believed, some of the benefits of cooperation should be distributed to the employees. The stockholders approved Cowden's proposal by establishing an employees' association to carry a $500 life insurance policy on every member. The company's profits on tire sales were set aside to pay the premiums.[7] One reason for offering group insurance to cooperative employees and officials was to get them to handle the company's tires and promote their sales.

At a special meeting of the stockholders on July 27, 1931, insurance policies for $500 were presented to all regular employees and to members of the Board of Directors.[8] When, the following year, the sale of tires exceeded expectations, the amount of each insurance policy was increased to $1,000.[9] Cowden reported that this program had stimulated among the employees keen interest in the Union Oil Company and its member companies and had generated greater concern for the cooperative movement as a whole. Also in 1932 employees of the Union Oil Company formed the Cooperative Oil Credit Union, with management's backing. When robbers blew up the office safe in August, 1932, and stole $148.38 belonging to the Employees' Credit Union, Cowden got the Directors to reimburse the money from company funds.

Cowden's desire to build employee loyalty only partly explains his support for this type of fringe benefit; he had a warm personal interest in the employees and a genuine concern for their welfare. Cowden expressed his true attitude when he told about a man who had given the best years of his life to the cooperative movement and died, leaving scarcely any estate. "What finer thing could we do if the families of some of our employees should be so left than to hand them a check for $500 or $1,000?" he asked.[10] In this period of the Union Oil Company's history he knew all of the employees well — there were forty-one persons on the payroll in 1932 — and there was a close relationship

---

[7] *President's 1930 Report* and *President's 1931 Report*.
[8] Stockholders' meeting, Minutes, July 27, 1931.
[9] *President's 1932 Report*.
[10] *President's 1930 Report*.

between Cowden and the other workers. It can be said that he was not a benevolent dictator, but a benevolent cooperator.

Cowden had more in mind than providing economic security for the Union Oil Company's employees. He wanted them to feel that they were participating in the great and exciting adventure of building a cooperative movement. "We are extremely anxious," he wrote, "to have our employees be the best informed and most enthusiastic cooperators in the country." [11] However, Cowden recognized that this condition would not come about by chance. Most regular employees of the Union Oil Company and the affiliated associations worked for a cooperative because it was a job, not because of devotion to cooperative business principles. Therefore, it was just as important — or perhaps more so — to educate company personnel as it was to inform farmers and the general public on consumer cooperation.

In discussing this problem Cowden and the Board of Directors decided that the best cooperative literature should be made available to employees in North Kansas City as well as to managers and officials of local cooperatives. Cowden announced in February, 1932, the establishment of a circulating library consisting of the best books, periodicals, and pamphlets dealing with the cooperative movement in the United States and the world.[12] More than a year elapsed, however, before the library was actually organized. In 1932, about $465 was spent on the library and in the next two years $586 and $834, respectively.[13] Meanwhile, a course was set up for Union Oil Company employees on salesmanship and business efficiency. Cowden told the membership in January, 1933, "In fostering this educational movement of employees, the Union Oil Company is taking a leading part for the future of the cooperative movement." [14]

This emphasis upon grounding workers thoroughly in cooperative principles arose from Cowden's belief that cooperatives had failed in the past because they lacked efficient and informed leaders. Although the company paid only average wages, employees did develop an intense loyalty that lasted even after CCA became a multimillion-dollar business and worker relationships much less personal. Picnics and old-fashioned family gatherings became the custom among Union

---

[11] *President's 1931 Report.*
[12] *Ibid.*
[13] See the Union Oil Company audits for 1932, 1933, and 1934, CCA Files.
[14] *President's 1932 Report.*

Oil Company employees early in company history. After a good supper the employees would present a program of music, group singing, and short talks on cooperative theory and practice. These events had both educational and social value.

The economic depression created a number of problems for the Union Oil Company, but expansion continued to characterize the company's policy. Shortly after additional office space was completed in July, 1931, Cowden informed the Directors that land immediately south of their property would soon be for sale.[15] He explained at a meeting of the Board on February 1, 1932, that the land and an adequate warehouse building together would probably cost no more than $10,000. The Board authorized him to buy the land for $3,000, and additional storage tanks were placed there. At this meeting the Directors discussed the feasibility of establishing a grease plant; a majority of the Board thought it would be advisable, but took no action.[16] The following day, Cowden announced in his annual report that plans were under way not only to buy more land but to double the size of the present properties. "These plans," he said, "are in line with our policy of developing our facilities as required, in order to give good service and at the same time not to overexpand." [17]

The next major construction project was the building in 1933 of a three-story structure, connecting the office and the original compounding plant. This building increased the space for blending and handling oil and provided warehouse space for tires, tubes, and batteries. Much of this work was done by regular employees at a minimum of expense.[18] As the business grew, more warehouse facilities became necessary in different parts of the Union Oil Company territory. By the end of 1933 the company was operating nine warehouses, all of which lost money except the one at Aberdeen, which continued to be the main outlet for business in the Dakotas.[19] The warehouse at McCook, Nebraska, showed a loss of $162, and the one at Sioux Falls was closed after a few months of operation, indicating that Union Oil Company's management still had a number of unsolved problems in the field of distribution.

Although the Union Oil Company's trade territory covered the six-

---

[15] Board of Directors, Minutes, November 13, 1931.
[16] Board of Directors, Minutes, February 1, 1932.
[17] *President's 1931 Report.*
[18] *President's 1933 Report.*
[19] Union Oil Company Audit, 1933, CCA Files.

state region of Missouri, Kansas, Colorado, Nebraska, and the Dakotas, large percentages of Union Certified products were sold in two of the states, Kansas and Missouri. During 1931, for example, 52 per cent of the total business was done in Kansas alone. The fact that the Union Oil Company held a contract to supply the Kansas State Highway Department with oil was partly responsible for this large business. However, local cooperatives were strong and numerous in Kansas, and, perhaps even more important, Cowden had many close friends in the state who worked hard to help increase the Union Oil Company's business.

The stockholders recognized this situation at their annual meeting on February 2, 1932, when they increased the number of directors representing Kansas from four to seven. This raised the membership of the Board to sixteen. Ralph Snyder, president of the Kansas Farm Bureau, was among the new directors elected from Kansas.[20] Snyder's election was a wise move because his reputation among farmers and farm leaders added strength and prestige to the Union Oil Company and to its program. Once elected to the Board, Snyder took every opportunity to boost the cooperative wholesale. Speaking over the radio in February, 1932, he explained that this was the first time that farm organizations in the Midwest had united to save money through cooperative purchases. In Kansas, he said, the Farm Bureau, the Farmers Union, the Grange, the Equity, and the Cooperative Grain Commission Company were all backing the Union Oil Company and helping to make it more effective.[21] This kind of publicity was invaluable to the company and to its program of expansion. Snyder praised Cowden for his good management and progressive ideas and stated in a letter to Cowden: "No effort should be spared, and no one's personal ambition or prejudice should be allowed to stand in the way of making the Union Oil Company the biggest farmer's cooperative purchasing concern in the United States. I am very much in hopes that ultimately this result may be obtained." [22]

Although the Union Oil Company had been operating for three years, there were still many independent oil companies within the adjacent trade territories that were not affiliated with the wholesale cooperative. Cowden informed the Board of Directors on August 27, 1932, that approximately three hundred cooperative companies were

---

[20] Stockholders' meeting, Minutes, February 2, 1932.
[21] Ralph Snyder, radio address, February 15, 1932, copy in Cowden Papers.
[22] Snyder to Cowden, February 16, 1932, Cowden Papers.

still buying petroleum products from sources other than cooperative. He announced his plan to mail friendly resolutions and testimonials about the Union Oil Company to the managers and directors of these local associations and then to follow up with a letter explaining the plans and accomplishments of the company.[23]

Too, Cowden was thinking of moving into new territory. Already a few sales had been made in Iowa and Montana, but not enough to permit either of those states to have representation on the Board of Directors. It was not until January 31, 1933, that a director was elected from Iowa, making seventeen members on the Board. However, in August, 1932, Cowden asked the Board about trying to open up a new area in Idaho, Washington, and Oregon. A majority of the Directors took the position that it would be better to concentrate on building up the local cooperatives then affiliated with the Union Oil Company than to spread operations too thin. Yet, the Board of Directors seldom, if ever, questioned Cowden's judgment, and in this instance authorized him and the Executive Committee to take what action they deemed best.[24] If arrangements were made with cooperatives in the Pacific Northwest, Cowden was to take whatever steps were necessary to supply those associations. He had received numerous letters from cooperative leaders in that region, asking for help and guidance in developing local cooperative oil companies and inquiring about the possibility of pooling their buying power with the Union Oil Company. This whole problem needed the personal attention of someone from the Kansas City office, so Cowden dispatched Homer Young, a new fieldman, to the Northwest early in 1933.

The career of Homer Young, who later became president of CCA, has many of the elements of the traditional success pattern in America. Born on a farm in Lewis County, Missouri, on May 2, 1902, Young attended a one-room country school a quarter of a mile from his farm home. He went to high school for three years in Lewistown and finished a fourth year in Columbia, where he then enrolled in the College of Agriculture of the University of Missouri. As short of funds as most farm boys, he worked at a variety of jobs to put himself through the university. He milked cows, fired the dean's furnace in exchange for a room, and waited tables at the Robinson Hotel for his meals.

After graduating from the university in February, 1926, Young at-

---

[23] Board of Directors, Minutes, August 27, 1932.
[24] *Ibid.*

tended Northwestern University's School of Commerce in Chicago during the following summer. His first job after finishing college was as a fieldman for the Missouri Farmers Association. Cowden was then secretary of MFA, and the two men became well acquainted. Among Young's first accomplishments was the organization of a cooperative creamery, which he managed for about three years. Young was thoroughly familiar with field and organizational work and had proven himself an effective salesman of both cooperative ideas and products. In the summer of 1932 Cowden offered him a job, and he went to work on August 1 at $175 a month.

When Young got to the Boise Valley in Idaho, he found a strong cooperative spirit among farmers, and he helped to form a number of local associations there and elsewhere in the region. For a short time several of these cooperatives bought grease, oil, and tires from the Union Oil Company. Cowden reported to the Board in May, 1933, that prospects in the Pacific Northwest appeared favorable.[25] At about the same time the company rented warehouses in Salt Lake City, Spokane, and Portland to take care of the business in that region.[26] Inventories of oil and grease were maintained at Salt Lake City until 1942. However, the distance between the Pacific Northwest cooperatives and Kansas City is so great that to continue to expand operations in the area would have required additional warehouse space. An alternative was simply to help those cooperatives form a separate wholesale.

In August, 1933, Cowden recommended to the Board of Directors that the cooperatives in Washington, Oregon, and Idaho be organized into a special regional group. He had suggested the same thing, he told the Directors, to the board of National Cooperatives.[27] Cooperators in the Northwest, however, were still depending on the Union Oil Company for leadership. Late in October Young, accompanied by his bride, traveled to Portland, where about thirty cooperative leaders met to discuss a new cooperative wholesale. Out of this meeting came the Pacific Supply Cooperative, a regional wholesale; the leaders of the new cooperative immediately voted to affiliate with National Cooperatives. Young was back in Kansas City early in November, and on November 13 he reported to the Board of Directors that the Pacific Supply Cooperative was off to a good start. In January, 1934, officials

[25] Board of Directors, Minutes, May 22, 1933.
[26] Union Oil Company Audit, 1933, CCA Files.
[27] Board of Directors, Minutes, August 29, 1933.

of the new wholesale, meeting at Portland, passed a resolution thanking the Union Oil Company for "the splendid work done by Homer Young for the invaluable assistance which he gave in helping to bring into being the new regional organization."[28]

What Young did in the Pacific Northwest highlighted his talent as an organizer about as much as any single incident in his career. Within a period of about nine months he convinced the leaders of some thirty local cooperatives that they should go into the oil business, and in several instances he actually helped found the associations. Then he brought the leadership group together at Portland, and these men, practically all of them strangers to one another, took Young's recommendations for membership on the board of directors. The board, on his advice, elected Charles Baker of Walla Walla, who had been secretary of the Washington State Farm Bureau, as the manager of Pacific Supply Cooperative. The local cooperatives in Pacific Supply included some built around local units of the Grange, some around local units of the Farm Bureau, some around local units of the Farmers Union. Some were in apple country, some in potato country, some in wheat country, and so forth. Young had brought them together with a convincing picture of what they could do in the handling of gasoline, oil, tires, and related supplies.

Young was now promoted from fieldman to supervisor of refined fuel sales. Although this was supposedly an office position, he continued to spend much of his time on the road, organizing cooperatives, selling Union Certified products to established cooperatives, and, in general, pushing company business. Young was away from Kansas City for days at a time. He would return to get clean clothes and answer his mail, and then he would be off again to hold meetings with directors and managers of local cooperatives. By the time Young became president and general manager of CCA, he was able to look back on meetings with boards of directors of more than a thousand cooperatives. He made a tremendous contribution by establishing an intimate relationship between the wholesale and the local cooperatives.

The assistance that Young and the Union Oil Company gave in forming another cooperative wholesale reflects the basic missionary spirit of Cowden and the Board of Directors. To paraphrase the greatest of all teachers, it was as if they had heard the admonition to go into all the world and proclaim the gospel of cooperation. Cowden

<hr>

[28] *Cooperative Consumer*, January 25, 1934, 4.

was not satisfied simply to operate a successful regional wholesale. This, of course, was essential as a base from which to expand, but he always insisted that cooperators should not rest until they had carried the message to the nation and to the world. His interest in the formation of National Cooperatives expressed this view, and he wrote in his annual report for 1933, "To enjoy the full privileges which the cooperative system can bring to us, we must build substantially at the bottom, and all the way to the very top," until cooperatives were among the strongest business organizations in the nation. Cowden constantly cited the Cooperative Wholesale Society in England as a mark at which cooperatives in the United States should aim.

As the financial depression became worse in 1932 and 1933, Cowden attacked the traditional business structure with increasing vigor. He argued that, in the long run, the farmer's major problems could be solved only through cooperation. If farmers were not satisfied with marketing conditions, he wrote in early 1933, they should cooperate and change the system rather than continue to let profits go to wealthy stockholders of "old-line" companies.[29] In his annual report to members in 1933, Cowden explained again that the cooperative movement "seeks to substitute the service-motive in business for the profit-motive." The depression, he said, had been caused by a system that "concentrated too much wealth in the hands of a few people." Cowden's remedy was to redistribute the wealth, to place more of it in the hands of those whose toil produced it. He wrote that the Union Oil Company was doing its part "in replacing a crumbling capitalistic structure, with a way of doing business which substitutes service for profit."[30]

Cowden's sharp and insistent verbal attacks against the "old-line" companies did not remain unanswered. As the cooperatives, especially the wholesales, increased their petroleum sales, the oil industry responded with a spirited campaign to discredit the cooperatives. It is no wonder that the private companies, especially the jobbers and wholesalers, complained of this new competition, since in some areas the cooperatives cut heavily into their business. For example, in 1933 the Mitchell County Farmers Union Oil Company of Beloit, Kansas, bought 10,060 gallons of lube oil, 12,232 pounds of grease, and 28.8 carloads of gasoline. At one time this cooperative had bought from a

---

[29] *President's 1932 Report.*
[30] *President's 1933 Report.*

distributor of one of the major companies, but now it obtained all of its petroleum products from the Union Oil Company.[31] The Union Oil Company by this time was buying most of its petroleum products from independent rather than major companies, although this was due more to the companies' policies than to the cooperative's choice. In December, 1932, the Board of Directors authorized Cowden to contract with the Globe Oil and Refining Company for the company's supply of gasoline, kerosene, and distillate [32] after Conoco canceled a five-year contract.

Cancellation by Conoco was part of that company's strategy to strangle the Union Oil Company. If the major suppliers could tell local cooperatives that the Union Oil Company had no reliable supply of gasoline, the local associations might be reluctant to contract with the wholesale cooperative. This situation actually occurred in late 1932, when Homer Young was appearing before a local board of directors at Beresford, South Dakota. He had made a strong sales appeal, urging the cooperative to buy its petroleum from the Union Oil Company. Much to his embarrassment, when he finished his talk the local manager showed him a message from Conoco that reported the company's cancellation of the contract; now, stated the message, the Union Oil Company had no dependable supply of oil products. Word of the cancellation had reached the Kansas City office too late for the staff to notify Young. Experiences of this type convinced Cowden, Young, and other officials of the Union Oil Company that it was essential to get control of their own basic supplies.

In the summer of 1933, when the oil code was being drawn up under the National Recovery Act, the major companies believed they had an opportunity to strike a telling blow against the cooperatives. Since one of the objectives of the NRA codes was to eliminate unfair competitive practices, the oil companies argued that patronage refunds paid by cooperatives were actually disguised price cuts and they should not be permitted under the oil code. However, Cowden was on hand in Washington during July to protect the cooperatives against any harmful decisions by the committee that was considering the regulations. He not only represented his own company, but he spoke also for the other regionals in National Cooperatives as well as for the Grange and the American Farm Bureau Federation. Explain-

[31] Sales Record, 1933, Union Oil Company Scrapbook No. 1.
[32] Board of Directors, Minutes, December 12, 1932.

ing that nonprofit cooperatives were required under their charters to distribute dividends to their members, Cowden argued that the code's provisions regarding deviations from regular prices should not prohibit cooperative associations from paying patronage dividends.

The cooperatives won the day, and when President Roosevelt approved the code on August 19, nothing in the provisions prevented the payment of patronage refunds to members or stockholders. However, membership in farm cooperative associations was to be limited to those whose chief source of income was farming. Cowden had obtained everything he wanted except for that insertion of the word "farm" before "cooperative societies." He did not want to confine the benefits of consumer cooperative membership to those on farms.[33]

The private oil companies insisted that they suffered because the code forbade them to reduce prices or to give discounts in order to meet the competition of cooperatives, which granted patronage dividends. They were especially agitated when, under pressure from the cooperatives, the President issued an order on October 31 that permitted cooperatives to pay patronage dividends to any legitimate member regardless of whether he was a farmer, a provision the cooperatives had been unable to write into the original code. This, oil company representatives argued, placed a patently unfair advantage in the hands of cooperatives. "They can go into the town, to the customers of established oil companies, and offer price rebates, in the form of patronage dividends, and the oil companies are powerless to meet this form of price competition with straight price cuts."[34] H. H. Champlin of Oklahoma wrote to C. C. Cogswell, Master of the Kansas Grange, that the cooperatives' sales and their membership should be confined to people actually engaged in farming.[35] The practice of permitting a patron of a cooperative to acquire a share of stock by withholding his patronage refunds and without his having to invest any cash was also criticized by the private firms. *The Super-Service Station*, a voice of the petroleum retailers, said that the code endangered "the business of scores of legitimate oil marketers in territory where cooperatives are active."[36]

---

[33] J. P. Warbasse to Cowden, July 31, 1933, Cowden Papers.

[34] Warren C. Platt, "Favoritism for the Farmer Co-operatives," *National Petroleum News*, XXVI (January 3, 1934), 13. See also "The Oil Industry Needs Higher Prices," *National Petroleum News*, XXV (August 9, 1933), 9.

[35] Champlin to Cogswell, January 15, 1934, copy in Cowden Papers.

[36] *The Super-Service Station*, January, 1934, 11–12.

Warren C. Platt, editor of the *National Petroleum News*, was among the sharpest and most persistent critics of the oil cooperatives, and during the latter part of 1933 and 1934 he constantly attacked what he considered the special consideration they received under the NRA code. In January, 1934, he delved into the whole principle and philosophy of cooperatives and accused them of retarding recovery. The cooperatives, he wrote, had been founded on entirely false ideas and misconceptions. He charged that cooperative organizers and officials had capitalized on hatred of monopoly among farmers and on the idea of retaining the profits of their own business. Actually, he wrote, oil cooperatives hurt the farmers because they reduced the incomes of people who worked for the regular petroleum corporations who then had less to spend on food and fiber produced on farms.

Platt declared that there was scarcely any subject — not even religion — about which there was more "narrow, fanatical bigotry than concerning cooperatives." He insisted that they "are really a religion, not business enterprises built on cold logic and individual initiative." Platt maintained the view that patronage refunds were price cuts, regardless of what they were called. "If one admits that the cooperative idea is right," he continued, "then . . . one must admit that the so-called capitalistic system is all wrong." He concluded by saying, "A blind administration at Washington, or maybe a weak administration, is playing gutter politics in giving its blessing to the cooperatives." [37]

Meanwhile, complaints against the cooperatives were reaching Washington in increasing numbers. In December, 1933, a convention of the Nebraska Petroleum Marketers at Omaha objected to the status of cooperatives under the code. At about the same time the Illinois Petroleum Committee of Zone 8 addressed a long letter to President Roosevelt, protesting against the unfair competition of Farm Bureau Cooperative oil associations in the state. On May 11, 1934, the Illinois Petroleum Marketers Association sent a letter to all dealers in Illinois, requesting them to initiate whatever pressure was necessary to modify the President's orders regarding cooperatives. Retailers and wholesalers were asked to join in the campaign because they were equally affected "by the serious inroads farm cooperative oil companies are making into their business through the latter's expansion into the

---

[37] Warren C. Platt, "Abuses of Co-ops Retard Recovery," *National Petroleum News*, XXVI (January 17, 1934), 5–6.

service station field, soliciting every type of customer on a patronage dividend basis, with disastrous results to the legitimate retailer." [38]

Cowden thrived on this type of controversy, and, as pressure developed against the cooperatives, he responded in his usual vigorous fashion. Convinced that the factor that decided issues in Washington was a flood of letters from home, he wrote a pamphlet reviewing the situation and mailed it to 2,402 cooperative leaders on February 23, 1934. Cowden explained that, because of the propaganda circulated by certain "old-line" companies, National Cooperatives had instructed him and President I. H. Hull to go to Washington again. When he arrived, Cowden said, he wanted hundreds of letters from cooperative leaders, setting forth clearly the cooperative position. One of the things that alarmed the cooperative officials was a change in the code, approved January 25, 1934, that would prohibit cooperatives from selling equipment to their members. Apparently this provision would cover such items as tires, batteries, tanks, and other supplies. If this order remained intact, Cowden wrote, cooperatives could never become completely cooperative because they would be forced to handle some "old-line" goods. This, he explained, would put the cooperatives at the mercy of "old-line" interests and help the system that had brought "agriculture to its present pitiful condition." [39]

Cowden sharply criticized the private oil companies in the columns of the *Cooperative Consumer* also. Attacks by private companies, Cowden wrote, only proved the effectiveness of cooperatives. Answering his question as to why the oil companies opposed cooperatives, he declared: "Obviously there can be but one reason. Cooperation is good for consumers. What is good for consumers cannot also line the pockets of selfish capitalistic interests with velvet. And so, they 'holler.' " [40]

Representatives of the cooperatives and of the private oil industry appeared before the Petroleum Administrative Board on May 2, 1934, to argue the definition of a legitimate cooperative and to discuss again the position of cooperatives under the code. That the oil cooperatives could exert political influence was demonstrated a few weeks later when Hugh Johnson, Administrator of the NRA, issued an order that upheld their every contention. For nearly a year Cowden had

---

[38] Printed statement, Cowden Papers.
[39] *An Appeal for Action*, February 24, 1934, pamphlet, Cowden Papers.
[40] *Cooperative Consumer*, March 10, 1934, 2.

been intermittently fighting the battles for cooperatives in Washington and, along with other farm leaders, had kept the private oil companies from damaging cooperatives in any way. The cooperatives were greatly assisted in their fight by James P. Warbasse, one of the nation's most distinguished authorities on cooperatives and president of the Cooperative League of the U.S.A. He was a member of the Consumers' Advisory Board of the NRA, and it was he who worked out the acceptable definition of a cooperative association, which Johnson had accepted. Warbasse and Cowden communicated almost constantly during the several months of the controversy.[41] In April, 1934, Cowden was named to the Planning and Coordination Committee of the code authority for the oil industry. His appointment further strengthened the position of cooperatives.

Farm groups were quick to express their appreciation of Cowden's work. For example, on October 27, 1933, the Kansas Farmers Union passed a resolution at its state convention, attacking the attitudes of the old-line oil companies which, it said, would "have ruined hundreds of successful local cooperatives." Since the Union Oil Company had taken the lead in fighting for the amendment that permitted cooperatives to pay patronage refunds, the resolution urged Farmers Union members "to patronize cooperative oil companies whenever possible" and recommended that all cooperatives handle Union Oil Company gasoline, tires, tubes, and batteries.[42]

Even while Cowden increasingly devoted his time and attention to various phases of the national cooperative movement, the depression made it mandatory that he give close supervision to Union Oil Company affairs. Problems faced by local petroleum cooperatives were reflected in the operation of the company's own retail and bulk stations, and the prosperity of the wholesale depended upon the financial health of its affiliated local associations. As to its own retail outlets, four of the twelve lost money in 1932; the next year, six out of fifteen failed to show a profit, and those that did make money made only a very small gain. A reflection of business conditions in many communities was the fact that three of the Union Oil Company's bulk plants showed losses in 1933.[43]

---

[41] *Ibid.*, May 25, 1934, 1. See also Donald Kirkpatrick to Edward A. O'Neal, May 15, 1934; and Warbasse to Cowden, July 31, 1933, Cowden Papers.

[42] Resolutions adopted at Farmers Union State Convention, Lawrence, Kansas, October 27, 1933, Cowden Papers.

[43] Union Oil Company audits, 1932 and 1933, CCA Files.

The problem of credit was becoming increasingly serious. In his annual report for 1932, Cowden mentioned credit as "one of our most difficult problems during the past year." [44] He constantly urged local associations to operate on a cash basis. If the local cooperatives granted credit it was almost certain that they would ask their supplier, the Union Oil Company, to carry their accounts beyond the normal thirty days. In February, 1932, Cowden advised, "We should operate on as nearly a 100 per cent cash basis as possible." He tried, with considerable success, to show local cooperatives that if they tied up their relatively small working capital in accounts receivable they could not provide the proper services to members. [45] Although the Union Oil Company paid extremely close attention to its own credit problem, it had $73,291.70 in accounts receivable at the close of 1933, and $29,-518, or about 40 per cent of this amount, was ninety days or more past due. [46] However, the auditor reported that the credit situation had improved after the company had employed a person to deal with this problem.

In spite of generally poor economic conditions, in 1932 the Union Oil Company exceeded $1 million in business for the first time. Total sales of both the wholesale and retail departments reached $1,328,-629.18. The volume of goods handled was also greater than ever before, but the increases over 1931 were modest. For example, the number of carloads of refined products increased from 1,766 to 2,032 — only a little more than half as much as the rise between 1930 and 1931. Sales of lubricating oil were up only about 34,000 gallons. Greater physical volume and dollar sales seemed to reflect a fairly healthy position, but net gain of the Wholesale Department was only $27,463.62, compared to $43,345.71 the year before. This condition resulted from continued heavy expenses and small margins of profit.

Gross income was sufficient, however, to provide funds for a vigorous educational and sales program that resulted in adding fifty-three local cooperative associations to the Union Oil Company federation in 1932. Traveling expenses amounted to $17,194.61, field and development work $9,692.88, and advertising $8,196.16. In other words, the expenses of acquiring new business and expanding the old accounts continued quite high.

---

[44] *President's 1932 Report.*
[45] *President's 1931 Report.*
[46] Union Oil Company Audit, 1933, CCA Files.

The question of refunds to member companies received extensive discussion by the Board of Directors on January 30, 1933. It was finally agreed to reduce the patronage dividends to 12½ per cent on gross savings for 1932, compared to 15, 20, and 25 per cent in 1929, 1930, and 1931, respectively. Moreover, members were required to take this 12½ per cent refund in book credit, payable at the discretion of the Directors, or to receive their patronage dividends in common stock. The reason for this decision was simple: As Vice-President Kearns explained, the Union Oil Company did not have the money to pay a cash dividend to member associations. Actually, the 1932 dividends were not paid until 1934.[47] The interest on capital stock was also lowered from 8 to 6 per cent.[48] These decisions, subsequently ratified by the stockholders, emphasized again that the immediate practical benefits of affiliating with the Union Oil Company were meager indeed. The profits were being retained in order to expand the company and its services, and member associations had to have faith in future benefits. The entire refund voted on 1932 business amounted to only $11,666.70, and, as has been mentioned, this was to be paid in credit or stock.[49]

In 1933 the company achieved another modest increase in sales and in volume of products sold, and fifty-six cooperatives were added to the Union Certified chain. The low point in profits had been passed in 1932; net gain of the wholesale climbed to $48,473.10, more than $20,000 above the preceding year. The entire profit picture was beginning to look more encouraging. While gross gain on sales increased only about 14 per cent in 1933 over 1932, net profits rose about 76 per cent. However, refunds to member companies were relatively small again in 1933. The Directors voted a 12½ per cent patronage dividend for the second consecutive year, amounting to only $14,439.-13.[50] Patronage refunds were figured, not on gross gain on sales, but on gross profits or savings — a much smaller figure. Deductions were first made for reserves and interest on capital stock. These items increased steadily, so that, despite a large increase in gross business by 1933, the patronage refunds were less than in 1930 or 1931. Management continued to plow back most of the company earnings into the firm in order to provide capital for necessary expansion. Sale of capital

[47] Board of Directors, Minutes, January 29, 1934.
[48] Board of Directors, Minutes, January 30, 1933.
[49] Union Oil Company Audit, 1932, CCA Files.
[50] Union Oil Company Audit, 1933, CCA Files.

stock progressed slowly; by the end of 1933 only $67,512 worth of common and preferred shares were outstanding.[51]

At the end of December, 1933, the Union Oil Company closed out its first five years of business. Although the firm was greatly under-capitalized in relation to its total business, the company's over-all position was sound. Total assets amounted to $245,999, which seemed like a very large figure to those who remembered starting out with less than $3,000. Perhaps the brightest part of the picture was the fact that fixed assets, consisting of buildings and equipment, were adequate for expansion. Valued at $83,387, these physical properties included land, buildings, pumps, tanks, furniture and fixtures, and automobiles and trucks.

Cowden reported that 291 cooperative associations would participate in the 1933 patronage refunds and that at least 100,000 consumers were benefiting from Union Oil Company service and products. The company had begun business with only six affiliated cooperatives and a few hundred members. In the five-year period the Union Oil Company had sold 7,789 carloads of refined fuels, 2,107,239 gallons of lube oil, and 1,525,720 pounds of grease, plus 12,942 tires, 11,937 tubes, and 3,084 batteries during the last two years of the period when these latter products were marketed. Profit on the wholesale operations, figured before deductions for depreciation and reserves, totaled $148,139.88 in the first five years of operation, and $70,293.81 had been paid or accrued in patronage refunds.

About four hundred cooperators, representing approximately one hundred local associations, met at the high school auditorium in North Kansas City for the Union Oil Company's fifth annual meeting on January 29 and 30, 1934. The delegates heard rousing speeches on cooperation, sang Union Oil Company songs, listened to reports on the company's progress, and enjoyed a free banquet provided by the company. They ratified the decisions of the Directors regarding all business affairs, including patronage refunds of only 12½ per cent. Stockholders discussed the question of patronage dividends for two hours before concluding that it would be better to leave most of the earnings in the company for future expansion and development than to pay it out in cash to themselves. As one leader expressed it, there was danger "in milking a cooperative to death." Tom DeWitt was honored for having signed contracts with eight cooperatives in that

---

[51] *Ibid.*

many days, and the whole convention was marked with harmony, enthusiasm, and optimism about the future. Utah was added as a ninth district, and the number of Directors was increased to eighteen. Cowden was re-elected president by the Board of Directors, without opposition.[52]

Although still a relatively small firm, the Union Oil Company was following some of the practices and taking on some of the characteristics of larger corporations. By 1932 expenses for entertainment appeared on the company books, and a small amount was spent for Christmas presents. Per diem and travel expenses for the Directors reached $2,740 in 1933, and premiums for employee insurance amounted to several hundred dollars.

The first five years of Union Oil Company's history is not especially significant because of the firm's growth, size, profits earned, or savings to member associations. Actually, the cooperative wholesale had not yet made any substantial economic impact on its trade territory. In a few communities like Garden City and Beloit, Kansas, where strong cooperatives sold Union Certified products, it could be said that the company was an important influence in the community's oil business, but throughout the length and breadth of the six-state area in which the company did most of its business, sales were literally only a drop in the bucket of petroleum distributed among farmers. These five years were significant because of the experiences gained in marketing, manufacturing, and cooperative educational effort. Cowden had proved that the cooperative way of doing business appealed to a growing number of farmers and that consumer cooperatives, if properly managed, could compete successfully with privately owned companies.

Even more significant, in the long run, was the fact that Cowden had aroused faith and confidence in what cooperatives could do for consumers in the future if they owned their own productive facilities. An increasing number of cooperators had begun to catch Cowden's vision of integration — cooperative control of petroleum from the well to the farmer's tractor and automobile. There were other successful cooperative wholesales, several of which did more business than the Union Oil Company, but "Cowden's outfit," as it was sometimes called, was distinctive in its plans for the future, which included the integration of production and distribution.

---

[53] *Cooperative Consumer*, February 10, 1934, 1.

Chapter 6

Education and Planning, 1934-1935

Bᴄ ᴛʜᴇ ᴇɴᴅ ᴏꜰ 1933 a number of vital concerns confronted the Union Oil Company's management. Besides the usual problems of credit, opposition from the private oil companies, lack of capital, and similar questions, the Board of Directors was faced with the issue of whether to establish a company newspaper. Cowden and his Directors were well acquainted with farm and cooperative publications, and they had a fairly good idea of the problems these papers encountered. It was very difficult, for example, to make a paper of this type pay its own way. This fact raised the question of whether the value of such a publication would equal or exceed the cost involved and whether the returns would be greater than those received from advertising in a number of established agricultural journals. Since 1929 the Union Oil Company had regularly edited two pages in M. R. Miller's *Cooperative Farmer* and had advertised widely in other farm papers.

By 1933 Cowden had become convinced that a company paper would be a real asset. The Board of Directors first discussed the matter of an official publicity organ at its meeting in January. Miller, publisher of *Cooperative Farmer*, was present and, among other things, suggested the possibility of his organization's publishing a paper for the Union Oil Company on a contract basis. The Directors consid-

ered Miller's proposal but finally voted to publish their own cooperative paper. They discussed various names, such as "Full of Pep," "Cooperative Oil Builder," and "Union Certified Builder." [1]

Nothing more was done to implement the Board's decision until
August 29, when the entire question was again considered.[2] Subsequently, arrangements for publication were worked out, and the first
issue of the *Cooperative Consumer* appeared on December 10, 1933.
It was a four-page tabloid paper, to be edited by Cowden and published twice monthly. The publishing venture had to be subsidized
from the beginning, as the subscription price was only 25 cents a year,
paid, usually, when a cooperator authorized his local cooperative to
withhold this amount from his patronage fund. The *Cooperative
Consumer* cost the company $4,053.38 in 1935 and $2,255.94 the following year.[3] Cowden now had an official outlet through which he
could regularly funnel his ideas directly to consumers. Moreover, the
paper provided a regular tie between the Union Oil Company and
its patrons.

The pattern established in the early issues of the *Cooperative Consumer* continued for many years. Cowden usually wrote two or three
editorial-type articles in which he tended to combine information,
propaganda, and appeals for support of the cooperative movement.
Naturally, the growth and activities of the Union Oil Company were
given central attention. News stories recounted the successes of local
associations that were affiliated with the company, and special notice
was given to new cooperatives that signed up to buy Union Certified
products. For example, a front-page story in the first issue carried the
headline, "Three Co-ops to Union Certified." Pictures of successful
cooperative gasoline and oil stations appeared frequently, accompanied by favorable accounts of the firms' business growth and their services to farmers. The *Cooperative Consumer* also carried testimonials
from satisfied customers and general news of consumer cooperation.
Advertising was held to a minimum and was confined mostly to company products or to the services and commodities of firms doing business with the Union Oil Company. Since the company had no printing facilities, a contract was made with the North Kansas City *News*
to publish the paper.[4]

---

[1] Board of Directors, Minutes, January 30, 1933.
[2] Board of Directors, Minutes, August 29, 1933.
[3] Consumers Cooperative Association, Audits, 1935 and 1936, CCA Files.
[4] Board of Directors, Minutes, November 13, 1933.

In the first issue Cowden explained that he hoped the *Cooperative Consumer* would "find a real place in bringing us all closer together in furthering our cooperative program." In his customary way of trying to give the members a feeling of belonging, he remarked, "It is your paper." He expressed the hope that the paper would help people catch the vision of consumer cooperation and "put new zeal into our efforts." There was certainly no indication that Cowden's zeal or faith was flagging. He attacked what he called the "old order of things" and the "old system" and insisted that "thousands of souls are hungry for an understanding" of the principles of consumer cooperation. There were those, he wrote, who wanted "to believe in cooperation but who have been so long schooled in the system which accumulates the wealth of our country into the hands of the few that much learning must be heaped upon them to give them the courage to change to a way of living contrary to that which they have known throughout their lives." Farmers who were satisfied with conditions should continue to deal with "old-line" companies, he continued, but "for those who are not satisfied, there is happily another course — they should patronize the cooperatives — and more than that they should spread the Gospel of cooperation among their neighbors." [5]

Cowden looked upon the *Cooperative Consumer* principally as an instrument of cooperative education. "Constant and persistent educational work is needed in every community," he wrote. He emphasized that cooperative leaders must take the message to others and "feed the life blood of growth into the arteries of the cooperative movement." [6] Here was one of his transfusions into the blood stream of consumer cooperation; by August, 1934, the *Cooperative Consumer* was reaching 9,840 homes.

Although Cowden and other officials of the Union Oil Company had from the first emphasized the need for cooperative education, by 1933 and 1934 much more time and money was being expended for this purpose. Cowden was interested in all phases of the project, ranging from informing people about the national and international cooperative movement to advising local managers and directors on how to operate a cooperative business more successfully. Considering education in its broadest sense, it was obvious that news articles, speeches, and other public statements were only part of the means to spread the

---

[5] *Cooperative Consumer*, December 10, 1933, 2.
[6] *Ibid.*, March 25, 1934, 2.

philosophy and practice of consumer cooperation. Somehow the Union Oil Company had to get down to the grass roots and provide local associations with practical help and advice. No amount of the usual kind of publicity and propaganda could be nearly so effective in winning the support of the individual farmer as his membership in a thriving local cooperative. And efficient management was a key to cooperative success.

As mentioned earlier, one of the main justifications for establishing and maintaining the Retail Department was to gain experience in operating retail stations and bulk plants. With this experience in hand, Union Oil Company representatives were in a position to advise local managers and officials on business methods. While this approach had some value, to consult with one manager or group of directors at a time was slow, and it was costly in terms of time and money. In addition to being costly, this procedure was not systematic. The Union Oil Company needed a plan of education that would bring cooperative managers and leaders together for intensive instruction in business affairs and in cooperative philosophy and understanding. Some kind of school or short course seemed to be the answer. This kind of instruction might be given either in various parts of Union Oil Company territory or at the Kansas City offices. The Indiana Farm Bureau Cooperative Association and some of the other regional wholesales had conducted cooperative schools, and Cowden was anxious to try this method of education.

The Board of Directors discussed the matter of conducting a school for cooperative leaders at its meeting on August 29, 1933. A representative who had conducted such schools in Indiana and elsewhere was present to outline the program for this type of educational effort.[7] It was agreed to hold a school at some time during the coming year if at all possible. The matter was discussed again at the next quarterly meeting, but no definite plans were made.[8]

Before any further action could be taken on the matter of cooperative schools, Cowden informed the Directors on June 19, 1934, that, along with four other cooperative leaders, he had been invited to attend a meeting of the International Cooperative Alliance to be held in London from September 4 to 7. He would represent the Cooperative League of the U.S.A. Cowden was eager to go. He had read widely

[7] Board of Directors, Minutes, August 29, 1933.
[8] Board of Directors, Minutes, November 13, 1933.

about the cooperatives in England, Scotland, and on the Continent, but he wanted to observe their operations at first hand. In addition, his attendance at the conference might well be put to practical use, especially if he could arrange to sell oil to foreign cooperatives. The Board readily agreed that Cowden should go, and they voted to pay his expenses, "including the tour studying European cooperatives." [9]

For a time, however, it appeared that local conditions would not permit Cowden to leave. A second year of searing drought struck much of the Union Oil Company's territory, and it seemed unwise for him to be absent at such a critical time. But the Board of Directors, as well as other cooperative leaders, insisted that he go. On August 25 he sailed from New York on the *Bremen* for Southampton. In his suitcase he carried twelve samples of Union Certified oils.

Cowden made no effort to hide his excitement as he approached London. He had become more and more enamored with the international cooperative movement, and at last he was about to see some of the world's strongest associations. As did other cooperative leaders, he viewed cooperatives as instruments of world understanding. In the past, he said early in 1933, Europe's troubles had been brought on by the selfishness of international bankers and capitalists, and cooperatives could promote international peace. He declared, "If we are to justify the faith Abraham Lincoln had in the common people, we must develop new leadership" imbued with the cooperative philosophy.[10]

When Cowden met with the 453 other delegates from 31 nations in the great convention hall in London, he thought,

> Here is the real "League of Nations." Here, not bankers, not politicians, but common people, consumers and producers, are represented in a mighty movement to reconstruct economic life on a service basis, and so bring plenty and peace to the world. These delegates represent big business — but big business run cooperatively, not for the profit of one but for the good of all.[11]

Besides listening to speeches and participating in discussions, the delegates had an opportunity to examine a large number of coopera-

[9] Board of Directors, Minutes, June 19, 1934.
[10] Speech delivered before the Indiana Farm Bureau Cooperative Association, March 9, 1933, Cowden Speech File.
[11] Cowden, *A Trip to Cooperative Europe* (1934), pamphlet.

tive-manufactured goods, on display in the Crystal Palace. These were provided by English and Scottish cooperatives. Cowden saw cooperative-produced coal, rope, twine, drugs, furniture, textiles, soap, and scores of other items. He later visited some of the factories that were owned and operated by the cooperatives. No visit to England, of course, would be complete without stopping at Rochdale. Here in 1844 a small group had organized the first successful consumers cooperative association. Standing before the weavers' cooperative store, Cowden felt a reverence that no monuments to kings or conquerors could produce in him. After visiting English and Scottish cooperatives Cowden went on to Sweden and Denmark. He sailed for home on September 22, full of ideas for promoting consumer cooperation in the United States.

Cowden returned to Kansas City with renewed enthusiasm and dedication. He had been amazed and gratified at the extent and variety of business carried on by the great English Central Wholesale Society, its counterpart in Scotland, and the Koperativa Forbundet, or K. F., in Sweden. These wholesales did millions of dollars' worth of business. Why, Cowden asked, could not this spirit and activity be duplicated in the United States? But in most of the countries he had visited, he had witnessed a different attitude toward cooperatives than that held by most Americans, and this convinced him that education on cooperatives must be expanded and improved in the United States.

The need for pushing international trade among cooperatives now seemed to be an immediate possibility and an important objective to pursue. The first shipment of CCA lubricating oil to foreign cooperatives was made on March 5, 1935, less than six months after Cowden had visited Europe with his oil samples. These sales to cooperatives in Estonia, France, and Scotland were small, but they marked the beginning of an international cooperative trade in oil.

Cowden had for long believed in integration of production and marketing; his trip abroad demonstrated to him the economic results of the cooperatives' expansion of their own manufacturing facilities. Why could not as much be done along this line in the United States as was being accomplished abroad? he asked. Or, as he wrote, "How can we speed the day when America will 'go cooperative' as these countries have done?" The answer, he felt, was in cooperative planning and cooperative education. In numerous speeches and articles written for the *Cooperative Consumer* late in 1934, Cowden told about his trip abroad, but his main concern was with education and planning for the future. It was clear that Cowden's contacts with foreign cooperatives and their leaders had given him new vision and fresh determination to increase the effectiveness of his own organization.

On October 17 Cowden reported to the Board of Directors that he had engaged a New York firm to prepare brochures, bulletins, and other publicity to be used in an active campaign of education and organization. Still excited by his observations in Europe, Cowden told the Board that the great need of the cooperative movement in the Union Oil Company's territory was a thoroughly planned program of education. "We need to go out to our members and show them the wonderful things these cooperatives in other lands, and in other parts of America are doing, and how we can match these achievements. We need to teach the philosophy as well as the business methods of Cooperation." [12]

Although a few educational meetings had been held earlier, this new emphasis upon education began with a series of sessions in the district for managers and officials of cooperatives affiliated with the Union Oil Company. These were to run from November 7 to 21, 1934, in cities as far north as Aberdeen, South Dakota, to as far south as McPherson, Kansas.[13] A special invitation was given to women and young people also to hear the principles of cooperation discussed. Besides considering business matters, these meetings were designed to stimulate educational work in local districts throughout the coming winter. Cowden was scheduled to attend each meeting to talk about his trip to Europe, and his presence was a strong drawing card.

Attendance at the nine meetings ranged from 90 to 160, with some managers and other cooperative officials traveling as much as 200 miles to attend. The meeting at Fort Dodge, Iowa, on November 7 was fairly representative of these gatherings. There, 125 cooperators heard Tom DeWitt, Homer Young, Harry Appleby, Oscar Cooley, who handled educational activities, and Cowden speak about different phases of cooperation. DeWitt emphasized that the Union Oil Company belonged to the locals: "It is your wholesale cooperative," he said, "set up to serve your needs." Young took much the same approach, but stressed the need of education: "We do not merely sell gas and oil," he declared. "We sell cooperation 90 per cent of the time

---

[12] *Cooperative Consumer*, October 25, 1934, 1–2.
[13] *Ibid.*

and gas and and oil 10 per cent. Education is the chief problem of the cooperative movement." Appleby described and exhibited CO-OP tires and accessories, while Cooley discussed the need to increase the circulation of the *Cooperative Consumer* and urged locals to advertise in newspapers and by means of roadside signs, leaflets, and similar materials. After a banquet, Cowden climaxed the meeting with an account of his European trip.[14]

Meetings of this kind generated a lot of local enthusiasm among cooperative officials. Furthermore, representatives of cooperatives that were not affiliated with the Union Oil Company attended some of the meetings, providing an opportunity to attract them into the wholesale family.

Meetings held for managers by Union Oil Company personnel were important and had practical value, but they were only a small part of the total educational effort required. The company's most serious need was trained local cooperative leaders who could educate their own membership and the people in the community without having to rely on more than general guidance from representatives of the Kansas City office, since the company did not have enough fieldmen and travelers. The Union Oil Company could exert its greatest influence by operating cooperative training schools to develop the cooperative philosophy and to improve business methods among members and officials of local associations. As mentioned earlier, this matter of holding a school had been discussed before Cowden left for Europe, but nothing definite had been done. However, on October 17, 1934, Cowden told the Board of Directors that the time had come to act. On December 25 it was announced that the Union Oil Company would sponsor a week-long school at North Kansas City, beginning on January 21, 1935.

To interest prospective students the school was advertised through the *Cooperative Consumer*, and the fieldmen talked it up throughout the trade territory. Bruce McCully, head of the Retail Department, presented the idea to local cooperatives in northern Missouri during December and received an encouraging response. The plan was to get the cooperative membership in each community to elect a committee on education. This group would then choose two or more individuals to attend the school. There was no tuition, but each student who en-

---

[14] *Ibid.*, November 25, 1934, 1–2.

rolled must promise to hold a local cooperative school in his own community after he returned home.[15]

The first Union Oil Company cooperative school opened on schedule in the North Kansas City High School auditorium with between fifty and sixty students. Most of them were from northern Missouri, but some came from as far away as Burlington, Colorado. V. S. Alanne, Executive Secretary of the Northern States Cooperative League in Minneapolis and a person who had wide experience in this work, acted as director. Alanne lectured on the history and principles of consumer cooperation. Students also heard Cowden talk on foreign cooperatives and explain how to manage and operate a cooperative oil association. Besides the talks emphasizing the history and principles of cooperation, discussions were led by employees of the company on salesmanship, organization, bookkeeping, and management. The students were kept busy from 8:30 A.M. to 9 P.M.

At the close of the school, Cowden wrote, "The week of Jan. 21–27, 1935, will go down in the cooperative history of this central West as an epoch-making period." Many cooperative schools had been held in other parts of the country, but this was the first one conducted in the region around Kansas City. Cowden reported, "The students have gone back to their home communities primed to the muzzle . . . with cooperative information, and also with enthusiasm." These students would now hold one session a week for six weeks in their home communities. As Cowden explained, "The student becomes teacher, and passes on the torch of knowledge." [16] The first of these local cooperative schools was held in northern Missouri during late January and early February of 1935. This entire educational venture was so successful that it started the Union Oil Company on an intensive and permanent program of cooperative schooling.

Another phase of the new educational effort was to organize a cooperative guild for women in communities that had a strong cooperative. The first of these was formed by employees and wives of workers of the Union Oil Company in North Kansas City on December 3, 1934. These women met once or twice a month and studied various aspects of the cooperative.[17] This was another of the ideas that Cowden brought back from Europe. The Women's Cooperative Guild in Eng-

---

[15] *Ibid.*, December 25, 1934, 1, 3.

[16] *Ibid.*, January 28, 1935, 4.

[17] *Ibid.*, December 10, 1934, 5.

land reportedly had 72,000 members who seemed to be playing an important role in cooperative education. A few other guilds were organized in towns where the Union Oil Company had strong affiliated cooperatives, but this part of the new educational program was never successful.

In keeping with its greater emphasis upon education the Union Oil Company now attempted to get cooperation taught in the public schools and colleges. Cowden discussed the matter with the Directors late in 1934, and at the annual meeting in February of the next year stockholders considered the question. Resolutions were passed "strongly urging" all publicly supported schools in the Union Oil Company's territory to include courses on cooperative marketing and purchasing. It was also suggested that courses in cooperation should be established in the vocational departments of high schools and should be added to the extension offerings of the state colleges. Failure to achieve this program was a deep disappointment to Cowden. Kansas State College taught some courses, but generally the schools proved to be poor avenues through which to spread cooperative ideas and principles.[18] A general lack of interest among teachers and unwillingness on the part of school boards to allow the schools to become associated with special interests worked against spreading the cooperative message in classrooms.

Cowden returned home from Europe as much concerned with long-range planning by cooperatives as he was with education. In fact, the two matters were directly related. He had found that European cooperatives were making plans and drawing up programs for as much as a decade ahead. About a month after he returned to Kansas City, the Cooperative League of the U.S.A. met in Chicago. Cowden was among those who suggested that the league set up the National Cooperative Planning Committee. But even before the national organization could get started on plans for business expansion, personnel training, education, and organizational activity, Cowden insisted that the Union Oil Company should have a long-range plan of its own for cooperative development in the central western region of the United States.

On October 17, 1934, the Board of Directors authorized Cowden to appoint a committee to draft a five-year plan and to work out a more systematic educational program. The idea of a five-year plan was dis-

---

[18] *Ibid.*, February 12, 1935, 5.

cussed at the managers' meetings during November, and appeals were made for suggestions for the company's plans and objectives through the columns of the *Cooperative Consumer*. When the stockholders met for their annual convention on February 5 and 6, 1935, the Union Oil Company's first five-year plan was ready for consideration and approval. As might be expected, it was adopted unanimously.

The five-year plan was divided into two principal parts: One dealt with cooperative education and the other with cooperative business principles and practices. The plans for education called for establishing an education department that would sponsor cooperative schools on a regular basis. The aim was to have at least fifty students in each school. A closely related objective was to expand the circulation of cooperative publications. A circulation of 55,000 by 1940 was set for the *Cooperative Consumer*, an annual increase of about 10,000 copies. The distribution of books, pamphlets, manuals, and other cooperative literature was to be multiplied many times. Moreover, the company proposed that local educational committees be set up on a permanent basis in each community. These committees would "spread the knowledge of cooperation," increase the trade and membership of local cooperatives, and "increase and enlarge the services rendered by the local cooperatives." The establishment of a cooperative college by 1940 was one of Cowden's main objectives. The company was prepared to underwrite the broader aspects of this expanded educational program by considering it as an ordinary part of operating expense. Local associations, in turn, were urged to invest a definite amount of money in their educational work.

Better cooperative education was obviously not an end in itself, but a means to the end of increasing cooperative business. The five-year plan included several specific objectives for expanding company business operations. The first objective was to add forty cooperatives to the Union Oil Company chain in 1935, forty in 1936, and then five less each year through 1939, for a total of 170. Besides bringing more existing cooperatives into the company organization, fifty-seven new cooperatives were to be organized. All together, by January 1, 1940, there were to be 486 cooperatives, representing 168,000 consumers, affiliated with the wholesale.

Other goals included acquiring a printing plant in which to publish the *Cooperative Consumer* and other company literature and advertising; expansion of the number and kind of commodities furnished to local cooperatives; and increase in manufacturing facilities.

"When a commodity can be manufactured more economically than it can be purchased," Cowden wrote, "we should then go into manufacturing." It was recommended that manufacturing plants for grease, paint, and batteries be established, in addition to a refinery. Finally, each local cooperative was urged to work out a five-year plan for its own development.[19]

During 1934 the company added a number of important commodities to the list of products supplied to members. A few automobile accessories had been handled since 1932, but late in 1934 a full line was made available under the CO-OP brand name. Also, CO-OP paint was sold for the first time, although sales amounted to only $2,978.81.[20] The Directors had discussed the matter of manufacturing paint at their meeting on August 29, 1933, but about a year later, when the Union Oil Company began handling this product, supplies were obtained from a private dealer.[21] Twine was another commodity that the Union Oil Company commenced marketing in 1934. A contract was made with International Harvester Company on June 19 to furnish the needed amount. Throughout 1933 and 1934 the Board of Directors studied the possibility of dealing in farm machinery. Some of the regional wholesales were selling implements, but as yet it did not seem practical for the Union Oil Company to branch out into this line.

Besides expanding the wholesale's services, Cowden and the Board of Directors continued to study the question of acquiring a refinery. In addition to providing cooperative-produced refined products, a cooperative-owned refinery would stop the rumors that the Union Oil Company did not have a dependable supply of refined fuels. This matter was never far from Cowden's mind, but there were many obstacles to be overcome. First was the problem of finding a refinery in good operating condition and available at a fair price. Lack of capital was another barrier to this avenue of expansion. After investigating several propositions in 1931 and 1932, the Directors discussed purchasing the Dickey Refinery at McPherson, Kansas, in June, 1934. The Dickey property was for sale at $160,000. The committee appointed to investigate the property at McPherson reported at the next meeting of the Board that no action had been taken because of demoralized market conditions. Actually, the company could buy its

---

[19] *The Five-Year Plan* (1935), pamphlet published by CCA.
[20] Union Oil Company, Audit, 1934, CCA Files.
[21] Board of Directors, Minutes, June 19, 1934.

petroleum products on the open market at very favorable prices. Consequently, nothing more was done, although the Board expressed the hope that a small refinery could be obtained through "the united efforts of the National Cooperatives, Inc." [22]

Lack of operating capital was still a major problem for the Union Oil Company, but this pressure had been greatly relieved when the Banks for Cooperatives were set up under the Farm Credit Act of 1933. Here was a new, cheaper, and more generous source of funds for operation and expansion. Cowden had been active in lobbying for the provision of the Farm Credit Act that permitted the new banks to make loans to consumer as well as to producer cooperatives. Once the Banks for Cooperatives began operating, Cowden was not slow to take advantage of them. He suggested to the Directors on November 13, 1933, that they should negotiate a loan for about $50,000 from the St. Louis Bank for Cooperatives. This amount, he explained, would be enough to take up the individual stockholdings and other indebtedness that bore 8 per cent interest. Since the company might borrow from the St. Louis Bank for Cooperatives at 4½ per cent, a considerable saving in interest would result.

With the Board's authorization, Cowden, on January 10, 1934, borrowed $35,000.[23] Repayment was scheduled at $5,000 a year for the next seven years. Actually, most of the new loan was used for expansion rather than to retire old debt. The long-range debt structure at the end of 1934 amounted to $131,781.10. Besides the $35,000 due to the St. Louis Bank for Cooperatives, there was outstanding $5,110 in certificates of indebtedness, of which $2,000 was owned by Cowden. Notes and mortgages due to individuals totaled $6,950. Vice-President Kearns held $5,200 of this amount in demand notes bearing 8 per cent. The company owed the Farmers Union Jobbing Association $3,200, and paid-in capital stock had reached $81,521.10. Although the company was still greatly undercapitalized, the availability of funds from the Banks for Cooperatives placed it in much more favorable financial position than before. As time passed, this source of credit became increasingly important in supplying money to expand services. Even the cooperatives found the helping hand of government a great asset.[24]

Both total business and net profits were up in 1934, despite linger-

---

[22] Board of Directors, Minutes, October 17, 1934.
[23] Union Oil Company, Audit, 1934, CCA Files.
[24] *Ibid.*

ing depression and drought conditions in much of the Union Oil Company's territory. About 800 more carloads of refined fuels were sold than in 1933, and oil and grease sales also made good gains. Sales of tires, tubes, batteries, antifreeze, and equipment represented only a small portion of company business. Total sales exceeded $2 million for the first time, and the wholesale showed a net gain of $51,052.25, the highest on record. Net income in the Wholesale Department was up about $17,701.13 over the year before.

Business in the Retail Department, however, presented a different story; this operation showed a loss of $373.58. The deficit was not large, but it indicated that the company was experiencing difficulty in operating retail outlets. Not only did the Retail Department fail to show profits, but it added to the over-all credit problem. Despite intensive efforts to collect accounts receivable and to put affiliated co-operatives on a cash basis, the company had a larger amount outstanding and more than 90 days delinquent than it had in 1933. The Retail Department was responsible for about 40 per cent of this total. When it is remembered that the Retail Department did only a very small percentage of the total business, it is easy to see that it was necessary to put the department on a better-paying basis or to get rid of it.[25]

Even though company savings were in favorable amount in 1934, the stockholders, upon recommendation of the Directors, voted a dividend of only 12½ per cent for the third straight year. Further, this dividend was to be paid at the decision of the Directors. By this time it had definitely become Union Oil Company policy to retain most of the savings rather than to pay them out in cash to local co-operatives. In this way the firm had a constant and cheap source of funds for expansion and enlargement of facilities. But, as mentioned earlier, these savings were not sufficient to provide capital for many of the projects the Union Oil Company wanted to undertake. This was especially true when it came to acquiring a refinery.

One matter that bothered the company's officials was the lack of a more closely descriptive name for the organization. As early as 1932 Tom DeWitt had headed a committee of the Directors to propose a new name. No action was taken at the time; a stockholders' resolution agreed to leave the matter up to the Board of Directors.[26] In an attempt to show the broad reach of the company, Ralph Snyder told

[25] *Ibid.*
[26] Stockholders' meeting, Minutes, February 3, 1932.

a radio audience in February, a more appropriate name was under consideration, but still the Board delayed action. By 1934 the original name was so nondescriptive as to be actually a misnomer; the cooperative wholesale was handling some sixty different products, many of which could not be classed as "oil." Furthermore, another Union Oil Company, a private profit concern on the West Coast, objected to the Kansas City firm's use of the name. Cowden believed that he had a good legal case if the controversy should ever be brought to court, but he had no desire to quarrel. Perhaps the strongest force for the selection of a new name for the company was the practical need to have a more accurate and descriptive name, one that would convey the idea of an association of consumer cooperatives.[27] By late 1934 there were 259 cooperatives affiliated and doing business with the Union Oil Company

At a meeting held on October 17, 1934, the Directors seriously discussed the change in name. Although at this meeting the name "Consumers Cooperation Incorporated" received the most support, on February 4, 1935, the Board finally recommended that the organization be called the "Consumers Cooperative Association."[28] The stockholders approved this name the next day. "Union Certified," which had been used to designate company products, was dropped from the bylaws and the term "CO-OP" was substituted. Union Oil Company stockholders had voted on January 29, 1934, to change the colors of their stations to red and black to identify them as members of National Cooperatives, Inc. The CO-OP insignia of National Cooperatives had been used on tires since 1932, and it now became the trademark for all of the Union Oil Company's products. CO-OP brands, it was hoped, would have a uniform advertising appeal over the nation.

Three weeks later Cowden explained that the new name, Consumers Cooperative Association, was a vital factor in telling people about cooperative principles. He thought a big step had been taken, and he urged all cooperators "to make this new, meaningful name known throughout the territory."[29]

The 259-member cooperative chain that made up the Consumers Cooperative Association had been built by constant and aggressive

---

[27] *Cooperative Consumer*, February 12, 1935, 1.
[28] Board of Directors, Minutes, February 4, 1935.
[29] *Cooperative Consumer*, February 25, 1935, 4.

work in the field, and, as might be expected, company representatives often ran into opposition from other state or regional wholesales. As more state and regional cooperative wholesales developed they often found themselves in competition for the same business, and this competition sometimes created heated disputes. Generally, the cooperative leaders worked out an understanding whereby a company would not solicit business in a territory where another cooperative was already supplying the local associations. This gentlemen's agreement avoided duplicating activities and services.

When the Union Oil Company moved into Nebraska it ran into difficulty with the Farmers Union, which maintained a wholesale, the Farmers Union State Exchange, at Omaha. Naturally, the Farmers Union State Exchange and many loyal members of the Farmers Union did not welcome competition from the Kansas City organization. Nonetheless, the Union Oil Company signed up a number of local Farmers Union cooperatives. As the Union Oil Company intensified its field work in Nebraska, the editor of the *Nebraska Union Farmer* expressed the home organization's opposition. He sharply attacked Cowden and referred to him as a "cuckoo Cooperator." The editor explained that a cuckoo was a bird that laid its eggs in the nests of other birds or took for its own use things that others had created. This situation, the editor continued, described Cowden, who had come into Nebraska to obtain business from cooperatives that had been established by the Farmers Union. Why proselyte, he asked, when there was so much territory in the United States where cooperatives needed to be organized?

This controversy continued for several years as the Consumers Cooperative Association continued to sign up additional cooperatives in Nebraska. At a meeting of cooperative leaders in Sioux Falls, South Dakota, on September 21, 1937, L. H. Herron, editor of the *Nebraska Union Farmer*, created a "spirited discussion" when he charged Cowden with trying to bring all of the oil business in the Midwest under his control.[30]

Nevertheless, CCA was unwilling to give up its search for business among Farmers Union associations in Nebraska. Cowden had several conferences with officials of the Nebraska Farmers Union, but their differences could not be resolved. The Farmers Union State Exchange obviously feared the growing competition from CCA and resented its

---

[30] Lincoln, Nebraska *Star*, September 22, 1937.

local associations' contracts with the Kansas City firm. By July, 1940, CCA had contracts with fifty-five cooperatives in Nebraska, many of which were Farmers Union organizations. In a letter to Cowden dated November 29, 1940, C. McCarthy of the Farmers Union State Exchange wrote that his organization would not willingly concede any of its Farmers Union oil stations to CCA. He explained that he would be "happy to work with CCA, but we cannot do so so long as you insist on undermining us with our own associations."[31] Other Nebraskans also expressed opposition to CCA. A cooperator near Gresham wrote Homer Young that there had been several protests against the Polk County Farmers Union Gas, Oil and Produce Association's affiliating with CCA.[32] When Editor Herron was invited to the dedication of CCA's Phillipsburg Refinery in early 1940, he refused to attend. The Nebraska Farmers Union could still work with CCA, he wrote, if the wholesale would agree "to leave our local cooperative associations alone and deal directly with the Farmers Union State Exchange."[33]

Some farm organization leaders objected to CCA's so-called "open membership" philosophy. They believed that each local cooperator must belong to a farm organization in conjunction with his membership in the cooperative. Indeed, this policy helped to increase membership in farm organizations because farmers joined in order to have the advantages of cooperative buying or selling. CCA, however, was interested primarily in gaining members for the cooperative, and it was of little interest to the company's officials if cooperators were members of a farm organization also. When Tom DeWitt told members of the Oklahoma Farmers Union that a consumer cooperative organization was needed which did not depend on farm organization membership for support, John Vesecky of the Kansas Farmers Union was quick to set him straight. Vesecky wrote that consumer cooperatives should "require membership in a general farm organization if they are farm cooperatives." He added that he and President Tom Cheek of the Oklahoma Farmers Union did not appreciate DeWitt's "preaching of such doctrine," especially to Farmers Union members.[34]

Another aspect of competition among cooperative wholesales developed between CCA and the Farmers Union Jobbing Association of Kansas City. In 1929, when Cowden began business, he made a

[31] McCarthy to Cowden, November 29, 1940, CCA Files.
[32] A. S. Torell to Young, June 12, 1939, CCA Files.
[33] Herron to J. W. Cummins, April 26, 1940, CCA Files.
[34] Vesecky to *Kansas Union Farmer*, May 19, 1938.

contract with the jobbing association that called for endorsement and support of his oil program among Farmers Union cooperatives in Kansas, in return for small brokerage fees paid to the jobbing association. Besides the brokerage fees, the Union Oil Company was to take at least $50 of advertising each month in the *Kansas Union Farmer*.[35] This contract was renewed, with some modifications, on September 1, 1932. From 1930 to the middle of 1935 CCA paid the Farmers Union Jobbing Association $19,748. However, this policy of giving the jobbing association what amounted to a discount on oil products prompted other cooperative wholesales that were sponsored by farm organizations to ask for the same privilege. For one instance, between 1933 and 1935 brokerage fees were paid to the Kansas Farm Bureau; these fees were much less than those paid to the jobbing association, nevertheless they were paid.

Early in 1935 CCA officials decided to eliminate all brokerage fees. Cowden wrote to H. E. Witham, a former Union Oil Company board member and now head of the Farmers Union Jobbing Association, explaining the new policy. "We understand this action is agreeable with you," Cowden concluded.[36] Almost immediately afterward representatives of the jobbing association began to consider wholesaling petroleum products to Farmers Union cooperatives in Kansas. This discussion excited Cowden and friends of CCA in Kansas, who saw the dangers of competition from another wholesale cooperative.

The Farmers Union had not decided to handle oil and gasoline just because CCA stopped paying brokerage fees. Their decision was a part of the union's attempt to build membership and support, in the belief that if Farmers Union cooperatives began buying their petroleum products from their own wholesale, the union's membership and patronage would grow. In addition, part of the jobbing association's profits would be returned to the parent organization for educational work in the state.

During the latter part of 1935 and early in 1936, Cowden, CCA fieldmen, and friends of CCA throughout Kansas exerted themselves to keep the Farmers Union Jobbing Association from going ahead with plans to handle petroleum products. In some instances Cowden came in for some stinging criticism. At one meeting a friend of the Farmers Union asked whether "the CCA would render any particular

---

[35] Contract dated June 17, 1929, Cowden Papers.
[36] Cowden to Witham, July 1, 1935, Cowden Papers.

service to anyone except Mr. Cowden." [37] On the other hand, Cowden's friends charged that the Farmers Union was not demonstrating a cooperative spirit. O. C. Servis of Winfield wrote that competition among cooperatives was playing into the hands of "the oil fraternity." [38] Cowden took this same approach in writing, "There is plenty of opposition directed at cooperatives from the outside, and we think that on the inside it is our duty to have cooperation between cooperatives and not competition." [39]

On April 2, 1936, it was officially announced that the Farmers Union Jobbing Association would begin handling petroleum products. Almost at once scores of protest meetings were held throughout Kansas, and resolutions were passed, opposing the jobbing association's action. President Vesecky resented these meetings in Farmers Union territory which, he said, had been called "at the instigation of the CCA or its employees and representatives." He argued that the jobbing association had supplied cooperatives with many commodities for years and between 1927 and 1929 had furnished oil. CCA's campaign against the Farmers Union's entering the oil business, he declared, hurt the whole cooperative movement. Attempts were made to reach some kind of understanding, but to no avail, and competition among cooperatives continued.

Differences of this nature between farm organization leaders and the CCA arose from time to time, but, generally speaking, Cowden and the fieldmen were able to keep opposition at a minimum. It was too much to expect that everyone would go along with the idea of one wholesale for all cooperative oil associations in the region. Habits of doing business, special interests, jealousy, personality conflicts, and other factors all had their influence. However, by 1936 CCA was by far the largest farm supply cooperative in the Kansas City trade area. Much of the credit for this dominance can go to CCA's insistence upon staying free of ties with any farm organization. The policy of trying to work with all groups kept CCA out of farm organization politics and permitted the wholesale to win broader geographical coverage than that enjoyed by any other farm supply wholesale.

As the Union Oil Company greatly expanded its business, the questions of organization and management became increasingly impor-

---

[37] Minutes of a joint meeting of the Kansas Farmers Union State Board of Directors and the FUJA Directors, July 19, 1935, Cowden Papers.

[38] Servis to Cowden, July 8, 1935, Cowden Papers.

[39] Cowden to T. C. Belden, March 9, 1936, Cowden Papers.

tant. By 1934 most of the firm's business was administered through three major departments or divisions. Bruce McCully headed the Retail Department; Homer Young was in charge of refined fuels; and J. H. Appleby directed the Tire and Accessories Division. The five or six fieldmen generally reported directly to Cowden. Early in 1935 an educational department was added, in line with the objectives of the five-year plan.

Cowden, as president and general manager, kept a tight hold on every aspect of the company's affairs. He usually made the final decisions, subject to approval by the Board of Directors, which very seldom disagreed with his policies. In fact, the Board considered Cowden so important to the company that in May, 1933, it took out a $25,000 insurance policy on his life. Cowden's very position of dominance and control created problems of which the Directors had been well aware early in company history. What if something should happen to him? Who would take over? It was suggested at a meeting of the Board of Directors in May, 1933, that someone in the organization should be working closely with Cowden. The implication was clear that this person should be qualified to assume the full management and direction of the company if the need should arise. However, the Board took no action on the suggestion, and the matter of developing another top administrator in the organization was postponed. Administratively, the Union Oil Company continued to be largely a one-man show.

By 1935 the wholesale had a new name, its trademark had been revised to emphasize that its products were the results of cooperative enterprise, more associations had become affiliated with the company, and total business had passed the $2 million mark. Educational plans and policies had been worked out and put into practice, and serious consideration had been given to expanding the company's services and productive facilities. Indeed, CCA was looking to new horizons.

Chapter 7

Factories Are Free

ALTHOUGH GENERAL ECONOMIC CONDITIONS had improved by 1935, the depression still cast its shadow over business. Despite the rather bleak outlook, Cowden and other officials of the Consumers Cooperative Association stepped up their plans to expand the company's physical facilities and to enlarge services to member cooperatives. Confidence in the continuing success and growth of CCA was nowhere better illustrated than in the move to buy additional property.

At a meeting on June 28, 1935, the Directors discussed the purchase of land and buildings owned by the Pennsylvania Petroleum Company at 1500 Iron Street in Kansas City, about three blocks south of the CCA office. A subsidiary of the Atlantic, Pacific and Gulf Oil Company, the Pennsylvania firm had gone bankrupt, and its property was for sale. This was the same company that five years earlier had refused to do business with the old Union Oil Company because the little cooperative did not buy in large enough volume. Now the situation was reversed. The Board of Directors was convinced that this property could be purchased at a favorable price, and the members voted unanimously to proceed with the negotiations. It was agreed to seek financing from the St. Louis Bank for Cooperatives.[1]

---

[1] Board of Directors, Minutes, June 28, 1935.

While the Board was meeting, Cowden received a telephone call from a representative of the Pennsylvania Petroleum Company, asking for an immediate appointment to consider the sale. After a short absence Cowden returned to the meeting and announced that he had offered $55,000 for the property, but that the creditors wanted $60,-000. He informed the Board that he had suggested the compromise figure of $57,000, a price which apparently included some furniture and equipment. (The *Cooperative Consumer* gave the price as $53,-000.)[2] Actually, $60,000 was a low price for the property, but Cowden hoped the bankrupt company would accept his offer. The Board was still in session when word arrived that CCA's figure had been accepted. "It was the unanimous opinion of the board," the Secretary recorded, "that this seemed very favorable to our interests."[3] Indeed, such was the case. In 1926, only nine years earlier, the main building of the Pennsylvania Petroleum Company's installation had been completed at a cost of $245,000.

The newly acquired property consisted of a large fireproof brick-and-concrete building providing 29,156 square feet of floor space. The plant had room for offices, a laboratory, and oil-blending facilities and equipment. Besides the principal building, there were thirty-one compounding tanks with a capacity of 55,800 gallons, and forty-two large storage tanks that could hold about 492,000 gallons of bright stocks and neutrals. Since twelve of the tanks were inside the main building, oil could be blended in the winter without special heating. This was the first really modern plant owned by CCA. The deal was closed on August 14,[4] and the company occupied its new quarters on September 3. "By evening," the *Cooperative Consumer* reported, "the office employees were functioning at their usual efficiency behind new desks in the commodious offices of the new quarters."[5] In November additional storage space was provided by enlarging the basement under the main building.

At the next meeting of the Board of Directors, the members sat for pictures around a large horseshoe-shaped mahogany table in the special directors' room. The general appearance of this new meeting place for CCA officials was an expression of prospering company fortunes. Except for the fact that their suits might have been a little more

[2] *Ibid.* See also *Cooperative Consumer*, August 26, 1935, 1.
[3] Board of Directors, Minutes, June 28, 1935.
[4] Kansas City *Star*, August 18, 1935.
[5] *Cooperative Consumer*, September 9, 1935, 1.

wrinkled and their faces somewhat weather-beaten, it would have been hard to distinguish CCA's Board in its new surroundings from the directors of any large private corporation.

While CCA was moving to its new home, the field force was being reorganized in order to increase sales. The main objective was greater frequency of fieldmen's visits to each local cooperative. The field force consisted of eight men who covered fixed territories, plus Tom DeWitt who ranged over all of the area in which CCA did business. Over all, Homer Young, who continued to direct the Petroleum Department, and Harry Appleby, director of the Tire and Accessories Division, were in charge of sales promotion. Young and Appleby traveled to all parts of the eight-state region. McCully, who managed the Retail Department, confined his traveling mostly to Missouri.[6] Sales efforts met with success despite drought conditions, and business during the first eight months of 1935 broke all previous records.

The new facilities purchased in 1935 were only the physical symbol of CCA's expansion; before another year passed the company had greatly enlarged its services. Late in the year CCA began to manufacture its own grease, and early in 1936 the company produced paint. Groceries, lumber, and tractors were the most important commodities added to the growing list of products that were being handled on a commission basis.

The plant at 1500 Iron Street included some crude equipment to manufacture grease, and plans were made almost immediately after the property was acquired to manufacture this product that farmers were using in ever-increasing quantities. The company's policy concerning new enterprises was announced in the Five-Year Plan, which stated that "when a commodity can be manufactured more economically than it can be purchased we should then go into manufacturing." Production of grease seemed to fit this criterion. On November 25 the *Cooperative Consumer* announced that production of grease was under way, although the facilities were suitable primarily for making only axle grease. The first deliveries of cooperative-made grease in the United States were scheduled for December 9.[7] Meanwhile, Homer Young was directing a campaign to obtain an order for grease from every member cooperative in CCA territory. This goal was not reached, but by December, 101 cooperatives had

[6] *Ibid.*, August 26, 1935, 1, 7.
[7] *Ibid.*, November 25, 1935, 1.

ordered 24,652 pounds.[8] Officials and friends of CCA boasted that they had won another "first" in the history of consumer cooperation in the United States. Only six years before, the Union Oil Company had been the first cooperative to blend oil, and now CCA took the lead in manufacturing a cooperative brand of grease.[9]

The first grease was manufactured in small, entirely inadequate kettles, but on March 10, 1937, a completely new and modern grease plant was placed in operation by CCA. This equipment could turn out almost fifty kinds of CO-OP grease and had a daily capacity of about 20,000 pounds.[10] George Bunce, who had some sixteen years of experience in the oil and grease business, was placed in charge of grease manufacture on January 1, 1937.[11]

In 1938 CCA sold 1,991,145 pounds of greases that had been manufactured in its own plant. Slightly more than 1,000,000 pounds were distributed to member companies, while the remainder went to other regional wholesales. By 1940 grease sales reached 2,522,033 pounds and was CCA's fourth best profit item. That year CCA produced about 13 per cent of total sales in its own plants.[12] This was a long way from the complete integration that Cowden so much desired, but it was a good beginning.

In November, 1935, at about the same time the decision was made to produce grease, the Board of Directors voted to purchase paint manufacturing equipment and to employ an experienced man to operate the new plant.[13] For about two years CCA had been supplying paint to its member cooperatives; now it seemed feasible to begin manufacturing this product. In line with the general policy, Cowden explained that paint could be produced in a CCA plant cheaper than it could be bought under the most favorable contract. On January 21, 1936, Cowden announced that equipment was being installed and that production would begin early in February. According to the minutes of the Directors' meeting, secondhand machinery for this operation was obtained at a little less than $2,000.[14]

Fortunately, CCA was able to employ Riley Brown, a well-qualified

[8] *Ibid.*, December 23, 1935, 1.
[9] *Manager's Report*, Seventh Annual Meeting, February 3–4, 1936, 5.
[10] *Cooperative Consumer*, March 22, 1937, 1.
[11] *Ibid.*, January 11, 1937, 1.
[12] *Twelfth Annual Report*, 1940, 7.
[13] Board of Directors, Minutes, November 6, 1935.
[14] Board of Directors, Minutes, February 3, 1936. In the published accounts $2,300 is the figure given.

technician, to supervise the paint-making division. When delegates came to the annual meeting on February 3 and 4, they were shown the new manufacturing facilities, and orders were taken for the CO-OP product. Cowden explained to readers of the *Cooperative Consumer*, "Making paint in our own plant insures to cooperative consumers the highest quality of products for the lowest possible price." [15] Early in 1937 new and improved machinery was installed, and during the year CCA sold 19,748 gallons of paint. For the year ending August 31, 1938, sales reached 30,156 gallons. [16]

Meanwhile, plans were going forward to establish a wholesale grocery department and to handle lumber and farm machinery. At its meeting on June 28 and 29, 1935, the Board of Directors authorized Cowden to survey the cooperative retail stores in CCA territory to see if enough business was assured to warrant setting up a grocery department. Although the minutes of the meeting do not indicate whether a decision was reached, within ten days the *Cooperative Consumer* announced that a grocery division would be established. [17]

A survey showed that there were seventy-six cooperative stores in Kansas and Missouri that were potential customers for a CCA grocery department. In September CCA officials sponsored managers' meetings throughout the two states in order to determine the needs and desires of local cooperative grocery stores. [18] Final plans to begin distributing groceries were made by the Directors at their meeting on November 6. Obviously worried about the credit problem, the Board established a cash policy that required weekly payment of grocery invoices. [19]

On January 13, 1936, it was publicly announced that CCA was ready to distribute groceries to cooperative stores. Arthur Katka, who had been employed by the Central Cooperative Wholesale of Superior, Wisconsin, was named manager of the new department. Within a few weeks Katka issued optimistic statements about the local support for this new service, [20] but privately, Cowden indicated that the grocery program was experiencing tough sledding. Writing to John Vesecky, President of the Kansas Farmers Union, Cowden said that

---

[15] *Cooperative Consumer*, January 27, 1936, 1.

[16] *Ninth Annual Report*, 1937, 9; and *Tenth Annual Report*, 1938, 5.

[17] Board of Directors, Minutes, June 28, 1935; and *Cooperative Consumer*, July 8, 1935, 1.

[18] *Cooperative Consumer*, October 14, 1935, 1.

[19] Board of Directors, Minutes, November 6, 1935.

[20] *Cooperative Consumer*, March 9, 1936, 1.

CCA's main objective in starting a grocery department was to rebuild the cooperative stores.[21] But, he explained in a subsequent letter, "we are finding the job of rebuilding the stores a very difficult one." By cooperation and hard work, he predicted, "we can save all of the stores now in operation, although at some points they are greatly discouraged."[22]

Except as a means of broadening cooperative business coverage as far as possible in CCA territory, it is difficult to explain why Cowden led his wholesale into the grocery business. Cooperative grocery stores had, historically, experienced difficult times, and the growth and development of chain food stores made their problems even greater. Cowden and other leaders in the Missouri Farmers Association in the 1920's had actually opposed establishment of cooperative stores because of their history of general failure in the late nineteenth century. Cowden may have thought that the buying power of a large cooperative wholesale could make the local stores really competitive, but this did not prove to be the case.

In a few small towns cooperative grocery outlets enjoyed a good business, but these were the exception rather than the rule. Poor management and the extension of too much credit plagued the cooperative's stores in the late 1930's just as they had the Grange's establishments in the 1870's and 1880's. In any event, the discouraging picture presented by Cowden did not brighten with time, not even after prosperity returned in 1941. But until the Grocery Department was finally abandoned in 1953, CCA sold many items under its CO-OP label. By the end of 1936 almost two hundred products were distributed by CCA under the CO-OP trade name,[23] and early in 1937 a large CO-OP truck was placed in service to make wholesale deliveries. Groceries, however, never became an important part of CCA business. For example, in 1939, out of more than $4 million worth of business, grocery sales accounted for only $140,699, and the margin of profit was extremely small.[24]

By 1941 CCA was providing merchandise bearing the CO-OP label to 121 cooperative stores in seven states. The first cooperative supermarket was opened at Winfield, Kansas, during that year. In his annual report of 1941 Cowden said, "The next great step forward for CCA

[21] Cowden to Vesecky, December 21, 1935, Cowden Papers.
[22] Cowden to Vesecky, February 18, 1936, Cowden Papers.
[23] *Eighth Annual Report*, 1936, 2.
[24] CCA, Audit, 1939, CCA Files.

in the grocery field is that of processing food products." However, as will be seen subsequently, it was many years before CCA began processing meat, and meanwhile the Grocery Department was abandoned. Probably the greatest value of the Grocery Department was that it could be used as a demonstration of how cooperative services might be expanded to meet all consumer needs. Its value was greater as propaganda for CCA than as economic benefit for farmers.

The attempt to supply tractors was another of CCA's enterprises to fail. By the middle 1930's several cooperative wholesales were handling tractors for their members on a limited basis. For example, the Indiana Farm Bureau sold B. F. Avery machines. As early as May 22, 1933, the Board of Directors discussed the matter of handling farm implements. Representatives of several farm machinery firms attended the meeting, but the Board took no action.[25] About two years later, on June 28, 1935, Cowden again discussed with his Directors the possibility of distributing farm machinery and implements on a cooperative basis.[26] Nothing was decided, however, except that a motion was passed to cooperate with National Cooperatives, Inc., if National should begin selling agricultural machinery. But Cowden was anxious to add this new service. He investigated the CO-OP tractor that had been designed by Dent Parrett, a highly qualified engineer, and that was being manufactured by the Duplex Machinery Company at Battle Creek, Michigan. Powered by a Chrysler-built Amplex engine and mounted on rubber tires, this machine had many advanced features, including a self-starter.[27]

Although only a few of these tractors had been produced by the fall of 1935, Cowden arranged a field test for the Board of Directors, who were to meet on November 5 and 6. Following this demonstration, the Directors discussed whether to begin handling the CO-OP tractor; only one member opposed the move. A motion was then passed, directing Cowden to get in touch with other regional cooperatives and to make a deal for tractors through National Cooperatives, Inc.[28]

CO-OP tractors were displayed at the annual meeting early in February, 1936, and later in the month a machinery department was established with George Batcheller, former manager of the Farmers

---

[25] Board of Directors, Minutes, May 22, 1933.
[26] Board of Directors, Minutes, June 28, 1935.
[27] *Farm Implement News*, February 27, 1936.
[28] Board of Directors, Minutes, November 6, 1935.

Union Brokerage Company of Sioux City, Iowa, as manager. Between March 21 and April 13 the new tractor was demonstrated in twenty communities throughout CCA territory, and the Cooperative Oil Company of Parsons, Kansas, sold the first tractor to Elmer Frerichs of Dennis. Encouraged by the initial response of farmers, Cowden optimistically predicted brisk sales. E. W. Barth, a veteran CCA fieldman, replaced Batcheller as manager of tractor sales in September, 1936.[29]

Although the CO-OP tractor was a good machine and favorably priced, it never sold well. In the first place, most local cooperatives were not prepared to service tractors, and farmers hesitated to purchase a machine for which parts and mechanics were not immediately available. More important was the fact that most cooperatives could not afford to tie up capital in expensive merchandise with a slow turnover. Furthermore, private dealers and spokesmen for the farm machine industry opposed the sale and distribution of a tractor under the CO-OP label. In November, 1935, for example, Stanley M. Sellers, representative of the National Federation of Implement Dealers Associations, made a strong plea "to curb the growing evil of co-operative buying of farm machines." [30] As did the local cooperatives, CCA found it difficult to finance tractor operations. In the fall of 1937, for instance, management was confronted with carrying eighty-nine tractors until the following spring. In order to do this a loan was negotiated from the St. Paul Bank for Cooperatives. The Board, when it met on October 23, discussed the "many difficult problems" connected with the sale of tractors thoroughly.[31]

After a brief surge during the first and second year, tractor sales practically stopped. During the first eight months of 1937, CCA sold $131,406 worth of tractors, priced in Battle Creek at $1,085 to $1,385, depending on the model. CCA probably moved between 100 and 120 machines. But in 1939 the Machinery Department sold only $30,662 worth of tractors and suffered a loss of $1,394. In 1940 losses on tractors amounted to $3,051, and the early enthusiasm for handling farm machinery on a cooperative basis turned to gloom.[32] Cowden and other CCA officials were reluctant to admit that their machinery program was a failure. Years later, CCA spokesmen declared that the company's

[29] *Cooperative Consumer*, February 24, March 9 and 23, April 13, 1936.
[30] *Farm Implement News*, November 21, 1935.
[31] Board of Directors, Minutes, October 23, 1937.
[32] CCA, Audits, 1937, 1939, and 1940, CCA Files.

experience with tractors had not been without some benefit to farmers. According to them, the major manufacturers of tractors had been pushed into including improved features on their own machines as a result of potential competition from the CO-OP model.

Other important action taken by the Board at the meeting of June 28, 1935, was the decision to arrange for jobbing lumber and building materials. Despite a unanimous vote to proceed, nothing definite was done until February 3, 1936, when the Directors voted to establish a lumber department at once.[33] On March 1, H. M. Gibney was named manager of the new department, and shortly afterward he left for the West Coast in search of a supply of lumber. As a result of his trip, Gibney reported in May that CCA could supply a complete line of shingles, posts, siding, flooring, and other items. This was strictly a commission business. CCA took orders from cooperative lumber yards and transmitted them to mills in Oregon which shipped carload lots directly to the local association. CCA did not carry any stock for reshipment at its warehouses in North Kansas City.[34] During the first year of operation, the Lumber Department did only $18,993 worth of business. By 1940 this figure had increased to $104,152, but like groceries, paint, tractors, and a number of other items handled by CCA, lumber was a relatively small part of the company's business.[35] This was also true of electrical appliances, which were added to the CCA commodity line early in 1937.

The establishment of a transportation department on May 1, 1938, was another important aspect of CCA's attempt to enlarge and integrate its operations. CCA acquired its first vehicle for distance hauling by trading refined fuels to an affiliated cooperative at Offerle, Kansas, for an International truck. A little later a fleet of eight trucks was purchased from the Union Transport Company of McPherson, Kansas, and soon additional units were leased from a firm in Salina. By the end of 1938 sixteen transports were being operated under CCA permits. Most of the equipment bought by CCA was secondhand and had to be thoroughly overhauled during the first year of operation. By March, 1939, CCA had $23,466 invested in transports and shop equipment. From headquarters in McPherson, the trucks were used to deliver refined fuels, oils, and greases to local cooperatives in Kansas, Colorado, and Nebraska. By the end of 1940, CCA had twenty-one

---

[33] Board of Directors, Minutes, February 3, 1936.
[34] *Cooperative Consumer*, May 11, 1936, 1.
[35] CCA, Audits, 1937 and 1940, CCA Files.

transports in operation, all painted with the conspicuous CO-OP insignia. Here was constant CO-OP advertising as the trucks rolled over the highways of several states.[36]

Cowden explained that, since transportation accounted for a substantial part of a commodity's price, CCA should keep this cost at a minimum. CCA could now develop a cost series on transportation that "will serve as a yardstick by which local cooperatives can determine the efficiency of their own trucking operations."[37] Between May 1, 1938, and January 31, 1939, the Transportation Department saved CCA $8,204. As the Production Committee reported, "This department has proved to be a money maker from the beginning."[38]

In order to make CCA's charter conform to its expanded business operations, important amendments were suggested in May, 1937, and finally approved by the shareholders on October 26. The original charter had specifically covered only petroleum products, but it was now changed to include buying, selling, processing, manufacturing, and transporting a wide range of commodities. This amendment gave CCA express rather than implied permission to do the things it was doing. In addition, the authorized capital stock was increased from $100,000 to $300,000, or 12,000 shares at a par value of $25 each.[39] By August 31, 1940, some three years later, the paid-in common and preferred stock amounted to $143,917.37,[40] but, as will be seen later, shortage of capital was still a major problem facing CCA management during the late 1930's. Also in 1937 the number of directors was increased from nineteen to twenty, and a new district, Oklahoma, was added, making nine districts eligible for representation on the CCA Board of Directors.

Under Cowden's leadership and fired with the enthusiasm generated by the Five-Year Plan, CCA experienced a strong and healthy growth after 1935. Despite the fact that the company was supplying a much wider range of services and commodities, the bulk of business continued to be the sale of gasoline, kerosene, distillate, tractor fuel, oil, and grease. In 1939 petroleum products accounted for about 82 per cent of the total sales and for nearly 70 per cent of the annual

[36] *Tenth Annual Report*, 1938, 17; *Twelfth Annual Report*, 1940, 20; and Report of the Production Committee to the Board of Directors, March 3, 1939, CCA Files.

[37] *Tenth Annual Report*, 1938, 17.

[38] Report of the Production Committee.

[39] Shareholders' meeting, Minutes, July 12, 1937. See also *Cooperative Consumer*, November 8, 1937, 11.

[40] CCA, Audit, 1940, CCA Files.

savings.[41] These figures emphasized that, while the additional lines had some value, the main growth in volume and savings was to be found by expanding the petroleum business. This meant an unceasing effort to add member oil cooperatives and to get them to use CO-OP products exclusively.

The first five-year plan, adopted in February, 1935, called for adding forty new cooperatives the first year. By late November, forty-seven membership agreements had been signed. Not only were the fieldmen busy, but Cowden, too, spent time and energy convincing cooperatives that they could benefit by joining CCA. In October, 1935, Cowden and Tom DeWitt arranged to sign up sixteen Farmers Union Cooperative oil companies in Iowa at a single meeting. By the end of the year fifty-four new members had joined CCA, fourteen more than the established goal. Most of the additions were already successful, operating cooperatives, but a few new cooperatives were constantly being organized under CCA direction and leadership.[42] By 1940, 486 local cooperatives were affiliated with the Consumers Cooperative Association.

Convinced that the growth of cooperative enterprise depended to a large extent upon informing consumers, CCA continued to promote a vigorous educational program in line with the objectives of the Five-Year Plan. Up to 1937 CCA's educational effort had been handicapped by lack of proper leadership and organization. Heads of the Education Department came and went with discouraging regularity, leaving most of the real work for Cowden, DeWitt, Young, Appleby, and other officials. For example, Dr. Joseph Myers, a Kansas City minister, was named manager of the Education Department and editor of the *Cooperative Consumer* on July 1, 1935, but he resigned the following April 15.[43] In order to give the Education Department more stature and to provide continuity in its operation, Cowden began looking for a strong and capable head. On December 28, 1936, it was announced that Merlin G. Miller, a professor of history and sociology at the College of Emporia in Kansas, would begin directing CCA's educational work on January 16, 1937.[44] Miller was a vigorous advocate of consumer cooperation, and he had written and lectured widely on cooperative principles and programs.

---

[41] CCA, Audit, 1939, CCA Files.
[42] *Cooperative Consumer*, November 25, 1935, 1.
[43] *Ibid.*, April 27, 1936, 1.
[44] *Ibid.*, December 28, 1936, 1.

As mentioned earlier, five cooperative training schools, usually lasting a week or ten days, were held in CCA territory during 1935. For some unexplained reason these were not continued in the following three years. It may have been thought that the students who had attended the schools in 1935 could carry on the work in their communities. In 1936 only one two-day school was held in North Kansas City for managers, directors, and employees of local cooperatives, at which most of the emphasis was on sales practices and techniques. Late in 1938 Miller proposed that a school of the same type as those organized in 1935 be resumed, because it was essential to give better training to employees and officers of member cooperatives.[45]

Following this recommendation, two schools were held in January, 1939. Later in the year CCA shareholders voted to hold schools annually so that "we may better supply competent employees, managers, and organizers to meet the needs of our expanding movement."[46] In February, 1940, about forty employees of cooperatives received a month's intensive training at North Kansas City. Shorter schools and cooperative courses were also given.[47] In the winter of 1936–1937, CCA cooperated with Kansas State College when the college offered a seven-week short course to train cooperative leaders. CCA immediately hired four of the students who finished this program.[48] Furthermore, beginning in 1937, the annual meeting became a greater source of education. Sectional meetings provided specialized training and discussion sessions for directors of local cooperatives, managers and other local employees, women, and educational leaders.[49] In other words, the educational effort was directed toward specific groups.

Meanwhile, CCA spread the cooperative gospel in its territory by sponsoring prominent speakers, distributing pamphlets and books, and pushing subscriptions for the *Cooperative Consumer*. Beginning with a circulation of only 8,500 in late 1933, the *Cooperative Consumer* reached 41,000 patrons by the close of 1936 and 62,058 by September 1, 1938. This paper was more than a house organ; it was a spokesman for the entire national and international cooperative movement. Besides keeping readers informed about CCA activities and advertising commodities bearing the CO-OP label, the *Coopera-*

[45] Proposed CCA Educational Program for 1938–1939, CCA Files.
[46] Resolution passed by the Eleventh Annual Convention, CCA Files.
[47] *Thirteenth Annual Report*, 1941, 26.
[48] *Eighth Annual Report*, 1936.
[49] *Cooperative Consumer*, January 17, 1937, 1.

tive Consumer carried articles of general educational value and interest.

During its first three and a half years, the *Cooperative Consumer* had not had an experienced and properly qualified editor. On August 9, 1937, however, J. W. Cummins, who had been director of information for the Farmers National Grain Corporation at Chicago, took over the editorial duties. Cummins was a man of wide experience and broad contacts in the cooperative movement. He had spent more than a dozen years writing for cooperative publications before he moved to CCA. From the beginning, Jim Cummins was more than an editor; he became a close friend and adviser of President Cowden.[50] Under his editorship the *Cooperative Consumer* was enlarged from eight to twelve pages in January, 1938, and the paper became more effective as a spokesman for the whole cooperative movement. Another regular publication distributed by CCA was the *CO-OP Homemaker*. It was first published in November, 1938, and was distributed through CO-OP grocery stores.

Some of CCA's educational program consisted of bringing nationally known leaders to the Kansas City area for speeches and discussions. For example, early in 1936 James P. Warbasse, president of the Cooperative League of the U.S.A., made fourteen addresses in CCA territory. At the annual convention in February, Toyohiko Kagawa, prominent Japanese Christian, told an overflow crowd of 1,000 persons, "We must learn to live together, and cooperatives offer the best way to do it." [51] Horace M. Kallen, a widely read authority on consumer cooperation and a man whose writings had greatly influenced Cowden, spoke in the Kansas City area in January, 1937.[52] Cowden's wide personal acquaintance with most of the cooperative leaders made it relatively easy for him to get outstanding speakers for almost every occasion.

But even the best speeches or the most carefully written articles and pamphlets could not substitute for face-to-face contact between men and women committed to cooperative principles and those who were not. Consequently, CCA developed a number of additional plans for promoting consumer cooperation in its territory. The CCA sponsored CO-OP Week for the first time, in October, 1936. Where possible, local ministers were enlisted to open the week's activities by

[50] *Ibid.*, July 26, 1937, 1.
[51] *Ibid.*, February 10, 1936, 1.
[52] *Ibid.*, January 11, 1937, 1.

preaching on the ideals of cooperation. During the following five days local members, employees, and managers were to make a concentrated effort to win new members and additional business.[53]

In the fall of 1936 a number of district councils were also established. These meetings brought together on one evening each month all employees, directors, and interested members of cooperatives in a given district. There, with representatives of CCA, both the business and philosophical aspects of cooperation were discussed.[54] District meetings for leaders and officials of local cooperatives were held annually in each of CCA's eight districts (nine after 1937). The monthly district councils emphasized general cooperative education and philosophy, while the annual district meetings concentrated on sales techniques and general business affairs. In 1938 CCA began an annual trade and membership drive throughout its territory, accompanied by an intensive publicity effort. These campaigns were modeled after the yearly drives of the London Cooperative Society.[55]

Efforts were made in 1936 to organize additional women's guilds, the first of which had been established in North Kansas City in 1934, but only a few were successful. After five years there were only twenty-five active groups. The limited size and activity of the guilds made it abundantly clear that this attempt to train a consumer-minded public was a failure. Efforts to form study circles and buying clubs in communities that had no cooperative also failed.

The formation of neighborhood councils was another attempt to promote consumer education through person-to-person influence. The plan called for monthly meetings in private homes at which the cooperatives' problems and opportunities could be discussed. These discussions were usually preceded by a recreation period, including the singing of cooperative songs. One of the most popular songs was the "Battle Hymn of Cooperation":

> Oh, we are a mighty army, though we bear no sword and gun.
> We're enlisted 'til the struggle for cooperation's won.
> O, we know our plan is righteous and we know our cause is just;
> For upon the brotherhood of man we firmly base our trust.
> Let us strive to win the victory, for win we can and must.
> Consumers marching on!

---

[53] *Ibid.*, September 28, 1936, 1.
[54] Merlin Miller, "Educational Program of CCA, A Record of Achievements, 1935–1936," CCA Files.
[55] *Cooperative Consumer*, December 15, 1938, 1.

Participation in these group activities was never large. By 1940 there were only thirty-six active councils in CCA territory, and the so-called neighborhood councils were gradually abandoned. CCA's attempts to develop responsible and informed local leadership through various community meetings and discussions were not generally successful. Even those persons trained in the cooperative schools did not usually return home and set up classes of instruction in consumer cooperation as had been expected. Very few local educational committees were appointed in keeping with plans adopted by CCA in 1935, and most of those that were named failed to function.[56]

CCA also carried on active youth programs. For example, it cooperated with 4-H clubs in sponsoring short schools on cooperative principles. In August, 1940, the wholesale held its first camp for cooperators at Estes Park, Colorado, and this became an annual affair except during the second World War, when transportation facilities were overloaded. CCA also sent representatives to the National Cooperative Recreational School conducted in Ames, Iowa, to train leaders who in turn would develop recreational activities among local cooperatives.

When CCA's first five-year plan was adopted early in 1935, the only well-established educational activity was publication of the *Cooperative Consumer*. During the next five years a great volume and variety of publications were distributed, annual membership and trade drives were conducted, a two-week or four-week school for employees and prospective employees was held after 1939, circuit councils for directors and employees were scheduled, and women's guilds and neighborhood councils were encouraged. Merlin Miller wrote in September, 1940, that this ambitious educational program had been somewhat of "a shot in the dark" and that some of its features had proven unsuccessful. Despite the failure of some programs, CCA did make important contributions to education concerning cooperatives.[57]

Perhaps the most effective education continued to be done by CCA's leaders, especially Cowden, who were ardently devoted to consumer cooperation. Cowden, Homer Young, Appleby, Merlin Miller,

---

[56] See Miller, "Educational Program of CCA." For comments on the neighbor-night type of activity in the cooperative movement, see Clarke A. Chambers, "The Cooperative League of the United States of America, 1916–1961: A Study of Social Theory and Social Action," *Agricultural History*, XXXVI (April, 1962), 72.

[57] *Ibid.* See also Miller, "Proposed CCA Educational Program for 1938–39," and Report of the Publicity and Educational Committee to the Special Five-Year Planning Conference of CCA, September 4, 1940, CCA Files.

and others from the Kansas City office traveled to district meetings and other gatherings, where they pounded away at the need for and importance of consumer cooperation. From the beginning Cowden depended heavily upon the radio, and he gradually made more and more use of this medium. During special campaigns, as for memberships, the CCA business territory was blanketed with broadcasts. For example, in February, 1938, Cowden made twenty-six speeches over six of the leading radio stations in CCA territory during the drive then under way to add 12,000 cooperators to member companies.[58]

Managers and directors of local associations generally took advantage of meetings and conferences sponsored by CCA, but even these leaders were usually more interested in having CCA show them how to increase their membership and sales than in the general principles of cooperation. Thus, the schools, meetings, and conventions that emphasized practical business matters generally had a good attendance and lively discussion. In contrast, the guilds and neighborhood sessions that were organized to promote the broad principles and philosophy of consumer cooperation failed to arouse much response. This situation emphasized the fact that most farmers joined cooperatives for practical benefits and that they were not really interested in changing the basic economy.

Cowden, however, continued to attack the capitalistic system and to appeal for support of the "middle way." In an address to a group in Indianapolis on December 30, 1935, he declared that it was not necessary to choose a dictatorship of the right or the left. Cooperatives, he said, provided a method and a means of social change by evolution rather than by revolution. The cooperative system was "building a new bridge for humanity to use in reaching the goal of an abundant life which a machine age can produce, while the old bridge of private profit through artificial scarcity is threatening to collapse."[59] In his annual report of 1940, Cowden wrote that people were looking for a better way than the "barren prospect held out by a dog-eat-dog economic system."[60]

In line with this philosophy and the general thinking in cooperative circles, early in 1937 the CCA Board of Directors voted to recommend amendments to the bylaws that would eliminate the basic capitalistic vocabulary. The words, *dividends, profits, capital stock,*

---

[58] *Cooperative Consumer*, January 24, 1938, 7.
[59] Cowden Speech File.
[60] *Twelfth Annual Report*, 1940, 4.

stockholders, and *stock* were dropped, and the terms, *refunds, savings, share capital, shareholders,* and *shares* were substituted.[61] These and other changes were made in the bylaws in October.

By the middle 1930's, much of the CCA publicity associated the cooperative movement with Christianity. The *Cooperative Consumer* carried scores of articles by ministers and cooperative leaders that emphasized this relationship. One Kansas City minister compared the fundamentals of Christianity and cooperation in an article entitled "The Cross And Cooperation." He asked that Christians "study the methods of the Cooperatives and seek to find in them a way to a social order in which the principle of the cross is paramount and not the rule of force." [62]

At the company's Christmas party in December, 1935, Harvey Hull, president of National Cooperatives, Inc., said that "as cooperative workers we can sing these Christmas songs with great joy, because we are giving a practical application to the ideals of Christianity every day in the year as we build the Cooperative Movement." Cowden added that "the organization of consumers into cooperatives to supply every need of life is the surest way to put the Golden Rule of Jesus into practice every day." [63] In his Christmas editorial, published in the *Cooperative Consumer* on December 15, 1938, Cowden called Christ "the first great Cooperator." This approach had a strong appeal to depression-ridden people who felt that the nation had fallen upon evil days because of the selfishness and greed of big business. Cowden and other cooperative leaders exploited this theme for all it was worth.

Although Cowden was primarily interested in building CCA in the Kansas City trade area, he was not satisfied with promoting cooperation on merely a regional or even a national basis. Following his trip abroad in 1934, he never ceased to advocate the values of world-wide business cooperation. In fact, Cowden's interest in world-wide cooperation gradually became more intense. In February, 1935, CCA became a member of the International Cooperative Wholesale Society. Meanwhile, Cowden was considering how to promote international cooperative trade in oil. On his second trip to Europe in 1937 Cowden addressed cooperative delegates in Paris on September 4 and urged the establishment of an International Cooperative Petroleum

[61] Board of Directors, Minutes, January 30–31, 1937.
[62] *Cooperative Consumer,* May 13, 1935, 7.
[63] *Ibid.,* December 23, 1935, 1.

Society. This suggestion was turned over to the executive committee of the International Cooperative Wholesale Society, but nothing was done for several years. Cowden argued that such a move would help maintain world peace by taking the oil business out of the hands of monopolistic cartels.[64]

After 1935 CCA began to ship small quantities of lubricating oil and grease to cooperatives in Estonia, France, and Scotland. For example, in December, 1937, the Scottish Cooperative Wholesale ordered 4,400 gallons of oil and 1,325 pounds of grease. In the spring of 1938, 4,760 gallons were shipped to a cooperative in Sofia, Bulgaria.[65] Between 1935 and 1940 foreign cooperatives earned patronage refunds amounting to only $1,005.56.[66] Nonetheless, CCA directors and stockholders believed they were helping to build "the economic foundation of world peace through international cooperative trade." In keeping with this objective, the stockholders passed a resolution on February 4, 1936, stating that CCA would not supply lubricating oil "to any nation engaged in aggressive warfare in violation of the Kellogg Pact outlawing war." [67] This was an obvious reference to Italy's attack on helpless Ethiopia and expression of a policy that might have been followed by the major oil companies. The *Cooperative Consumer* frequently carried articles critical of European dictators who curbed and destroyed the cooperatives.[68]

By 1935, as one authority has written, CCA was "still a depression phenomenon in the petroleum industry." [69] However, during the next five years CCA's services and commodity base were greatly enlarged. Much of this expansion was made possible by retaining patronage refunds for capital needs. In February, 1937, the shareholders first voted to defer payments of cash dividends to member cooperatives for five years: the patronage refunds due in 1936, would be paid in 1941. Previously, patronage refunds had been returned to member companies after about eighteen months, but always at the discretion of the Board of Directors. Often, refunds were taken in common

[64] "Proposal for International Cooperative Trade," September 4, 1937, Cowden Speech File.
[65] *Tenth Annual Report*, 1938, 13–14.
[66] Statement in Cowden Files.
[67] Shareholders' meeting, Minutes, February 4, 1936.
[68] *Cooperative Consumer*, October 28, 1935, 5.
[69] Charles W. Merrifield, "The Cooperative Association: An Institutional Case Study of the Consumers Cooperative Association of Kansas City, 1929–1951," unpublished doctoral dissertation, Claremont Graduate School, 1952, 85 ff.

stock. The shareholders also voted to defer payment of the refunds
due in 1935 for five years. Patronage dividends for 1935 and 1936
amounted to $70,490.28, which now became available for company
expansion.[70] Speaking in favor of the plan, one local cooperative
manager declared: "It is one of the great steps forward in giving CCA
the power for maximum service to us all. Our growth has been phenomenal, and we must keep it sound by providing the sources necessary for providing new services." [71] The effect of this new policy was
to give to CCA's management an interest-free loan, or what might be
called voluntary forced savings. Of course this could not be done
without the shareholders' approval. At the end of the five-year period,
the oldest deferred refunds would be paid in cash, but the new dividends would be withheld for continued use as capital.

Directors and shareholders of CCA justified this policy in the belief
that, although consumers would not receive their savings immediately, they would receive greater benefits in the future. "It is not as if this
revolving fund was costing us anything," said one cooperator. "It represents merely the savings we have been able to make by using cooperative products. If these funds can be used by CCA so that later
our returns may be even greater, then we shall all back the move 100
percent." [72] A pamphlet, entitled *Deferred Refunds — for Power and
Plenty*, explained that deferring patronage refunds was like building
a dam across a river. The dam represented power — in this case, power
to expand cooperative facilities and factories so that in the long run
patronage refunds could be doubled, trebled, and even quadrupled.
The refunds, so the argument went, "halted momentarily to generate
this tremendous power," would "sweep on down stream to enrich the
farms and homes of cooperative members." Another brochure, *Factories Are Free*, stated:

> Why rob yourself of factories? You rob yourself of factories by
> not trading at your cooperative! Your buying dollar is an eco-
> nomic ballot! You can spend it, to be used to build privately-
> owned factories, or you can spend it with your cooperative, to
> be used in buying cooperative factories! The first cost of launch-
> ing a factory must be met, but the difference between the cost
> of a product and the selling price — the thing known in private-
> ly-owned business as profit — *is the margin that enables con-*

[70] *Cooperative Consumer*, February 8, 1937, 1.
[71] *Ibid.*, 5.
[72] *Ibid.*

sumer cooperatives to buy factories of their own! Why rob your-
self — you're paying for factories — do you hold title to them?

In the late 1930's and early 1940's CCA published scores of leaflets,
brochures, and posters based on the theme, "Factories are free — for
cooperators." By withholding the patronage refunds, or profits, CCA
could raise money to begin manufacturing paint and grease and to
handle many other commodities on a commission basis. In his annual
report of 1937 Cowden stated that the original paint plant had paid
for itself in six months. New equipment installed in 1937 was also
paid for "out of manufacturing profits." [73] By following a policy of
retaining refunds belonging to members for five years or more, CCA
eased, but by no means solved, its problems concerning capital. However, private business attacked CCA and other cooperatives because
they were not required to pay federal income taxes on these allocated
but undistributed savings.

By July 31, 1939, undistributed savings amounted to $187,915.45,
and the revolving fund reached $128,399.94. While these amounts
played an important role in CCA's expansion between 1935 and 1939,
they were less significant than the company's publicity would indicate.
Actually, loans from the St. Louis Bank for Cooperatives played a
larger role in the company's growth than did the firm's own savings.
In every large expansion after 1935, CCA turned to the Banks for Cooperatives for at least a part — in some cases a large part — of its capital
requirements. Yet, the "Factories are free" propaganda was effective, and much of CCA's educational effort after 1935 was directed
toward convincing farmers that it was sound business to defer patronage refunds and to invest this money in plants and equipment to supply themselves with additional commodities and services.

---

[73] *Manager's Report*, 1937, 6.

Chapter 8

Cash Trading

ONE OF THE PROBLEMS that had, historically, plagued consumer cooperatives was credit management. Many cooperatives had run into financial difficulties by failing to keep accounts receivable under control. Part of this situation was due to the fact that local managers disliked rejecting friends' and neighbors' requests for credit. By 1936 buying on credit posed a major threat to the economic health of CCA and its member cooperatives, and the Board of Directors began to consider remedial action.[1] The decision to move toward a cash basis in 1937 was one of the most important managerial decisions made during the first decade of CCA history. The term, "cash trading," did not mean cash on delivery, but payment on receipt of invoice.

On May 25 and 26, 1936, the Directors discussed the problem of credit, but took no definite action, despite the fact that accounts receivable then totaled nearly $150,000. By August 31, 1937, the figure had risen to $301,979.69.[2] This condition reflected the fact that local cooperatives were extending credit to individual patrons and then expecting CCA to carry member accounts. As one CCA official later explained, "Credit trading was slowly sapping the vitality of Consum-

---

[1] Board of Directors, Minutes, May 25–26, 1936.
[2] CCA, Audit, 1937, CCA Files.

ers Cooperative Association." CCA, he said, was "suffering from a form of 'creeping paralysis.' "[3]

Although the problem was grave, CCA's management faced it directly. On November 6, 1936, the Board resolved to adopt uniform terms of sale and to reduce total accounts receivable. It was agreed to present the problem to local directors and managers and then to inaugurate a policy after January 1, 1937, setting "sales terms as nearly uniform as possible and a definite credit policy providing for as short term credits as is consistent with efficient operation of a cooperative wholesale association, which shall be uniform and strictly enforced by the credit department."[4] Nothing much more than talk came from this initial effort to discontinue sales on credit, but in October, 1937, the Board of Directors voted to encourage prompt payment by giving small discounts for cash and to charge 8 per cent interest on all accounts more than thirty days old. At the annual meeting in October shareholders voted to work toward a cash basis during the next fiscal year. "Many managers were going home," said the *Cooperative Consumer*, and would "call meetings of their membership, and put the matter of cash trading up to them on a dollar and cents basis."[5]

So far as CCA's management was concerned, the crux of the matter was to convince the local cooperatives that cash trading was the best policy. Having accomplished this end, management would then help the member associations reach their goal of operating on a cash basis.

Beginning immediately after the annual meeting in 1937, CCA launched its campaign to promote cash trading. The subject of sales for cash versus sales for credit was discussed in every part of CCA territory, and it was one of the main questions considered at the district meetings that autumn. The principal argument advanced in favor of cash sales by cooperatives was that credit added greatly to the cost of doing business; it caused economic waste. Besides the losses due to bad debts, CCA officials explained that when capital was tied up in credit by either the wholesale or the retail associations, the amount of funds available for expansion was reduced. Further, the cost of extending credit had to be added to the price of commodities; the customer who paid cash was really subsidizing his neighbor who received credit. According to some studies, credit costs, including loss of discounts and

---

[3] Glenn S. Fox, "Buy for Cash," speech delivered October 16, 1940, CCA Files.
[4] Board of Directors, Minutes, November 6, 1936.
[5] *Cooperative Consumer*, November 8, 1937, 1.

bad debts, transformed into an interest rate that amounted to between 13 and 17 per cent for cooperatives in CCA territory. This was a penalty very few associations could bear.[6] Finally, it was explained, cash business would reduce the worries of management, eliminate disputes and hard feelings over accounts, and actually improve the loyalty of patrons.

Early in 1938 CCA's officials began an intensive cash-trading educational program among managers, directors, and patrons of member cooperatives. Letters went to cooperative managers, fieldmen discussed the advantages of cash business in local meetings, thousands of pamphlets were distributed, and Cowden made several radio broadcasts on the subject. In one speech Cowden declared that cooperatives should not serve as banks and that extension of credit should be left up to financial agencies. "If it's necessary to have credit, it should be extended by the Production Credit Association, where it's a matter of production credit, or otherwise by a credit union," he said.[7] Articles opposing the use of credit appeared in the *Cooperative Consumer*. Readers were confronted with front-page stories under such titles as "Can CO-OP Serve as Bank Successfully?" and "Another CO-OP Gets Free From Credit Trading."

In order to emphasize and substantiate the points that credit was slavery and that credit added materially to the cost of doing business, CCA sponsored some special studies of the situation. Starting early in 1938, Joseph G. Knapp, an economist in the Cooperative Division of the Farm Credit Administration, began investigating the problems of credit among local associations in the CCA region.[8] Knapp concluded that it had cost CCA $40,000 to extend credit in 1937–1938.[9] Meanwhile, Vance M. Rucker, an extension specialist at Kansas State College, was employed to study and analyze CCA's business operations between September 1, 1937, and August 31, 1938. Rucker pointed out that CCA's credit position was improving, but that cash reserves were still low.[10] Other studies that showed the expense of credit included a Master's thesis by Glenn S. Fox of Kansas State College, "Retail Credit in Southwestern Kansas Cooperative Elevators." Fox con-

---

[6] Fox, "Buy for Cash."

[7] *Credit and Collections Handbook* (Kansas City: Consumers Cooperative Association, 1939).

[8] *Cooperative Consumer*, February 14, 1948, 1; and *Eleventh Annual Report*, 1939, 6.

[9] *Cooperative Consumer*, October 31, 1938, 2.

[10] Vance M. Rucker, "Report to CCA Board of Directors, October 6, 1938," CCA Files.

cluded, after studying the retail business of fifty-one cooperative elevators in 1936–1937, that credit costs were excessive and that "it is best to operate on a cash basis." [11]

Following almost a year of intense study and discussion, the Board of Directors voted, on October 9, 1938, to begin operating strictly on a cash basis as of February 1, 1939. This policy was confirmed by the shareholders at their annual meeting two days later. On October 17 a headline in the *Cooperative Consumer* announced, CCA TO A CASH BASIS. In order to encourage the shift to cash business, a system of discounts for immediate payment was worked out; it offered 1 per cent discount on refined products and 2 per cent discount on building materials. Commodities on which there was no discount were to be paid for within ten days of receipt. If payment was not received by the tenth of the month, future orders would be sent C.O.D. Adjustment or modification of this policy was permitted by the Board of Directors "only if occasion demands." [12]

The cash-trading policy was really a decision by the wholesale to cease furnishing operating capital to member cooperatives in the form of credit. In approving this action, the shareholders, as Glenn S. Fox wrote later, "took no halfway measures once their minds were made up to get a divorce from credit trading." [13] To help prepare member companies for the switch to cash business, a special edition of the *Cooperative Consumer* was included in the issue of January 23, 1939. Under a large black headline, CREDIT IS SLAVERY, were articles on the value and importance of operating on a cash system.

It took real courage for CCA to move to a cash basis. The risk, of course, was that some member cooperatives might quit buying from CCA. The wholesale's policy would force most local associations to insist upon cash payments from their individual customers, and it was easy to imagine that many farmers might take their business to a competitor of the local cooperative. As one cooperative manager reported, "Our biggest problem is to get customers to try and supply their own credit when other competitors extend them credit." [14] If it did nothing else, cash trading would test the loyalty of farmers to their local cooperatives and the loyalty of the member associations to the wholesale.

----

[11] Glenn S. Fox, "Retail Credit in Southwestern Kansas Cooperative Elevators," unpublished Master's thesis, Kansas State College, 1938.

[12] Board of Directors, Minutes, October 8–9, 1938; and *Cooperative Consumer*, October 17, 1938, 3.

[13] Fox, "Buy for Cash."

[14] Quoted in *Credit and Collections Handbook*.

It is surprising that the cash-trading policy met so little opposition. It can be explained by the fact that CCA fieldmen and auditors had shown local managers the high cost of credit. Simple arithmetic convinced many member associations that they could save their patrons more money by doing business on a strictly cash basis. The propaganda campaign against credit trading by the entire CCA organization had penetrated to the grass roots. A survey of twenty-one cooperatives that adopted cash trading showed that they lost an average of only 2.1 customers each and that these losses were only temporary.[15] Improved economic conditions among farmers after 1938 made it much easier to shift to a cash basis; CCA inaugurated this policy at a fortunate time. By May 1, 1940, 201 local cooperatives, or approximately 35 per cent of CCA's members, were operating on a cash or strictly controlled credit basis.[16] The Board of Directors and the shareholders were so impressed with this record that they resolved at the annual meeting in November, 1939, to push cash trading until it was adopted by 100 per cent of CCA members. A large banner, stretched across the stage of the North Kansas City High School auditorium, greeted delegates to the 1939 convention with the announcement: "They said it couldn't be done — but we're doing it." [17]

At the end of 1938, just before CCA shifted to cash trading, accounts and notes receivable amounted to $237,717; by August 31, 1939, this figure had been reduced to $163,021; after another year receivables stood at only $115,099. Here was concrete evidence that CCA could put its finances in order.[18]

Even before CCA began operating on a cash basis, plans were developed to collect open accounts, some of which were long overdue. Under a policy that was worked out early in 1937, local associations signed notes calling for regular monthly payments to CCA and bearing 5 per cent interest. The first note was signed in March, 1937, by a Missouri cooperative which owed about $5,000 to CCA, plus other debts.[19] By August 31, 1937, payments were being made on $26,967 worth of notes, and a year later notes receivable amounted to $78,522. All together, CCA transferred $101,963 of its receivables from open accounts to notes on which regular payments were made. By August

[15] Fox, "Buy for Cash."
[16] *Ibid.*; Shareholders' meeting, Minutes, November 13, 1940.
[17] *Cooperative Consumer*, October 31, 1939, 4.
[18] CCA, Audit, 1940, CCA Files.
[19] Fox, "Buy for Cash."

31, 1939, notes receivable were down to $51,824, and by 1940 they totaled only $38,599.[20]

The signing of a note by a local cooperative did not assure payment, but, generally, CCA was successful in collecting its old accounts in this fashion. Higher farm prices and a brighter economic outlook in 1939 and 1940 also contributed to the program's success. However, since some cooperatives were in a very weak financial position, CCA did not simply demand payment and then ignore the local association. It was, of course, to CCA's advantage to strengthen every member cooperative, and, beginning in 1937, the wholesale gave cooperatives a great deal more help in improving their business practices.

In response to requests from member companies, a special auditing and business analysis service was set up in 1937 to advise and assist member cooperatives in solving their financial problems. An auditor employed by CCA would analyze the financial and operating statements of cooperatives and would then help to project plans for the future. This service sought to initiate uniform accounting practices, to set up balance sheets, to classify accounts, and to make recommendations for change or reform in financial and business matters. By the end of 1938 more than fifty cooperatives were using the new service, and in 1940 audits were made for ninety-one associations.[21]

Local cooperatives saw their need for better business methods and asked CCA to help them — a benefit for CCA too, because in the long run a stronger local cooperative meant more business for the company. Also, CCA assisted local cooperatives to strengthen their financial position by helping them obtain long-term credit from sources like the Banks for Cooperatives. In other words, CCA attempted to get cooperatives to abandon rule-of-thumb business practices and to adopt more efficient methods. To improve its own business techniques CCA began developing a budget system about 1937. Sales goals were projected, and general costs of operation were anticipated. Strict budgeting and extensive planning, however, did not come until after the second World War.

To help inaugurate and carry out these financial reforms, Cowden brought Glenn S. Fox to CCA on February 15, 1938. Born in 1911 and reared on a wheat and livestock farm in Pawnee County, Kansas, Fox had a strong interest in agriculture and in the problems of farmers.

---

[20] CCA, Audits, 1937, 1938, 1939, and 1940, CCA Files.
[21] *Tenth Annual Report*, 1938; and *Thirteenth Annual Report*, 1941.

After taking a degree in agronomy at Kansas State College in 1933, he worked briefly for the cooperative grain elevator at Phillipsburg and then served for a short time as county agent in Stafford County. He then returned to Kansas State College as a marketing specialist, working under Vance Rucker. In his extension work Fox traveled thousands of miles, studying and analyzing the financial operations of grain elevators. Fox was transferred to the economics department of the college, where he divided his time between teaching and research, holding the rank of instructor. Meanwhile, he fulfilled the requirements for a Master's degree and completed his thesis, "Retail Credit in Southwestern Kansas Cooperative Elevators," in January just before taking the position with CCA.[22]

With this wide background of training and experience it is not surprising that Fox seemed to Cowden to be qualified for a place on CCA's staff. Fox was fully convinced that cooperatives must adopt modern business methods if they intended to survive and grow. His own research had shown the importance of better financial and credit practices. After arriving at North Kansas City, Fox created and directed the auditing and analysis service that supplied experts to help the local associations inaugurate credit and sales reforms. Fox and Merlin Miller later wrote two pamphlets on the subject of reading and understanding cooperative financial statements, *Learning the Language*, and *Reading Between the Lines*. These were distributed widely among cooperators in CCA territory. Fox was also deeply involved with collecting the slow-paying note accounts. One of his first responsibilities was to analyze the condition of fifty-two cooperatives that owed CCA long-overdue accounts. He also assisted local cooperatives to negotiate loans to strengthen their capital position. This was really the beginning of a financial division within CCA, with special emphasis upon service to member associations. Fox was made director of the Finance Department in April, 1938, after Clifford Miller resigned.[23] Although Miller left CCA for other employment, he continued as a member of the Board of Directors, to which he had been elected in February, 1935. Before joining CCA he had managed the Farmers Cooperative Association at Brewster, Kansas, and had been active in cooperative educational work.[24]

[22] *Cooperative Consumer*, February 28, 1938, 1–2.

[23] *Ibid.*, April 11, 1938, 1.

[24] Miller was still serving on the Board in 1964 and was the oldest member in terms of tenure.

Besides moving to a cash basis and helping to strengthen the financial position of local cooperatives, CCA sought to increase its capital position by urging member companies to deposit excess funds with the wholesale. A resolution, passed at the tenth annual meeting of the shareholders on October 11, 1938, declared that cooperative associations "should be entirely financed by their own members or other cooperative associations."[25] It was agreed to pay 2 per cent interest to local companies on their average monthly balance deposited with CCA. This was referred to as "loan capital." Cowden argued that cooperatives should deposit their extra money with CCA rather than in local banks, which often fought cooperatives. He explained that "the loan capital plan is a mechanism for keeping our excess funds under our own control instead of allowing such funds to be drained to the money centers and, perhaps, to be used against us."[26] This scheme had been used successfully by the Scottish Cooperative Wholesale, and Cowden believed the plan would work well for CCA.[27] By August 31, 1939, loan capital deposited with CCA amounted to $13,850, but by 1940 it had declined to $6,000.[28] The figure increased later, but this plan of getting cheap operating capital was far less successful than Cowden and other CCA officials had hoped. In his annual report for 1941 Cowden admitted that the plan had been less helpful in financing CCA "than it should be."[29] Most member cooperatives did not have large amounts of idle and unneeded funds, so it is not surprising that the loan capital plan failed temporarily. Later in CCA history, however, loan capital was provided by member associations and others in sizable amounts.

To support the new credit policy and to encourage improved business practices in local cooperatives, CCA shareholders formally launched a "100 per cent co-op products plan" drive at their annual meeting in October, 1939. This program was designed to get each patron to give 100 per cent of his business to his local cooperative; it urged the member associations to buy 100 per cent of their needs from CCA. Editorializing on this question, Cowden declared, "We believe consumers will serve their interest best by making full use of the cooperative instruments which they have set up and capitalized.

[25] *Cooperative Consumer*, October 17, 1938, 6.
[26] *Eleventh Annual Report*, 1939, 6.
[27] *Ibid.*
[28] CCA, Audits, 1939 and 1940, CCA Files.
[29] *Thirteenth Annual Report*, 1941, 24.

It is the easiest way to increase volume and to improve service."[30] Cowden had always recommended that patrons keep their business within cooperative channels, but very few farmers followed this policy. Cooperatives did not handle many commodities that farmers needed, and most consumers were likely to buy where they could get the cheapest price, regardless of whether it was a cooperative source. As with most of the new programs, Cowden expressed confidence and enthusiasm for the "100 per cent plan" and predicted that by January 1, 1940, one hundred member cooperatives would adopt it.[31] This program moved slowly, however, and late in 1939 only eighteen cooperatives had signed 100 per cent agreements.[32]

Another attempt to help local cooperatives was made by CCA in May, 1937, when the Cooperative Insurance Association was established. The purpose of this service was to pool the bond and insurance purchases of local associations. The association bought fidelity bonds, fire insurance, and other types of protection for cooperatives on a group basis and at considerable savings.[33] The Cooperative Insurance Association provided the additional service of giving advice to member associations on their insurance needs.

Both the dollar value and volume of CCA business advanced steadily after 1935. Neither the move to a cash basis nor the recession of 1937 interfered seriously with the company's growth. Total sales in 1936 reached $3,310,411, almost $400,000 above 1935. Since the fiscal year was changed in 1937 to end on August 31, the sales figure for 1937 covered only eight months. Despite the short year, business totaled $3,090,116, or only a little more than $200,000 less than for the full twelve months of 1936. Sales of CCA products exceeded the $4 million mark for the first time, in 1938. CCA saw one of its smallest gains in the year of 1938–1939. Both drought and general business conditions were responsible for the gain being small — only 3.27 per cent. But in the year ending August 31, 1940, CCA sold $5,110,163 worth of merchandise, an increase of 15.48 per cent over 1939.

At the same time, savings mounted rapidly and in about the same proportions as total sales. Between 1936 and 1940 annual net savings rose from $60,347 to $129,327. As mentioned earlier, these savings

---

[30] *Cooperative Consumer*, October 31, 1939, 4.
[31] *Ibid.*
[32] Cowden Memorandum, November 18, 1939, Cowden Papers.
[33] *Cooperative Consumer*, August 23, 1937, 1. See also *Eleventh Annual Report*, 1939, 25.

were retained by CCA in undistributed dividends, reserves, and in the five-year revolving fund. By 1939 the equity of members totaled $464,-083, and a year later it reached $564,415. The first payment from the revolving fund was due in 1941, and it amounted to $17,136. Meanwhile, CCA had the use of this money for expansion and growth.[34]

An analysis of CCA's business at this period shows that in 1939 the company was handling twenty-one major commodities. These included a full line of petroleum products, and auto accessories, paint, twine, fly spray, tractors, wire, lumber, roofing, groceries, and electrical appliances. Gasoline continued to command the largest dollar sales, but it ranked behind oil as a producer of savings. The high return from oil can be seen in the fact that from $365,200 worth of sales in 1939, the profit amounted to $140,607. On the other hand, only $121,443 was realized on $2,380,024 worth of gasoline sold. There was a surprisingly good margin on tires, although the volume was relatively small; profits reached $45,416 on sales of $235,361 in 1939. Grease ranked fourth in profits.

Out of gross savings of $427,145 in 1939, four commodities, gasoline, oil, tires, and grease accounted for $334,982. As mentioned in another connection, CCA officials talked in glowing terms about the benefits of handling groceries, tractors, lumber, electrical appliances, and other products on a cooperative basis, but all together these items represented a relatively small part of the total business. They were more important as symbols of cooperative growth. On some of these lesser products the margin was good enough, but CCA was unable to generate sufficient volume to make any substantial savings. For example, in 1939 the company made $4,864 on sales of only $10,155 worth of fly spray. This was a remarkable profit, but the total volume was so small that it did not make much difference one way or another in the company's total business or in service rendered.[35] It took CCA a long time to learn that it could perform the greatest service by concentrating on supplying farmers with a relatively few commodities — those which entered largely into agricultural production costs. It did not make much difference to a farmer if he saved a little money on fly spray, roofing, groceries, paint, or antifreeze, but it was of vital importance to him to save as much as possible on petroleum products because they were becoming increasingly important in his cost of

[34] CCA, Audits, 1937 and 1939, CCA Files.
[35] CCA, Audit, 1939, CCA Files.

production. CCA officials gave a great deal of attention publicly to nonpetroleum products in the late 1930's, but basically, they realized, gasoline, oils, and greases were the company's mainstays. This realization formed part of the basis for the company's decision to build a refinery.

While the wholesale showed a healthy growth, this was not duplicated by the Retail Department. Instead of standing as shining examples of successful cooperatives, CCA's bulk and retail stations struggled along, making very little gain and, in many cases, losing money. How was it that CCA could advise its member associations on how to operate profitable retail cooperatives, but failed to earn satisfactory returns on its own bulk and retail stations? The reason was that CCA often established its bulk and retail stations in communities where there was little support for cooperative enterprise, as a sort of missionary work for cooperatives. Interested individuals were either sold a $10 share in the Retail Department or, more often, earned a share of stock by having CCA withhold dividends until their dividends reached that amount. In time, some of these patrons raised or earned enough money to set up a local cooperative, a development which CCA encouraged. However, CCA continued to operate outlets in communities that could not raise enough money to finance a local association. This meant that the weakest territories always remained in the Retail Department. Moreover, CCA had management and credit problems like those of independent cooperatives. These and other difficulties made the Retail Department a cause for worry and concern.

In 1938 CCA operated twenty-one bulk plants and ten service stations. Of the latter, seven lost money, while five bulk stations failed to show a profit. The next year, seven of the twenty-one bulk plants experienced losses. During 1938 and 1939 the Retail Department made only $3,483 and $3,439, respectively.[36] There was no real object of operating a Retail Department from a savings viewpoint, but quite a number of cooperatives in northern Missouri were started by CCA's Retail Department.[37]

Burdened with an unprofitable and troublesome operation, CCA's Directors voted in February 2, 1937 to abolish the Retail Depart-

---

[36] CCA, Audits, 1938 and 1939, CCA Files.
[37] Interviews and correspondence with Homer Young, Howard A. Cowden, and Glenn S. Fox.

ment.[38] The plan was to push the formation of local cooperative associations at points where CCA operated retail outlets and then turn the business over to the local cooperative. For example, in April, 1937, United Cooperatives was formed for the purpose of absorbing the assets and inventories of CCA's Retail Department in North Kansas City, Smithville, and Liberty, Missouri. This new cooperative simply took over from CCA the retail business at these three points. This idea did not work particularly well, and CCA was still operating twenty-five stations in 1940. By that time economic conditions had improved to such an extent that all of these businesses were showing a small saving.[39]

Both the growth of fixed assets and the expansion of the commodity base were financed to a large extent after 1935 by the St. Louis Bank for Cooperatives. Despite the bold talk about "loan capital" and financing its own growth through profits — that is, retaining member refunds and placing them in a five-year revolving fund — CCA placed increasing reliance upon the Banks for Cooperatives. Loans were fairly easy to obtain, and interest rates were low, usually 3 per cent. At the end of 1935 CCA owed the St. Louis Bank for Cooperatives only $25,000, but a year later this debt reached $96,511. By 1937 about $173,311 had been borrowed, and CCA's debt to the St. Louis bank remained near that figure over the next two years. These were both facility and commodity loans. For example, on August 15, 1935, CCA borrowed $57,760 at 4 per cent to purchase its new building, and on April 15, 1937, it negotiated a $100,000 loan at 3 per cent for the purpose of handling certain commodities. These were referred to as operating loans. Fewer commodity loans were needed after CCA went on a cash basis. In 1939 CCA shifted most of its business to the Wichita Bank for Cooperatives, of which Ralph Snyder, a former member of CCA's Board, was president.[40]

As CCA enlarged its operations, it was necessary to pay closer attention to administrative organization. By 1937 the company had 123 employees, some of them part-time, with an annual payroll of $109,-740. During the next two years the number of workers rose to 171, and the payroll reached $196,107. Up to the summer of 1937 Mrs. Cowden was in fact, if not in name, the office manager. Although Mrs. Cowden continued with CCA until June 3, 1940, she assumed other

---

[38] Board of Directors, Minutes, February 2, 1937.

[39] CCA, Audit, 1940, CCA Files.

[40] CCA, Audits, 1935 to 1939, CCA Files.

company duties after accompanying her husband abroad in August, 1937. Meanwhile, in June Cowden hired Lawrence Fulton as personnel director and office manager. Fulton had been a bookkeeper for the Missouri Farmers Association when Cowden was secretary of that organization in the 1920's, but he had left MFA in 1928 to take a position with General Mills in Kansas City. When Fulton took over his duties with CCA there were about 35 employees in the main office.[41]

There was little change in CCA's organizational pattern before 1939. Actually, the company's administrative structure was loosely organized, and Cowden continued to direct most activities from his office. The main divisional organization fell under the sales, finance, education, and retail departments. Young was in his sixth year as head of the Sales Department in 1939. In 1938 Glenn Fox had assumed direction of finances, and Merlin Miller continued to manage the Education Department. Bruce McCully had the unenviable job of trying to make the Retail Department a success. Although Jim Cummins was listed officially as editor of the *Cooperative Consumer*, Cowden relied heavily upon him, in addition, for counsel and advice on a wide range of matters.

Young, McCully, and Fox represented the second level of administration, but they were all overshadowed by Cowden. As mentioned earlier, Cowden found it hard to delegate authority, and, consequently, these second-line executives were not administrative decision-makers.

The tight rein that Cowden held over CCA prompted David M. Hardy, president of the St. Louis Bank for Cooperatives, to raise the question of future management. In a letter dated January 31, 1936, Hardy called attention to the fact that CCA owed the St. Louis bank $115,000, and that before CCA broadened its operations further it should carefully consider certain specific problems. In regard to leadership, the letter continued: "We feel that your association has enjoyed strong and capable management headed by Mr. Howard A. Cowden, who has a national reputation in the cooperative movement." But, Hardy stated, "In our judgment a capable understudy to Mr. Cowden should be employed at once, in order to safeguard the association against the fatal mistake of centering all decisions and responsibilities in one executive." He also warned that nepotism was

---

[41] Interview with Lawrence Fulton, August, 1961.

not good for cooperative businesses. President Hardy added that the
St. Louis bank had no desire to influence the operations or policies
of its borrowers beyond safeguarding its loans and assisting associations in adopting sound business practices.

Confronted with this communication from its main source of capital funds, the Board of Directors, at its meeting on February 2, discussed the questions it raised. After lengthy deliberations, Cowden
left the room, and Vice-President DeWitt took the chair. A committee
was named to answer Hardy's letter, and the committee quickly composed a letter and mailed it the next day. It explained that, in Cowden's absence, the bank's queries had been carefully considered. In
regard to future management the Board of Directors had

> given much thought and consideration to the development of
> a successor for [Mr. Cowden]. We reiterate our former position
> that as a matter of policy we employ and train only those indi-
> viduals who have a vision and understanding of the true pur-
> poses and possibilities of our cooperative organization. We
> believe we are meeting the need you suggest and are developing
> several men who are capable of attaining a degree of efficiency
> that will qualify them for the place. However, we do not intend
> to pass any opportunity to get executive ability into the organi-
> zation if and when adequately qualified ones are available.

If the Board had anyone specifically in mind as an understudy for
Cowden, it failed to say so. Actually, CCA was drifting, so far as top
management was concerned, and there is no indication that the Directors wanted to come to grips with the problem presented by Hardy.
After all, Cowden was only forty-three years old and in the prime of
life. Moreover, he was a close personal friend of all members of the
Board, and it would have been embarrassing for them to take any
action that might indicate lack of confidence in his leadership. In
fact, year after year the Board and the shareholders praised CCA's
management in formal resolutions. On February 4, 1936, for example,
the shareholders commended "the board of directors and the management for the vision, the judgment, and the vigor of their administration of our mutual welfare."[42]

The committee's letter assured the St. Louis bank that nepotism
was no problem in CCA. Yet, it is evident that the Board was sensitive
on this point, especially in regard to Mrs. Cowden's continuing em-

[42] Board of Directors, Minutes, February 2 and 3, 1936.

ployment by CCA. At an evening session on the very day the letter was written, the Directors resolved that "the services of Mrs. Cowden have been indispensable in the development of this association and its successful operation and we approve of her continuance on the payroll at any and all times that may suit her convenience." This motion was approved unanimously. Other cases of nepotism were McCully who, as mentioned earlier, was a son-in-law of Vice-President DeWitt, and Miles Cowden, a nephew of Howard, who held a responsible position in the Production Division. However, there is no indication that relatives of CCA officials held their positions for any reason other than their devotion to cooperative principles and their competence. Mrs. Cowden had grown up with the business and indeed was a valuable employee in the office. She had prepared copy for early issues of the *Cooperative Consumer,* and she had written bulletins and copy letters to managers, besides taking care of Cowden's secretarial work. The same was true of Miles Cowden.[43] He had been one of the company's original employees and was at the time manager of the oil-compounding operations.

At its meeting on October 23, 1937, the Board of Directors sought to improve its own administrative efficiency by setting up five permanent committees — finance, publicity and education, organization, production, and welfare. The responsibilities of the Finance Committee were to deal with credits, collections, audits, and loans. The Publicity and Education Committee was to handle technical training, cooperative schools, the women's guilds, and other types and methods of cooperative education. The Committee on Organization was to deal with sales, soliciting new members, and supervising the fieldmen. The Production Committee was given the task of guiding plant operations, purchases, contracts, new products, and research. The Welfare Committee was to work with health and accident prevention. President Cowden was to appoint all of these committees, and he sat on each one as an ex-official member, a further illustration of Cowden's close personal supervision of even the most minute details of CCA business.[44]

Whatever the criticisms of Cowden, it could not be said that he profited personally from his management of CCA. He was working for the principles of consumer cooperation and gave little thought to

[43] *Ibid.*
[44] Board of Directors, Minutes, October 23, 1937.

his own financial welfare. He could have drawn a much higher salary in private business. Despite the fact that in the middle 1930's he was running a company that did several millions of dollars' worth of business a year, he continued to receive a salary of only $6,000 from CCA. On October 11, 1938, the Board voted to increase his compensation to $7,000 annually.[45]

Between 1935 and 1939 CCA inaugurated credit and financial reforms in its own organization and among member cooperatives that helped put the company in a much better position. Cash trading, regular discounts, and auditing and business services to member cooperatives all helped to build a stronger cooperative structure in CCA's territory. Partly as a result of these reforms, which gave the company an improved credit rating, CCA was able to expand its services to member associations, which grew from 313 to 452 in those five years. Moreover, it seemed that at last CCA was in a position to realize Cowden's dream of nearly a decade by building a refinery.

---

[45] Board of Directors, Minutes, October 11, 1938.

Chapter 9

Phillipsburg, U.S.A.

F ROM THE BEGINNING of operations in 1929, Cowden and the Board of Directors had periodically considered the acquisition of a petroleum refinery. Over the years Cowden had discussed the matter before cooperative groups also, both in and outside of CCA territory. At district meetings during the winter of 1937–1938 he spoke frequently of the need for CCA to produce and refine oil. There was never any doubt but that he saw the acquisition of a refinery as a major goal for the company. Without it, CCA could never achieve the integration Cowden and other of the company's leaders so greatly desired. But there were many formidable obstacles in the path of a relatively small firm like CCA trying to acquire refining facilities.

Between 1929 and 1937, company officials had investigated numerous deals for a refinery. The reports of these investigations were invariably unfavorable: the price was too high; the property was in poor condition; or some other factor stood in the way. During 1937 the question of acquiring a refinery was discussed at practically every meeting of the Board.[1] It became evident that the company was nearing a decision on this important matter. On July 25, 1938, Cowden headed his editorial in the *Cooperative Consumer* with the question,

---

[1] Board of Directors, Minutes, June 14–15 and October 23, 1937.

"Do You Want a Refinery?" He asked: "Are member cooperatives of CCA ready to build a refinery of their own? Are they ready to go even back of refining to the production of crude oil, if that becomes necessary? Are they willing to help finance a program that extends all the way from primary production to ultimate consumption?"

Cowden then explained why he thought it was necessary for CCA to take this step: The margins for handling petroleum products had declined, and the big earnings were in production rather than distribution. "The major companies," he said, "are looking less and less to distribution for their profits and more and more to production, refining, and the operation of pipe lines." Answering the question, "What does this mean to cooperatives?" Cowden pointed out that "organized consumers must take those steps that lead to production, refining, and perhaps the operation of pipe lines. Otherwise, the cooperatives are going to find themselves more and more at a competitive disadvantage as time goes on." [2]

It was, then, only after years of discussion and study that the Board of Directors voted, on August 12, 1938, to build a refinery — undoubtedly the most important decision in the company's history. Subsequent enterprises undertaken by the wholesale were larger and involved much more money, but in constructing a refinery, CCA broke new ground for cooperatives in the United States and laid an earnings base for a multimillion-dollar expansion of its commodity and service programs. Moreover, by entering the refining, transportation, and, eventually, the production of oil, CCA began to emancipate itself from reliance upon private firms for its chief sales item — gasoline.

At the meeting on August 12 each Board member was given an opportunity to express his views on the new venture. Not a single voice of doubt or opposition was raised. One member declared that the best time to expand was during hard times, and another agreed that conditions were then ideal to enter the refining business. Kansas had a large surplus of crude oil, as potential production had jumped from about 300,000 barrels a day in 1934 to 3,485,000 barrels a day in 1938. In other words, CCA would have available an abundant supply of raw material, and at the same time it could help producers of oil by reducing the surplus. Cowden had always argued that crude oil was a farm product and that farmers should get greater financial returns

[2] *Cooperative Consumer*, July 25, 1938, 4.

from this commodity.[3] Another favorable circumstance was that during the previous year CCA had built up a good demand for the products that it planned to manufacture; in one month during 1938 it had sold more than nine hundred cars of refined fuels.

Adequate financing was, of course, the main problem facing the Board of Directors. Ralph Snyder and David M. Hardy, respective presidents of the Banks for Cooperatives at Wichita and St. Louis, attended the meeting on August 12 and discussed some of CCA's financial problems. Although neither Snyder nor Hardy made any definite commitments at that time, it was generally assumed that one of their banks would provide substantial financial help. It was known, however, that Hardy was not enthusiastic about CCA's entering the refining business, so the Board looked more directly to Snyder. Despite their uncertainties, the Board voted to incorporate the Cooperative Refinery Association as a wholly controlled subsidiary of CCA.[4]

On September 12 the *Cooperative Consumer* announced the Board's decision. Bold headlines declared: CCA TO BUILD REFINERY. The story reported that at some time later in the year a refinery with a daily capacity of 3,000 barrels was to be started somewhere in northwestern Kansas, near a major oil pool. No decision had yet been reached on the exact location of the plant. The news story estimated that the entire project would cost more than $500,000, and Jim Cummins declared editorially that the announcement was "the best news these columns ever contained." The new program was met with enthusiasm in all parts of CCA's territory.[5] At last CCA was to produce synthetic hay for iron horses.

A refinery could not be built with enthusiasm alone. It demanded hard, cold cash, and a lot of it. By 1938 CCA was in a fairly strong financial position, but it required considerable faith to try to raise capital for an enterprise of this size. At a meeting of the Board on October 9, the bylaws of the Cooperative Refinery Association were written. They called for issuing $425,000 worth of stock, to be divided between 40,000 preferred shares with a par value of $10 each that would be sold to cooperatives and individual patrons, and 1,000 shares

[3] Kansas City *Star*, August 28, 1938. The Kansas oil situation is also discussed in *Cooperative Consumer*, September 12, 1938, 3.

[4] Board of Directors, Minutes, August 12, 1938. The first cooperative refinery was built by the Consumers Cooperative Refineries, Limited, near Regina, Saskatchewan. It began operations in May, 1935. *Cooperative Consumer*, October 11, 1937, 2.

[5] *Cooperative Consumer*, September 12, 1938, 1–3.

of common stock, valued at $25 each. The common stock was to be purchased by CCA in order to give control to the parent company. The officers and directors of CRA were to be the same as those of CCA. The Directors of CCA were each required to own a share of common stock in the refinery, but these shares were to be held in escrow by the company. If a Director should leave the Board of CCA he was automatically removed from his position with CRA and was required to give up his share of stock in the new company. This precaution was taken in order to remove every possibility of CRA falling under any control other than CCA's.[6] These bylaws were approved at the annual meeting on October 11, 1938. The Cooperative Refinery Association's charter was filed at Topeka on October 24 and signed by Kansas' Secretary of State on November 8.[7]

Even before the refinery program was publicly announced, CCA's officials were obtaining promises of stock subscriptions. No money could be accepted until CRA's charter was approved, but almost immediately afterward, patrons of CCA were approached for support. On August 18 a meeting of employees in North Kansas City resulted in promises to buy nearly $10,000 of Cooperative Refinery Association stock. The next day, Cowden presented the program to directors of the Mitchell County Farmers Union Cooperative Association of Beloit, Kansas, the largest cooperative affiliated with CCA. This group voted to invest $10,000 in the refinery. The Mitchell County organization was the first local association to subscribe for stock, and on September 12 the *Cooperative Consumer* pictured President Lee Vetter and Secretary-Manager John L. Schulte signing the company's subscription.[8] The next year, Schulte was elected to the Board of Directors of CCA, and in 1961 he became chairman of the Board. On August 27 Cowden sent an enthusiastic letter to the president of each member cooperative; he predicted that the money could be easily raised, "so great is the enthusiasm of our people for a refinery of their own."[9]

A general appeal was made through the *Cooperative Consumer* to prospective purchasers of stock. A subscription blank was included in each issue to encourage individuals and cooperatives to buy one or more shares of stock at $10 each, to be paid for not later than March

[6] Shareholders' meeting, Minutes, October 11, 1938.
[7] Cooperative Refinery Association Charter, CCA Files.
[8] *Cooperative Consumer*, September 12, 1938, 1.
[9] Form letter, dated August 27, 1938, CCA Scrapbook.

31, 1939. A specially designed button was given to those who took stock. Officials spoke throughout the territory, and Cowden used every avenue of publicity to win support for the new program. In the *Co-operative Consumer* he asked, "Will You Do Your Share?" Building a refinery, he wrote,

> will be notice to the world that consumers are building an economy of their own in which service rather than profit is the guiding motive. It will provide new jobs for men and women, and by returning savings to the people will make them better consumers. It will be building assets, not for the few, but for the many.[10]

The field force also presented the refinery program to local cooperatives.

At the annual meeting on October 10 and 11, it was announced that approximately $124,000 had been pledged for the refinery. While presiding at the general session, Cowden called for additional pledges, and delegates promised another $16,000 on the spot, making a total of $140,000. This was a favorable beginning, but it was only a beginning. Cowden did not pull any punches; he told *Consumer* readers, "We still have a long way to go; we still have much more money to raise." [11] Consequently, intensive drives were carried on in CCA territory during November and December, 1938.

Purchases of stock through almost sacrificial effort were publicized by CCA officials. After Homer Young explained the problems of financing a refinery at a district meeting in South Dakota, Ed Mickelson of Selby bought a share for one of his sons with 1,000 pennies.[12] Other stories told of farm women who took the egg or cream money from the sugar bowl to pay for a share of stock, and one man was reported to have walked into the CCA office and bought 100 shares with ten $100 bills.[13] A writer for the *Cooperative Consumer* declared:

> Pennies from the baby's bank have gone into the purchase of shares in the proposed refinery. Widows have contributed toward its building. Men old in years and experience, who seldom buy shares in any business enterprise, have made the refinery an exception to the rule. Money that gives evidence of

[10] *Cooperative Consumer*, September 12, 1938, 4.
[11] *Ibid.*, October 17, 1938, 4.
[12] *Ibid.*, November 30, 1938, 1.
[13] *Ibid.*, January 9, 1939, 1.

having been out of circulation for years; money all but worn
out from frequent handling; the large "saddle blanket" bills
of other days — it's all coming in as a result of appeals to cooperators to build their own refinery.[14]

Cowden liked to repeat instances like these, and he used them to advantage in explaining the eagerness of many people to achieve the
dream of a cooperatively owned refinery.

Although the effort to raise capital was great, the financing of the
refinery encountered difficulties during the winter of 1938–1939. By
March 1, 1939, $243,910 had been promised, but many of the subscrip-
tions remained unpaid. Hundreds of farmers found it difficult to raise
enough cash to meet their payment for stock on time.[15] Moreover, the
financial requirements of the new enterprise were increasing because
of the need to construct a network of pipelines. The Board voted on
March 1 to set up a second subsidiary corporation, the Cooperative
Pipeline Association, with a capitalization of $260,000, later changed
to $250,000. It was chartered on May 5. The common or voting stock
was limited to $10,000 and was to be owned entirely by CCA; the pre-
ferred shares were to be sold to patrons and local cooperatives.[16] Since
it had been estimated that the refinery would cost $436,000 and the
pipelines about $250,000, the entire refining operation was to require
approximately $700,000.[17] The main reason for developing a small
system of pipelines was to assure a regular supply of crude oil, once
refining operations were begun.

It was already evident that some of the major companies, especially
Standard Oil, did not favor CCA's entering the refining business. Believing that these major companies would do everything in their power to thwart the development of a cooperative oil refinery, Cowden
sought assurance that the CCA enterprise would be able to obtain
crude oil under the Kansas proration act. He was convinced that, if
they could, the major oil companies would deny crude oil to CCA
either directly or by putting pressure on the Kansas Corporation
Commission. Cowden wrote to Governor Payne S. Ratner on February 9 to inform him that, since CCA had announced its refinery
project, the major companies had shown an unusual interest in the

---

[14] *Ibid.*, 6.
[15] Board of Directors, Minutes, March 1, 1939.
[16] *Ibid.*
[17] Minutes of a meeting of the Cooperative Refinery Association, March 1, 1939; and
Minutes of a meeting of the CRA Executive Committee, April 19, 1939.

purchase of crude oil in northwestern Kansas. Because of this development, Cowden continued, CCA hesitated to proceed with construction until its officials could feel certain that sufficient crude oil would be available when needed. He wanted to be sure that control by monopoly would not deny raw material to the CCA refinery. Governor Ratner replied that there was no reason to believe "that an ample and continuous supply would not be available to a refinery located at Phillipsburg." Ratner wrote that state laws were adequate to protect any prospective purchaser of crude oil against monopolistic practices or unfair discrimination.[18]

Although CCA proceeded on the Governor's assurance that crude oil would be available when the cooperative's refinery commenced operations, it teamed with independent oil firms to try to block amendments to the oil proration law then being considered by the Kansas legislature. Cowden felt that the amendments gave the major companies too much control of oil supplies through their network of pipelines and did not give the Corporation Commission enough power "to allocate allowed but unused quotas."[19]

Bruce McCully went to Topeka on March 16 to lobby for CCA. He entertained members of the House at dinner and thought he was making progress in blocking the amendments that were desired by the major companies. However, when the Governor "started calling the boys down to his office and talking to them one at a time," and when he held up some state appointments, support among the legislators for the views of CCA and the independents vanished. But McCully was not entirely discouraged. He reported to Cowden that Governor Ratner had told several legislators that the prospective CCA refinery would get the needed supply of crude oil.[20] This coincided with what the Governor had written to Cowden.

Amendments to the proration law were not so important in themselves, although they seemed to constitute a victory for the major companies. However, this fight in the Kansas legislature was significant in CCA's history because it was the first time that the cooperative engaged actively in political lobbying. Some friends of CCA told McCully that it was a mistake to become involved in politics, but he did not agree. He told Cowden that CCA was now in a better position to deal

[18] Cowden to Ratner, February 9, 1939, and Ratner to Cowden, February 17, 1939, CCA Files.
[19] *Twelfth Annual Report*, 1940, 24.
[20] Report of McCully to Cowden, March 28, 1939, CCA Files.

with the Governor and the Corporation Commission. McCully believed that political power was essential to achievement of economic goals.[21]

During the spring of 1939, as financial problems mounted and the controversy over a future crude oil supply intensified, the location of the refinery remained indefinite. In November, 1938, members of the Board had visited several communities in northwestern Kansas with the view of locating the refinery, but no decision was reached. These investigations continued into 1939, and the *Cooperative Consumer* kept predicting that the location would soon be revealed. Cowden had told Governor Ratner early in February that the refinery would be built in or near Phillipsburg, but it was not until May 8 that the *Cooperative Consumer* headlined a story with REFINERY TO PHILLIPSBURG.

In 1939 Phillipsburg, Kansas, was a town of some 1,500 people, located approximately 250 miles west and a little north of Kansas City. It was on the edge of the Great Plains and about sixteen miles from the Nebraska border. Agriculture provided the economic base of Phillips and surrounding counties, although in recent years oil had been discovered in the area. One of the main reasons for locating the refinery there was the abundant supply of cheap crude oil. More important, however, was the fact that Phillipsburg was not far from Superior, Nebraska, which had a favorable freight rate to Omaha and points north and west.[22] CCA's officials expected a comparable rate, which they considered competitive. Also, Phillipsburg provided about 75 acres of land without cost to the refinery, and businessmen in and around the town bought $20,000 worth of CRA stock. Moreover, Phillipsburg was located in a region where CCA had some strong member cooperatives.

Governor Ratner greeted the announcement of the refinery's location as "welcome news" and added: "The new refinery . . . will open up an increased market in northwest Kansas, and as an important industrial development, the state welcomes its announcement and offers its fair and impartial cooperation." Cowden called the prospective refinery "cheering news to thousands of our people. They've worked hard for it." [23]

On May 6, only two days earlier, Cowden announced that the Mid-

[21] *Ibid.*
[22] Cowden to Western Trunk Line Committee, September 11, 1939, CCA Files.
[23] *Cooperative Consumer*, May 8, 1939, 1, 4.

Continent Engineering Company of Dallas would build the refinery — including storage tanks and an office building and laboratory — and the 70 miles of pipeline. Construction was scheduled to be completed in 100 days. Later Cowden declared that at least two other companies had been asked to bid on the job, but they had been forced to withdraw by the major oil companies with whom they customarily did business.[24]

A fresh burst of enthusiasm followed the announcement that actual construction would soon be started. But CCA still confronted some knotty financial problems. Cowden reported that as of June 10 total paid-in stock subscriptions amounted to only $127,407, while unpaid pledges totaled $75,277. A down payment of $75,000 had been made on the refinery, but another $75,000 was due July 27 — barely a month away — and only $40,000 was on hand to be applied on this next installment. It would be necessary, Cowden said, to raise $35,000 in about four weeks.[25] Although the Wichita Bank for Cooperatives had promised to loan CRA $259,900, to be repaid at a minimum of $30,-000 a year, the money was to be used as the final payment on the refinery. The bank's agreement meant that individuals, member cooperatives, and CCA needed to raise nearly $450,000. The situation was not quite so bad as it at first appeared because, as will be shown subsequently, much of the cost of the pipeline was to be paid for on an installment basis after completion.

Another problem was the demand of the Mid-Continent Engineering Company for a revision of the original contract because of changes in specifications and equipment. The office building and laboratory was to be enlarged from 800 to 1,900 square feet. It was originally intended to use some secondhand materials in the refinery and pipelines, but this did not prove feasible, so new equipment had to be purchased. All together, these changes meant increased costs of about $49,000, or $17,000 more for the pipeline and an additional $32,000 for the refinery. To ease the financing, the executive committee of the Cooperative Pipeline Association agreed to add all of this extra cost to the pipeline contract, making it $299,000. The refinery contract was left at $436,000. The total cost for both projects was $735,000.[26]

The pipeline contract called for an advance of $50,000, and since

[24] *Twelfth Annual Report*, 1940, 23.
[25] Cowden to Board of Directors, June 28, 1939, CCA Files.
[26] Executive Committee of the CPLA, Minutes, June 26, 1939.

this amount was not available in June, 1939, when it was due, Cowden was authorized to borrow that amount. Actually, CCA supplied these funds by purchasing $50,000 of CPLA common and preferred stock.[27] There was no further immediate pressure to meet pipeline obligations because the remaining $249,000 was to be met in monthly installments, beginning thirty days after completion. These payments were to run for eighteen months. By that time, it was expected, the refinery and pipeline would both be making good earnings.[28] By August 31, 1940, CCA had $65,900 invested in CPLA stock and $50,000 in the CRA, or a total of $115,900 in both subsidiaries.[29]

Although CCA faced serious financial difficulties in raising funds to build the refinery and pipeline, the Board of Directors had decided as early as March 3 that CCA would support the Cooperative Refinery Association with whatever assets might be required. There was, of course, some danger to CCA if it had to commit too much of its resources to underwrite this new project. However, a motion had been passed by the Board at its meeting on March 3 that, as a last resort, CCA would endorse the refinery's obligations if necessary and if the Bank for Cooperatives would permit it. Fortunately, this endorsement did not become necessary.[30]

During the summer of 1939 an intensive campaign was launched to collect unpaid stock subscriptions. By August 31, $207,663 had been received, leaving unpaid pledges of $105,661. About $41,185 of these pledges was being paid by local cooperatives at the rate of one-eighth of a cent a gallon on the refined fuels they bought from CCA. Enough money was being collected to meet the contract obligations. Eventually, member companies and nearly 7,000 individuals invested about $362,000 in the refinery.[31] Despite this response, financing the refinery was a herculean task for CCA. Cowden admitted that CCA's efforts probably would not have been successful without the credit furnished by the Wichita Bank for Cooperatives. He wrote in his annual report, "We could not have succeeded on our own resources alone."[32]

On June 26 it was announced that construction of the refinery would begin at once. L. M. Johnston had been employed as refinery

[27] *Eleventh Annual Report*, 1939, 30.
[28] *Ibid.*
[29] CCA, Audit, 1940, CCA Files.
[30] Board of Directors, Minutes, March 3, 1939.
[31] *Eleventh Annual Report*, 1939, 29; and *Cooperative Consumer*, February 14, 1931, 6.
[32] *Twelfth Annual Report*, 1940, 23.

superintendent and was in immediate charge of over-all building operations.[33] Mayor William L. Faubion of Phillipsburg turned the first shovelful of dirt in a ceremony on July 20, and the next day excavation for the office building and laboratory began.

An elaborate program was planned in connection with laying the cornerstone of the office building on August 2. Some 2,000 enthusiastic cooperators from six states were on hand when the formal program began at 2 P.M. The Phillipsburg High School band provided lively music, addresses of welcome and congratulation were delivered by local dignitaries, and the deed to the refinery property was presented to Cowden by Hugh Starr, president of the Phillipsburg Chamber of Commerce. The climax came, however, when Neal S. Beaton, president of the Scottish Cooperative Wholesale Society, delivered the main address and then spread mortar on the cornerstone with a gold-plated trowel. Calling the event "a history-making occasion," Beaton praised CCA and its leaders for this forward move in cooperative service.

Cowden did not let pass this opportunity to promote the principles of cooperation. He declared, "We are met here this afternoon to lay the cornerstone of a building which will belong to the people." The cooperative refinery, he said, "was not conceived to enrich one man, or a handful of men. Rather, it was fashioned by a movement which any man may join, regardless of race, color or creed." The refinery was being built, Cowden continued, to bring service and savings to the common people. He concluded by saying that the cornerstone symbolized "the solid rock on which the cooperative movement was being built." [34]

Even while the refinery was under construction, Cowden was discussing the next step in his plan to achieve complete integration in the petroleum business. At meetings held at Aberdeen and Sioux Falls, South Dakota, and at Fort Dodge, Iowa, on November 20, 21, and 22, Cowden talked with directors, employees, and members of local associations about cooperative production of crude oil. He emphasized again that production of crude oil, which he considered a farm product, would not only be profitable for CCA, but would provide the cooperative wholesale with security of supplies which it had never known.[35] According to the *Cooperative Consumer*, leaders in

---

[33] *Cooperative Consumer*, June 26, 1939, 1.

[34] *Ibid.*, August 14, 1939, 1, 5.

[35] *Ibid.*, November 30, 1939, 1.

the communities visited by Cowden expressed keen enthusiasm for this expansion by CCA.

Meanwhile, construction of the refinery was proceeding rapidly. By October nearly two hundred men were working three shifts a day, and it was predicted that the project would be completed by the middle of December.[36] At the eleventh annual shareholders meeting on October 13, 1939, prospective refinery operations held the center of delegates' attention.

The 70-mile network of pipelines and the refinery were completed almost on schedule. The first crude oil ever gathered by a cooperative pipeline was emptied into a storage tank on December 18, 1939. The topping plant produced its first gasoline at 6:06 A.M., January 1, 1940. It was several weeks, however, before the 3,000-barrel-a-day unit was in full operation.

Cowden had great faith in special days and celebrations as means of advertising cooperative achievements, and he missed no opportunity to publicize the new refinery. Saturday, March 2, 1940, was set as "Celebration Day" in the entire Phillipsburg region. The idea behind this special day was to promote the sale of the first run of cooperative-produced gasoline. Managers of the 150 cooperative gasoline and oil stations were urged to push toward the goal of retailing 30,000 tanks of gasoline during that single day. Radio programs were sponsored by CCA to attract new customers to the cooperative stations, and on February 28 Cowden spoke to the area from Station KMMJ at Grand Island, Nebraska, to emphasize the economic importance of the new refinery. Handbills were distributed, urging the reader to picture himself driving his car "filled with CO-OP gas. The crude oil from which it came was produced on some farmer's farm in either Rooks, Ellis, or Phillips County, Kansas. It was moved from the oil well through the first cooperative pipeline in the world's history, on to Phillipsburg, Kansas, where the world's first complete cooperative refinery is now operating at capacity."[37] This would be a great day, Cowden editorialized in the *Cooperative Consumer*, because citizens of "these semi-arid, drouth-stricken regions" would have a chance to burn gasoline in their cars and tractors without paying any toll "to absentee owners in eastern cities." This, Cowden wrote, would be "a great day for the Plains."[38]

[36] *Ibid.*, October 18 and 31, 1939, 1.
[37] Handbill, Cowden Files. See also *Cooperative Consumer*, February 15, 1940, 1.
[38] *Ibid.*, 4.

Unfortunately, a severe snowstorm in much of the area around Phillipsburg on March 2 kept many people from buying their first tank of gasoline from the farmer-owned refinery on that day. But despite adverse weather, station managers reported doing business with customers who had never previously bought CO-OP products.[39]

But the really climactic day was May 4, the day the new plant was formally dedicated. For more than a month before this big event news of the dedication was publicized by a variety of means. A full day of activities was promised the thousands that were expected to attend. Early on Saturday morning, May 4, the roads around Phillipsburg began to fill with traffic as people came from near and far. One caravan started from Kansas City shortly after midnight in order to reach Phillipsburg in time for the festivities. Local, regional, and national cooperative leaders were all on hand to participate in the program.

Beginning at 7 A.M., the refinery was open to all visitors. Then at 11:30 a mile-long parade, consisting of visiting dignitaries, marching bands, the cooperative's transport trucks, cowboys, and early-model automobiles, moved from near the center of town to Rodeo Field. By noon about 25,000 — some estimates were as high as 30,000 — people had gathered to enjoy a free barbecue. Eighteen serving lines formed, and before 2 P.M. the crowd had consumed 1,700 pounds of CO-OP beans, 3,000 pounds of beef, 30,000 buns, and 900 gallons of coffee. It was certainly the biggest crowd in Phillipsburg's history, and it may have been the largest meeting ever sponsored by a cooperative.[40]

Filled with beans and barbecue, people settled down to a rather long afternoon program. Cowden gave a speech on "Dreams Come True," in which he traced some of the refinery's history. "This project," he said, "brought into being before our eyes, has the quality of romance, the glow of the impossible suddenly realized, which we associate with dreams." But Cowden could not resist striking a blow against what he considered the oil monopoly. He declared: "We have reached the vitals of the oil octopus." [41]

The main address was delivered by I. H. Hull, an old friend of Cowden and president of the Indiana Farm Bureau Cooperative Association. In praise of the project Hull said that it, the "beautiful refinery," stood for the beauty and soundness of the cooperative movement. Continuing in a more practical vein, he told the audience that

[39] *Ibid.*, March 15, 1940, 1.
[40] *Ibid.*, May 14, 1940, 3.
[41] *Ibid.*, 7.

the refinery was "your declaration of independence and your bill of rights to solve your economic problems." The formal act of dedication was performed by Ralph Snyder, president of the Wichita Bank for Cooperatives. Snyder poured a vial of gasoline into an old horse-drawn tank wagon that had been used many years earlier by the farmers' cooperative at Kirwin, Kansas, a few miles away. As the gasoline ran into the old tank, Snyder said: "Let it represent new ideas, new and better ways, trickling through and permeating and modifying the old [economic] structure." Cowden then accepted the refinery on behalf of the shareholders, and the dedication of the nation's first cooperative refinery was completed. This indeed had been, as the *Cooperative Consumer* said, "drama on the Plains."[42]

The enthusiasm connected with dedicating the refinery was dampened somewhat by the fight to obtain a supply of crude oil adequate for the refinery to run at capacity. Opposition to CCA's entering the refinery and pipeline business had developed early among some of the major firms, and the fight was led by Standard Oil. J. B. Runnels, who was in charge of the CPLA at Phillipsburg, wrote to Cowden on December 31, 1939, that the assistant manager of the Continental Supply Company of Wichita had reported that "he had never seen the Standard more disturbed over anything in the mid-continent field than the construction of our refinery and pipeline." Runnels said that Standard Oil employees had taken pictures of CCA operations and had done "a general first-class job of sleuthing."[43]

A crisis occurred in April, 1940, when CRA needed about 90,000 barrels of crude oil to operate at capacity for the month. It had connections with only 37 wells, with allowables, under the law, of 26,000 barrels. An application was immediately filed with the Kansas Corporation Commission, requesting increased allowables from the wells that were being tapped by CPLA. The petition was promptly dismissed. Chairman Andrew F. Schoeppel took the position, "We cannot raise the allowable of the wells connected to the cooperative pipeline, without raising the allowables of our other wells of a like kind."[44] Cowden wanted the Kansas Corporation Commission to allocate to CRA unused allowables that other refiners did not need. Actually, the commission was not empowered to grant CCA's request even if it had wanted to.

[42] *Ibid.* Entire issue.
[43] J. B. Runnels to Cowden, December 31, 1939, CCA Files.
[44] Schoeppel to D. P. Misner, June 30, 1940, copy in CCA Files.

The only way CRA could get the needed crude oil was to transport it over Stanolind or other privately-owned pipelines connected to wells that possessed adequate allowables, or to build more pipelines of its own. Bruce McCully went to Tulsa in the hope of working out an arrangement with Stanolind, but no satisfactory agreement could be reached. This is not surprising, in view of Cowden's continuing attacks on the major oil companies and their subsidiary pipelines.

Cowden and other CCA officials were aroused; they urged the United States Department of Justice to investigate the oil monopoly in Kansas. But this action did not get any crude oil to the cooperative refinery. On May 17 Cowden telegraphed Governor Ratner that the Phillipsburg refinery would close within a week if more crude oil could not be obtained.[45]

Cowden pictured the fight over crude oil as a struggle between the people and the greedy oil monopolists who had an undue influence over the state government of Kansas. Deciding that political pressure was necessary, he urged friends of CCA in Kansas to write or to wire the Governor or the Corporation Commission and urge "a broad gauged . . . interpretation of the oil proration law."[46] He told Governor Ratner that there was plenty of oil "for Standard Oil Company pipelines which carried it outside the state for refining," but not enough for CRA. Cowden charged that this condition had resulted from a monopoly created by amendments to the oil proration act that had been forced through the legislature by Ratner's administration "and the powerful oil lobby."[47] Cowden declared that if the state could not cope with these powerful economic forces, CCA would have to take other action, presumably an appeal to the courts, to get relief from what he considered a conspiracy against the cooperative refinery.[48] As early as April 17 the Executive Committee, in considering its difficulties with Standard Oil, discussed the possibility of suit to enjoin the Corporation Commission from limiting the allotment of crude oil below the requirements for operation of the refinery at full capacity.[49] However, no such action was taken.

To make matters worse, CCA was accused of violating the Connally "hot oil" Act, a law passed to prevent interstate shipment of crude oil

[45] Cowden to Ratner, May 17, 1940, CCA Files.
[46] Cowden to E. G. Tharpe, April 26, 1940, CCA Files.
[47] Cowden to Ratner, May 18, 1940, CCA Files.
[48] *Ibid.*
[49] Executive Committee, Minutes, April 17, 1940, CCA Files.

in excess of state allowables. This charge was investigated and dismissed, but it was another example of the opposition CCA was experiencing in getting a refinery into operation. Rumors were also circulated that CRA was about to go bankrupt and that some of the major companies were hovering like vultures, ready to gobble up its financially broken remains.[50]

Unable to get oil through Standard Oil pipelines or to get the Corporation Commission to increase the allowables of wells with which it was connected, CCA faced another hard decision. On May 24 the Board of Directors voted to build an additional 22 miles of pipeline to tap about fifty-five wells in several Ellis County pools. This was to cost $45,000 — an amount that had not been anticipated in considering total financial obligations.[51]

The building of additional pipelines undoubtedly was a major factor in weakening Standard Oil's determination to harry and thwart the cooperative refinery project. More important, however, was the fact that the Globe Refining Company of McPherson, Kansas, an independent from which CCA bought gasoline, and Sinclair, which sold oil for CCA's blending plant, both provided CRA crude oil through their pipelines.[52]

By early June it was evident that CCA had won the battle for adequate supplies of crude oil. The refinery had actually been forced to close for a very short time, but now an abundant supply of raw material was available, and the refinery was soon turning out about 3,400 barrels of refined fuels daily. Even Standard Oil fell into line. Cowden explained to Ralph Snyder that CCA could run "any amount of crude oil we wish to run from Standard's line during the completion of our pipeline extension now under construction."[53]

Political pressure exerted by CCA and its friends was a factor in this outcome. McCully explained that "the change in attitude of Stanolind (Standard Oil of Indiana) was brought about by the Corporation Commission and the Governor, who in turn was brought about by the pressure which was brought to bear on Topeka."[54] The fact that Governor Ratner was running for a second term the following No-

[50] *Twelfth Annual Report*, 1940, 25. On the question of oil allowables, see Andrew F. Schoeppel to Cooperative Pipeline Association, May 17, 1940, CCA Files.
[51] *Cooperative Consumer*, May 28, 1940, 1.
[52] See article, "Co-op Gets Its Oil," in *Business Week*, June 15, 1940, 23–25.
[53] Cowden to Snyder, June 7, 1940, CCA Files.
[54] McCully to Cowden, August 30, 1940, CCA Files.

vember may also have been important. In any event, McCully's interpretation seems to be accurate. When McCully first approached Stanolind in Tulsa to get additional crude oil, he was summarily refused. But when he visited Tulsa again on June 10 at the suggestion of Schoeppel and Governor Ratner, the attitude of Stanolind officials had completely changed. They still did not like cooperatives, but they readily agreed to give CCA whatever connections it wanted. This change indicates that Schoeppel and Ratner may have used their influence with Stanolind and that CCA's political influence had not been without effect.[55]

Cowden urged consumers to act politically in their own interest. Writing in the *Cooperative Consumer* after the fight for supplies for the refinery was over, he said: "The cooperatives, without playing politics at all, can well become a new and salutary influence in the public interest regardless of what party comes to power." [56]

The fight over crude oil during April and May, 1940, confirmed Cowden's belief that CCA must add production to its refining business. As mentioned earlier, he and other CCA officials had discussed this move in meetings attended by cooperative members and leaders during the fall of 1939. The popular response was encouraging. On May 3, the day before the dedicatory celebration, the Board of Directors met at Phillipsburg and voted to set up a subsidiary corporation to engage in the production of crude oil.[57] After the meeting Cowden announced,

> Local cooperative associations and more than 6,000 individual members provided most of the capital for building the refinery. I feel sure they will underwrite the cost of producing an adequate supply of crude oil, knowing as they do the importance of having their own sources of supply.[58]

A third subsidiary company, the Cooperative Oil Producing Association, was chartered on September 24.[59]

COPA bought for $13,500 a 26 per cent interest in a 160-acre Rooks

---

[55] Office memoranda, McCully to Cowden, June 12 and August 30, 1940; and Cowden to Ralph Snyder, June 7, 1940, CCA Files.

[56] *Cooperative Consumer*, July 16, 1940, 4.

[57] Minutes of a meeting of the Board of Directors, May 3, 1940; and *Cooperative Consumer*, May 14, 1940, 2.

[58] *Cooperative Consumer*, May 14, 1940, 2.

[59] *Twelfth Annual Report*, 1940, 26.

County lease that already had one producing well. Plans were made immediately to begin drilling three additional wells. The *Cooperative Consumer* headlined its September 30 issue with CCA PRODUCING OIL NOW. On October 12 COPA brought in its first oil well at 3,200 feet, near Laton, Kansas.[60] Cowden was on hand when the well came in, and he wrote jubilantly, "It's a high privilege to be oil-spattered when the oil is the crude product from the first well ever drilled by a cooperative."[61] By November 9 two additional wells were completed, and CCA had begun a major production program.

Cowden could not let pass this opportunity to denounce big business. He told *Consumer* readers that oil had made more millionaires and billionaires than "any other one farm product." But, he said, regardless of how large COPA became, it would never produce a single millionaire. These oil wells were for the benefit and enrichment of thousands of consumers. "Too much rural wealth has been piped away to the centers of large population in a one-way pipeline," he continued, but the wealth from cooperative wells would largely remain in the communities which produced it.[62]

Cowden believed that the value of a refinery and producing properties went far beyond assuring supplies of refined fuels for wholesale distribution. He was vitally concerned about the effect a cooperative oil industry would have on the Phillipsburg area. Here was a region hard hit by drought and almost entirely dependent upon agriculture. Moreover, much of the wealth of the region was drained off to distant centers of trade and finance. Cowden declared that "this constant drain of our wealth to other areas is just as disastrous to our region as it is to have our soil blow away or washed down the river." Cowden explained the problem for areas like northwestern Kansas when he said in his dedication address that the need was "for industry to balance agriculture."[63] The refinery, Cowden said, was an answer "to the unbalanced economy of the Great Plains." He wanted to use the full natural resources of the region for the benefit and improvement of the community; he took social values into consideration. The refinery was an important asset to Phillipsburg, and it helped in a small way to provide the economic balance so badly needed in that part of the

[60] *Cooperative Consumer*, October 15, 1940, 1.
[61] *Ibid.*, 4.
[62] *Ibid.*
[63] *Ibid.*, May 14, 1940, 7. See also Cowden's radio address on February 28, 1944, "Our Refinery — Our Answer to the Needs of the Great Plains."

Great Plains. It stimulated building and, initially, provided employment for nearly seventy-five persons. But if the region was benefited, so was CCA. The cooperative wholesale had important interests in this area, and Cowden saw that the interests of CCA and the region were interdependent. If one prospered, so would the other.

Successful completion and operation of the refinery carried many significant implications for the present and future of CCA. In the first place, it called on the loyalty and support of rank-and-file members to such an extent that the entire cooperative movement in the Midwest was strengthened. Upon seeing the refinery actually turning out petroleum products, the faith and vision of many cooperators enlarged.

Second, the development of large-scale manufacturing affected the general structure of CCA. With the establishment of three subsidiary companies controlled directly by the wholesale — all of the subordinate corporations had the same Board of Directors — the responsibility of the parent company increased. The production cooperatives did business only with each other: COPA sold all of its crude oil to the pipeline cooperative; CPLA transported oil only to CRA; and all refined fuels were sold to CCA, which distributed them to member cooperatives. The savings of each company passed along the same line and were eventually disbursed by CCA.[64]

Most important of all was the fact that the refinery soon began to provide large earnings that were available for investment in other productive enterprises. In Cowden's words, petroleum products "literally lubricated our way into other commodities." [65] By July 31, 1941, the close of the first full year of operation, CRA showed net savings of $204,314, and they rose rapidly in succeeding years.[66] This was an extremely handsome return on an investment of some $850,000, which included not only the cost of the refinery but also the cost of pipelines and operating capital. In the same fiscal year CCA's net savings, excluding those of the subsidiaries, amounted to only $173,652 — the refinery made better earnings during its first full year of operation than did the parent company, which had been in business for thirteen years.[67] Earnings of the refinery were so good that $108,213 was paid on the debt in 1940–1941, and Cowden predicted that the entire plant

[64] *Thirteenth Annual Report,* 1941, 11.
[65] Merrifield, "The Cooperative Association," 142.
[66] *Thirteenth Annual Report,* 1941, 51.
[67] *Ibid.,* 12, 51.

would be paid for early in 1943. The plant, he said, would be another example of "free" factories for cooperative consumers.[68]

An important aspect of the initiation of the refinery program was CCA's exploiting the increased loyalty of its members for political purposes. In the struggle to obtain crude oil, CCA abandoned its neutral role in politics and exerted political pressure to achieve economic goals. CCA was not concerned with party politics but with protecting its economic interests. As time would reveal more clearly, CCA led a new pressure group with which Kansas politicians would be forced to deal in the future.

Throughout its history, CCA enjoyed some sheer good luck in its plans for expansion. If a refinery, for example, had been built in 1934, when the oil industry was depressed, instead of in 1939–1940, the story might have been different. But in 1940 prosperity was rapidly returning to farmers, under the impact of the European war and defense spending. America's entry into World War II assured to every refinery, both large and small, all of the business it could possibly handle if crude oil was available. Consequently, the Phillipsburg property, which had been built when prices were still low, began doing business in a period of rising prices. Thus, the refinery became the prosperous base for further cooperative expansion into manufacturing.

---

[68] *Ibid.,* 12.

Chapter 10

CCA and World War II

ENTRANCE OF CCA into the refining, transport, and production of oil coincided with the end of the first five-year plan, adopted in February, 1935. Besides celebrating the success of these new ventures in 1940, it was appropriate to look back and survey CCA's over-all progress. Most, but not all, of the important objectives laid down in the first five-year plan had been realized. A strong education department was in operation, subscriptions to the *Cooperative Consumer* had increased from 12,500 to 77,250, and leadership training sessions and schools for the cooperative's employees had become regular affairs by 1939 and 1940. Increased manufacturing facilities included plants for producing paint, grease, and, the crowning achievement, oil. Failure of efforts to purchase a printing plant and to manufacture batteries was disappointing, but CCA had not entirely abandoned these projects. The aim of having 486 member cooperatives by January 1, 1940 — 170 more than in 1935 — was not reached until November of that year, but the units affiliated with CCA were getting larger and were doing more business.

The value of setting definite goals for the organization seemed obvious to the management of CCA, and on January 31, 1940, Cowden called on patrons to help write a new five-year plan. He announced a contest in which the twenty-five persons who presented the best programs for building CCA would win all-expense trips to Kansas City, about September 1, to discuss their ideas with the Board of Directors. The basic questions to be answered, Cowden said, were: "Where do we go from here?" and "What should we do in the next five years?" [1] On September 4 seventy-four cooperators, including the twenty-five winners, met with CCA officials to consider the company's objectives.[2] At this meeting the main features of CCA's second five-year plan were developed. After undergoing some refinement, the plan was adopted at the annual shareholders meeting on November 13.

The second five-year plan was somewhat more comprehensive and sophisticated than the first, but it followed the same general pattern. Principal emphasis was again placed upon education concerning cooperation and on expansion of manufacturing facilities. Because of CCA's experience with cash trading and business services to local associations, a great deal of stress was laid on improved business methods and better organization. Continuing the policy, established five years earlier, of manufacturing a product if it was cheaper to make than to buy, the second five-year plan called for setting up a battery factory, a printing plant, facilities for the manufacture of soap and related products, a flour and feed mill, a bakery, a salt refinery, and a plant for manufacture of building supply materials. The production of crude oil was recommended, although this program was already under way. It was stated that, if National Cooperatives, Inc., should begin the production of any of these commodities, CCA would expect to share the investment and ownership. Besides enlarging manufacturing facilities, the new plan aimed at getting all member associations on a cash basis, increasing the loan fund, and creating more cooperative credit unions. Several kinds of business and advisory services were also to be provided to local members. This included help in membership trade drives, auditing and business analysis, and forming new cooperatives. The membership goal was to add 150 cooperative associations, for a total of 636 by 1945.

Educational objectives in the first five-year plan were, as Merlin Miller pointed out, "planned in the dark," without any basis in experience. Now, however, the aims of cooperative education fell into three main categories. The first aim was an informed public, which would require greater circulation of the *Cooperative Consumer* — at least 125,000 fortnightly — the distribution of books and pamphlets,

---

[1] *Cooperative Consumer*, January 31, 1940, 1.
[2] *Ibid.*, September 17, 1940, 1.

film strips, movies, and regular radio broadcasts. Second, this educational program was to result in an active membership among individual cooperators. It was hoped that this could be achieved through neighborhood councils, women's guilds, summer camps, youth activities, and recreation. The third aim was the training of local leadership through circuit councils, schools for cooperative employees, district meetings, and, possibly, a cooperative college.[3]

The Consumers Cooperative Association was already performing many of the services and educational features of the second five-year plan. In most instances, furthering the plan was a matter of expanding and improving the current programs. Even the new plans for manufacturing were only a formalization of projects that the Board of Directors had been discussing for several years. Now these plans became the agreed goals of both CCA and the member associations. Although the second five-year plan had been developed essentially by Cowden and the CCA staff, discussion of the proposals at local and district meetings and the popular contest for ideas produced the appearance of grass-roots origin. Cowden's ability to make individual patrons and local associations feel that they were helping to determine company policy was one of the secrets of his success as a cooperative leader. But more than this, he had the knack of learning what local cooperatives wanted, and then he implemented their ideas.

The twelfth annual meeting of shareholders in November, 1940, not only approved the second five-year plan, but also heard President Cowden report a record business for CCA and its subsidiaries. Total sales reached $5,110,163 — exceeding $5 million for the first time — and net savings amounted to $129,327. This was an increase of between 15 and 16 per cent in both sales and savings. When the subsidiaries were included, total sales climbed to $6,211,401 and net savings to $166,621. CCA controlled $2,038,609 worth of assets, and its debt position had improved over past years despite extraordinary heavy expenditures in connection with the refinery. By July 31, 1940, $47,939 had been repaid already to the Wichita Bank for Cooperatives on the refinery loan.[4]

This was indeed a record of success, but no responsible administrator could be oblivious to the problems attending the growing threat of war. Conflict in Europe had been raging for more than a year, and although most Americans wanted desperately to avoid active partici-

---

[3] *Ibid.*, November 19, 1940, 5.
[4] CCA, Audit, 1940, CCA Files; *Twelfth Annual Report*, 1940, 12, 13, and 35.

pation, Cowden frankly warned delegates that the United States might become involved. In any event, he wrote in his 1940 annual report, war would undoubtedly affect business operations in the months ahead. "Even if continuing war left American cooperatives largely unaffected, it is certain that postwar conditions would affect them vitally," he stated. To meet either war or postwar problems, Cowden urged the building of strong local cooperatives that would join in supporting a powerful regional wholesale. He urged further expansion of service to members because, he wrote, if petroleum products were rationed and local associations were handling only gasoline and oil they might be ruined.[5]

In November, 1940, war seemed far away to most Americans, but when Cowden reported to CCA's shareholders in October, 1941, the United States was rapidly approaching a war economy. As Cowden wrote, during CCA's 1940–1941 fiscal year there had been a transition from production for civilian needs to production for national defense. He predicted "further dislocations and increasing difficulties before the emergency has ended." Cowden explained that cooperative business would be plagued with shortages, delays in delivery, high prices, rationing, and other complexities. To deal with all these problems, Cowden's solution was the same: Local cooperatives should "broaden the bases of their operations" and plan carefully for expansion.[6]

In order to carry out the objective of strengthening local cooperatives, CCA sponsored an intensive drive to win new members, early in 1941. This was the greatest effort made thus far by the wholesale to build cooperative support at the grass roots. More than 220 local associations took part in the drive, and nearly 4,000 new members, the second highest number reported for any previous campaign, were added to cooperatives throughout CCA's territory.[7] At the same time an attempt was made to foster community pride in CCA's recent accomplishments. Local cooperators were encouraged to visit Phillipsburg — *their* refinery — and the home office in North Kansas City. In January eighty-nine persons from South Dakota made the trip to Phillipsburg in eighteen automobiles, each of which bore a large CO-OP sign painted on the side. In March a delegation from Iowa made a similar journey.[8] Cowden and other leaders believed that these

[5] *Twelfth Annual Report*, 1940, 3–4.
[6] *Thirteenth Annual Report*, 1941, 3–4.
[7] *Cooperative Consumer*, February 14, 1941, 1; and *Thirteenth Annual Report*, 1941, 16.
[8] *Cooperative Consumer*, January 31, 6–7; and March 17, 1941, 9.

visits were important as a means of convincing local cooperators that CCA really belonged to the patrons.

On February 14, 1941, the *Cooperative Consumer* carried a popular story on the company's history, entitled "The Romance of CCA." More romance than history, this account described past accomplishments and future prospects in glowing terms. Cowden and his staff were skillful publicists, and they drew heavily on past experiences to make their points. Cowden never tired of repeating the story of the wholesale's growth from a small company to one doing a multimillion-dollar business. And he was always careful to credit this to grass-roots support.

Further evidence of the vigorous effort to strengthen cooperatives is seen in the four-week school held in February and March. At the end of the course forty students were awarded diplomas.[9] In August a second man was added to the Education Department. In announcing the appointment of Guy Williams, Cowden said, "With the kind of times we are going through right now, education is more important than ever before in the history of cooperatives."[10] Late in 1941 CCA began to sponsor regular radio newscasts from Wichita, Kansas, and Scottsbluff, Nebraska.[11] CCA put tremendous effort into its educational program throughout 1941 in recognition of the need of strong support from CCA territory in order to expand business operations in line with the second five-year plan.

The first new expansion under the second five-year plan was the purchase of a printing plant. On March 17, 1941, it was announced that CCA had bought the Cooperative Farmer Publishing Company in North Kansas City. This deal had been made two weeks earlier when Cowden paid $500 in cash and 120 shares of preferred CCA stock, valued at $3,000, for the plant.[12] The new printing plant immediately began to turn out letterheads, forms, and other materials for the home office. It also did job printing for some other wholesales. Local associations were urged to patronize the CCA plant, which was organized on a cooperative basis. "When you need printing," readers were told, "think first of your own plant which will be expanded grad-

---

[9] *Ibid.*, March 17, 1941, 3.

[10] *Ibid.*, August 14, 1941, 1.

[11] *Ibid.*, November 29, 1941, 4. Despite bold talk, the women's guilds and the neighborhood councils gradually died out completely. In 1942–1943 there were only ten active women's guilds and eight neighborhood councils in CCA's ten-state area. The following year there were only six and seven groups, respectively.

[12] Board of Directors, Minutes, March 3, 1941.

ually to serve your every need." The *Cooperative Consumer* could not
be printed in the new plant, however, until a larger and faster press
was obtained.[13]

During its first six months of operation, the printing plant lost
$1,139, but by 1942 it realized the very small net gain of $290. A year
later, however, the printing plant showed net savings of $4,218 out of
business totaling $56,535. Originally, the plant was not capable of
doing all of the job printing required by CCA and its member cooperatives, and some business had to be contracted with outside firms,
but with improved machinery and additional personnel the printing
department was able very shortly to take care of most of CCA's needs.[14]

When the shareholders gathered for their annual meeting on October 16, 1941, Cowden created general excitement by announcing that
another refinery might soon be acquired. Delegates responded enthusiastically to this suggestion and passed approving resolutions. They
also supported a program looking toward manufacturing salt and
lumber and toward the development of a complete insurance service.[15] By this time the success of the Phillipsburg refinery had been
proven, and it seemed like sound business to refine even a greater percentage of the fuels needed by CCA customers.

On October 31 the *Cooperative Consumer* carried a banner headline to announce that the Cooperative Refinery Association had purchased a 1,500-barrel refinery located at Scottsbluff, Nebraska, from
Terry Carpenter, Inc. A front-page picture showed Cowden and Carpenter signing the contract. Besides the refinery, the purchase included 71 acres of land, a warehouse, administration building, grocery
store, laundry, bottling works, some scattered service stations, and several gasoline transports. These facilities cost approximately $750,000,
and CCA took possession on December 1.[16] When the bombs dropped
on Pearl Harbor, Miles Cowden and other workmen were taking inventory at the Scottsbluff plant.[17]

Word that CCA had bought its second refinery brought resounding
praise from the cooperative world. J. P. Warbasse, founder and past

---

[13] *Cooperative Consumer*, March 17, 1941, 1, 15; and *Thirteenth Annual Report*, 1941,
30.
[14] See CCA audits, 1941, 1942, and 1943, CCA Files.
[15] *Cooperative Consumer*, October 20, 1941, 1.
[16] Executive Committee, Minutes, November 1 and 25, 1941. See also the Scottsbluff
Star-Herald, December 14, 1941.
[17] Interview with Miles Cowden, August 10, 1961.

president of the Cooperative League of the U.S.A., wrote to Cowden: "Your organization represents cooperation at its best. . . . What you are doing with petroleum is of historic importance." Murray D. Lincoln, president of the Cooperative League, also extended hearty congratulations for "establishing your own refinery and in drilling our own cooperatively-owned oil wells." Cowden himself told readers of the *Cooperative Consumer* that acquisition of a second refinery was the result of careful planning and sound business practices. "We did not go into refining," he wrote, "we grew into it." [18] At the district meetings which were held between December 2 and 16, local cooperative leaders applauded the action of their wholesale and urged management to drill more oil wells and to expand production in other lines.[19] The slogan, "Factories are free for cooperators," acquired greater meaning in the knowledge that the Phillipsburg refinery, the pipeline, and the producing wells had netted $250,246 in the 1940–1941 fiscal year, or about one-third the cost of the facilities. On May 25, 1942, a dedication ceremony was held at Scottsbluff, but it was attended by relatively few people because of wartime restrictions on travel.[20]

The Scottsbluff refinery actually processed about 1,350 barrels of crude oil daily rather than the advertised 1,500. However, CCA was now in a position to produce in its own refineries around 50 per cent of the refined fuels that it sold. The company was another step closer to the goal of 100 per cent production and distribution by cooperative-owned plants and equipment.

The impact of a defense economy made itself felt on CCA long before December, 1941. In July Cowden was appointed a member of the marketing committee for District Two, which included most of the Midwest, by Harold L. Ickes, Petroleum Coordinator for National Defense. Cowden was the only representative of cooperatives on any of Ickes' oil committees. Even before his appointment, Cowden wrote Ickes that great savings could be made in the oil industry by wider trading among refiners in the transportation of refined fuels. This, he said, would reduce much of the need for long-distance hauling. Cowden also urged that no more lubricating oil be marketed in cans. "To end the canning of oil during the national emergency would

---

[18] *Cooperative Consumer*, November 15, 1941, 1, 4, 6, 7.

[19] *Ibid.*, December 17, 1941, 1.

[20] *Ibid.*, June 1, 1942, 1.

release both men and materials to better uses," he wrote. Cowden declared further that the 125,000 consumer families of CCA wanted to eliminate waste in the interest of national defense.[21]

Cowden was vitally concerned also about the effect of rising prices. He complained about the sharp advances in the prices of bright stocks and neutrals, the ingredients in motor oil, and he early advocated congressional action to halt runaway inflation. CCA, he said in July, 1941, had not yet raised prices of lubricating oils and preferred not to do so, but eventually upward changes would be necessary "if the spectacular price advances we have seen recently are permitted to stand." He concluded his statement by arguing that cooperatives should follow a price policy that would be "in the best interest of consumers, on the one hand, and in the best interest of the nation, on the other. Certainly we do not want to go as high and fall as hard as we did in World War No. 1." [22]

In order to give their customers some protection against mounting prices, CCA officials urged patrons throughout the fall of 1941 to lay in a supply of oil and grease at once. Higher prices and, perhaps, shortages were bound to come, CCA salesmen explained, and by making their purchases before any price advances occurred, farmers could assure themselves of supplies for the spring of 1942 at reasonable prices.[23]

At its meeting on June 13, 1941, the Board of Directors discussed in some detail the possible effects war might have on CCA's future. Board members agreed that there would be a strong, inflationary economy during the war — it seemed to be assumed that the United States would become actively involved — but that peace would bring depression. Consequently, the Board decided that the war period would be a good time to strengthen the company's financial position by paying debts, establishing reserves, and building surpluses.[24] Cowden urged local cooperatives to follow similar policies.

President Cowden was especially critical of those member associations which did not hold firmly to cash trading. As farmers became more prosperous during 1941, there was a tendency for local management to extend more credit and to abandon strict cash business. In his annual report for 1941 Cowden wrote that sixty-one cooperatives

[21] *Ibid.*, July 15, 1941, 1.
[22] *Ibid.*, 4.
[23] *Ibid.*, August 30 and October 20, 1941, 1, 2.
[24] Board of Directors, Minutes, June 13, 1941.

that had been on a cash basis a year earlier "had gone back to a credit business." This, he said, was "progress the wrong way." [25] After the United States entered the war, Cowden listed cash trading as a major objective for all cooperatives. It was the only sound business method for member associations, he argued; moreover, credit trading was inflationary and harmful to the general welfare in wartime.[26]

During the entire war period, officials of CCA were convinced that deflation and hard times would follow a return to peace. Having lived through post-World War I, they based their judgments on what had happened in 1920 and 1921. Consequently, all cooperatives, from the grass roots to the wholesale, should prepare for this eventuality by strengthening their financial position.

Although the second five-year plan had already called for more oil production, the operations of drilling, transportation, and refining were pushed even more rapidly because of the war. The growing needs for petroleum products to increase the farmers' agricultural output coincided with shortages of refined fuels. To assure supplies to member cooperatives as well as to help the war effort, CCA management concentrated on enlarging all phases of its oil operations.

By August 31, 1942, the Cooperative Oil Producing Association had nine producing wells, but Cowden insisted that more were necessary to support the two refineries. During the following year COPA drilled four additional producers and acquired two blocks of oil land in Kansas, totaling 1,960 acres. Also, an 80-acre tract was leased near Midland, Texas, where prospects of production were good. All together, by 1943 COPA held leases in seven fields.[27]

A severe fuel drought for farmers in the Middle West during the early summer of 1943 speeded up plans already under way to expand greatly CCA's production of refined petroleum products. On July 14, Cowden reported to his Executive Committee that the Globe Oil and Refining Company of McPherson, Kansas, had been purchased by CCA and four other cooperative wholesales, which had formed the National Cooperative Refinery Association. Chartered under the laws of Kansas on July 7, the National Cooperative Refinery Association was created by CCA; the Central Cooperative Wholesale of Superior, Wisconsin; Midland Cooperative Wholesale, Minneapolis; Farmers Union Central Exchange, St. Paul; and the Farmers Union State Ex-

[25] *Thirteenth Annual Report*, 1941, 23.
[26] *Fourteenth Annual Report*, 1942, 34.
[27] *Ibid.*, 15; *Fifteenth Annual Report*, 1943, 19; and CCA, Audit, 1943, CCA Files.

change of Omaha. Although five wholesales participated in the purchase, CCA owned one-third interest in the properties, which included land, storage tanks, and a refinery with a daily capacity of 17,500 barrels of crude oil. There was also an oil-compounding plant and 229 miles of six-inch pipeline for refined fuels, linking McPherson, Kansas, and Council Bluffs, Iowa. The new plant and equipment cost $3,500,000. CCA's share of the cash payment, through its subsidiary the Cooperative Refinery Association, was $500,000, which was invested in NCRA preferred stock. The National Cooperative Refinery Association borrowed $2,800,000 from the Central Bank for Cooperatives. When the inventories and working capital were added, the cooperatives had made an outlay of nearly $5,000,000. On August 2, 1943, NCRA began actual operation of its new refinery.[28]

Cowden was elected the first president of the National Cooperative Refinery Association. One of his first moves was to sponsor a dinner for the new cooperative employees at McPherson. "We are serving this dinner," he said, "because we wanted to meet all of you, our new employees. . . . If we get together, talk together, we most assuredly will work together." He then began educating the employees in the principles of cooperation by giving them a brief history of the cooperative movement. Harry Appleby led the crowd of nearly 360 persons in singing co-op songs.[29]

Since CCA received one-third of the refined products from the McPherson plant, the wholesale was now in a position to supply a large percentage of the fuels needed by member associations. Actually, shortages of crude oil kept the McPherson refinery from operating at capacity, but CCA was able to supply almost all requirements from Phillipsburg, Scottsbluff, and McPherson. In addition, CCA realized savings of about $196,400 as a result of its membership in NCRA during the first eleven months of operations at McPherson.[30]

If cooperators in CCA territory were enthusiastic over the joint purchase of the Globe Oil and Refining Company, there was much more important and exciting news ahead. Following a technique that he frequently used, Cowden brought the thousand delegates to the fifteenth annual meeting to the edge of their chairs when he predicted that by the next year CCA would be in a position to supply 100 per

---

[28] Executive Committee, Minutes, July 14, 1943; Board of Directors, Minutes, August 12, 1943; and *Cooperative Consumer*, July 21, 1943, 1, 8.
[29] *Cooperative Consumer*, August 2, 1943, 1, 8.
[30] *Sixteenth Annual Report*, 1944, 14.

cent of its members' needs for refined fuels. Cowden added that he could not then make any definite announcement of how this was to be accomplished, but he indicated that something vital to cooperative history was about to happen. Although they had no knowledge of the nature of this event, the shareholders enthusiastically urged Cowden to proceed with further expansion of productive facilities.[31]

About a month later, on November 29, Cowden announced the big story: CCA had bought a refinery at Coffeyville, Kansas, which had a capacity of 13,500 barrels of crude oil daily, or some 81,000,000 gallons of refined fuels each year. The purchase was made from the National Refining Company for $3,940,703 and was by far CCA's biggest single business transaction. The wholesale took over active management on January 1, 1944.

Besides the gasoline refinery, the Coffeyville purchase brought CCA much other valuable property. There was a lubricating oil refinery for making bright stocks, neutrals, and finished oils, with a yearly capacity of around 10,000,000 gallons. Now CCA would have the basic ingredients from which lubricating oil was compounded. Moreover, there were 269 producing oil wells — many of them strippers of low productivity — 786 miles of pipelines, and 104,408 acres of undeveloped leases in Illinois, Kansas, Oklahoma, Texas, and New Mexico. One well was currently being drilled in Illinois. Finally, there were storage tanks, several truck transports, and a sizable inventory.

But what turned out to be the best facility was not even completed when the deal was closed. At that time the Defense Plant Corporation was building a $6,500,000 aviation gasoline plant adjacent to the Coffeyville refinery. Although this plant was not ready for operation until the summer of 1944, CCA operated it for the government during the final year of conflict and ultimately bought it.[32]

Cowden gave several reasons for purchasing the Coffeyville property. In the first place, he wanted to protect member associations against shortages such as had occurred during the previous spring and summer. Also, he was interested in having CCA contribute as much as possible to the war effort. Moreover, if CCA could buy the aviation gasoline plant after the war, it would be in a good position to supply the demand for high-octane fuels required by the newer engines.

Most important, in the long run, was CCA's desire to make its oil

[31] *Cooperative Consumer*, November 8, 1943, 1, 16.
[32] *Ibid.*, November 30, 1943, 1–7; *St. Louis Post-Dispatch*, November 29, 1943.

operations completely self-sufficient and independent of privately owned companies. This was the type of integration that Cowden had been seeking ever since he started business in 1929. Cowden noted in his annual report for 1945 that "for the second straight year CCA has met the needs of its patrons for refined fuels from its own facilities." These results, he continued, confirmed "the essential soundness of the decision made six years ago . . . to move into petroleum production, pipe line transportation and refining."[33] Furthermore, the margins in oil were so good that CCA's petroleum operations provided funds to expand services and production in other directions. For example, the net savings at Phillipsburg, Scottsbluff, and Coffeyville, not including the aviation gasoline refinery, totaled $1,381,388 in fiscal 1945.[34]

During World War II, CCA emerged as an important independent oil company. In 1944–1945 it sold 21,544 tank cars of refined fuels, compared to only 10,185 cars in 1940–1941, the last prewar year. Sales of lubricating oil jumped from 1,275,134 to 20,839,456 gallons, much of which went to the government. Grease sales increased from 3,090,768 pounds in 1940–1941 to 4,577,746 pounds five years later. In the year ending August 31, 1945, CCA furnished patrons $26,560,150 worth of merchandise, of which the Cooperative Refinery Association supplied about 70 per cent. Petroleum products continued to be the commodities on which CCA grew and prospered.[35]

By 1945 CCA had 369 producing wells that provided 1,014,330 barrels of crude oil annually, about 18 per cent of the needs for CCA refineries. The company also held undeveloped leases on 49,762 acres of land. The pipeline network had been extended around Phillipsburg until it totaled 134 miles. Although the Cooperative Oil Producing Association had been fairly successful in its explorations for oil, CCA management decided in 1945 to transfer COPA's assets and activities to the Cooperative Refining Association. This was done on May 1. Actually, after CRA bought the Coffeyville properties, which included producing wells and undeveloped leases, CCA in effect had two oil production departments. Thus it seemed best to place all production under CRA.

The operation of a large oil enterprise required the establishment of a geological division. Besides maintaining a geology staff at North

[33] *Seventeenth Annual Report*, 1945, 12–13.
[34] *Ibid.*
[35] *Ibid.*, 30, 46.

Kansas City, district offices were located at Mattoon, Illinois; Wichita, Kansas; and Midland, Texas.[36]

Although CCA's principal business expansion after 1940 came in petroleum, the second five-year plan called for manufacturing in several other fields. At the first meeting of the Board of Directors after war was declared, Cowden discussed enlarging the printing plant, engaging in the manufacture of flour and feed, producing household and electrical appliances, manufacturing food items and lumber, and developing insurance and finance associations.[37] Investigations were also made in regard to establishing a soybean processing plant and another for manufacturing salt.[38] At every opportunity Cowden promoted the idea of operating additional productive facilities to supply the needs of local cooperatives.

With the increase in the number of cooperative lumber yards, the acquisition of one or more lumber mills seemed desirable. In his annual report of 1939 Cowden wrote, "There is no reason why cooperative lumber yards, by centralizing their purchases through this regional wholesale, cannot one day own lumber mills of their own." [39] The Board of Directors discussed this matter from time to time in subsequent months, but the main attention in late 1939 and 1940 centered around the Phillipsburg refinery.

In August, 1941, Cowden, Homer Young, and other CCA staff members discussed with representatives of cooperative lumber yards in Iowa the matter of setting up a lumber office on the West Coast. These dealers from Iowa believed that they could get better service from suppliers if they had an agent on the ground to negotiate for their needs. Something of this nature seemed especially desirable at a time when government orders were getting high priority. While Cowden suggested that a special representative to serve cooperatives would be helpful, he really wanted a CCA-owned lumber mill. "All we need to do to acquire ownership of shingle mills and lumber mills," Cowden said, "is to centralize this volume of purchasing. We can make shingles, or mill lumber, and sell it at the going price. The difference between the cost of doing that, and the selling price, is the margin that will pay for these factories." Then, Cowden explained, "We can do in the building supply field just what we have done in the petroleum field." [40]

[36] *Ibid.*, 7–10.
[37] Board of Directors, Minutes, February 13 and 14, 1942.
[38] Board of Directors, Minutes, August 28 and 29, 1942.
[39] *Eleventh Annual Report*, 1939, 21.
[40] *Cooperative Consumer*, August 30, 1941, 1, 11.

By 1940 and 1941 Cowden was constantly boosting the "factories are free" principle.

The first move toward gaining control of a lumber supply came on March 23, 1942, when CCA agreed to take the entire output of the W. Richtman Lumber Company of Custer, South Dakota, in the southern Black Hills. The Custer plant could turn out 20,000 board feet of Ponderosa pine a day. This contract, according to Cowden, would assure cooperative lumber yards a dependable source of lumber and was "a first step toward cooperative ownership ultimately of mills needed to supply cooperative yards in CCA-land." [41]

The contract between CCA and the Custer mill was canceled, however, early in 1942 when the federal government required the output for war purposes. This left cooperative yards in the Dakotas, Iowa, Nebraska, and Kansas without supplies, as shipments from the West Coast had also been cut off. To meet their needs CCA officials began an intensive search for a suitable mill to purchase. At a meeting of the Board on August 28, 1942, Tom DeWitt reported that there was a lumber mill at Hill City, South Dakota, which would meet at least some of CCA's needs. After further consideration the Board, on October 6, voted to buy the Hill City plant. [42]

The Hill City mill was small and produced only about a carload of of lumber daily. However, it did provide a beginning for CCA in this field. Officials of CCA held no illusions regarding the immediate importance of the new property. Cowden explained in his annual report of 1942 that the Hill City operation would provide facts and figures that would be helpful to CCA in "getting into the production of building supplies after the war." [43] Apparently, Cowden regarded it as a kind of yardstick of experience.

Even before the Hill City deal was closed, CCA officials began discussing the acquisition of additional lumber facilities. At the annual shareholders' meeting on October 9, it was announced that property was available in Oregon at an attractive price. A motion was passed to investigate the Oregon proposition. On February 10, 1943, the Board of Directors instructed the CCA staff to purchase the Oregon property if satisfactory arrangements could be made. Cowden announced on March 31 that CCA had bought the Swisshome fir mill, located about 60 miles west of Eugene, Oregon. Besides the mill, CCA

---

[41] *Ibid.*, March 31, 1942, 1.
[42] Board of Directors, Minutes, October 6, 1942.
[43] *Fourteenth Annual Report*, 1942, 30.

got logging equipment and 80,000,000 board feet of standing timber, enough to last for five or six years. The entire property cost $272,000, of which amount $200,000 was loaned by the St. Louis Bank for Cooperatives.[44]

Since the government took about 80 per cent of the output at Swisshome, it is clear that 1942 and 1943 was not a favorable time for CCA to enter the lumber business. Of the 208 carloads produced between April and August, 1943, only about 40 were available to cooperative yards.[45] An almost mortal blow hit the Lumber Department on August 28, 1944, when the Swisshome mill burned to the ground. There was an actual and immediate financial loss of $25,000 because the plant was not fully insured, but much greater losses resulted from the fact that more than a year elapsed before operations could be resumed. The Board voted to build a larger and more efficient mill immediately, but it was November, 1945, before production could be resumed. To ensure an adequate supply of raw materials CCA also bought an additional 18,000,000 board feet of timber in 1945.[46] The Hill City mill was sold in 1945, primarily because it was too small to permit efficient and profitable operation. Sales of lumber, building materials, and roofing reached $635,084 in 1944, but fell to $321,751 the following year, when the Swisshome mill was being rebuilt. The savings of only $2,789 made by the lumber mills for the year ending August 31, 1943, must have caused some observers to doubt whether CCA should engage in the lumber business.[47]

During 1942 and 1943 CCA expanded its manufacturing operations in other directions. Following an inspection trip by the Board of Directors in May, 1942, CCA purchased a cannery from the Otoe Food Products Company at Scottsbluff, Nebraska, on June 17. Located in the North Platte River valley, this processing plant had an annual capacity of about 290,000 cases of peas, corn, beans, tomatoes, and tomato juice. About 35 per cent of the pack went to the federal government, but the remainder was available to supply cooperative food stores. At that time CCA was furnishing nearly 150 cooperative retail food outlets. Cowden emphasized that this new project was significant because "it is a first step toward doing in the food field what we have done to a greater degree in the petroleum field; namely, a step toward

---

[44] Executive Committee, Minutes, April 2, 1943.
[45] *Fifteenth Annual Report*, 1943, 8.
[46] *Seventeenth Annual Report*, 1945, 1, 14.
[47] CCA, Audit, 1943, CCA Files.

an integrated food setup that will include other processing plants."[48]
On October 3, Neal S. Beaton, president of the Scottish Wholesale
Society, who had laid the cornerstone for the Phillipsburg refinery,
dedicated the cannery to "the ability of the people to serve themselves."

Late in December, 1942, Cowden announced that CCA would begin dehydrating potatoes at Scottsbluff as soon as equipment could be
obtained and installed.[49] When the projected plant was in full operation, he said, CCA expected to dehydrate 35 tons of potatoes daily for
the War Food Administration.[50]

But Cowden was not satisfied with the canning and dehydration
operations at Scottsbluff. He wanted to obtain additional facilities,
he told the Directors, perhaps in Wisconsin, Iowa, or Missouri.[51] As a
result of his interest in food processing, on March 20, 1943, CCA purchased a plant at Milan, Missouri. This was primarily a tomato cannery, but a sorghum mill was also included in the property.

The first canning season was a sharp disappointment to CCA because an early freeze greatly reduced the tomato pack. All together,
131,328 cases of vegetables were canned and marketed in 1942. Some
improvements were made in the plant, and a warehouse was added,
with the idea of enlarging operations greatly. Savings made by the cannery during the first full year, ending August 31, 1943, amounted to
$17,825. Besides arguing that CCA should furnish cooperative-manu-
factured canned goods to cooperative grocery stores, Cowden justified
the purchase of food processing plants on their help in providing a
better market for farmers. In this fashion, he said, CCA was providing
a direct link between producers and consumers.[52]

The cannery program furnished good copy for CCA publicity, but
even with the tremendous demand for food during World War II it
was not successful. Inadequate management and poor weather conditions were among the factors that plagued the food-processing operations. The Scottsbluff cannery never achieved full capacity. Instead
of packing between 200,000 and 300,000 cases a year as expected, it
turned out 76,455 cases in 1944 and 121,159 in 1945. Unfavorable
growing weather in 1945 reduced business at Milan, and only 7,021

[48] *Fourteenth Annual Report*, 1942, 21–22. See also *Cooperative Consumer*, June 17, 1942, 1.
[49] *Cooperative Consumer*, December 31, 1942, 1.
[50] *Fifteenth Annual Report*, 1943, 10.
[51] Shareholders' meeting, Minutes, October 9, 1942.
[52] *Cooperative Consumer*, June 17, 1942, 4.

cases of tomatoes were canned, compared to 18,226 the year before. CCA's federal contract calling for 1,800,000 pounds of dehydrated potatoes was canceled late in August, 1945, leaving this facility with little or no outlet for its production. Despite these problems, the Scottsbluff cannery showed net savings of $52,971 in 1945, but the future did not hold promise of substantial margins in this business.

In November, 1943, CCA purchased a 75-ton-a-day feed mill at Enid, Oklahoma, to supply member cooperatives in that immediate area with commercial feeds.[53] Many local cooperatives that were trying to mix their own feeds found their operations hampered by shortages of minerals and various concentrates. It was believed that a central plant could be much more efficient in obtaining the needed raw materials, manufacturing the finished products, and distributing them to consumers. Part of the six-point feed program looked toward a testing and research laboratory, a standard cooperative label on all bags, and the acquisition of further facilities, including soybean plants, alfalfa meal works, and cottonseed oil mills.

In keeping with these aims, CCA built an alfalfa dehydration plant at Pond Creek, Oklahoma, not far from Enid, in 1944. At about the same time it began construction of a soybean mill, near the refinery at Coffeyville, which began operation on July 3, 1945.[54] Thus, by 1945 CCA was able to offer member cooperatives mixed feeds from its Enid mill or concentrates from other plants. This entire program was designed to assure farmers a high quality of commercial feed and to provide another service to local cooperatives. The rapid increase of sales indicated farm support for this program. In 1944 CCA supplied cooperatives with $853,874 worth of feeds, and by 1945 the figure had nearly doubled, to $1,571,999.[55] The immediate success of the feed program indicated that CCA had hit upon another highly worth-while service to its farm customers — something both desired and needed. It is significant that CCA's feed business in the first year exceeded its grocery business in the tenth.

In 1943 CCA joined other cooperatives in helping to buy a milking machine factory and a farm implement plant. Homer Young explained to the Board on October 9, 1942, that National Cooperatives, Inc., had bought the Universal Milking Machine Company at Wauke-

---

[53] *Ibid.*, November 8, 1943, 1.
[54] *Sixteenth Annual Report*, 1944, 20; and *Seventeenth Annual Report*, 1945, 16.
[55] *Consumers Cooperative Association, Prospectus*, prepared for the Securities and Exchange Commission, February 24, 1949, 11.

sha, Wisconsin, and that CCA had loaned National $15,000 as its
share of the deal.[56] Early in 1943 National Cooperatives, Inc., began
operating the Waukesha plant.[57] On August 13, CCA's Directors voted
to buy $10,000 worth of stock in the National Farm Machinery Co-
operative, Inc., of Shelbyville, Indiana. Although earlier experiences
of CCA with farm machinery had not been reassuring, the Board felt
that the Shelbyville plant, backed by several regional wholesales,
could succeed.[58] By 1942 and 1943 CCA's farm machinery program
had declined; this department sold only $12,341 and $15,317 worth
of products, respectively, in those years. After CCA joined other cooperatives in manufacturing farm machinery, sales in 1945 rose to
$113,365, but this was an insignificant part of the wholesale's business.

The Consumers Cooperative Association met one major defeat in
its wartime manufacturing program. At its meeting on May 25 and
26, 1942, the Board voted to form a subsidiary company to manufacture alcohol from farm products. Senators George Norris of Nebraska,
Guy Gillette of Iowa, and other midwestern leaders had been advocating the establishment of several plants to produce alcohol from
grain, to be used in the manufacture of synthetic rubber.[59] A new
subsidiary, the Farm Products Cooperative Association, was chartered, and an application was made to federal authorities to permit
construction of a $1,000,000 alcohol plant at Kansas City. Cowden
wired President Roosevelt early in June, asking that the Midwest,
which had suffered from chronic grain surpluses, be given "its fair
share of the alcohol-rubber industry." [60]

Cowden made several trips to Washington in an effort to get a favorable decision on CCA's application for critical materials. Young also
worked on this project. Cowden later reported good relations with
W. M. Jeffers, head of the government's rubber program, but he ran
into strong opposition from men in the War Production Board,
which had the last word on priorities. He charged that these officials
were "close to the petroleum and whiskey distilling interests." In the
ensuing struggle for permission to build the grain alcohol plant, CCA
was no match for the large private interests, which were interested not
only in wartime output, but also in control of the synthetic rubber

[56] Board of Directors, Minutes, October 9, 1942.
[57] *Fifteenth Annual Report*, 1943, 12.
[58] Board of Directors, Minutes, August 13, 1943.
[59] *Cooperative Consumer*, June 1, 1942, 1.
[60] *Ibid.*, June 15, 1942, 15.

industry after the war. On December 18 it was announced that a contract for the Kansas City facility had been granted to National Distillers Products Corporation.[61] The *Cooperative Consumer* carried the story with the headline, FAVOR LIQUOR CROWD. In March, 1943, it appeared as though CCA would get a 10,000,000-gallon plant at Keokuk, Iowa, but suddenly the War Production Board announced that it had a sufficient capacity.[62]

Failure to get an alcohol plant prompted Cowden to intensify his blasts against monopoly. Editorializing on the synthetic-rubber situation in August, 1942, he wrote that "farmers and business men in this area suspect that the petroleum interests were determined to seize control of a billion dollar industry and keep it monopolized after the war."[63] So far as Cowden was concerned, failure to get the alcohol plant proved his worst suspicions. He had always pictured the cooperatives as representing the little people in their struggles against the exactions of big business and concentrated wealth, and he now gave even greater emphasis to this theme. He accused the distillers and oil companies of combining to keep smaller, independent businesses, especially the cooperatives, from getting a fair share of the wartime and postwar synthetic rubber business. He wrote on January 20, 1943, that the distillers and oil men were all "one big happy family."[64]

Throughout the war Cowden attacked the oil industry, the large insurance companies, financial monopoly, and other aspects of big business. The *Cooperative Consumer* gave prominence to stories dealing with monopoly, the paper carried numerous cartoons designed to discredit big business, and Cowden considered business concentration in many of his editorials. Thurman Arnold, one of the Roosevelt administration's most vigorous trust busters, was quoted frequently and liberally, and the results of Senator Joseph O'Mahoney's Temporary National Economic Committee were given conspicuous coverage. Headlines like the following were common in CCA's official organ: "Warns Against Industrial Super Government"; "Great Chicago Speech, Vice-President Wallace Blasts Monopoly"; and "Cartels Cast Lustful Eyes Upon World."[65] Cowden called for Co-op Minute Men

---

[61] *Ibid.*, December 31, 1942, 1.
[62] *Fifteenth Annual Report*, 1943, 12.
[63] *Cooperative Consumer*, August 17, 1942, 4.
[64] Cowden, "Heart-to-Heart Talk," January 20, 1943, leaflet.
[65] For typical articles, see *Cooperative Consumer*, September 15, November 8, and December 15, 1943.

"to support cooperative associations in fight-to-the-finish battles which may develop as co-ops expand into new fields." "We may again," he said, "come to grips with entrenched monopolies." Cowden continued to play on the antimonopoly sentiment of farmers to win support for CCA and the entire cooperative movement.[66]

As was true with many businesses, CCA's growth and expansion gained impetus from World War II. Farmers were prosperous, and demands were heavy for all kinds of services and commodities supplied by the wholesale. Between 1940 and 1945, total dollar business of CCA and its subsidiaries rose from $5,110,163 to $26,560,150. Price rises accounted for part of this increase, but most of the expansion came from greater volume. Net savings had made even more astonishing gains, rising from $166,621 in 1940 to $1,765,367 five years later, an increase of almost 1,000 per cent.[67] This record seemed to prove that the program of getting into manufacturing was paying off. It is no wonder that Cowden, members of the CCA staff, and local leaders kept calling for more production as well as for wider distribution of cooperative-manufactured products.

Although CCA shared in the general business benefits of wartime, its gains were greater than those of other regional wholesales because of its operations in the critical and strategic field of petroleum. Without oil CCA would have experienced only modest growth. Moreover, most of the high savings made during the war were retained as deferred patronage refunds, thus providing much of the capital for further expansion. While this policy of retaining savings had been started several years before the war, it was probably easier to withhold such large sums after 1941 because farmers were prosperous and did not need their dividends as they would have in hard times.

Another important factor in the rather phenomenal record that CCA set during the Second World War was Cowden's continued leadership. He was always thinking in terms of expansion, growth, additional services, and an integrated program, whether in oil, feed, or food products. While he was willing to take a chance in new programs, however, Cowden was careful not to move ahead without firm and widespread backing from local associations; he never lost contact with the grass roots. The district and annual meetings were used as sounding boards to test new ideas and as a means of educating local

---

[66] *Ibid.*, July 15, 1942, 7.
[67] *Twelfth Annual Report*, 1940, 35; and *Seventeenth Annual Report*, 1945, 7.

cooperators. Cowden, his staff, and the field force built a cooperative spirit in CCA-land that provided a solid basis for CCA's ever-expanding operations. Cowden fully knew the dangers involved if business success outran member participation and understanding. He wrote in his 1943 report, "Many a local association is realizing that an educational program, planned and executed to solve its problems, is essential if the co-op is to avoid the dangers of becoming successful financially without true cooperative understanding among its members." [68]

During the war CCA increased both its personnel and its expenditures for education. It provided on-the-job training for new employees, held schools for cooperative leaders, helped with membership drives, and distributed cooperative literature and movies. By 1942 there were about six hundred volumes in CCA's library, and in April the library instituted a policy of lending any of these books for two-week periods at no charge except return postage. [69] In addition, CCA produced several movies to be mailed to groups in the wholesale's territory. In 1945 a color-and-sound movie, entitled "Up from the Earth," pictured the company's history; it proved to be a very popular film.

The increase in manufacturing facilities between 1941 and 1945 necessitated large amounts of capital. The financing of these enterprises came mainly from three sources: deferred patronage dividends, loans from the Banks for Cooperatives, and the sale of CCA preferred shares. Some funds were provided by loan capital from member associations, but this sum was never very large.

By 1943 CCA had sold $653,701 worth of capital shares, but in that year the wholesale sponsored an intensive drive to raise a much larger sum from patrons. The preferred shares were valued at $25, bore 4 per cent interest, and were redeemable in ten years. In appealing to potential investors, the *Cooperative Consumer* asserted that CCA was helping to build economic democracy in America. "If you believe," the article asked, "that monopolies breed unrest at home and dissension in foreign lands, why not step in and oppose them with your dollars?" [70] Cowden sent out thousands of letters to "Dear Cooperator," explaining that by investing in CCA "your money will be working,

---

[65] *Fifteenth Annual Report*, 1943, 31.
[69] *Cooperative Consumer*, April 15, 1943, 11.
[70] *Ibid.*, August 30, 1943, 1.

not to make profits for a few men, but savings for many, many people."[71] As a result of these and subsequent appeals for capital, investments in preferred shares by individual patrons and local associations reached $1,597,162 by 1945.[72]

The largest single source of capital, however, was the member equities that were classified under the revolving fund, deferred patronage refunds, and equity reserve. Total member equities reached $2,810,439 by 1943 and $4,787,944 by 1945. Meanwhile, the company was paying deferred patronage refunds that had accumulated in the late 1930's on the basis of the five-year revolving plan. During the period from 1943 to 1945 these refunds were paid at a rate of less than $50,000 annually.[73]

But even the retention and reinvestment of savings, most of which came from the refineries, was not enough to finance the company's wartime expansion. Therefore, increasing reliance had to be placed on the Banks for Cooperatives in St. Louis and Wichita. These institutions made large and frequent loans to CCA. In 1943 the wholesale and its subsidiaries had long-term debts, secured by notes and mortgages, totaling $504,805.[74] Two years later, notes and contracts payable after one year had reached $4,361,025.[75] The Banks for Cooperatives furnished most of this capital.

The growth of CCA after 1940 was accompanied by many aggravating problems that were common to many businesses during World War II. One of the most serious difficulties was the loss of experienced workers to the armed services. By August, 1942, thirty-nine CCA employees were in the military forces, and this number had increased to eighty-seven a year later.[76] Member cooperatives also had a hard time maintaining qualified personnel, and CCA was required to intensify its programs of educating workers in cooperative principles and of providing on-the-job training. Furthermore, the rationing of gasoline and tires created hectic days around the Kansas City offices, as when local cooperatives ran out of fuel. One employee remembers getting 138 telephone calls in a single day from frantic customers. Also, rationing restricted travel for CCA's staff members as well as for local

---

[71] Form letter, December 21, 1943, Cowden Files.
[72] *Seventeenth Annual Report*, 1945, 41.
[73] *Fifteenth Annual Report*, 1943; *Sixteenth Annual Report*, 1944; and *Seventeenth Annual Report*, 1945.
[74] CCA, Audit, 1943, CCA Files.
[75] *Seventeenth Annual Report*, 1945, 41.
[76] *Fourteenth Annual Report*, 1942, 3.

patrons who wanted to attend district and annual meetings. Cowden urged farmers and local cooperative leaders to form car pools and travel together.

Some aspects of the company's business suffered heavily because of the war. Sales of wire and of fencing supplies dropped sharply for a time because of the general shortage of steel. The principal casualty, however, was paint. In 1941–1942 CCA manufactured and sold 70,690 gallons of paint, the largest amount distributed up to that time, but a shortage of linseed and other oils reduced production to 55,277 gallons in 1943 and to 57,301 in 1944.[77] There were periods when some of CCA's factories failed to earn any margins. R. R. Zurbuchen, director of manufacturing, reported to Cowden that up to January 31, 1944, the dehydration operations had shown a net loss of $48,487. The difficulties, he said, were managerial inefficiency and failure of some equipment. At the lumber mill at Hill City, Zurbuchen explained, low production, lack of uniform output, shifting of employees, and some inefficient milling operations resulted in losses. On the basis of this report, Cowden discussed the operating losses in the lumber, canning, and dehydration enterprises with the Board on February 18, 1944. After considering the report, the Board passed a resolution to close the dehydration plant at an early date if it did not begin to show a profit.[78]

Other problems arose as CCA expanded into new fields and added hundreds of new member associations. Following an inspection trip through Missouri, Kansas, and part of Nebraska, Ivan Lanto reported on some of these difficulties. He told Cowden that many local cooperatives needed new or better-trained managers and that CCA fieldmen were definitely "oil minded" and spent very little time or effort pushing the other lines handled by CCA. For instance, most sales of appliances, he said, were to managers or tank-wagon drivers, who bought a washing machine or refrigerator for themselves at wholesale prices. Lanto added that the grocery and appliance departments were "treated as stepchildren or after-thought or something like that."[79] Some of the negative aspects described by Lanto continued for several years or until the unprofitable departments were discontinued.

Rapid business expansion created problems of personnel and man-

---

[77] *Fifteenth Annual Report*, 1943, 17; and *Seventeenth Annual Report*, 1945, 30.
[78] Memorandum, Zurbuchen to Cowden, February 17, 1944; and Board of Directors, Minutes, February 18, 1944.
[79] Memorandum, Lanto to Cowden, September 17, 1940, CCA Files.

agement also. The number of employees increased steadily, but rather slowly, before 1939. Beginning with 6 employees in 1929, by 1941 CCA employed 365 persons and had an annual payroll of $400,982. Between 1939 and 1941 the number of employees more than doubled, largely because of the acquisition of oil properties. There were, for example, nearly 50 workers at Phillipsburg, and with the purchase of other plants hundreds of employees were added. The Coffeyville re- finery employed 542 persons in 1945, and Swisshome 300. At the close of the war CCA and its subsidiaries employed 1,857 persons, with a yearly payroll of $3,458,251.[80] It should be emphasized that some of these employees worked only part time. In order to handle the in- creasing problems of employment, a personnel department was estab- lished in May, 1942, and later a safety office was added.[81]

Of the 1,857 employees in 1945, about 300 worked at the Kansas City administrative offices. The headquarters building at 1500 Iron Street was far too large when the staff first occupied it on September 3, 1935, but less than a decade later the facilities were completely in- adequate. Some workers had to be housed at the old location at 1721 Iron Street, and other office space was rented elsewhere. In order to bring all of the office and staff personnel together, CCA purchased the five-story Insurance Building in Kansas City on June 15, 1944, located at 10th and Oak streets, and providing 5,800 square feet of space on each floor. In 1944 it accommodated the company's office needs. After remodeling and redecorating the building, the wholesale occupied its new home about November 1.[82]

The rapid growth of CCA put a severe strain upon the company's administrative organization as well as on the physical facilities. By 1942 it was evident that the old three-division organization of sales, finance, and education was inadequate. Firmer lines of authority needed to be drawn, with division heads only reporting to President Cowden. CCA did not undertake any general overhauling of its ad- ministrative structure, but through gradual shifts and some reorgani- zation, a new pattern emerged by late 1944.

One important addition to the administrative staff was the position of general counsel. As early as 1939 Cowden told the Board that CCA should employ an attorney and establish a legal department "to pro-

[80] Typewritten statement in CCA Files; *Seventeenth Annual Report*, 1945, 39.
[81] *Fifteenth Annual Report*, 1943, 33.
[82] *Cooperative Consumer*, June 15, 1944, 1; and *Sixteenth Annual Report*, 1944, 16.

tect our interests of a legal nature, and give service of that kind to our member associations."[83] It was not until June, 1941, however, that Daniel C. Rogers was employed as a staff attorney to handle the company's legal affairs. In 1944 a legal division was created, consisting of a general counsel and two other attorneys.

F. R. Olmsted became CCA's first general counsel. Admitted to the Colorado bar in 1929, Olmsted practiced in Denver and Lamar before becoming general counsel for the Ninth Farm Credit District at Wichita in June, 1934. Three years later he was assigned to the Wichita Bank for Cooperatives. It was here that Olmsted and Cowden became well acquainted, and Cowden was soon depending upon Olmsted to protect CCA's interests as well as those of the bank. Olmsted accompanied Cowden to Washington in 1938 to obtain the approval of the Central Bank for Cooperatives for the Phillipsburg refinery loan. Late in 1943 Olmsted was transferred to the staff of the Associate Solicitor of the United States Department of Agriculture. There he served the Cooperative Bank Commissioner and the Central Bank for Cooperatives. Olmsted had been in Washington only a few months when Cowden asked him to join CCA and establish a legal division. He assumed his new position of general counsel on May 15, 1944.[84]

The General Counsel was concerned with contracts, leases, general litigation, tax matters, and many other questions. His office was administered under the Services Division in the new organizational structure, along with education, publicity, personnel, and research. The research branch was formed in October, 1942, after the Directors voted to spend $10,000 a year on research in whatever fields would be most helpful to the wholesale.[85]

Late in 1941 Bruce McCully was made supervisor of the COPA and CPLA, and Dwight D. Townsend, a cooperative manager in Iowa, replaced McCully as head of the Retail Department.[86] Despite Townsend's vigorous efforts to put the Retail Department on a paying basis, it continued to be more a liability than an asset to CCA. By even the most liberal bookkeeping devices, the retail business showed only $5,119 in net savings for 1943.[87] In 1944 Townsend was made head of the new Management Division, a position that gave him super-

---

[83] Board of Directors, Minutes, March 1, 1939.
[84] Memorandum of F. R. Olmsted, June 1, 1962, CCA Files.
[85] *Cooperative Consumer,* October 19, 1942, 13.
[86] *Ibid.,* August 14, 1941, 1.
[87] CCA, Audit, 1943, CCA Files.

vision over the managed stations and stores as well as over the Retail Department.[88]

Besides the new divisions, Services and Management Services, the Board created the Treasury and Control Division in 1944. J. D. Lawrence, who had been deputy commissioner for cooperative banks in the Farm Credit Administration, was brought in to head this new branch.[89] Other new administrative divisions included Manufacturing, headed by R. R. Zurbuchen, and Procurement, directed by S. A. White. Homer Young and Glenn Fox continued to head Distribution and Organization, and Finance and Credit, respectively. In summary, the seven major administrative divisions of CCA in 1944 were Manufacturing, Procurement, Distribution and Organization, Finance and Credit, Treasury, Management Services, and Services.

By 1945 CCA had come a long way from the two-car garage to which Cowden now so fondly and frequently referred. CCA had become a large and complicated business, manufacturing 64 per cent of the products that accounted for its sales. In addition, it supplied products to 907 member associations. The company owned and operated oil-compounding, grease, and paint plants; three refineries and one-third interest in another; 868 miles of trunk and gathering pipelines; and 369 producing oil wells. The oil operations were sustained by geology and research departments. The wholesale also owned a lumber mill, two canneries, one dehydration factory, a printing plant, two feed mills, a soybean plant, and a transportation department that operated 38 tank transports and 12 semitrailer merchandise trucks, plus auxiliary units. It owned a five-story office building and employed 1,857 workers. With fixed assets valued at $5,923,660, CCA did $26,560,150 worth of business and had net savings of $1,766,507.

But Cowden was not satisfied with this record. He was not content to operate a successful cooperative wholesale for nearly 150,000 consumers in ten midwestern states. Writing on "The Shape of Things to Come" in his 1943 report, Cowden declared that what had been done was "only a beginning. . . . The time is not far distant when people in this area will be providing themselves . . . with $100,000,000 or more of goods and services annually." [90] This must have sounded like the musings of an impractical daydreamer to many cooperators in

---

[88] *Sixteenth Annual Report*, 1944, 25.
[89] *Cooperative Consumer*, June 15, 1944, 6.
[90] *Fifteenth Annual Report*, 1943, 34.

CCA-land, but in the year Cowden left the presidency, 1961, CCA did $193,000,000 worth of business.

During the early years of the depression, Cowden had talked a great deal about consumer cooperation as a way to provide immediate and practical help for depression-ridden farmers. While he never discounted this function of the wholesale, he also saw cooperatives as something more than an agency for agricultural relief. Cowden viewed a strong cooperative movement as a tool to fight economic monopoly at home and to preserve peace abroad. Throughout the war years, he stressed increasingly the role of cooperatives in international trade. Cooperation, he wrote, was "the only business force on the horizon that has the resources to match the business giants for profit who would build business into super-states known as international cartels, and all that they have stood for in the past." [91]

Cowden came to view cooperatives as a genuine and effective instrument for world peace. He had proposed a world oil cooperative as early as 1937, and in September, 1945, he attended a meeting of the International Cooperative Alliance in London to help promote international trade of all kinds. After his return from London he explained to shareholders at CCA's seventeenth annual meeting that cooperatives were

> recognizing the fact of one world where people, without regard to race, color or creed may come to know one another, trade goods and cultures with one another, and otherwise develop through cooperatives a peoples' economic system that will strengthen the foundations of the United Nations Charter.[92]

He added that the time was "ripe for a world-wide swing to cooperatives" and indicated that CCA should play a leading role in the move toward international cooperation. From World War II onward, Cowden devoted an increasing amount of his time and energy to international cooperation and preached the gospel according to Rochdale all around the world.

---

[91] *Seventeenth Annual Report*, 1945, 38.
[92] *Ibid.*, 3.

Chapter 11

CCA under Attack:
Tax and Charter Problems

So long as cooperatives remained small and did relatively little business, they were not subject to much open criticism. The major oil companies had opposed CCA from the beginning, but Cowden and other company officials had skillfully turned this opposition into an asset by emphasizing CCA's struggles against the great monopolies. However, when CCA and some other regional cooperatives began to do a multimillion-dollar business and to earn net savings for patrons running into hundreds of thousands of dollars, these wholesales, especially CCA, were criticized for bigness. The attacks on CCA that developed during the 1940's in Kansas, where the firm was incorporated, were only a part of the nationwide effort by private companies to remove what they charged were the special privileges that cooperatives enjoyed under both state and federal laws.

The steep increase in wartime corporation taxes prompted business groups to come out openly and vigorously against the cooperatives. The corporate interests declared that cooperatives like CCA were able to expand their operations by withholding patronage refunds, which were not taxable like corporate profits. This situation, they charged, gave cooperatives an unfair advantage in accumulating capital for expansion, a condition that needed to be corrected by changing the income tax laws.

The special tax position of cooperatives had been written into the Revenue Acts of 1921 and 1926 with a clear intent on the part of Congress to help farmers by encouraging cooperative enterprise. Many agricultural states had also provided favorable tax treatment for cooperatives. The principal privilege that the federal tax laws gave to cooperatives was their exemption from income taxes on patronage refunds, which made up the bulk of gross income. Moreover, it was not necessary for cooperatives to pay the patronage refunds in cash in order to receive the tax exemption. These refunds could be allocated to patrons in merchandise, stock, revolving fund certificates, or letters of advice. Even though these dividends were held and used by the cooperatives, they could be deducted from gross income for tax purposes. This kind of tax treatment was justified on the basis that cooperatives were not organized for profit, but for service to members; therefore, they had no profits in the strict sense. Practically all of the earnings were allocated to members, who were required to pay taxes as individuals.

Under the law there were two classes of cooperatives, exempt and nonexempt. Neither class was required to pay income taxes on patronage refunds, but exempt cooperatives were not even required to pay corporate income taxes on stock dividends, capital gains, incidental income, or income from government business. On the other hand, nonexempt cooperatives had to pay income taxes on these types of income. Also, of course, all cooperatives paid local real estate and other taxes, and individual members paid income taxes on their patronage refunds, whether or not the amount was received in cash. Since the cooperatives had not previously had to justify their special tax position, there was a general lack of understanding of the tax system's apparent favoring of one type of business enterprise over another.

The formation of the National Tax Equality Association in 1943 caused deep concern among cooperatives. Promoted by a group of grain merchants in Minneapolis who had seen the cooperative Farmers Union Grain Terminal Association in St. Paul grow into a large business, NTEA was eager to remove the federal income tax exemption on cooperatives. Ben C. McCabe, head of the International Elevator Company, became president of NTEA. The National Tax Equality Association argued that cooperative savings were no different from ordinary company profits and that refunds to patrons were identical to dividends to stockholders. Expressing this view, a writer for *Fortune* declared that when the cooperatives withheld refunds to patrons and used the money for capital expansion, the situation worked "for the aggrandizement of the co-operative in competition with the ordinary corporation, and this may be unfair if the withholdings of the corporations are heavily taxed as they are at present." [1]

In May, 1944, Fulton Lewis, Jr., wrote two widely circulated columns that were highly critical of cooperatives. Lewis declared that the annual savings of a large cooperative were not divided among the patrons, but were kept for business expansion. "The money from the stock sales, plus the plowed back profits, plus government low-interest loans provide the financing by which the past expansion has been possible," Lewis argued. Besides dealing with cooperatives in general, Lewis specifically cited CCA as one of the octopus-type organizations that were expanding on untaxed profits. He not only criticized the tax-exempt position of cooperatives, but he also opposed the cheap credit that they received from the Farm Credit Administration. [2]

After 1943 the cooperatives were subjected to a steady barrage of unfavorable publicity, much of which was instigated and supported by the NTEA. Speaking in Kansas City, which he called "one of the bailiwicks of cooperation," Vernon Scott of the NTEA told the Chamber of Commerce on February 21, 1945, that cooperatives were among the worst "tax profiteers" of the war and the "pets of bureaucracy." [3]

The notable success of CCA made the company a special object of attack, and Cowden's factories-are-free propaganda helped to open the way for criticism by private business. His argument that additional productive facilities could be built with undistributed patronage refunds that were not subject to the corporate income tax led critics to charge that these savings were nothing more than an interest-free loan from patrons. In the case of CCA these undistributed dividends were revolved on a five-year basis.

The attack on the tax status of cooperatives touched a tender nerve, and the associations reacted indignantly. As one of the largest cooperative wholesales in the United States, CCA immediately took the lead to counteract the organized opposition. On October 28, 1943,

[1] "Big Business Without Profit," *Fortune*, XXXII (August, 1945), 153.
[2] *Salt Lake Tribune*, May 14, 1944; and *San Francisco Examiner*, May 15, 1944.
[3] *Cooperative Consumer*, March 3, 1945, 1.

Cowden wrote to a large number of cooperative leaders, inviting them to a conference in Chicago on November 9 to "devise ways and means of combating the nationwide fight now developing against cooperatives of all types." At the meeting, cooperative leaders agreed to set up a committee of nine members to work with cooperative organizations "in carrying on the fight to preserve the present income tax status of cooperatives." Cowden was named to this committee. Representatives of the cooperatives met again in May, 1944, and formed the National Conference of Cooperatives, of which C. L. Brody became chairman. Brody did not mince words in announcing the purpose of NCC. It would "combat and defeat" attacks made on cooperatives by the National Tax Equality Association. For the cooperatives, Brody said, it was "a call to arms." [4] Under a new name, National Association of Cooperatives, the new agency was incorporated in Illinois on June 28, 1944.[5] CCA promised to support NAC with $10,000 annually over a three-year period, although the actual contribution was slightly less. The NAC immediately began to set up state organizations and to distribute publicity to combat the anticooperative propaganda.

CCA's officials were worried about the widespread effort to change the federal tax position of cooperatives, but they had a more pressing and practical problem near home. When the Kansas legislature met in January, 1945, bills were introduced in the House and Senate to strike out Section 11 of the Kansas Income Tax Act, which exempted cooperatives and certain other organizations from state income taxes. Since CCA was chartered in Kansas, this action appeared to be the initial move to cripple the wholesale that critics now insisted was too big. Cowden had learned a long time before this that it was essential to use political power to achieve economic objectives, and he was an effective politician when the occasion required.

Two days after legislative hearings were held on the tax question, Cowden sent out hundreds of mimeographed letters addressed to "Dear Cooperator." He declared that "the time has come for cooperative leaders in Kansas to write letters and wires to their state senators and representatives." He added that he did not know what the House and Senate committees would decide, but said, "We should not take chances either on this measure or some successor to

<hr>

[4] Minutes and reports of the meetings of cooperative leaders, November 9, 1943, and May 27 and 29, 1944, CCA Files.
[5] This organization held its last meeting in Chicago on November 22, 1948. It was discontinued because the National Council for Cooperatives was beginning to do a better job of defending cooperative interests.

it." In their letters, Cowden urged, cooperators should insist that the Kansas Income Tax Act should be left "just as it now stands." Any break in the tax dike, he warned, would be the first step toward taxing patronage refunds. He continued, "This is an all out fight against all cooperatives. . . . Kansas has been chosen as the testing ground for the enactment of laws that will hamstring the movement." [6] Referring to the bills before the Kansas Senate and House, the *Cooperative Consumer* said, "It's time to start slugging." [7]

Despite the opposition of Cowden and cooperative leaders in Kansas, the legislature seemed to be giving way before the pressures of those who favored changing the law that dealt with taxation of cooperatives. Early in March, 1945, C. C. Cogswell, State Master of the Grange, wrote to Grange leaders throughout the state, saying that big business, with seemingly unlimited finances, had made some progress in moving the bills through the legislative committees. Then he asked Grangers to descend on Topeka to help defeat the "stop cooperatives" program.[8] Cowden also urged farmers to take positive action. He wired a large number of the cooperatives' supporters on March 6 and asked every local association to have at least one carload of leaders in Topeka two days later to work against the tax bills. This action came none too early, because on March 7 the Senate passed Bill No. 170.

On the morning of March 8 Kansas legislators must have thought the spirits of Mary Lease and William Peffer were running amuck in the State Capitol. By 10 A.M. about eight hundred cooperators filled the corridors of the building. "Flood of Farmer Objectors Swarm Capitol Third Floor As Legislators Seek Cover," announced the *Topeka Daily Capital*.[9] One observer remarked, "Old-timers around the legislature asserted that they had never seen so many farmers in the corridors since the days of the Populists." [10] Farmers first went to Governor Andrew Schoeppel's office and then up to see their senators and representatives on the third floor. Lawmakers scuttled for cover, but when they ventured into the open, home-town voters seemed to be everywhere. One correspondent wrote that "bewildered legislators who ventured into the corridors were surrounded promptly and

---

[6] Cowden to "Dear Cooperator," February 10, 1945, Cowden Papers.
[7] *Cooperative Consumer*, March 3, 1945, 1.
[8] Cogswell to Grange Leaders, March 3, 1945, Cowden Papers.
[9] *Topeka Daily Capital*, March 9, 1945.
[10] *Cooperative Consumer*, March 19, 1945, 1.

backed up against the walls, and there were hearings 'on the hoof' around every corner." A reporter for the *Daily Capital* said that before noon it was evident that the House bill was dead and that "the farm pallbearers could go home and worry no more." [11]

The next evening, Cowden addressed a dinner meeting of legislators and explained how important the cooperative movement was to the economic life of Kansas and to the country as a whole. He urged the lawmakers not to change the tax law. Cowden did not threaten the legislature; he preferred to rely on reason and persuasion. Nevertheless, he and his cooperative friends in Kansas had made it abundantly evident that they could exert strong political pressure. Undoubtedly this fact made some legislators much more responsive to the arguments advanced by representatives of the cooperatives.

The House bill died on March 16, and the anticooperative measure passed by the Senate was killed by the House six days later on a voice vote of 52 to 42.[12] However, the cooperatives dared not relax, because the legislature passed a resolution directing the Kansas Legislative Council to study and report on the legal position of cooperatives. It was evident that the whole question would come up again, and probably at the next session. To keep in close touch with the situation F. R. Olmsted, CCA's general counsel, went to Topeka as an observer.[13]

Although it was settled by March that no action harmful to the cooperatives would be taken at the current session, public argument over the tax position of cooperatives continued. The main criticisms were leveled against the large cooperative associations like CCA, which was often mentioned by name. No one argued against the principle of cooperatives, and most critics claimed to favor small farmer-owned associations, but they opposed what they called the "super-duper" cooperatives. Cowden spent much time and effort refuting the charges directed against CCA and its size. He wrote several columns for the *Cooperative Consumer* in which he argued that CCA could not perform the services farmers needed unless it was a large, integrated operation. Cowden also pointed out that CCA was small compared to the really big businesses in the United States. He insisted that larger farmer associations were desperately needed to meet the growing concentration of economic power in business organizations. Coopera-

[11] *Topeka Daily Capital*, March 9, 1945.
[12] *Cooperative Consumer*, March 31, 1945.
[13] Board of Directors, Minutes, July 25–26, 1945.

tives, he wrote, were "the only rock of defense in a monopoly-ridden land." [14]

After eighteen months of study by a special committee of the Kansas Legislative Council, a report was submitted in November, 1946, only a few weeks before the opening of the next session of the legislature. Agreeing with the assumption that cooperatives had been beneficial to Kansas producers, the committee said that the building of large regional associations had not been anticipated by those enacting the original cooperative acts. These corporations, said the committee, were now very definitely big business. The committee continued with the statement that one of the major factors in the rapid expansion of larger cooperatives had been their ability to withhold tax-exempt patronage refunds for capital expansion. Then, examining the tax question, the committee reported that under both state and federal laws "the total burden upon the ordinary corporation has been very much heavier than that upon cooperatives, and that the latter's ability to build up reserves has, consequently, been much greater than that of a competing corporation transacting the same amount of business." Going further, the committee suggested that the "tax inequality" could be remedied by the cooperatives' discontinuing their present practice of deferring patronage dividends. Finally, the committee recommended that specified reserves set aside by cooperatives should be considered as property of the corporation and subject to taxation, and that the remainder of the net earnings should be paid annually in cash. If these recommendations were carried out, the patronage refunds of cooperatives would be taxed, and the cooperatives could not hold members' dividends for several years and use them for capital expansion. [15]

These recommendations brought cries of anguish from the Kansas Cooperative Council, CCA, and other cooperative groups. A few days after receiving the report Olmsted wrote to eighteen national and regional cooperatives, charging that the recommendations were unsound. If the legislature should act on this report, he said, "irreparable injury to farmer cooperatives" in other states as well as in Kansas would result. He thought that other cooperative leaders "may want to offer some suggestions to assist us in meeting the threat which it [the report] presents." [16]

---

[14] *Cooperative Consumer*, March 31, 1945, and other issues.
[15] Linn T. Woods, "Committee Report," November 14, 1946, Cowden Papers.
[16] Olmsted to Eighteen Cooperative Leaders, November 25, 1946, Cowden Papers.

A letter written by a representative of the Kansas Independent Businessmen's Association soon after the legislature convened indicated that CCA was the main object of the anticooperative attack. Referring to the study of the Legislative Council's special committee, this observer declared that the report was good news for Kansas businessmen. Implementation of the recommendations, he said, would require big cooperatives like the Consumers Cooperative Association to pay income taxes just like any other corporation. He added that this should result in tax equality for businessmen in Kansas and help in the national campaign to force cooperatives to pay their full share of federal income taxes. Finally, the writer called on businessmen to back legislators who favored changing the tax laws because the cooperatives were marshaling their strength to keep their unfair advantages. In February the Kansas Independent Businessmen's Association mailed out hundreds of postcards and letters attacking the cooperatives.[17]

Although several bills were introduced into the Kansas legislature early in 1947 to change the tax status of cooperatives in Kansas, it was soon apparent that none of them would be passed. The Kansas Cooperative Council, representatives of CCA, and other cooperative leaders were all doing effective work to curb the anticooperative move. The *Cooperative Consumer* carried one or more articles supporting the cooperative cause and denouncing opponents in nearly every issue during the early months of 1947. The cooperatives won a real victory when a special subcommittee was appointed to study the tax problem; the membership of this group was such that any legislation that might cripple or handicap cooperatives was most unlikely. It was even rumored that the subcommittee had been set up to relieve Governor Frank Carlson of any political embarrassment over this touchy question. After an interview with Carlson, Olmsted reported that the Governor would oppose any legislation that would be detrimental to the cooperatives. However, Carlson did cause uneasiness by talking about some kind of compromise. From the cooperatives' standpoint no compromise was feasible, because any measure that would satisfy the critics would undoubtedly be highly injurious to the cooperatives.[18]

Although there was slight chance that anticooperative legislation would be passed, vigorous argument and behind-the-scenes maneuver-

[17] Thomas M. Green, mimeographed letter, January 24, 1947, Cowden Papers.
[18] Olmsted to Cowden, January 31, 1947, Cowden Papers.

ing over the tax question continued. In March a compromise measure, H.B. 370, was killed, and, as the cooperative leaders announced, they had "scored another great victory." [19]

The fight in Kansas over taxing cooperatives as well as the nation-wide efforts of the NTEA raised fundamental questions that caused some deep soul-searching among cooperative officials. Initial reaction by cooperatives to the challenge of their tax position was that selfish big business interests and grasping middlemen were attacking the "rights" and "privileges" of cooperatives. The cooperatives' special tax status, although they had enjoyed it for many years, did not involve any rights. The tax laws could be continued or canceled as the state legislatures and Congress saw fit. Thus, the cooperatives needed to explain and justify their tax status in positive terms; denouncing their opponents was not sufficient to present their argument to the public. It was not enough to argue that private business did not actually pay income taxes, but passed the tax on to consumers as a cost of doing business, nor was it enough to insist that the ordinary corporation was a taxgatherer rather than a taxpayer and that many businesses enjoyed direct or indirect federal subsidies of one kind or another. The task of CCA and other cooperatives was to show fully and effectively how they contributed to economic progress and to the general welfare of agriculture. Until this message was made clear, cooperatives were likely to be on the defensive when subjected to the criticism of competing businesses and to the scrutiny of a public looking for more revenue from taxes. A basic understanding of the contributions made by cooperatives was not general even in Kansas, and when the campaign to modify the tax laws began, the cooperatives had to rely on direct political pressures rather than on general support unaffected by self-interest. In any event, the tax fight in Kansas emphasized as never before the need for a more effective program of broad education in principles of cooperation.

Olmsted, as general counsel for CCA, was deeply involved in the fight, and he discussed this problem fully in a memorandum to Cowden when the first attack against CCA was made, in 1945. He explained that legislators and others felt that cooperatives were able to accumulate risk capital much faster than private business by withholding untaxed patronage refunds and that this ability gave the cooperatives

---

[19] Kansas Cooperative Council, undated newsletter, Cowden Papers.

an unfair advantage. He then warned that CCA could no longer rely on a defensive program based on the argument that, since cooperatives had no income, they were not subject to income taxes. Henceforth, Olmsted wrote, CCA must carry on an aggressive campaign "to let the public know what cooperatives are and to convince the public that the cooperative form of enterprise should be encouraged and developed as a means of improving the condition of the average citizen and as a means of protecting the public from the dangers threatened by monopolies and cartels." [20] Here was a positive approach, one that emphasized the economic contributions of cooperatives to the entire country as well as to individual patrons. Cowden had talked in these terms, but so far the results had not been encouraging.

The move to tax cooperatives was only one of the problems that CCA dealt with in the middle 1940's. An equally serious matter was the effort of Kansas' Attorney General Edward F. Arn to dissolve the company charter and oust the wholesale from Kansas. Arn took this action following a dispute between CCA and the Kansas State Charter Board over a request by CCA to increase its capital stock.

On February 27, 1946, the Board of Directors voted to increase the company's capitalization from $2 million to $12 million. When the request was presented to the State Charter Board in Topeka various reasons, mostly of a trivial nature, were offered as to why the application could not be approved. On January 25, 1947, shortly after Arn took office, the Charter Board denied the request for increased capitalization on the grounds that CCA had abused and exceeded its corporate powers as granted under the Kansas Agricultural Cooperative Marketing Act. Olmsted's personal efforts to change this decision were to no avail. Arn insisted that some provisions of the Marketing Act were not clear and that a friendly suit should be filed so that certain important questions could be settled by the Supreme Court of Kansas. Moreover, there was a problem of whether CCA was required to register its securities with the Kansas Corporation Commission. Consequently, on March 12 CCA instituted a mandamus suit to compel the Secretary of State to file an amendment to the company charter, allowing CCA to increase the firm's capitalization, and on April 8 the Attorney General filed a proceeding of quo warranto, asking for the dissolution of the Consumers Cooperative Association and for-

[20] Olmsted to Cowden, March 24, 1945, Cowden Papers.

feiture of its Kansas charter and requesting a court order enjoining CCA from doing business under the Cooperative Marketing Act.[21]

Attorneys for the state relied on two basic contentions. In the first place, they argued, the extensive business and industrial enterprises of CCA went far beyond that permitted by the Cooperative Marketing Act. Second, they charged that up to February 28, 1947, CCA had sold $7,120,644 of securities that were not registered with the Corporation Commission as required by law. For these reasons the Attorney General asked the court to dissolve CCA and annul its corporate existence under the Marketing Act. Earl Hatcher and Olmsted, who represented CCA, denied that the corporation had exceeded its privileges under the Marketing Act, but admitted that the company had sold unregistered securities. However, the law was not clear on the latter point, and CCA's attorneys said that if their firm had, through a misunderstanding of the law, exceeded its authority or breached its obligations CCA should be so informed and given an opportunity to correct the same.

In reviewing the case, the Supreme Court of Kansas noted that it was "the culmination of considerable agitation before at least the last two sessions of the legislature. The complaints seemed to center in the main about the fact that the cooperative societies were engaged in general business activities and did not have the tax burden borne by ordinary business." However, the court said that the question of taxes had nothing to do with the case. The main point to be decided in the ouster suit was whether CCA had the power and authority to manufacture supplies — particularly petroleum products — produce its own oil, and move it through company-owned pipelines. After considering this whole matter, the court held that supplying gasoline, oil, and other commodities for farming operations came within the purview of the Marketing Act. Therefore, the ouster was denied.

On the charge of selling unregistered securities, the court pointed out that up to 1946 the state Corporation Commission had knowingly permitted CCA and its subsidiaries to sell stock without requiring registration. This had been done pursuant to consultations between state officials and representatives of CCA and was in line with a long-established policy of "permitting farmer cooperative societies to sell securities . . . without requiring their registration." The court

---

[21] Consumers Co-op Ass'n v. Arn *et al.*, 183 P. 2d 453; and State *ex rel.* Arn v. Consumers Co-op Ass'n, 183 P. 2d 423.

made it clear that there "was no contention by anyone in this action that CCA is not sound and solvent and in a flourishing condition." In other words, there was no implication that CCA was selling stock of doubtful worth, although the company had technically violated the so-called Blue Sky Law with the permission of state officers. The court concluded that CCA should not be penalized for nonregistration; in the future, however, it must register its stock and certificates of indebtedness, but not its patronage refund certificates.[22] On the same day, July 12, 1947, the court decided the mandamus suit instituted by CCA, and it ordered the Secretary of State, who was a member of the Charter Board, to file an amendment to CCA's Articles of Incorporation that would raise the capitalization to $12 million, as the company had requested about a year earlier.

The unanimous decision of the Supreme Court of Kansas in these cases was a complete victory for CCA. On July 15 the *Cooperative Consumer* headlined its story, CCA IN SMASHING VICTORY, and with a subhead, "Kansas Supreme Court Denies Writ of Ouster." As the editor reported, this decision removed "all doubt about the right of CCA to carry on its many activities under the marketing act." Actually, there is no indication that CCA was worried about the outcome. Olmsted reported to the Board of Directors on May 14, about two months before the decision was rendered, that he believed CCA would get a favorable verdict. However, CCA's officials used this suit to rally their friends and supporters behind CCA and the cooperative movement. Cowden wrote that the suit had been a needless affair, but that he did not resent the worry and expense if the outcome would serve the cooperatives' cause.[23]

Beginning on September 1, 1947, CCA voluntarily gave up its status as a tax-exempt cooperative under Section 101 of the United States Internal Revenue Code.[24] In order to maintain the exempt status, sales to nonmembers could not exceed 15 per cent of total business, and CCA might surpass that amount. However, the Board announced that the main reason for this action was "the fact that the sale of lubricating oil and other commodities to others than cooperatives resulted

---

[22] In 1951 CCA began registering its stock with the Securities and Exchange Commission.

[23] *Cooperative Consumer*, July 15, 1947, 4.

[24] Shareholders' meeting, Minutes, November 7, 1947. In the ouster suit, briefs of *amicus curiae* were filed by the Kansas farm organizations, the National Council of Farmer Cooperatives, and the National Association of Cooperatives.

in substantial patronage refunds being paid to a number of firms, some of which are openly hostile to cooperatives."[25] In other words, CCA did not want to provide savings for those who might use them to fight cooperatives. The Board emphasized that this action was not a "running for cover" in face of the fight being waged against cooperatives and that the move had been made for the best interest of CCA and its patrons.

CCA's political and legal victories in Kansas caused no letup in the growing opposition to cooperatives. CCA was the principal target of an article, entitled "Co-operatives or Free Enterprise," which appeared in the *Tulsa Daily World* on February 2, 1947. "Unless Congress immediately curbs the sweeping advances of the cooperative movement," wrote Walter Biscup, the United States would become the center of world socialism. Referring specifically to CCA, he declared that the petroleum cooperatives had grown rapidly by "utilizing tax-free swollen profits" and had benefited from other governmental favors and special privileges. Oil men in Tulsa, he said, had paid no attention when six small cooperatives had formed the Union Oil Company in 1929, but now the unnoticed baby had developed into a grasping giant. Biscup referred to Cowden as an executive of singular ability, but intimated that this made him all the more dangerous to free enterprise.

The National Tax Equality Association now intensified its efforts to get Congress to tax undistributed patronage refunds held by cooperatives. Garner M. Lester, president of the NTEA, wrote early in 1949 that the most important thing needed to win the fight for tax equality was "to make the *average person* aware that income tax favoritism affects his own tax bill and the security of the business with which he is identified." The ordinary citizen, he declared, could not understand legal and mathematical technicalities, so the NTEA had prepared an object lesson for general distribution in the form of "Co-op Tax-Free Bucks." These looked much like a dollar bill, but they bore the picture of a bloated businessman, labeled "Big Business Co-op." The slogan was "In tax exemption we trust." According to the caption these tax-free bucks could be used to buy out or bankrupt an income-taxpaying business and "make your tax bill higher." Lester said that this simple and impressionistic advertising would be effec-

---

[25] Board of Directors, Minutes, May 14 and July 14, 1947.

tive. "We must get MILLIONS of these bucks into circulation," he wrote to secretaries of trade associations and chambers of commerce.[26]

The NTEA had at last hit upon a technique to reach the general public with its anticooperative publicity. Tax-free bucks were soon turning up in letters, invoices, shipments of merchandise, and elsewhere. On May 12, 1949, Jerry Voorhis, executive secretary of the Cooperative League, wrote to hundreds of cooperative leaders to warn them against what he called the "phoney dollar" campaign.[27] But Voorhis admitted that the tax-free buck was "probably the most effective — and therefore dangerous — device yet used by the NTEA."

How could this admittedly effective propaganda and direct attack on the tax position of cooperatives be counteracted? Some of the cooperatives' officials thought that local associations should run advertisements to refute NTEA's arguments, but Cowden did not want to try the case in the public press. He felt that to do so would only give additional publicity to the opposition's charges. Cowden believed that more could be accomplished by political action and economic pressure. The American colonists, he wrote, had overthrown the English tyrants, and it was time for "a few 'Boston tea parties' in our territory." On June 8 he wrote to Representative Wright Patman, Chairman of the Small Business Committee, to inform him that NTEA was flooding the country with tax bucks and was using other unfair tactics. He declared that some harm had already been done to cooperatives, and he asked Patman's committee to investigate NTEA. Nothing came of Cowden's request. Within the cooperative family, some local cooperatives did buy advertisements in response to Cowden's urging. A few even reprinted the bucks, but printed over them in bold, black type, "Phoney bucks tell phoney story." Another device was to list the amount of taxes a cooperative paid.

During the next two years there was an all-out battle between the cooperatives and those who wanted to modify the tax laws. CCA helped finance the cooperative cause, and its officials lent personal support to the campaign. Political pressure was exerted wherever CCA had any influence. However, most of the fighting was left up to the National Council of Farmer Cooperatives and other national groups. The nation's need for more revenue during the Korean War worked

---

[26] Garner M. Lester to All Trade Association and Chamber of Commerce Secretaries, early 1949, Cowden Files.
[27] Copy in Cowden Files.

in favor of those who were pushing the program to levy income taxes on cooperatives. Representatives of the Treasury Department, the NTEA, other business groups, and a growing number of senators and representatives all combined in 1951 to push a revised tax law through Congress. This law only slightly modified the income tax position of cooperatives, and — most important from their viewpoint — it did not levy corporate income taxes on allocated but undistributed patronage refunds. Despite what may have seemed to be the loss of this tax campaign, it was not a very important battle, and the cooperatives came out reasonably well.

There is no question but that the income tax laws were favorable to cooperatives, otherwise, the cooperatives would not have fought so hard to retain their tax status. The special tax provisions enacted by Congress for cooperatives in the 1920's were similar in principle to certain other tax laws, such as depletion allowances for minerals, which Congress thought were in the national interest. Whether the laws were right or wrong, they had become public policy. It was in the American political tradition for economic groups to advance and protect what they considered their own best interests in the halls of government, although these interests often conflicted with those of other groups. Once a group enjoyed any type of governmental favor it usually sought to justify its position by identifying its particular interests with national welfare. As mentioned earlier, the general educational effort of CCA and other cooperatives on the tax question had not been very successful, and they were forced to use direct political pressure to prevent detrimental changes in the tax statutes.

In a democracy, where public policy is shaped in the forum of public opinion, it was entirely reasonable to raise the question of whether the tax privileges of cooperatives were sound and desirable. But it was ridiculous and somewhat hypocritical to single out cooperatives, as some critics did, when in fact many groups benefited economically in one way or another from government policies. Those who opposed the cooperatives were more interested in destroying the cooperative movement than they were in the public welfare. This may have been the reason why Congress did not heed the cries of this particular group of critics.

Chapter 12

Postwar Developments

IN SOME WAYS the decade of the 1940's was a trying time for CCA. Besides the problems connected with war and reconversion, the company was confronted with large-scale opposition for the first time. It was forced to spend an increasing amount of time and money to present a favorable public image. But none of CCA's difficulties were serious enough to interfere with the pattern of rapid expansion.

Although during the last year of World War II CCA had broken all previous records in volume of business, net savings, and number of patrons served, Cowden announced that it was no time for complacency or self-satisfaction. CCA, he said, must move ahead to greater achievement. Speaking to delegates at the annual meeting late in November, 1945, Cowden told an overflow crowd in Kansas City's Continental Hotel that although CCA was now a big business, the company continued to operate on the same basic principles as it had in its beginnings. Figures denoting the size of CCA had changed, but the cooperative was still "a story of the common people working together and achieving together." Cowden was always careful to present CCA as a people's organization.[1]

Already a third five-year plan was under consideration. On Septem-

---

[1] *Cooperative Consumer*, November 30, 1945, 1.

ber 29, 1945, Cowden had asked readers of the *Cooperative Consumer*, "Where Do We Go From Here?" The main question, he said, was how could CCA and the local cooperatives be of greater service to patrons. Despite widespread discussion of objectives for the future, Cowden told the Board on November 27 that plans had not matured sufficiently to recommend anything for approval by the shareholders even though the period of the second five-year plan had expired. The Board agreed to discuss the plans for the future at the coming district meetings and to take definite action later. It was not until November 21, 1946, that shareholders formally approved plans and objectives for the next five years.[2]

On the flyleaf of the booklet outlining the third five-year plan were the words that had become a CCA slogan: "Make No Little Plans." Having more than achieved the goals established in the second five-year plan, both management and patrons were optimistic. This attitude was reflected in the shareholders' setting $104,000,000 as the amount of business to be reached by 1951, a quadrupling of the figure for 1946. The aim was to have 1,500 member associations, serving a half-million farm families. To achieve this goal a "March of Progress" trade and membership drive was inaugurated throughout CCA territory in early 1946. The trade drives had become annual affairs, but efforts were now intensified.[3]

The third five-year plan was similar to those adopted in 1935 and 1940. Emphasis was placed upon education and development and on the expansion of business services. The educational goals included increasing the circulation of the *Cooperative Consumer*, developing radio programs, employing a full-time, paid educational field secretary to work among groups of member associations, organizing local study groups, youth programs, and a school for cooperative leadership, and instituting job training for managers. In order to serve CCA's customers more adequately it was recommended that additional manufacturing plants be established and that more raw materials like crude oil and timber be acquired. The financial objectives called for selling more preferred shares to strengthen CCA's capital position and for a higher degree of cash trading by member associations. Here was the same pattern that CCA had been following for a decade or more. It was based on the philosophy that CCA must build broader

---

[2] Shareholders' meeting, Minutes, November 21, 1946.
[3] *CCA, 5 Year Plan*, pamphlet, CCA Files.

cooperative support through an intensified educational effort and that production in cooperative-owned factories should be increased to meet the growing demand of more and larger local associations.

In keeping with the objective to engage in more manufacturing, early in 1946 CCA officials gave careful consideration to buying the United States Ordnance Plant located about ten miles north of Des Moines, Iowa, consisting of 800 acres of land, a power plant, and five large buildings. The Board of Directors discussed this purchase in a long session on February 27 and again on May 15 and 16.[4] It appeared that if CCA could obtain this property from the government it might integrate most of its manufacturing in a single location. After much investigation, however, Cowden reported to the Board on November 17 that the ordnance plant could not be obtained on a favorable basis, and the matter was dropped.

The dollar value of goods distributed by CCA declined slightly in 1946, and net savings dropped 5.7 per cent. The decline was due to the fact that in 1945 the company had sold about $4.5 million worth of petroleum products to the federal government, and this market vanished with the end of the war. But the record of business for 1946 was only a temporary leveling off, and during the following two years phenomenal gains were made. Between 1946 and 1948 the value of merchandise furnished to patrons more than doubled, rising from $26,243,652 to $54,071,409. Savings rose even faster, going from $1,665,289 to $8,320,206. Much of the dollar gain came from postwar price increases, but the volume of goods supplied to customers also rose substantially. By 1948 about 77 per cent of the merchandise furnished to patrons was produced in factories that were owned entirely or in part by CCA.[5]

Petroleum products continued to provide by far the largest value of goods sold by CCA and its subsidiaries. In 1946 about 70 per cent of sales was of refined fuels, oil, and greases, and this pattern did not change much during the next few years. Following World War II, the wholesale further expanded its petroleum operations by purchasing more crude oil reserves and increasing refinery capacity. In December, 1946, CCA bought the Corolena Oil Company of Tulsa, and in November, 1947, it purchased the Stelbar Oil Company, which controlled extensive leases and 155 producing wells. At about the same

---

[4] Board of Directors, Minutes, February 27 and May 15–16, 1946.
[5] *18th Annual Report*, 1946, 3, and *22nd Annual Report*, 1950, 27.

time CCA gained a controlling interest in the Bridgeport Oil Company of Wichita.[6] However, the most important development was purchase of the high-octane refinery at Coffeyville from the War Assets Administration. As mentioned earlier, CCA had leased the refinery from the War Plants Administration and operated it until August, 1945. The property, which had cost the federal government $4,659,-804, was now obtained by CCA for $1,200,000.[7] Moreover, as a result of the modernization program at the Coffeyville refinery, CCA began producing a higher grade lube oil in April, 1947. Additional petroleum capacity was acquired late in 1948 when the wholesale bought a 2,000-barrel-a-day refinery at Newcastle, Wyoming, and began operating it on January 1, 1949. These acquisitions gave CCA outright ownership of four refineries, besides a one-third interest in the plant at McPherson. By 1950 the company also owned 911 oil wells.

By the 1940's CCA was distributing a wide range of commodities, including groceries and home appliances, but most of the company's business was concentrated in a half-dozen lines. Besides the petroleum products, which held a place of commanding importance, the fastest growing services were those connected with supply of feed and fertilizer. Although lumber provided the fourth largest dollar volume by 1950, expansion of this enterprise was slow and erratic. Other leading commodities, all of which were responsible for more than $1 million in business, were tires and accessories, groceries, and farm machinery.

As already emphasized, CCA's early success was closely associated with its petroleum program. The petroleum business was an ideal activity for a cooperative, from two viewpoints. In the first place, CCA was providing to farmers commodities that had become important in the cost of farm production, and second, margins were good for CCA, especially on oil and grease. When CCA began to manufacture feed and fertilizer in the 1940's it moved into another area of production where opportunities to serve agriculture were great and advantages many for the company. Cowden had originally hoped to establish a genuine consumers cooperative on the order of the Scottish Cooperative Wholesale, which distributed hundreds of items to consumers. CCA did handle many commodities, but it was essentially a farm-supply cooperative, and it tended to concentrate on the products that

[6] *19th Annual Report*, 1947, 6; *Co-op Prospectus*, September 22, 1951, 15–16.
[7] *Cooperative Consumer*, March 31 and July 15, 1947.

were most important to agricultural producers. The expansion into feed and fertilizer was in this pattern.

The feed program, which had been started with the purchase of a mill in Enid, Oklahoma, in November, 1943, was greatly enlarged in the postwar years. In 1946 CCA started to build a $100,000 plant at Eagle Grove, Iowa, to produce animal proteins, mainly meat scrap and tankage, needed in the preparation of open-formula feed. The plant was completed in August, 1947.[8] After failure to get a consistent and adequate supply of alfalfa around Pond Creek, Oklahoma, the alfalfa dehydration plant was moved to Longmont, Colorado, in 1949. By that time the soybean mill at Coffeyville, the dehydration plant at Longmont, and the mill at Eagle Grove were producing millions of pounds of concentrates. These were sold to some of the larger member cooperatives, which had their own mixing plants. CCA also handled feed ingredients that it did not produce and distributed mixed feeds directly to local associations from the Enid mill.

Officials of CCA argued that by its furnishing concentrates, providing formulas, and giving general advice on the manufacture of feed farmers would be assured of buying high-quality products. All of the feed, whether produced at Enid or in a local cooperative plant, was sold under the CO-OP label, and the ingredients were clearly designated. In 1950 CCA had distributed about 75,000 tons of CO-OP feed to poultrymen, dairymen, livestock feeders, and others in the Midwest.[9] Margins on the feed operations were initially small, although by 1950 the dollar volume of sales had climbed to $5,926,466.[10]

Commercial fertilizer was something like prepared feeds, in that prior to World War II most Midwestern farmers used it sparingly, if at all. For example, Iowa producers bought an average of 49,297 tons of commercial fertilizer annually during 1940–1944, but this figure had grown to 520,130 tons a year in the period 1950–1954. CCA officials were quick to recognize this changing situation. On February 27, 1946, Homer Young explained to the Board of Directors how rapidly farmers were increasing their use of commercial fertilizer, and he reported on the possibility of CCA getting into this business. The following November Young, Zurbuchen, and Fox again discussed the matter with the Board.[11]

---

[8] *19th Annual Report*, 1947, 10.
[9] *22nd Annual Report*, 1950, 8–9.
[10] *Co-op Prospectus*, September 22, 1951, 6.
[11] Board of Directors, Minutes, February 27 and November 17–18, 1946.

While these discussions were under way, CCA began handling fertilizer on a very small scale. It sold only $2,356 worth in 1946. The next year fertilizer sales rose to $148,214, but this figure was near the bottom of the list of the returns on CCA enterprises. But selling fertilizer on a commission basis was not in line with the third five-year plan, which called for more cooperative-owned manufacturing facilities. Also, Cowden was convinced that fertilizer prices were "rigged by a trust," and he thought fertilizer ought to be produced close to the final market.[12]

The first step in CCA's fertilizer program was to build a mixing plant at Eagle Grove, Iowa, in 1948. Since this enterprise would serve only a limited region, most of the $200,000 necessary was raised from cooperatives and individual patrons in the general area. Meanwhile, the Board of Directors was considering further expansion. On June 28 it voted to buy a fertilizer mixing and acidulation plant from the Best Brothers Plant, Inc., at St. Joseph, Missouri. The price of $130,000 was probably somewhat excessive for the physical facilities, but this was overbalanced by the fact that the plant, well located for CCA business, was ready to operate. To build a new facility would mean at least a year's delay in commencing distribution.[13] The St. Joseph plant was remodeled, and it was officially dedicated on March 17, 1949.

At the same time studies and surveys were being made to determine the feasibility of locating a fertilizer plant in eastern Oklahoma. On August 18, 1948, the Board of Directors authorized management to decide on a location and to begin construction. It was soon announced that a plant would be built at Muskogee. Construction was completed about ten months later, and manufacturing operations began in July, 1949.[14] Ownership and operation of three fertilizer plants, plus membership in the Central Farmers Fertilizer Company of Chicago, which was owned by regional cooperatives, permitted CCA to expand its fertilizer business at a very rapid rate. In only five years, between 1946 and 1950, fertilizer sales jumped from $2,356 to $2,509,758.[15] Although CCA had started another service helpful to member associations, the most important part of its fertilizer program, the building of a nitrogen plant, came later.

[12] *20th Annual Report*, 1948, 10.
[13] Board of Directors, Minutes, June 28, 1948.
[14] Board of Directors, Minutes, November 3, 1947, and August 18, 1948; *21st Annual Report*, 1949, 11.
[15] *Co-op Prospectus*, September 22, 1951, 6.

While CCA was enlarging and instituting important new programs in the late 1940's, some of its older services confronted serious difficulties. Its enterprises in farm machinery, groceries, the Scottsbluff cannery, the Retail Department, and lumber all presented perplexing problems.

During World War II sales of farm machinery dropped to only a few thousand dollars annually. In 1944 the Board voted to invest $25,-000 in the National Farm Machinery Cooperative, which was owned by twelve regional associations. A year later, however, Homer Young reported to the Board that NFMC had suffered heavy losses, of which CCA's share was $14,600. The Board voted to pay the loss and to continue in the business.[16] By 1947 two plants owned by NFMC at Bellevue, Ohio, and at Shelbyville, Indiana, and the Cockshutt Plow Company in Brantford, Ontario, were turning out a full line of farm machinery for cooperatives. Cowden declared that the National Farm Machinery Cooperative was a challenge to the "four giant companies" that controlled most of the farm machine business.

With the coming of peace in 1945, CCA made an intensive effort to push cooperative-produced farm equipment. The *Cooperative Consumer* advertised machinery, fieldmen promoted it, and Cowden talked endlessly about the importance of this program. Between 1946 and 1949 sales rose from $285,000 to $2,746,000. In order to help local associations to give full service, CCA sponsored tractor and farm machinery schools for servicemen and also advised member cooperatives on sources of credit necessary to carry a full line of equipment.[17]

Despite all this effort, the results from dealing in farm machinery were disappointing. Local associations found the cost of handling slow-moving equipment high and margins low. Moreover, it was expensive for member cooperatives to provide satisfactory maintenance and service. Only a few of the large locals could carry a full line of machinery. By 1950 CCA had sixty-one authorized dealers, but there was nothing to warrant optimism for the future. To the Board of Directors in June, 1950, Young reported that there had been a 65 per cent reduction in sales of machinery during the current season and that CCA must drastically reduce its orders in the coming year. Other regionals would have to do the same, and this reduction in orders, he said, would cause difficulty for the National Farm Machinery Coop-

---

[16] Board of Directors, Minutes, May 24–25, 1945.
[17] *Cooperative Consumer*, February 28, 1949, and March 16, 1950.

erative.[18] These problems continued until, as will be shown subsequently, CCA discontinued handling farm machinery.

The lumber operations were equally frustrating and discouraging. The building of a new mill in Oregon in 1945 did not eliminate problems there. In December Zurbuchen, director of CCA's manufacturing, was forced to discharge the superintendent of Swisshome for inefficiency. It was difficult to get labor because of inadequate housing near the mill, and, in addition, the supply of timber was not assured. Difficulties of this kind occupied the Board's attention at almost every meeting after 1945, and consideration was given frequently to trading or selling the property.[19] Although $1,720,000 worth of lumber was sold in fiscal 1949, the cooperative sustained a substantial loss. In 1950 the situation improved slightly, but net savings amounted to only about $50,000. Cowden was fond of pointing to the Swisshome community as an ideal in cooperative enterprise, but the records present another picture.

The Grocery Department was another worrisome problem. During the last year of World War II CCA sold $1,423,629 worth of groceries, but sales subsequently fell off and did not surpass this figure until 1950. During the late 1940's an intensive effort was made to open new cooperative stores, to modernize old outlets, and to push the distribution of groceries. Ross Denison, supervisor of CCA's food department, urged cooperative grocery stores to improve their service, equipment, and general appearance. CCA's "store engineer" Ivan Lanto advised local cooperative stores on decoration, fixtures, and other matters. But, despite improvements in number and quality of cooperative grocery outlets, they were unable to generate enough volume to warrant the expenses of warehousing, distribution, and service functions.[20]

The cannery operations at Scottsbluff that provided part of the food products distributed by CCA had an uneven record. The cannery turned out 149,815 cases of vegetables in the year ending September 1, 1946, but due to cancellation of the government's contract in late 1945, losses at Scottsbluff reached $22,390. The situation improved somewhat in later years, and, outwardly, optimism was high among CCA officials, but one problem after another plagued the food pro-

---

[18] Board of Directors, Minutes, June 19–20, 1950.

[19] Board of Directors, Minutes, February 27, 1946, November 3, 1947, and February 8–9, 1949.

[20] *Cooperative Consumer*, May 31, 1947, 3; *Co-op Prospectus*, September 22, 1951, 6.

duction and distribution operations. By December, 1950, operating losses at the Scottsbluff cannery had reached $279,000.[21] The other cannery operation — the tomato cannery at Milan, Missouri — burned to the ground on December 16, 1945. Indeed, the distribution of groceries and the cannery operations were aspects of CCA's business that caused much distress throughout the company's offices.

As previously mentioned, the Retail Department had been pregnant with problems from the beginning. The cost of management services, inability to strengthen weak locals operated by CCA, and other troublesome factors caused officials to consider abolishing the department. Cowden disliked any sign of retreat by CCA or the cooperative movement, but, finally, business judgment had to prevail over unrealistic sentiments. On October 21, 1947, the Board ratified the earlier decision to close out the Retail Department as of September 1. Assets of the department were sold to a new cooperative known as the "Cooperative Stores Association."[22]

Although CCA was not free of difficulties at home, Cowden now gave an increasing amount of time and effort to promoting cooperation on a world-wide basis. It will be remembered that he had proposed an international oil cooperative at Paris in 1937; during and immediately after World War II, Cowden pushed this idea with renewed vigor. He argued that a world oil cooperative could assure good quality and fair prices to local associations all over the world and could help to rehabilitate cooperatives in war-torn countries. But, more important, Cowden believed an international cooperative petroleum association might help to reduce tensions in areas like the Middle East and might be a major factor in promoting world peace. He was fully convinced that competition for control of rich oil fields was a direct threat to peace and international stability.

At a meeting of the International Cooperative Trading Agency in London during September, 1945, a committee was set up to explore the practical problems of establishing a world oil cooperative. Cowden was named secretary of this group. Another meeting of world cooperative leaders was held in Zurich, Switzerland, in October, 1946, at which time it was agreed to incorporate the International Cooperative Petroleum Association and begin doing business on a brokerage basis as soon as member cooperatives had pledged $500,000 in capital.

[21] Board of Directors, Minutes, December 11, 1950.
[22] Board of Directors, Minutes, October 21, 1947.

The ICPA was chartered in the District of Columbia on April 15, 1947, and soon commenced doing business. As of September 9, CCA had subscribed to $400,000 worth of stock, by far the largest amount promised by any cooperative in the sixteen countries where the member associations were located. This subscription, of which only $25,000 was at first paid in, reflected Cowden's intense concern for the success of this international venture.[23]

The ICPA started modestly and never developed to the extent Cowden had so fondly hoped. In 1948, the first full year of operation, business totaled only $560,088. By 1950 it reached nearly $2 million, but never exceeded $4 million in any year during the 1950's. Savings were usually small.[24] CCA, however, shipped substantial quantities of petroleum commodities to overseas customers after World War II. In the eighteen months prior to September 1, 1947, for example, shipments to twenty-one cooperatives in eighteen countries totaled $3,264,-262. Cowden's interest in world cooperation never lagged, and he continued to spend a great deal of time promoting the international cooperative movement.

As CCA's business developed rapidly in the late 1940's, the need for reorganization of management and of the internal structure of the company became apparent. As has been indicated, most of the major decisions throughout CCA's history had been made by Cowden, and he continued to keep a close rein on all activities even after the company jumped into the multimillion-dollar class. By 1949, twelve directors of divisions were reporting directly to him. The question of making any basic changes in the organization of the management was a delicate one and a matter with which the Board did not like to come to grips. It should be recognized, of course, that the Board, made up mostly of farmers, was hardly qualified to make independent recommendations on management problems of a large corporation. The Board necessarily depended on Cowden or on a professional management consultant.

The first outside study of CCA's management structure was undertaken in the spring of 1949 by representatives of the Farm Credit Administration, following a meeting of FCA and CCA officials on March 28. The most important observations were that too much authority was centered in Cowden's office, and there was no one to assume Cow-

---

[23] Secretary's Report to the Board of Directors, ICPA, September 25–26, 1947, typescript, Cowden Files.

[24] Analysis Report of ICPA, May 1, 1958, to April 30, 1959, Cowden Files.

den's responsibilities during his absence. Moreover, division heads sometimes found it difficult to discuss problems with Cowden because of his crowded schedule, and there was overlapping and duplication of functions among several departments. The FCA officials proposed that the company reduce the number of people who reported directly to Cowden and create two new positions, each of them with the functions of assistant general manager. Finally, they recommended that Cowden designate one of the new assistant general managers to act as general manager when he was not available.[25]

Shortly after this report was made, Cowden announced what appeared to be a major reorganization, to become effective on July 15. The new plan called for three assistant general managers who would work under him as president and general manager. Bruce H. McCully was named Director of Crude Oil Production and Procurement, which gave him control of all the oil operations except distribution to the local cooperatives; Homer Young became Assistant General Manager in Charge of Distribution. Except for oil production, Young was to manage the manufacturing and distribution of all products. Glenn Fox assumed the position of Assistant General Manager in Charge of Finance. Personnel, information, education, management services, and related matters also came under his jurisdiction. McCully and Young had both grown up with CCA, and Fox had been associated with the company for more than ten years. In announcing the appointment of the three assistant general managers, Cowden explained that he would now have more time "to think and plan ahead — something which is vitally necessary for an organization as large as CCA." [26]

Although the new arrangement may have seemed to be a basic reorganization, the changes were more apparent than real. The major decisions were still made by Cowden, and many relatively minor matters were also funneled through his office. Perhaps even more significant was the fact that the big question of grooming a successor for Cowden was left unsettled. About a month after the appointment of the three assistant general managers, the Board of Directors voted to employ the Trundle Engineering Company of Cleveland, Ohio, to study the efficiency of CCA's operations.[27] Reporting in October, the

---

[25] Report on the organizational study of the Consumers Cooperative Association, April 22, 1949, CCA Files.
[26] *Cooperative Consumer,* July 16, 1949, 3.
[27] Board of Directors, Minutes, August 16–17, 1949.

Trundle firm recommended many changes in CCA's business methods and procedures, but it skirted the problems of top management. The report said that the appointment of three assistant general managers was "considered sound" if the lines of responsibility were clearly divided and defined. But it, too, left the matter of Cowden's successor undetermined.[28]

Meanwhile, Cowden hired as his first full-time administrative assistant W. Gordon Leith, who joined the CCA staff on March 15, 1949. Leith, who had been born on a farm in Wisconsin, held a Master's degree in economics from the University of California at Berkeley and had spent his entire working career with cooperatives. Previous to joining CCA, he had worked in Washington for the Farmer Cooperative Service and the National Council of Farmer Cooperatives. In 1953 Leith organized CCA's Economic Research Division.

The business slump of 1949 put a severe strain on CCA's management. While 1948 had been a banner year, with savings of $8,320,206, total business increased only about $1.5 million in 1949, and net savings dropped to a mere $86,334, or about 1 per cent of what they had been a year before. The main problem for CCA, as well as for other businesses in the Midwest, was the drastic decline in farm income, about $5 billion. More specifically, however, CCA was caught by a sharp decrease in petroleum prices and extremely narrow margins between crude oil and refined products. Unfortunately, CCA had bought large quantities of oil in the fall of 1948 only to find within a few months that it had bought on a high market and had to sell on a declining one.

Other dark clouds loomed on the horizon. Glenn Fox reported in February that seventeen cooperatives with equities in CCA had gone into liquidation since the beginning of the current fiscal year. Also, more local associations were being served on a C.O.D. basis, and some cooperatives were leaning heavily on CCA's patronage refunds to counteract business inefficiencies. Too, borrowing during fiscal 1949 had increased by nearly $7 million, and by May consolidated indebtedness of CCA and its subsidiaries to the Banks for Cooperatives was $19,835,770. After the Board of Directors had discussed these and other problems, the Secretary recorded, "Neither the board nor management correctly anticipated or forecast the effect on CCA's

---

[28] Report of the Trundle Engineering Company, October 4, 1949, CCA Files.

operations of the economic changes that came about in the past year." [29] The situation in 1949 made one thing abundantly clear: The success of CCA was heavily dependent upon its oil operations.

As usual, Cowden expressed nothing but enthusiasm and confidence in the future. The small net savings in 1949, he told delegates at the annual meeting, were not discouraging because people knew that the regional wholesale supplied better products, provided a dependable source of supply, and served as a yardstick by which to judge fair prices. Cowden recalled some of the events in CCA's twenty-one-year history, but his main interest was in the future. He predicted that during the next twenty-one years CCA would challenge big business, not only in oil, but in fertilizers, farm machinery, and even food processing. Within five years, he added, CCA would own flour mills, bakeries, and meat processing plants "which will serve as yardsticks for the four large companies that now dominate the packing industry." [30] Cowden asserted that within another twenty-one years CCA would be doing $231 million worth of business annually. Perhaps not all of the 3,100 people who attended the annual meeting in December, 1949, were as optimistic as Cowden, but it was a happy crowd that ate the all-CO-OP supper and enjoyed square dancing afterward. As had been true from the first such occasion, the annual meeting was a time to arouse enthusiasm, renew commitment, and stimulate confidence in the future of CCA and the cooperative movement. And Cowden was a master at inspiring his fellow cooperators.

Although 1949 was a poor year, CCA was in a sound position, and total business and net savings made good gains in both 1950 and 1951. At the end of the third five-year plan in 1951, CCA was considerably short of its goal of $104,000,000, although it had done a record business of more than $74 million. The number of member associations declined from 1,455 in 1949 to 1,417 in 1950, but this was primarily due to better and more accurate means of counting. It should be kept in mind always that most of CCA's volume was with approximately 600 of its large member associations, some of which did several hundred thousand dollars' worth of business annually.

Each year CCA sponsored an intensive trade and membership drive throughout its territory. In March, 1949, it published the first sales catalogue, listing about 1,000 products CCA could supply to its pa-

[29] Board of Directors, Minutes, May 17–18 and December 5–6, 1949.
[30] *Cooperative Consumer*, December 16, 1949, 1.

trons. By 1950 most of the direct contact with local members and associations was in the hands of seventy-seven fieldmen, of whom seven were area supervisors. These representatives offered a wide range of talented service, including auditor analysis, special commodity advice, and specialized knowledge in cooperative organization. Beginning in 1951, neighbor nights were held in CCA territory at which local cooperatives sponsored suppers and programs to generate enthusiasm and support for cooperatives. These became important social and educational events to which both members and nonmembers were invited.

The Education Department sponsored schools and clinics for all types of cooperative employees. For example, in 1948–1949 schools were held for petroleum managers, station servicemen, bookkeepers, appliance salesmen, food-store managers, and others connected with cooperative enterprises. Management training received heavy emphasis, and in 1949 CCA offered local cooperatives nineteen different management services at a cost to the company of $386,887. Bus trips to CCA's facilities were sponsored by both the member associations and the wholesale in order to carry out the slogan, "You know what you own when you see what you own." Besides this kind of practical information, CCA gradually enlarged its programs of general cooperative education. Youth conferences, programs for employees, general meetings, radio talks, distribution of the *Cooperative Consumer* and other literature, and the showing of movies were all a part of CCA's effort to increase understanding of cooperatives. Some of the earlier education programs like the neighborhood councils, circuit councils, and women's guilds had to be abandoned because of lack of local support.

In an effort to build greater loyalty and efficiency among employees, CCA adopted its first full-scale retirement plan, and it became effective September 1, 1946. The program called for contributions by both CCA and its employees and set sixty-five as the age for retirement. According to Cowden, CCA wanted its workers to be able to retire "on incomes that will permit them to maintain their dignity and self-respect in their declining years." The number of workers remained about the same, slightly over 1,800, following the purchase of the Coffeyville refinery in 1944. Another upward trend in the number of employees began in 1947 and reached a high of 2,414 in 1949, with an annual payroll of $7,465,547. The number of employees decreased in 1950, following a rather bad business year.

In the postwar period CCA had to spend considerable time and money defending itself and the entire cooperative movement. Neither the attacks in Kansas nor at the national level, however, caused the company any real difficulty. Meanwhile, CCA expanded its productive facilities, especially in the important fields of feed and fertilizer. The company got caught in the general agricultural recession of 1949, but it recovered quickly and continued to enlarge its many activities and to increase both its physical and dollar volume. But a big test was in the offing. In 1950 the Board of Directors voted to build a nitrogen plant to provide basic ingredients for fertilizer. This was the most important decision made by CCA management in the 1950's; when the facility was successfully completed the wholesale had experienced the greatest difficulties in its history.

Chapter 13

The Battle of 1954:
Building the Nitrogen Plant

T HERE IS A FILE tucked away in the records of CCA that is labeled, "The Battle of 1954." It contains the letters, memoranda, and records that relate to the hopes, plans, and problems connected with building the most expensive productive facility constructed by CCA or by any other American cooperative up to that time. Cowden's memo in the front of the file reads: "This is the story of the struggle to finance the nitrogen plant which had placed a financial burden on CCA during its period of construction." Later he added, "This is the story of the cutback in expenses of $100,000 a month beginning in March, 1954, and of the successful completion of other goals, some set by CCA itself, some set by the Bank for Cooperatives." Indeed, building the $16,000,000 plant at Lawrence, Kansas, tested as never before in CCA history the nerve, dedication, and managerial abilities of Cowden and the entire staff, as well as the loyalty of the member associations.

Their experience with mixing fertilizer convinced management that CCA should enter into the business of producing the basic ingredients. This meant the production of ammonium nitrate, anhydrous ammonia, and other components. On December 11, 1950, following several months of discussion, the Board of Directors authorized

Cowden and his staff to investigate the possible development of an ammonia producing plant. Three days later shareholders enthusiastically approved this decision.[1]

At its next meeting, in April, the Board devoted a great deal of attention to the matter of constructing a nitrogen plant. By that time engineering reports were available, and locations had been investigated. It was estimated that a plant might cost as much as $20,000,000, but Cowden told the Board that the principal part could be secured through government loan.[2] The Board authorized management to continue its studies and voted to apply for a certificate of necessity under the Defense Production Act. Because of restrictions on the use of scarce materials during the war in Korea, CCA was required to have government authorization to proceed.

In August, 1951, the Board voted to incorporate the Cooperative Farm Chemicals Association, a wholly owned subsidiary of CCA, which would construct and operate a nitrogen fixation plant at a cost not to exceed $25,000,000.[3] The Board decided also to build the plant at Lawrence, Kansas, which was well located in CCA territory and had an abundant supply of water and natural gas. A few days later, while Cowden was attending the American Institute of Cooperation meeting at Logan, Utah, he approached Charles E. Wilson, head of the Office of Defense Mobilization, about the possibility of getting a loan to build the nitrogen facility. Wilson explained that credit could not be obtained for this purpose under the Defense Production Act. Shortly afterward, Cowden visited with Fred Merrifield, president of the Wichita Bank for Cooperatives, who agreed that a nitrogen plant would be a fine addition to CCA properties. Merrifield said he hoped such a plant could be financed, and he promised to discuss the matter with the bank's loan committee. From these discussions Cowden gained the impression that the Farm Credit Administration would provide the necessary financing. On the basis of this understanding, CCA's Board now decided to go ahead. Although detailed plans had not been developed, it was thought that CCA could sell $6,000,000 worth of certificates of indebtedness to individuals and local associations and borrow the remainder, or most of it, from the Farm Credit Administration.

---

[1] Board of Directors, Minutes, December 11, 1950; Shareholders' meeting, Minutes, December 14, 1950.

[2] Board of Directors, Minutes, April 26–27, 1951.

[3] Board of Directors, Minutes, August 22–23, 1951.

On October 11 Cowden made the first public announcement that CCA would build a $16,000,000 nitrogen plant at Lawrence. This, he said, was the largest project ever undertaken by the wholesale, and he added: "I believe we can repeat in nitrogen what we have done in petroleum." Cowden declared that, since farmers were the sole users of fertilizer, they should control its production.[4] Furthermore, he argued, a nitrogen plant would serve as a measuring stick by which to judge prices and profits of the private firms.

When CCA's shareholders gathered for the annual meeting late in November, 1951, they enthusiastically endorsed the Board's decision to move ahead with the nitrogen project. At the time there was little more than enthusiasm on which to proceed. The Defense Production Authority had not yet issued a certificate of necessity, and the Farm Credit Administration had given no official indication that it would loan the amount CCA required. Cowden reported that CCA had sold about $2,000,000 worth of securities toward financing the plant, but this was far short of the project's needs. Although CCA held an option on 375 acres of land two miles east of Lawrence, it had not closed the deal. In other words, all CCA had on which to begin was an option on some land, a verbal commitment for credit by a single officer of a co-operative bank, and a small amount of borrowed funds. To undertake a huge expansion program on such slender support seemed almost foolhardy. Would CCA overextend itself to the point where the company's very existence might be threatened? This was a possibility.

While CCA officials were waiting for the Farm Credit Administration to act upon their loan application, an intense campaign was carried on among patrons and local associations to win financial support for the nitrogen plant. A few months earlier, in August, 1951, Cowden had brought in Harold Hamil as an administrative assistant. Hamil's first assignment was to help publicize and promote the nitrogen program. A professional journalist, Hamil had spent most of his life close to agriculture and farm problems. He had grown up on a ranch in northeast Colorado, and, among other jobs, he had worked for twelve years on a daily newspaper at Hastings, Nebraska. Prior to going to CCA, Hamil had been an editorial writer for the St. Louis *Star-Times*. Within a short period after joining CCA, he became Director of Information and editor of the *Cooperative Consumer* and worked closely with Cowden on press releases, speeches, and public

---

[4] *Cooperative Consumer*, October 12, 1951, 1.

statements. Part of this work had been done previously by Jim Cummins, who had died in June, 1950. As events proved, CCA never needed a strong promotion and publicity campaign more than in its efforts to finance the nitrogen project.

On March 7, 1952, the Defense Production Authority issued a certificate of necessity that permitted CCA to buy materials and supplies for its projected plant. About five weeks later Glenn Fox reported to the Board that $4,765,200 worth of securities had been sold, but that the application for a loan was still pending. At this meeting on April 16 the Board voted to pick up its option on the 375 acres of land near Lawrence, at a cost of $119,000.[5]

Hesitation by the Farm Credit Administration to approve the application for funds was beginning to cause real worry among CCA officials. Fred Merrifield appeared before the Board on June 20 to inform its members that the Wichita Bank for Cooperatives could not itself make the needed loan. If a loan were granted, he explained, it must be made by the Central Bank for Cooperatives. In any event, Merrifield thought a decision from Washington would be forthcoming very soon. In May, General Counsel Olmsted went to Washington to discuss the application with Robert L. Farrington, chairman of the Farm Credit Administration's board of directors. Doubts soon turned to shock when Farrington frankly stated that he could not support CCA's application.

On July 23 Farrington wired Merrifield that the Farm Credit Administration would not approve the loan. By this time officials of the Farm Credit Administration had explained their position in detail. The main obstacle to the loan, they said, was CCA's lack of sufficient equity and permanent capital. In addition, the cooperative had relied too heavily on debt capital for expansion purposes. As of May, 1951, CCA had $1.84 of debt capital for every dollar of permanent capital. This was not considered a satisfactory position. Moreover, the ratio of current assets to current liabilities was 1.6 to 1; this figure averaged 2.6 to 1 among 22 other regional cooperatives. Officials of the Farm Credit Administration had indicated earlier that an aggressive expansion program by CCA might require more capital than FCA could supply; they believed that loans from the Banks for Cooperatives should not exceed the equity of members.[6] In going over

---

[5] Board of Directors, Minutes, April 16, 1952.
[6] "A Study of CCA's Financial Structure," August 22–23, 1951, CCA Miscellaneous Statements.

the situation with Olmsted, Farrington declared that patronage refunds, certificates of indebtedness that were redeemable at the end of a fixed period, and other revolving funds, could not be considered permanent capital in any sense; before any large loan could be made to CCA on new facilities the company must improve its capital structure. One way to do this would be to sell preferred stock.

But there was another matter. Farrington told Olmsted that the FCA disapproved of operations that demanded heavy capital investment and produced narrow margins or none at all. He mentioned the grocery department, the cannery at Scottsbluff, the Swisshome mill, and other operations as being in this category. It appeared that if FCA should loan additional money it would insist that some departments be abandoned.[7] Officials of the Wichita Bank for Cooperatives also told a representative of CCA that the wholesale must get rid of the "cats and dogs," meaning the poor-margin departments.[8]

In late July Olmsted returned to Washington in hopes of getting Farrington to change his mind. He argued that certificates of indebtedness for a cooperative were, in effect, equity capital for the cooperative as common or preferred stock was for a regular corporation, but Farrington did not agree. According to Farrington, there could be no reconsideration of the matter. During these discussions Farrington also revealed that Cowden's health had been a factor that had influenced FCA's decision to reject CCA's application. Cowden had been ill early in 1951, and in April the Board told him to take as much time off at full pay as was necessary to rest and to restore his health. The question of Cowden's ability to continue as president and general manager raised the problem of who might assume the top managerial position if anything should happen to him. This was a matter that had concerned officials of the Banks for Cooperatives since 1936.[9]

To make matters worse, the certificate of necessity was to expire on September 7, 1952. If the nitrogen plant were to be built, a start must be made before that time, or it would be necessary to get the certificate extended. Olmsted thought this would be difficult. Consequently, he recommended that CCA immediately employ a superintendent, complete acquisition of the site, get a contractor started, open corporate records for the Cooperative Farm Chemicals Association, and then

---

[7] Olmsted to Cowden, June 3, 1952. Unless otherwise indicated, all of the memoranda and letters cited in the footnotes of this chapter are in "The Battle of 1954," CCA Files.
[8] Max Wasserman to Olmsted, August 6, 1952.
[9] Olmsted to Cowden, August 5, 1952.

announce plans to proceed with construction. He thought there was very little chance of getting a loan from the Banks for Cooperatives, and he urged exploring other sources of credit, including offering part ownership to other regional cooperatives.[10]

Meanwhile, representatives of the Wichita Bank for Cooperatives suggested that future certificates of indebtedness sold by CCA should be subordinated to the claims of the bank. At this time CCA was making application to the Wichita bank for seasonal operating and facility loans totaling $14,502,689.[11] The high point of credit furnished to CCA by the Wichita bank in 1952–1953 was to be $22,000,-000. Although CCA opposed subordinating its certificates of indebtedness to bank loans because of the effect it might have on their sale, it had little choice. On August 25 Cowden wrote to Merrifield that the next certificates would be registered with the Securities and Exchange Commission on that basis. He then asked Merrifield if CCA could begin construction of the nitrogen plant. CCA depended so heavily upon the Banks for Cooperatives for both facility and operational loans that it could not act contrary to the wishes of officials of the Farm Credit Administration without risking a loss of credit. Any specific loan for the nitrogen plant would have to be in excess of already heavy borrowings by CCA and would stretch the wholesale's credit very thin. At least this was the view of FCA officials.

On September 18 Farrington called Merrifield to inform him that the Farm Credit Administration had no objection to CCA's beginning construction, but it should be clearly understood that the Banks for Cooperatives would not make any loan for the fertilizer project. Merrifield quickly conveyed this information to Cowden. If CCA brought about improvements in its financial structure, Merrifield said, the Wichita bank would, after two years, consider a loan for the nitrogen plant without prejudice.[12]

Three days before the Banks for Cooperatives had given official approval to proceed, the *Cooperative Consumer* carried a story under the headline, "Nitrogen Plan Moves Ahead."[13] Cowden announced that a plant superintendent had been employed and that preliminary agreements had been made with two engineering firms to construct

[10] *Ibid.*

[11] P. A. Nichols to Cowden, September 24, 1952.

[12] The essence of this conversation is found in Glenn Fox to Merrifield, September 18, 1952.

[13] *Cooperative Consumer*, September 15, 1952, 1.

the facilities. This looked like real progress, but it was actually a bold front. A few days later the discouraging facts were presented to the Board by Glenn Fox, who warned that a crisis in CCA's finances was at hand. CCA, Fox explained, was one of the largest borrowers from the Wichita bank, and yet it had the weakest balance-sheet ratio among the large cooperatives. Despite this situation, CCA had made plans and commitments to build a $16,000,000 nitrogen plant and had sold $7,000,000 worth of securities, mostly to members who had faith and confidence in the soundness of CCA. Now CCA was about ready to break ground and to begin spending the $7,000,000 without a definite idea of where the remainder of the necessary money could be obtained. If there were any lingering hopes that FCA might relent, Farrington and Merrifield exploded them when they later met with the Board and told the members that they could not make any commitments on financing the nitrogen plant.[14]

Undeterred by this bleak outlook, CCA laid the cornerstone for the administration building at the plant site on December 3, 1952. Nineteen busloads of people who had been attending the annual meeting in Kansas City went to Lawrence to participate in what one writer called "a real red letter day in the history of CCA."

In the light of the financial situation, it was emphasized at the annual meeting that CCA's investment program must continue if the plant were ever to be completed. As if things were not bad enough already, Cowden had to report that savings had dropped drastically in 1952. When plans for the nitrogen plant were being made the year before, savings were high, totaling $6,746,723, the second largest amount on record. But in 1952 savings declined to only $2,836,727 on a total business of more than $82,000,000.[15] This situation resulted from narrower margins in petroleum and continued losses in some of CCA's unprofitable operations like farm machinery.

Laying the cornerstone of the nitrogen plant was a surface indication of progress, but CCA's main problem still remained. Where could the necessary capital be obtained? The CCA organization continued to push the sale of certificates of indebtedness and to explore credit sources outside the Banks for Cooperatives. Fox reported to the Board on March 5, 1953, that regular lenders were reluctant to

[14] Board of Directors, Minutes, September 25–26, 1952.
[15] *24th Annual Report*, 1951–1952, 19.

consider the nitrogen loan because of the cooperatives' business methods.

Besides the search for credit to finance the nitrogen plant, CCA faced some difficult problems within its current operations. One of the most serious of these was the excessive inventory, especially in farm machinery. But, as mentioned earlier, conditions in the lumber and grocery departments and at the cannery at Scottsbluff were unfavorable, too. Confronted with a major financial crisis, CCA was forced to analyze its whole program more closely than ever before, centering finally on the question of just what commodities and services CCA should provide.

CCA's growth had been Topsy-like. It had added one department after another, without much view of the company's ultimate objective. Expansion for expansion's sake seemed good, and the announcement of each new enterprise was cheered at the annual meetings. As mentioned earlier, Cowden had wanted to develop a true consumer cooperative on the European pattern. He had been greatly influenced by what he had seen on his numerous trips to England, Scotland, Scandinavia, and elsewhere. In the early 1930's he expressed the hope of being able to distribute a large variety of consumer goods to both rural and urban patrons. His early appeal to labor unions as well as to farmers to join the old Union Oil Company indicated the direction of his thinking. The addition of groceries, appliances, and other consumer items to the list of goods represented an attempt to establish a genuine consumer cooperative. But in reality CCA was not so much a consumer cooperative as it was a farm supply cooperative. Now the question facing the management was, should CCA concentrate on providing farmers with a limited but highly essential number of commodities, thereby frankly admitting its position as a farm supply cooperative, or should it continue the delusion that it was a true consumer organization?

Apparently the first time the Board ever considered this matter in a serious way was on March 6, 1953. A member of the Board, Frank Dreyer of Colorado, raised the issue of the practicality of the broad scope of CCA operations and questioned the soundness of the Swisshome mill. Secretary Clifford Miller joined Dreyer and stated his opinion that the company should study "at once and very carefully the effect of CCA's operating rather unsuccessfully a great number of small departments and sidelines" that detracted from the more substantial departments of petroleum, feed, and fertilizer. Miller suggested disposing of some departments and urged that consideration be given to confining "future operations to the developing, processing, and distribution of a limited number of relatively important items, possibly as few as petroleum, feeds, and fertilizer." [16] Here was an expression of the belief that CCA should confine its business to a limited number of commodities which, on the basis of experience, could be handled successfully and were important in farm production costs. Miller seemed to be moving perilously close to applying the same criterion to a cooperative as to any ordinary business, namely, figures on ledger sheets. The company's financial condition, so it seemed at the moment, was more important than giving service or generating a cooperative spirit among patrons. Cowden maintained that the broader program had many advantages; it was evident that he was not ready to retreat. Nonetheless, the attitude of officials of the Farm Credit Administration and of some members of the Board and the difficult financial situation in which CCA found itself in 1952 and 1953 helped to force the wholesale away from handling consumer goods and toward confining its activities largely to the farm supply field.

Of course, more than principle was involved. The dollars-and-cents record of some CCA operations presented a dismal picture: The vegetable cannery had lost $244,435 in the five years ending August 31, 1952, and during the same time the alfalfa plant at Longmont showed a deficit of $112,414. The Swisshome mill had savings of $606,-487 from 1947 to 1952, but this would have been wiped out if an appropriate share of the company's general business expenses, including interest on an investment of $2,500,000, had been charged against it.[17]

Meanwhile, every effort was being made to improve CCA's operations in order to reach a position where the Farm Credit Administration would consider approving a $5,000,000 loan for the nitrogen plant. Cowden explained to the Board in June, 1953, that expenses had been cut by $25,000 a month. These savings had resulted from reducing the field force, closing the grocery warehouse at Aberdeen, South Dakota, and other reductions. But these developments were not enough to satisfy the officials of the Farm Credit Administration. Fox reported that the Central Bank for Cooperatives had asked that

---

[16] Board of Directors, Minutes, March 5–6, 1953.
[17] Financial Comments, undated, 1953, CCA Miscellaneous File.

a person be designated to work with the Wichita bank and CCA in order to analyze and improve the company's over-all business position.[18] Present at the meeting to consult with the Board, Merrifield explained that CCA's operating expenses were very high; some departments were not producing savings and were therefore objectionable from a lender's viewpoint; there was no economic justification for a grocery department; and the farm machinery program was doing more harm than good. Merrifield repeated that the Wichita bank would not as yet make any commitment on a loan for the nitrogen plant.[19]

It was evident from Merrifield's remarks that CCA could expect no help from the Banks for Cooperatives on the nitrogen project, at least until it met the operational requirements of the banks' officials. In the light of Merrifield's position, the Board voted to close the Grocery Department and to liquidate the inventory and equipment as soon and as advantageously as possible. The grocery program was actually discontinued on September 1, 1953.

Problems of financing the nitrogen plant placed severe strains on CCA's management, especially on Cowden. But there is no evidence either in the public or the private records that he ever considered giving up. Neither frightened nor panicked by events, he moved ahead in calm confidence. Part of Cowden's strength lay in his firm belief that the patrons of CCA would stand behind the wholesale they had helped to build. Moreover, he believed that eventually the Banks for Cooperatives would extend the needed credit. Referring to forthcoming meetings with bank officials, Cowden wrote to members of the Board on September 29, 1953, that bank representatives might require stipulations that would be difficult to meet, "but in the end I think they will approve the application for the nitrate plant loan."

However, the financial crisis seemed to be worsening. Construction at Lawrence progressed during 1953, but the funds raised by selling certificates of indebtedness were nearly exhausted. Unless additional financing could be found at once, building at the plant site would have to be halted by February, 1954.[20] Such a development would certainly cause doubt in the minds of prospective investors and discourage the sale of CCA's securities. In addition, returns from the ordinary

[18] Board of Directors, Minutes, June 16–17, 1953.
[19] *Ibid.*
[20] Board of Directors, Minutes, November 30, 1953.

operations were everything but favorable. Beginning with the new fiscal year on September 1, 1953, CCA's operating losses reached $870,-000 during the next five months. A decline in over-all margins and the need for capital funds presented problems to CCA's management that would have plagued a Solomon.

Cowden was still depending on the Banks for Cooperatives, and his faith was finally rewarded. Following much correspondence, many telephone conversations, and numerous conferences, an arrangement was finally worked out whereby the Wichita Bank for Cooperatives promised to loan CCA $5,000,000 to help complete the Lawrence plant, provided CCA met certain strict requirements. These conditions were incorporated in a Memorandum of Understanding agreed to on October 22, 1953.

Before the loan would be approved CCA had to agree to sell $500,-000 of common stock, $1,000,000 of preferred stock, and $2,500,000 of additional certificates of indebtedness. Such measures were necessary, bank officials said, to strengthen the company's capital position. Also, CCA was to sell the Newcastle refinery, the Swisshome mill, and the Eagle Grove rendering plant. Informally, bank officials said that CCA should make a permanent reduction in its inventories of roughly $500,000. Moreover, the Cooperative Farm Chemicals Association must set up a separate board of directors, and CCA had to guarantee all CFCA loans. Finally, CCA must agree to have in its offices a representative of the Central Bank for Cooperatives who would have full access to company records and the right to attend meetings of the Board.

On November 25 a conference was held in Cowden's office between staff members of CCA and the Wichita Bank for Cooperatives, including its President Merrifield, at which time these requirements were fully discussed. Five days later Cowden explained the situation to the Board of Directors. The Board quickly approved having a resident bank representative in the CCA offices, and James R. Isleib, already appointed by the Central Bank for Cooperatives, was brought into the meeting and introduced to the Board. Isleib explained that bank officials thought CCA had expanded too rapidly, was using too much borrowed capital, and had been slow to discontinue unsuccessful enterprises. The purpose of his appointment, Isleib said, was to keep the bank fully informed on CCA's business condition. It should be added that Isleib's presence was to assure the bank that CCA's affairs moved in the direction the Farm Credit Administration thought desirable. Isleib, though, did not have any management functions.

However sound these requirements may have been from a purely business standpoint, they were nonetheless humiliating to a firm that was doing more than $80,000,000 in business annually. But pride could not stand in the company's way to financial stability. CCA's borrowings from the Banks for Cooperatives were then too large to permit any other course. The bank's main conditions centered around raising additional permanent capital by selling more common and preferred stock, getting rid of unprofitable enterprises, and reducing inventory.

After Cowden explained the situation, the Board immediately moved to meet the bank's demands. Besides accepting the general conditions, it voted to sell the Swisshome mill at the earliest possible date, to close the Coffeyville soybean plant temporarily, and to offer the Eagle Grove rendering plant for sale. It was estimated that CCA could free as much as $4,000,000 for capital investment elsewhere by getting rid of these and other enterprises.[21] The cannery at Scottsbluff had already been closed and placed on the market, and the alfalfa plant at Longmont was not being operated in 1953 because of the low price of meal. Homer Young explained to the shareholders a few days after the Board's decision to sell several properties that "we can not continue to operate non-paying plants."[22] Finally, on November 30, the Farm Credit Administration officially approved the $5,000,000 loan, to be made by the Wichita Bank for Cooperatives to CFCA, $4,052,-700 for facilities and $947,300 for operating capital.[23]

CCA met another of the bank's requirements in December when shareholders voted to set up a separate board of directors for CFCA. However, some of the same men sat on both boards, and CCA continued to control its subsidiary by maintaining a majority of the CFCA stock and directors. Part of the reason behind the Farm Credit Administration's insistence upon a separate board for CFCA was to spread administrative responsibility. J. D. Lawrence, deputy governor of the Farm Credit Administration, told Cowden in December, 1953, that it would be a mistake for him to act also as chairman of CFCA.

---

[21] *Ibid.*
[22] *Cooperative Consumer*, December 15, 1953, 5.
[23] B. F. Viehmann to Fred Merrifield, November 30, 1953; Cowden to Merrifield, December 14, 1953.

Cowden deeply resented the implications of Lawrence's remark and responded, "Maybe you want me to resign from all of my jobs," to which Lawrence replied, "No." [24]

Establishment of a separate board of directors for CFCA left completely unanswered the question of changes in CCA's management. Although officials of the Central Bank for Cooperatives had been opposed to Cowden's being a member of the Board of Directors as well as the Board's president and general manager, no change had been made in the top administrative positions. However, on February 16, 1954, bank representatives met with the Directors and insisted that someone be named as first assistant general manager. Before bank officials went into the meeting Cowden suggested to the Directors that Bruce McCully be appointed to the new position. J. D. Lawrence later told the Board in executive session that it was a serious weakness to have a member of the Board serve both as president and general manager, and that this was "very objectionable from their [Farm Credit Administration's] standpoint." Lawrence's statement amounted to an ultimatum to which, obviously, Cowden had previously agreed. Consequently, a resolution was promptly passed by the Board, naming McCully as first assistant general manager in accord with Cowden's expressed wishes. The idea was that McCully, who had been with CCA since 1930, would gradually assume more and more of Cowden's duties as general manager.[25]

The tightening-up process that the Banks for Cooperatives had required continued relentlessly during 1954. Operating expenses were cut to the bone. Employees were laid off, the cooperative school program was reduced, some warehouses were closed, and mileage was lowered for fieldmen. Even telephone costs were cut. By February, expenses had been reduced by $76,100; the aim was monthly savings of $100,000.[26] A number of properties were disposed of as quickly as possible. The Newcastle refinery was sold on February 1 for $400,000, resulting in a loss of $136,000. In April the Longmont alfalfa plant and the Scottsbluff cannery were sold. Other properties brought total sales to $663,227 between September 1, 1953, and April 13, 1954. This was $59,332 less than the book value and only about half the original cost of the facilities. Arrangements were also being made to get out

---

[24] Cowden, Memorandum of discussion with Lawrence, December 29, 1953; Cowden to Lawrence, December 30, 1953.
[25] Board of Directors, Minutes, February 15–16, 1954.
[26] Cowden to Fieldmen, April 8, 1954.

of the farm machinery business by turning over all inventory on May 1 to the Cockshutt Plow Company, which had assumed control of the plant and equipment of the unsuccessful Cooperative Farm Machinery Association. As of December 31, 1953, CCA had $2,430,000 invested in farm machinery, and liquidation proved to be extremely slow.[27] It was not until February, 1956, that all of the farm equipment inventory was sold and CCA was entirely out of the business.[28] Rigid controls had been placed on inventories, and an intensive campaign was started to sell additional preferred shares. All of this was necessary to meet CCA's loan and repayment commitments to the Wichita Bank for Cooperatives.

The disposition of several manufacturing plants, especially Swisshome, was distressing to Cowden. He suggested that fieldmen should not discuss this matter unless local directors or managers raised questions.[29] The Swisshome properties were not actually sold until November, 1955, at which time Cowden declared that he was "terribly disappointed" that sale of the lumber mill had become necessary.[30] The mill had given Cowden something dramatic to discuss before cooperative groups, but he had usually avoided the economics of the operation. It had not been a sound enterprise at any time, in part because the mill turned out nothing but fir lumber and it was not easy to sell a carload of exclusively fir lumber to the small cooperative yards. This meant that CCA had to buy lumber from other mills to fill out most orders.

In explaining the disposition of some manufacturing plants and lines of commodities that did not pay, Cowden told patrons that CCA was acting like a wise farmer "who shifts his land use from wheat or corn to pasture or back again, where it will yield the best returns." [31] But Cowden failed to mention that CCA had taken this action under pressure from the Farm Credit Administration.

At a meeting on February 16, 1954, Lawrence explained to the Board in detail why it had been necessary for the Farm Credit Administration to place such strict and exacting requirements on CCA. He emphasized that CCA must meet its obligations and the bank's

---

[27] Board of Directors, Minutes, February 15–16, 1954.
[28] Board of Directors, Minutes, February 27–28, 1956.
[29] Cowden to Fieldmen, March 30, 1954.
[30] Board of Directors, Minutes, November 8, 1955; Cowden, "The Farmers' Own Program," address delivered November 29, 1955.
[31] *Heart-to-Heart Talk*, April 30, 1954.

demands or face receivership.[32] Here, at last, the awful word had been used frankly and openly. It was not likely that the member associations would have permitted such an eventuality or that CCA could not have weathered the storm somehow. The depreciated value of its fixed assets was then more than $27,000,000, and total assets exceeded $66,000,000. At that time, however, loans from the Banks for Cooperatives amounted to about $20,000,000. But the fact that the word "receivership" had been used indicated a crisis of unprecedented proportions.

By its rapid expansion and its failure to build up enough permanent capital CCA had got itself into a position where its creditors could apply preponderant influence on general policy matters. J. D. Lawrence was no J. P. Morgan, but his power over CCA was as effective as that exerted by Morgan over companies to which his bank had made loans in the early twentieth century. Officials of the Farm Credit Administration were determined, and rightfully so, to exercise every prerogative to protect their loans. At the same time it should be said that the FCA was also vitally concerned about helping CCA and did everything it thought wise to improve the wholesale's operations. There may have been a difference of opinion in FCA and CCA offices over what practical policies were good for the cooperative, but there was no disagreement on the ultimate end — a strong regional wholesale to serve the needs of farmers.

In order to ease the financial situation the Board voted to sell part of its interest in the CFCA. At its meeting on February 15, 1954, the Directors voted to issue $8,000,000 worth of common stock, of which three fourths would be held by CCA and one fourth would be sold.[33] On April 28 the Central Farmers Fertilizer Company of Chicago bought the $2,000,000 in common stock and became one-fourth owner of the plant. In addition, beginning early in 1954 CCA staged an intensive campaign to get member associations to transfer their certificates of indebtedness to new 4 per cent preferred shares in order to increase the permanent capital.

During the spring of 1954 rumors were widespread that CCA was deep in financial trouble. The question was often asked, "Will the nitrogen plant ever be completed?" While Cowden admitted that CCA had tremendous problems, he wrote to the fieldmen on March

---

[32] Board of Directors, Minutes, February 16, 1954.
[33] *Ibid.*

30, "I have no doubts about the future of CCA." In an effort to buoy sagging spirits in the field — some fieldmen were wondering if their jobs would continue — Cowden wrote that CCA had experienced some dark days before, but that "determination, team spirit and righteousness [had] won." CCA had always met its challenges, he wrote, and within a few years everyone would look back on the victory of 1954 "because of the rightness of the cause and the determination of every member of the team."

Meanwhile, construction at Lawrence proceeded nearly on schedule, which called for completion of the main units by July 1, 1954. Throughout the spring CCA pushed the sale of fertilizer among local associations, preparatory to the beginning of operations. Although some delays occurred, the plant was in partial operation by September. The facilities had an annual rated capacity of 83,000 tons of ammonium nitrate, 13,200 tons of anhydrous ammonia, and 13,200 tons of solutions.

Dedication ceremonies were held on August 31. It was a beautiful day, and nearly 12,000 visitors arrived to inspect the plant — an "orderly silver-painted array of towers, tanks, and buildings" — to eat barbecue, and to hear the glowing tributes by several speakers. Cowden set the theme of the dedication with an address entitled, "For Peace and Plenty." He paid tribute "to the countless men and women who provided the rivulets of devotion that grew into brooks, then into creeks, and finally merged into the mighty river of force that made possible the largest and most complex industrial plant ever built by farmers' cooperatives." He then discussed the value of the nitrogen plant to farmers in the Midwest. "This plant — built by farmers, operated by farmers — has a noble destiny. It is an instrument of peace and plenty." [34]

Although only a few months earlier the ugly word "receivership" had been bandied in some quarters, CCA's position by the fall of 1954 had improved considerably. As Cowden put it, CCA was "over the hump." Loans due to the Banks for Cooperatives had been reduced from nearly $20,800,000 in January to $11,863,500 by August 31. Most encouraging was the completion of the nitrogen plant that, in all probability, would produce good margins. Writing to a number of cooperative leaders on September 13, Cowden explained some of CCA's recent difficulties and then concluded: "I think we are all glad

---

[34] *Cooperative Consumer*, September 15, 1954, 11.

now that we weren't satisfied with handling fertilizer on a brokerage basis and that we took whatever chance was necessary in order to secure a farmer-owned nitrogen plant." [35]

Throughout the next year CCA continued to operate on a rather conservative basis and paid off much of its bank loans. By March 31, 1955, loans from the Banks for Cooperatives were down to $8,734,447, and by November to $4,188,000. By the spring of 1955 bank officials were encouraging CCA to pay off its certificates of indebtedness, which stood at $19,233,100, rather than to lower the bank debt. [36] But Cowden wanted to make sure that CCA would never again be subjected to the credit strain of the previous eighteen months. Cowden also wanted to reduce the banks' friendly interference with CCA business affairs and to get Isleib out of the headquarters office.

During the two years Isleib acted as the banks' resident representative, relations between him and CCA officials generally had been good. However, at times Isleib and Cowden had sharp differences. In one memo Cowden recorded that he had found Isleib in "a very bad mood" and that they had argued over a number of things. [37] Consequently, on November 28 the Board asked the Farm Credit Administration to rescind the Memorandum of Understanding that placed a bank representative in CCA's office. The presence of such a representative, the Board said, was frequently "misconstrued by the membership." Further, the conditions that seemed to require the representative no longer existed. Governor Robert B. Tootell agreed, and Isleib's work with CCA terminated on December 31, 1955. [38]

Throughout 1955 Cowden attempted to get the Banks for Cooperatives to provide long-term financing for CCA, perhaps as much as $30,000,000, so that the wholesale could be more independent and flexible in its operations. But FCA would not agree, [39] and CCA continued for several years to rely on short-term credit from the Wichita bank, budgeted for specific purposes. At a meeting of the Board on February 28, 1956, Merrifield commended CCA for the improvements that had been made in the company's financial structure. Until the Cooperative Farm Chemicals Association began to show larger earnings and further reduced its loans, however, the Wichita bank must

---

[35] Cowden to M. W. Thatcher, September 13, 1954.
[36] Merrifield to Cowden, March 11, 1955.
[37] Cowden, Memorandum, November 15, 1954.
[38] Cowden to Tootell, December 2, 1955; Tootell to Cowden, December 8, 1955.
[39] Cowden, Memorandum, April 29, 1955.

continue certain restrictions on CCA's fiscal operations. These included a guarantee of CFCA loans, the bank's approval for large cash disbursements, and a limit on outstanding certificates of indebtedness.[40]

Earnings of the nitrogen plant developed somewhat more slowly during the first two years of operation than CCA officials had hoped. Neither 1955 nor 1956 were particularly good years. In fact, so-called "start-up" deficits of several hundred thousand dollars occurred. During the year ending August 31, 1955, the plant was in full operation only after January, and production reached 51,282 tons of nitrogen products. The next year output climbed to 92,708 tons, but sales were under expectations because of widespread drought in CCA's territory. Prices declined, and storage problems developed. A drop in price was beneficial to farmers and was one of the reasons for building the plant, but it meant small margins. By 1957, however, production and earnings were both up; net savings at the nitrogen plant were $733,416.[41]

In the midst of the company's worst financial crisis, CCA celebrated its silver jubilee. There were no signs of discouragement when about 3,000 patrons gathered in Kansas City on December 1, 2, and 3, 1953, six weeks before CCA was actually twenty-five years old. Employees had been paid partially in silver dollars to emphasize the occasion, and a portrait of Cowden that had been authorized by the Board was unveiled before an admiring crowd. Despite CCA's critical financial situation, Cowden and the entire staff radiated outward confidence and talked in terms of the value of the completed nitrogen plant to farmers in CCA-land. A pamphlet containing congratulatory messages from Secretary of Agriculture Ezra Taft Benson and from other national and world cooperative leaders was distributed,[42] and *25 Co-op Years, How Farmers Built Consumers Cooperative Association* was published to show in words and pictures how CCA had developed.

While CCA faced its many problems in financing the nitrogen plant in 1953 and 1954, plans got under way for a new headquarters. The old building at 10th and Oak streets that the company had occupied in 1944 was entirely inadequate. Even after the Mutual Building at 13th and Oak was rented in 1948, space was at a premium, and office arrangements were neither convenient nor efficient. At its March meeting in 1953 the Board discussed moving to the edge of the city

---

[40] Board of Directors, Minutes, February 27–28, 1956.
[41] *29th Annual Report*, 1957, 13.
[42] *Cooperative Consumer*, December 15, 1953; *25th Annual Report*, 1953.

where there would be room for an adequate office building, perhaps a cooperative college, and other facilities.[43] Following a great deal of study, during which many sites were investigated, twenty acres of land were purchased on North Oak Trafficway, the route followed by U.S. Highway 169, and immediately north of the North Kansas City boundary. The land was on the hills just above the Missouri River bottoms. In July, 1955, the contract was let to construct the new office building. About fifteen months later, on October 26, 1956, employees moved into CCA's new home. It provided nearly 63,000 square feet of space, was modern in every way, including air conditioning, and housed about 375 employees. Cowden's office compared favorably with that of any business executive in Kansas City. Financed through the Employee Retirement Fund, the land and building cost $1,500,000.

The "Battle of 1954" had been crucial but by meeting its problems and getting the nitrogen plant into successful operation, CCA greatly added to its prestige and to the services it could provide farmers. Furthermore, the struggle to finance this new facility had forced the wholesale to analyze its entire operations more closely than ever before. The pressures that forced CCA to eliminate several departments of doubtful economic value either to patrons or to CCA were at first opposed and resented, but the results proved to be good for CCA business. With few exceptions, mainly appliances, true consumer items were no longer handled by CCA, and emphasis was given to the farm supply and service field. It had taken CCA more than a quarter of a century to find its true position in the agricultural economy of the Midwest. Indeed, there was now doubt if the word "consumer" had any rightful place in CCA's name.

By the late 1950's CCA's officials began to give much more attention to general farm problems and the role cooperatives could play in solving them. The distribution of $97,622,533 worth of commodities in 1956, almost entirely to be used in farm production, was CCA's answer to the cost-price squeeze and to other economic difficulties that beset farmers.

---

[43] Board of Directors, Minutes, March 5–6, 1953.

14

Maturity and Expansion

B Y THE LATE 1950's CCA was entering a new phase of its development; both the company's physical facilities and its ledger sheets reflected business maturity and prosperity. From modern headquarters that would have been a credit to any corporate enterprise, CCA officials managed a vast domain of refineries, oil wells, pipelines, grease and paint factories, fertilizer plants, feed mills, warehouses, transportation, and other properties. In 1957 the consolidated volume of CCA and its subsidiaries reached $113,348,657, passing the $100,000,000 mark for the first time. According to *Fortune* magazine, the company was 327th among the nation's 500 largest industrial corporations. It ranked among the half-dozen biggest cooperatives, and probably was Number One in value of assets. This growth had all occurred within twenty-nine years. It is no wonder that there was a fierce pride and loyalty among old-time employees and administrators who had played a part in this development.

With growth in size CCA had assumed many of the characteristics of big business in modern America. It had a retirement plan for its 1,785 employees and in 1958 added group insurance. The Economic Research Division under Gordon Leith was producing information on which to base managerial decisions, and the Technical Research Division's work was constantly being expanded to improve CO-OP products. An increasing amount of care was going into the preparation of annual budgets, under the direction of Assistant Treasurer D. E. Ewing. Meetings with economists from the nearby land-grant universities were becoming more frequent as CCA officials studied the general position of agriculture in their trade territory and analyzed the role CCA could play in helping farmers. Much greater emphasis was also being placed on advertising and public relations.

Accompanying CCA's great expansion and the development of improved management and business organization were some signs of maturity. Although CCA was not yet thirty years old, there was frequent discussion of the need for a history of the company. This indicated a belief by management that the wholesale had reached a place where there was something worth recording.

The first official mention of Cowden's retirement came in 1958 when he told the Board that, since he had nearly reached the retirement age of sixty-five, he must soon be relieved of many responsibilities. The very thought of Cowden retiring must have emphasized to old-timers that a new era was at hand. In the minds of many people CCA and Howard A. Cowden were almost synonymous.[1] Another change in the offing was construction of new laboratory, factory, and warehouse facilities in North Kansas City, which began in 1963, and the ultimate abandonment of the properties at 1500 and 1721 Iron Street, where the old Union Oil Company had started operations.

Some changes and modifications in the annual meetings also presented a new image. At these yearly sessions much time and attention had always been devoted to practical business affairs, and this continued to be the case, but by the late 1950's patrons were exposed to a level of culture that would have been scoffed at by the depression-ridden farmers of the 1930's. It was then expected that members would be entertained by singers of western ballads who had more nerve than talent. But in 1958 patrons were treated to an exhibit of paintings borrowed from the William Rockhill Nelson Gallery of Art, and the highlight of the entertainment at the 32nd annual meeting in December, 1960, was a performance of the Kansas City Philharmonic

---

[1] Board of Directors, Minutes, February 25–26, 1958.

Orchestra. This may have been the first time a major orchestra played before virtually an all-farm audience.

In December, 1957, shareholders adopted a new trademark and identification program that gave CCA products a new look. This change reflected the new emphasis on merchandising and distribution. An interesting aside, which tells much about what was happening in CCA as the sixties approached, was the fact that fieldmen were expected to wear suits instead of sport shirts or other informal attire at their annual sales conferences.

Despite the increase in size and the signs of sophistication that were unknown in the company's early years, CCA continued to maintain close relations with patrons at the grass roots. This was accomplished through advertisements, radio and television programs, the *Cooperative Consumer* (which had a circulation of more than 300,-000 in 1960), the annual meetings, and in other ways. But the most important and effective work was done by personal contact. CCA's fieldmen were, of course, highly significant in presenting the wholesale's program, but officials from the front offices spent what must have seemed to most business leaders an inordinate amount of time talking to, and working with, local cooperative groups. The annual district meetings were particularly useful opportunities for Cowden, McCully, Young, Fox, Hamil, and other company officers to keep in close touch with patrons. Cowden continually stressed the importance of grass-roots support; CCA, he maintained, had always been a people's organization. One year Homer Young attended each of the eighteen district meetings throughout CCA territory and was out of the office at least three days a week over a period of six weeks. CCA's executives, it is obvious, did not confine their work to an administrative chain of command, but consulted frequently with the patrons on whom they depended for support.

One new problem that accompanied CCA's industrial growth was that of labor relations. So long as the company only did a brokerage business that required only office workers and employed a few men in the oil-compounding plant, there was no need for union representation. Cowden maintained a close association with employees and tried to encourage the development of a happy CCA family, all working toward a common goal. To do this the personal achievements, marriages, deaths, and other events in the lives of CCA employees were often noted. Even after the number of employees increased in the grease and paint plants and in the warehouses and transportation services, no unions were organized. Attempts to unionize workers at the Phillipsburg refinery had failed.

When the Coffeyville refinery was purchased in 1943 no CCA workers were unionized, but acquisition of this plant brought with it a well-established union. Later, the truck drivers and employees in the grease and paint plant in North Kansas City voted to affiliate with Local 41 of the Teamsters Union. Workers at the St. Joseph fertilizer plant and at the Lawrence nitrogen plant were also unionized. Consequently, while CCA had not faced any problems of dealing with organized labor during its first fifteen years, by the late 1950's hundreds of its workers were employed under contracts arrived at through collective bargaining.

CCA had relatively little difficulty in labor-management relations, however, and up to 1963 it was confronted with only one serious and prolonged strike. There had been a number of short strikes and labor disputes, but these were relatively minor. The most serious conflict developed in 1958 when the truck drivers and workers in the grease and paint plant at North Kansas City struck on April 18. CCA truck drivers at Enid also joined the strike, and the unions posted pickets at CCA facilities in Coffeyville, Lawrence, and St. Joseph.

The dispute was mainly over wages. The union wanted a 13-cent-an-hour increase for warehousemen in North Kansas City, while CCA offered 8 cents. Truck drivers asked for higher mileage rates, which would give them about $56 additional per month, plus a slight increase in some categories of hourly pay. CCA proposed a mileage increase of $18.75. Negotiators for CCA claimed that the new wage demands were unreasonable, but the union insisted that wages at North Kansas City were low compared to other CCA warehouses and that truck drivers had to drive an excessive number of miles to earn decent salaries.

CCA supervisory personnel kept the paint and grease plants in operation throughout the strike, but the company was forced to buy some grease from noncooperative sources. The union was successful in shutting down trucking operations even though eleven truck drivers were dismissed. To eliminate picketing at its other plants, restraining orders were obtained to stop picketing at CCA factories outside of North Kansas City. On May 14, after nearly a month on strike, the drivers at Enid went back to work and voted against continuing their affiliation with the Teamsters Union. Through a series of letters Cowden appealed directly to workers. He explained that CCA was concerned about its employees and had always paid good wages, and he expressed sorrow for the hardships experienced by families of workers on strike. Cowden blamed the pressure of union representatives for the continued strike and said the CCA had jobs for those who wished to return.[2]

The union also sought popular backing and issued a statement entitled, "Why Are We on Strike at Co-op?" The workers took full responsibility for the strike, indicating that CCA was failing in its efforts to divide union members from their leadership; they argued that wages were less in North Kansas City than in Coffeyville or Lawrence. The statement concluded by asking the question, "Don't you think management could have stopped this with a little sincere co-operation instead of so much bullheadedness?"[3]

Following several weeks of fruitless negotiations, CCA notified the striking employees that they were being replaced by men who were willing to work. Cowden said this decision had been made reluctantly and only after it was clear that CCA and the union could not reach agreement on a new contract. Before a showdown occurred, the union agreed to accept CCA's original offer, and the strike ended.

There is no indication that CCA was more or less friendly to organized labor than other large business and industrial enterprises in America. Over the years the company had built up a loyalty and *esprit de corps*, particularly among office and field workers, which was fairly strong. The insurance, retirement, and other welfare programs had done much to achieve this end. But in a crisis such as that of 1958, management would fight hard to resist demands that it considered harmful to CCA's over-all development. When the truck drivers insisted on higher wages than CCA thought feasible, Cowden declared that such increases would price CCA out of the transportation business. This, he would not tolerate.[4]

---

[2] Cowden to All Employees, April 25, May 19, June 9, and July 11, 1958, CCA Files.
[3] Statement in CCA Files.
[4] For accounts of the 1958 strike see the following memoranda in the CCA Files: Young to Earl Bailey, April 21; Bailey to Young, April 23; Fred Claxton to Cowden, May 19, June 3 and 18; *Cooperative Consumer*, April 30, May 15 and 29, 1958.

Even though CCA had grown into the $100,000,000 class by 1957 there was no thought among company officials of leveling off. Difficulties encountered in financing the nitrogen plant did not scare or discourage CCA, and its executives looked ahead to bigger and better things. In February, 1957, the Board authorized management to move ahead with an expanded feed manufacturing program.[5] The next year a new plant was opened at Ida Grove, Iowa, and other mills were completed in 1960 at Muncie, Kansas, and Fremont, Nebraska. Additional plants were then either being built or in the planning stage.

Expansion in fertilizer production was even more rapid. Facilities at Lawrence were scarcely completed before it was found that they were inadequate. The Board voted to enlarge the plant in 1959 at a cost of $5,200,000.[6] In 1960 McCully told the Directors that more nitrogen was needed, and he proposed constructing an $8,000,000 anhydrous ammonia plant at Hastings, Nebraska. Without the slightest financial strain, this plant was completed in less than two years and was dedicated on April 25, 1962.[7] Meanwhile, in 1959, CCA acquired 75 per cent interest in an ammonium phosphate plant at Joplin, Missouri. During 1960 and 1961 eleven fertilizer blending plants were built in CCA's territory. At the same time oil refining facilities were improved, and the exploration and production programs were pushed ahead. In 1960 alone, $4,500,000 was spent to acquire proven leases, mostly in Texas.[8]

All of these facilities were added without any financial difficulties. This ease must have been a pleasant relief to CCA officials who had gone through the dark days of 1953 and 1954. Most of the funds for growth in assets came from operations. Large net savings, depreciation, and oil depletion allowances were the main sources of capital funds. There was also an adequate demand for company securities. In any event, CCA was no longer beholden to bankers. Both CCA and the Cooperative Refinery Association consistently ended each fiscal year after 1957 without any bank loans, and the CFCA had only relatively modest outstanding bank obligations. Even though CCA paid increasingly large patronage refunds in cash, there were enough savings remaining to provide, when added to the other sources of funds,

---

[5] Board of Directors, Minutes, May 27–28, 1957.
[6] Board of Directors, Minutes, November 20 and December 1, 1959; *32nd Annual Report*, 1960, 11.
[7] *Cooperative Consumer*, April 30, 1962, 8–9.
[8] *32nd Annual Report*, 1960, 11.

for capital expansion. Total consolidated savings reached $8,869,000 in 1960 and jumped to $14,900,000 the following year.

Petroleum products continued to account for most of CCA's business, although their predominance gradually declined after 1957. In that year sales of refined fuels, greases, and oil made up about 70 per cent of the total dollar volume. With the expansion of fertilizer and feed facilities, however, petroleum commodities dropped to 47 per cent of CCA's business by 1962. Fertilizer, which was coming up fast, accounted for 23 per cent, feed 13 per cent, and other farm supplies, mainly paint, appliances, steel grain bins and feed tanks, twine, dairy equipment, and lumber, 17 per cent. Because margins in petroleum were subject to wide fluctuations, more reliance on other basic commodities helped CCA to level out its savings.[9]

After 1955, total volume moved steadily and sometimes dramatically upward. By 1961 it reached $193,676,000, more than double the figure of six years earlier. Savings for the year amounted to $14,889,000, of which $2,404,000 was refunded to member cooperatives. Cash refunds paid to patrons from 1929 to the end of the fiscal year 1961 totaled $8,296,000. This amount exceeded the total volume done in 1940. By any business standards, CCA's was an outstanding record.

It must be emphasized that by the late 1950's CCA was committed to continued growth and larger size. According to Cowden, size was necessary in order to serve farmers better. Cowden wrote in the annual report of 1959: "I urge upon farmers that they think about their regional cooperative in terms of bigness and be proud of the bigness it has attained. We must be big to be effective. We must be big to protect farmers. We must be big to survive." [10] Unlike some old-line agrarians, Cowden recognized that big business had become a permanent part of the American economy, and he wasted no time advocating a return to a simpler existence of some bygone generation. Large-scale, corporate enterprise, Cowden insisted, was not interested in the welfare of agriculture, therefore farmers should build large cooperatives as a means of protecting their own interests. In other words, size could be a virtue rather than a curse if the power, opportunities, and advantages associated with bigness were based on the principle of service.

[9] *34th Annual Report*, 1962, 6.
[10] *29th Annual Report*, 1959, 4.

By the late 1950's CCA officials began giving much greater attention to general farm problems and to the role cooperatives could play in their solution. Back in 1930 and 1931, Cowden had talked about cooperatives' being a kind of practical farm relief, but throughout most of CCA's history the broader aspects of agricultural policy had been neglected. Emphasis upon building the company had taken precedence over consideration of the cooperative movement as a factor in the over-all solution to farm problems. Cowden and other CCA officials had quietly backed the government's agricultural programs, but their support had been passive rather than active; they did not want to involve CCA and the local associations in farm politics. However, after 1957 CCA turned its attention to general farm problems and emphasized the contributions that large and efficient cooperatives might be expected to make. The *Cooperative Consumer* carried many articles on this theme.

The cost-price squeeze suffered by farmers after 1952 and the popular attack on the federal agricultural programs were the main factors that stirred Cowden and CCA into action. In 1951 net income to farm operators reached more than $16 billion, but by 1957 it had declined to less than $12 billion. The main causes for this decline were a drop in farm prices and a rise in production expenses, which climbed by more than $1,200 million in the same period. With prices dropping and operating expenses rising, farmers found themselves in a harsh and destructive cost-price squeeze. The federal price-support programs came under bitter criticism as surpluses piled up in government warehouses. In 1959, *Life* magazine called the situation "a national scandal," and in his book, *The Great Farm Problem*, published the same year, William H. Peterson argued that farm difficulties were really caused by government intervention. In the light of these circumstances, where should CCA stand? What action should it take?

For the first time CCA's Board of Directors and shareholders began giving close attention to the broader problems of agriculture. When President Eisenhower, in April, 1956, vetoed a bill designed to peg prices of major crops at 90 per cent of parity, Cowden pointed to the President's action as evidence that farmers could not depend on federal programs. "It is not easy to solve the current farm problem in Washington," he said.[11]

In a "Heart-to-Heart Talk" distributed widely in August, 1957,

[11] *Cooperative Consumer*, April 16, 1956, 1.

Cowden asked the question, "What Course for American Agriculture?" This analysis of the agricultural situation, later revised and published in pamphlet form, was probably the most comprehensive discussion of over-all farm problems presented by Cowden up to that time. He explained that the cost-price squeeze was "one of the most pressing issues of our time." Federal price-support programs, he said, had failed largely because they could not be removed from politics or "kept aloof from sectional and partisan pressures." Even with the many years of government help farmers had received, they still did not get parity prices or parity income. Cowden discussed how farmers sold their products — except those under price supports — in a free market that was determined by supply and demand, while they bought supplies from industries that operated under set or administered prices. Farmers, he wrote, had no way to pass increased costs along to consumers or any effective means of limiting supply in the face of price declines. On the other hand, labor and industry had improved their position through organization and various protective devices, and it was up to farmers to strengthen their bargaining power. Lack of bargaining power was the farmers' greatest weakness, and until they could bargain effectively, Cowden thought, there was little chance for fundamental improvement in agriculture. Since government programs had at best been only partially successful, he insisted that cooperatives were the means by which farmers could solve their marketing and purchasing problems. He not only advocated greatly expanded cooperative buying and selling, but he envisioned the development of cooperative machinery to regulate production and handle surpluses.

There was nothing new about Cowden's analysis of farm problems or in his suggestion that cooperatives play a greater role in trying to solve them. However, the degree of emphasis placed upon the general farm situation was new in CCA history. Beginning in 1956 the Board of Directors and shareholders regularly discussed these problems and passed resolutions directed toward their solution. In 1956 CCA's shareholders declared that strong cooperatives were more positive in their benefits than government programs.[12] The next year they resolved: "Through cooperatives, farmers can build economic strength and improve their bargaining power. While our cooperatives are not large enough yet to match the power of big business and big labor, they

---

[12] Shareholders' meeting, Minutes, November 29, 1956.

must be developed with such a goal in mind. We must either have strong cooperatives in this country or surrender to the concept of an agriculture dominated by corporate industry and giant commercial farms." Then the resolution asked that the national government give greater support and encouragement to cooperatives.[13] In 1959, CCA's shareholders declared that cooperatives represented the only kind of power that could help farmers — economic power.[14] CCA's officials frankly admitted that cooperatives had not yet "attained the power and prestige necessary for full effectiveness," but they insisted that they represented the farmer's best hope.[15]

It was one thing to talk in general terms about cooperatives helping farmers to solve their basic problems, but it was something else to implement positive programs to achieve this objective. So far, CCA had confined its services to the supply field. Any savings to farmers in the cost of production contributed just that much to raising net farm income. CCA had kept abreast of the rapid agricultural changes and had concentrated its activities in those areas of cost that had been developing so rapidly. Since the old Union Oil Company had been formed, a mechanical, biological, and chemical revolution had occurred in American agriculture. In 1929 most of the energy used on farms had been supplied by horses, but by 1960 tractors had replaced animal power, and the horse was an object of curiosity on most American farms. When Cowden opened his little brokerage firm on Iron Street, commercial fertilizers, insecticides, and other chemical products that had been developed to increase agricultural production were scarcely used by farmers in the Midwest, but by the time CCA moved into its new headquarters on North Oak Trafficway chemical products were a part of the cost of production for practically all producers. By expanding its oil and fertilizer facilities CCA had developed a practical program to help farmers in this period of technological and chemical change.

A third aspect of the agricultural revolution of the mid-twentieth century was also taking place. This was commonly called "integration," and in its most complete form it meant control over a farm product through all of the phases of production, processing, and marketing. By the 1950's integration had become most common in the broiler industry. Feed processors supplied the chicks, feed, and

---

[13] Shareholders' meeting, Minutes, December 5, 1957.
[14] Shareholders' meeting, Minutes, December 4, 1959.
[15] Shareholders' meeting, Minutes, December 5, 1958.

other needs for production, while the farmer furnished only his labor. The actual grower was little more than a hired man who received a fixed fee or a percentage of the net profit. Despite cries of protest by many farmers and farm organizations against so-called "contract" farming, integration in the broiler industry expanded rapidly, especially in the South. Also, feed companies, packers, and chain stores became interested in an integrated hog program. Some of the advantages of the program were improved efficiency and uniform, high-quality products that were in demand by mass distributors like chain stores.

Throughout its history CCA held to an established policy not to engage in farm marketing. There were many problems and difficulties associated with marketing agricultural products that CCA officials wanted to avoid, but by concentrating on cost factors, the wholesale had attacked only half of the cost-price squeeze problem. Farmers were vitally interested in better prices, and if cooperatives were an answer to agricultural problems, how could they avoid dealing with the price factor? Of course, there were many fruit, vegetable, grain, and other marketing cooperatives that assisted farmers to get better prices. Some of the fruit associations like Sunkist had been very successful.

Despite CCA's historic policy, grass-roots pressure to add marketing services began to develop by the middle 1950's. At the shareholders' meeting in December, 1955, John Mathews of Mount Pleasant, Iowa, offered a resolution from the floor, asking that CCA's Directors investigate the possibilities of establishing a meat-packing plant in Iowa.[16] Shortly afterward, the Economic Research Division began to study the matter. Three years elapsed, however, before the Board of Directors voted to reverse its long-held policy not to engage in marketing. On December 1, 1958, the Board agreed to move into marketing livestock and livestock products "in an effort to protect the best interest of our farmers." It encountered relatively little opposition to this departure from the company's traditional policy.[17]

The real question, however, was whether CCA would simply enter some phases of processing and marketing or whether it would move into a whole program of integration. Throughout 1957 and 1958 management moved slowly and cautiously. Cowden took the position that integration of production and marketing was a fact that must be recog-

[16] Shareholders' meeting, Minutes, December 1, 1955.
[17] Board of Directors, Minutes, December 1–2, 1958.

nized, and that the important matter was whether it should be expanded "from the top down or from the bottom up." Would farmers control the integration process through their cooperatives, he asked, or would it be dominated by private business, which would deny the farmer his "traditional right to make decisions about buying, feeding and selling?" Cowden wrote, "Through cooperatives farmers can improve their production methods. Their cooperatives can help them obtain the right breeding stock, the right equipment, the right information about feeds and feeding methods, about sanitation and medication." By means of cooperatives, he continued, farmers could get together and provide themselves with "a collective efficiency to match that of the big operation which gets its capital and direction from a private business." [18]

Early in 1958 the Board took the official position that "wherever an integration project might be tied in with any of CCA's services or merchandise programs, CCA would participate to whatever extent was feasible and in the best interest of farmers involved." [19] Homer Young outlined an integration program to those who attended the annual meeting in 1958.

Since the principal move toward integration in the Midwest was in the raising of poultry and hogs, CCA took its first action in these fields. In December, 1957, the Board agreed to experiment in a limited way by financing feed for turkey production through the Cooperative Finance Association, a fully-owned subsidiary that had been set up in 1942 to provide some short-term capital to local cooperatives. [20] With its expanded feed program CCA seemed to be in an ideal position to work with farmers in poultry production. A few weeks later, on March 26, 1958, the Board voted to set up boar-testing stations at Eagle Grove and Ida Grove, Iowa, to assist farmers in developing the best meat-type hogs. [21] This was to be the beginning of a program that looked toward integration in breeding, testing, slaughtering, and marketing hogs in a limited area. An egg-marketing program was also considered at about the same time.

When the Board met on February 24, 1959, Cowden reported that CCA could purchase the Crawford County Packing Company at Denison, Iowa. Since Denison was fairly close to Ida Grove, where a new

[18] Cowden, *Integration and What To Do About It*, 1959, pamphlet.
[19] Shareholders' meeting, Minutes, December 5, 1958.
[20] Board of Directors, Minutes, December 2, 1957.
[21] Board of Directors, Minutes, March 26, 1958.

feed mill had been built, the location was ideal for carrying out an integrated swine program. After considerable discussion, the Directors passed a motion to buy the Denison property.[22] In May, CCA completed the transaction, and on June 5, Farmbest, Inc., a wholly owned subsidiary, was incorporated to own and operate the plant.

The new pork-packing facility was strictly a slaughtering plant that killed and processed hogs under contract for the Coast Packing Company of Los Angeles. Because of contractual agreements, CCA continued this arrangement until the spring of 1962, but beginning on January 1, 1962, Farmbest began operating the plant as a cooperative marketing association.

Although the plant slaughtered about 10,500 hogs weekly and had sales totaling more than $22,000,000 for the year ending August 31, there were no savings or patronage refunds. Many difficulties plagued the meat-packing operations from the outset. These included scarcity of good markets, some labor trouble, and management and transportation problems.[23] By September 30, 1962, CCA had $1,367,755 invested in Farmbest, but many problems remained as the wholesale sought to get a successful integration program on hogs into operation. Selling hog carcasses was one of the least profitable aspects of packing, and CCA needed to process ham, bacon, and other items for the ultimate consumer.

While CCA was getting into the hog-processing business, it also greatly expanded its poultry-feeding program. In conjunction with the poultry-feeding program, the Cooperative Finance Association loaned several million dollars to producers after 1958, and in 1960 alone about 1.5 million turkeys were fed under CCA financing.[24] In the 1961 season 145 turkey growers in seven states borrowed $5,516,000 to finance their operations.[25] At the same time the question of cooperative egg marketing was being studied. Finally, in May, 1962, an egg-marketing service for local Midwest cooperatives was opened at Sioux City. The Farmbest Egg Division was set up, and contracts were made with local associations to provide an adequate supply of high-quality eggs that CCA sought to market advantageously.[26] CCA also joined cooperatives around Erie, Kansas, to establish a cooperative

[22] Board of Directors, Minutes, February 24–26, 1959.
[23] Board of Directors, Minutes, August 25–27, 1959; *34th Annual Report*, 1962, 23.
[24] *32nd Annual Report*, 1960, 19.
[25] Executive Committee, Minutes, April 25, 1961.
[26] *Cooperative Consumer*, May 15, 1962, 1.

cow pool in order to help determine the feasibility of pool milking.[27] After three years it became apparent that this project would not succeed, and it was finally liquidated at some cost to CCA and the participating cooperatives. To permit CCA to engage in these various marketing activities, the wholesale amended its Articles of Incorporation in 1959.

While CCA was expanding its traditional activities and exploring new fields of service, the first really fundamental change occurred in company management. After Cowden announced his pending retirement early in 1958, a committee was appointed by the Board of Directors to study CCA's management structure. This group reported to the Board in August. It praised Cowden for his long years of distinguished service and said that "in the decade ahead CCA needs the practical idealism, the mature wisdom, and the influential leadership of Mr. Cowden" in order that CCA might continue to progress. The Board then invited Cowden to continue as president, "subject to action of the Board on the basis of a two-year notification."[28]

Thus, the question of a successor for Cowden was left unanswered, as had been the case so many times before. Earlier, however, the Board had voted to study CCA's management structure and subsequently hired Rogers, Slade and Hill, a New York consulting firm to make the study.[29] On August 26, 1959, the New York specialists presented their report. The most important recommendation called for establishing the position of general manager. For years various consulting experts had been suggesting that Cowden should not act both as president and general manager. Following some discussion, the Board, with Cowden's support, approved the idea of assigning the offices to two men and immediately appointed their first assistant general manager, McCully, to the new post. In announcing the change in managerial structure, Cowden told the membership in his annual report that he had been looking forward to relief from the responsibilities of day-to-day operations and would now devote more time to "overall policy and planning."[30]

The new arrangement was not entirely satisfactory, and in January, 1961, Cowden told the Executive Committee that management was

27 *31st Annual Report*, 1959, 17; W. Gordon Leith, "Serving Farmer Needs in Purchasing and Marketing," 1963, CCA Files.

28 Board of Directors, Minutes, August 19–20, 1958.

29 Board of Directors, Minutes, January 14, 1958.

30 Board of Directors, Minutes, August 26, 1959; *31st Annual Report*, 1959, 5.

considering the employment of another consulting firm to study CCA's corporate structure and operating methods. Within a few weeks the Board employed George Fry and Associates of Chicago to make a new survey and to report to the Board of Directors. Meanwhile, friction developed between Cowden and McCully, and on April 21 McCully angrily left his office. This quarrel created an internal crisis that affected the entire organization. The Executive Committee promptly declared the managership vacant, but on May 5 McCully discussed at length with the Executive Committee his problems and disagreements with Cowden. Essentially, the company's two chief executives failed to agree on the lines and division of authority. McCully's main complaint was that Cowden, as president, went around him and gave orders to personnel who were supposed to report to the general manager. Cowden, however, declared that McCully was offended at the appointment of the George Fry agency. McCully expressed regret for walking off the job, but the Executive Committee refused to re-employ him, and later the full Board postponed taking any action until it could study the Fry company's recommendations.[31]

The preliminary report prepared by the Fry consultants was placed before the Board on June 26. It recommended that Cowden, now sixty-eight years of age and three years past retirement age, should retire as president and that a new position, chairman of the board, be created. It was assumed that Cowden would be named to the new post in recognition of his long years of service. He left the meeting, and the Board immediately elected him chairman of the board. The report called for the president to be chief administrative officer, and the Directors promptly elected Homer Young. McCully was gone, and unless the Board wanted to go outside the CCA organization to fill its top post, Young was the logical choice. He had been in cooperative work ever since he finished college at the University of Missouri, and he had joined CCA in 1932. Since 1949 he had been assistant general manager in charge of distribution and was well known and respected throughout CCA territory.[32]

As chairman of the board, Cowden was to devote his time to broad planning and to international cooperation, in which he was so intensely interested. But he found his new position unsatisfying after so many years as CCA's chief executive. It was understandably difficult for him

---

[31] Executive Committee, Minutes, May 5 and 24–25, 1961.
[32] Board of Directors, Minutes, June 26–27, 1961.

to turn over the reins of management of a company that he had founded and directed. Consequently, on November 28, 1961, Cowden resigned his job with CCA and accepted a position as consultant with Nationwide Mutual Insurance companies, headed by Murray Lincoln. There he found outlets for his tremendous energy, much of it directed to the world-wide cooperative movement. He was president of the International Cooperative Petroleum Association and played an active role in other cooperatives. Cowden continued to serve on CCA's Board of Directors as one of the two directors-at-large until 1963.

Meanwhile, Cowden had been working to establish an agricultural Hall of Fame. He first suggested this idea to CCA's Board of Directors in August, 1957, and in December the Board voted to appropriate $25,000, or any needed part of that amount, to set up an organization to implement this idea. At the annual meeting a few days later, Cowden declared that an agricultural Hall of Fame was needed to give agriculture the recognition it deserved in American life and culture.[33]

From then on Cowden took the lead in gaining national support for this project. On May 15, 1958, about 175 persons from twenty-six states met for an organizational meeting in Kansas City. Former Secretary of Agriculture Claude R. Wickard and former President Harry S Truman were among the dignitaries present. Cowden was elected chairman of the Board of Governors, which assumed the responsibility of carrying the project forward.[34] Eventually the organization decided to locate the Agricultural Hall of Fame on a 409-acre site near Bonner Springs, about eleven miles west of Kansas City, Kansas. Farm groups and businesses dependent upon agriculture responded slowly to Cowden's active efforts to raise funds. However, when the project was completed, it stood as a monument to the vision of Howard A. Cowden and to his deep concern for both the historic and contemporary aspects of American agriculture.

It is difficult to overemphasize Cowden's contributions in building CCA. He not only founded the company, but he gave it direction and leadership for more than thirty years. He led the company into some unprofitable and not particularly useful ventures, such as groceries and food canning, but these failures were much more than counterbalanced by the tremendous successes in petroleum and fertilizer. As

33 Board of Directors, Minutes, December 2, 1957
34 *Cooperative Consumer*, May 15, 1958, 1.

a leader he was colorful, dynamic, imaginative, courageous, articulate, and wholly dedicated to the principles of cooperation. His intellectual honesty and personal warmth won support and inspired others to action. Cowden never lost his strong agrarian bias. His whole purpose was to make farm life better and more rewarding, results that he believed could be best achieved through cooperation. Perhaps his most significant work was building an organization that could go ahead smoothly and efficiently under a more institutionalized type of leadership after he retired. He was undoubtedly one of the most successful entrepreneurs in the entire cooperative movement in the twentieth century.

Chapter 15

Homer Young and the
Burgeoning Sixties

W<small>HEN HOMER YOUNG</small> took over the leadership of CCA in the summer of 1961, the company faced some difficult problems. McCully's resignation and Cowden's continued presence in a kind of advisory capacity discouraged good management. Moreover, he had barely got settled in the presidency when some employees urged him to investigate certain operations at the exploration and production office at Great Bend, Kansas. He eventually employed an independent investigating firm whose findings confronted Young with a big challenge. There was evidence that some Cooperative Refinery Association resources such as fencing had been diverted to the farm of a former employee in Missouri. But more disturbing was the evidence that people connected with CCA were part owners of a drilling firm that was in a position to profit from dealings that might otherwise have gone to CRA.

Young and Fred F. Claxton, former personnel director who had been promoted to assistant general manager, estimated that as much as $250,000 might have been involved. Claxton wanted to file a civil suit or even initiate criminal action. Young, however, held out for direct negotiations and he finally settled the matter for much less than $250,000. He believed that CCA stood to lose more in prestige and public confidence by going to court than could possibly be recovered through a lawsuit. Young kept the Board informed of every move, but all of this was carried out without injurious rumors or publicity. Young later considered the settlement of this matter as one of his major achievements, but at the time it was a touchy and difficult problem.

Meanwhile, Young announced some major changes in the company's management and organization. From the outset it was obvious that he was broadening the base of management. He was fond of referring to CCA's "management team," which indicated that CCA was moving into a more highly institutional type of management that was characteristic of large corporations. Fry and Associates had proposed an organization that included a number of top positions to be filled from the outside. Young, however, was determined that employment of outside men at the top management level should be held to a minimum.

During the first few months after Young took office, a nine-man management council was in control of the company. Emmet Stead, who had been brought into CCA from the packing industry in 1961 as general manager of Farmbest, Inc., was now responsible for other pending developments in the marketing field; A. H. Stephenson, who had come to CCA in 1954, was made assistant general manager in charge of distribution; manufacturing was placed under Merle A. Blue, who had joined CCA in 1949; D. Ross Denison, who had once worked with the Grocery Department, was named executive director of field services; personnel and membership services came under the direction of Claxton, who joined CCA in 1958; Miles F. Cowden, nephew of Howard Cowden and one of the original employees of the Union Oil Company, became general manager of the Cooperative Refinery Association; W. Gordon Leith, formerly Cowden's administrative assistant, was made secretary; Harold Hamil became assistant general manager of information and public relations.

D. E. Ewing was named treasurer. Ewing had started working for the Union Oil Company in July, 1933, at one of its retail petroleum stations at Parsons, Kansas. In December, 1935, he was transferred to the North Kansas City office and gradually moved up through the accounting departments. He became director of the budget in 1946 and assistant treasurer in 1955. Thus the new management team consisted of old-timers like Young, Ewing, and Miles F. Cowden, a middle group who came to CCA in the late 1940's and early 1950's, including Leith, Denison, Blue, and Hamil, and the relative newcomers Stephenson, Claxton, and Stead. Glenn S. Fox, a former assistant general manager, was made executive director of the new School of Cooperation.

It was generally understood that this administrative reorganization was temporary; basic changes were soon made. The top management group came to consist of the three assistant general managers and the corporate secretary and treasurer, who met weekly with Young. This group included Stephenson, Ewing, Leith, Claxton, Hamil, and Miles F. Cowden. In 1963 Ernest T. Lindsey replaced Cowden and became assistant general manager in charge of manufacturing and production. These six, plus Blue and Denison, and Young, constituted the Executive Council. This group, together with eleven men with the rank of executive director, became the Management Council. A third headquarters group, which embraced the two councils mentioned above, plus some thirty other men, made up what was known as the Management Conference. The Field Operations Council was established later to coordinate the field and distribution programs.

The new organization was accepted with few complaints and without any interruption in CCA's business progress. Over the years it appeared to many that CCA was too much a one-man operation, but the relatively smooth managerial change indicated that people of solid executive talents had been developed within the organization. The Board of Directors had held this position all along, even in the face of criticism from management specialists.

While Young had some problems getting his administration organized and operating to his satisfaction, CCA's business continued to increase in the early 1960's. At the end of Young's first full year as president total volume reached $215 million, exceeding the $200 million figure for the first time. By 1964 sales rose to nearly a quarter billion, or $249,640,696. Savings before income taxes amounted to $18.7 million in 1964 which was more than 80 per cent of the total volume in 1945. The sales of petroleum products continued to be the largest single aspect of CCA's business.

Whatever degree of success a quarter-billion-dollar year may have represented, however, it was not considered good enough by CCA's management. While the company's physical and financial growth might be viewed with satisfaction, there was some danger that success could encourage apathy rather than stimulate further momentum. Indeed, Young sensed a kind of leveling off or slowdown in company activity. This deeply concerned him. CCA, he believed, needed some new thrust, a spurt of energy, a challenge that would rally the company and its local associations to greater business achievement. But just what course should be taken?

Rather than think through the problem alone as Cowden might have done, Young turned to his associates for ideas and suggestions. During the early part of 1964 there was much discussion around corporate headquarters about CCA's future, and what actions should be taken to assure company progress in the years ahead. Company officials believed that CCA should set some definite goals that might be reached between 1964 and August, 1967, when Young would be sixty-five and scheduled to retire. The idea was to have the new programs and initiatives reaching their high point by the close of the Young administration. While the plan would have a kind of revival effect on the company, it involved evaluation of the corporate image and systematic future planning, something that had not been a high priority of CCA earlier.

Throughout May and June, 1964, executive officials began to outline new approaches and directions for the company. Over the Memorial Day weekend Hamil brought the various ideas together and drafted a program that dealt mainly with means or, as he put it, "the way we do things, rather than with long-range volume . . . and savings goals." In a document of some nineteen typewritten pages, Hamil outlined a plan to "reassess CCA's policies and programs."[1] He recommended that once CCA's Executive Council had agreed on the program, it should be presented to farmers and local associations throughout CCA territory. After further in-house discussions, the Board of Directors approved the program. In July CCA executives, led by Young, held a series of ten meetings throughout the company's service territory to obtain grass-roots opinion and support. Some 1,525 cooperators from 575 member cooperatives attended those gatherings. Farmers and managers of local associations agreed that CCA should not only reappraise its objectives, but its methods and procedures as well. Out of those discussions came Project 67 that received wide publicity during the fall of 1964.[2] Project 67 was a plan of action that would guide CCA during the next three years.

The purpose of Project 67 was to make "whatever changes are necessary and desirable to help CCA's farmer-patrons meet the chal-

---

[1] "Project 67—To Open the Doors of the Future For CCA and Member Associations," undated [1964], preliminary mimeographed draft, CCA Files; interview with Harold Hamil, August 30, 1977; "Project 67, A Plan of Action to Help Farmers, Their Local Cooperatives, Their Regional Cooperative—CCA," August, 1964, mimeographed. See also Young's reference to the plan in the *36th Annual Report*, 1964, 7.

[2] "Project 67, A Plan of Action to Help Farmers, Their Local Cooperatives . . . ," August, 1964, 1; *Cooperative Consumer*, July 15, 1964, 2.

lenge of new conditions in agriculture and in our national economy."[3] Hamil expressed the dominant thinking around CCA offices when he spoke to a group of cooperative managers in June, 1963. He declared that CCA must be responding constantly to changing needs and conditions on the farm. "CCA's relationship to the new businessman-farmer," he said, was the most important thing the company would have to contend with in the years ahead. "If we can find ways to better identify CCA with the new farming business of tomorrow," he declared, "we can expand and embellish the image of CCA and make it more acceptable to the people who need it most—the farmers."[4]

By the 1960's it was clear that CCA was committed to the efficient commercial farmer. There was no sentimentality or mystical agrarianism among company officials. They viewed farming as a business and believed that the contribution of cooperatives would be in direct proportion to how they helped farmers become better producers and more effective businessmen. Young told representatives at the 36th annual meeting on December 9, 1964, that farming as a way of life and as a family business could not "survive in our industrial society unless it takes on many of the vital aspects of successful industry. It must adapt itself to its industrial environment."[5] CCA leaders operated on the assumption that in the years ahead farmers would require huge amounts of off-farm inputs in the form of petroleum, fertilizer, herbicides, insecticides, prepared feeds, and other products. These inputs were among the key needs of the large, commercialized, businessman farmer of the 1960's. A revolution in production was occurring on American farms and CCA wanted to be in the forefront of helping farmers meet their changing needs.

One of the farmer's basic difficulties was that he had no control over the quality or price of the growing number of off-farm inputs. High prices for nonfarm commodities and low prices for farm products left farmers periodically in a cruel cost-price squeeze. "As an individual," resolved CCA's shareholders at the 1964 annual meeting, "the farmer is a victim of his lack of bargaining power in a society where contending forces are backed by powerful corporate concentrations."[6] In reviewing company business halfway through the fiscal

---

3 *Ibid.*
4 Harold Hamil, "Future Image of CCA," speech delivered June 17, 1963, CCA Speech Files.
5 Young, speech, December 9, 1964, CCA Speech Files.
6 Shareholders' meeting, Minutes, December 11, 1964.

year, Young told CCA employees in the company cafeteria on March 6, 1964, that "CCA's primary purpose is to earn money for farmers. If ever there is a challenge to do so," he continued, "it is at a time when the general economy is working against the individual farmer. We have to look at lower farm income as more reason than ever to do everything we can to earn savings for our farmer members."[7] Thus CCA's main goal was to increase the bargaining power of farmers in the market place through strong farmer-owned cooperatives.[8]

To achieve this objective both CCA and local member cooperatives must be big and efficient. As Young said, cooperators must get over "an innate fear of bigness." "We must," he continued, "clear the way for a cooperative structure of sufficient size and strength to hold its own in an era of big agriculture and big industry." CCA officials declared that they recognized a new concept of bigness "in which we make bigness do things 'for farmers' instead of 'to farmers.'"[9] Small, weak organizations could not successfully compete with the large oil and chemical companies such as Standard Oil and Phillips Petroleum Company that were selling supplies to many Midwestern farmers. It was essential, CCA spokesmen said, for the company to be competitive in supplying products for sale by member cooperatives. In turn the local associations must distribute the commodities and provide the services so efficiently and effectively that more and more farmers would see the advantages of belonging to a cooperative association. Most farmers would not join cooperatives unless they believed they would receive tangible benefits in terms of products, service, or price. As Hamil wrote in 1964, farmers were looking for an organization that "offers business advantages and improved income."[10] So, the overriding question was, how could CCA and its 1,791 member cooperatives best serve American farmers?

Project 67 outlined six major areas for special attention. The first of these was "operation leadership." Young and other CCA officials believed that in all agricultural matters cooperatives should become the "power center" for farmers and give "general leadership for all of agriculture." They would not leave this initiative up to the regular farm organizations such as the American Farm Bureau Federation and the Farmers Union, or to the federal government. Farmer-owned

---

[7] *Cooperative Consumer*, March 14, 1964, 1.
[8] Shareholders' meeting, Minutes, December 11, 1964.
[9] *36th Annual Report*, 1964, 8; "Project 67, District Meeting Presentation," 1964.
[10] Hamil, "CCA: A Look at the Future," 1964, mimeographed.

cooperatives, they insisted, must become strong enough to protect farmers against the monopoly power of huge corporations and guarantee producers control over their own businesses. To fulfill its leadership role, CCA would in the future speak out more forcefully on particular problems of farmers, stress that cooperatives were a vital part of the agribusiness picture, better communicate the farmers' message to both farmers and nonfarmers through public programs, and would work harder to attract individual farmers to cooperative membership. In short, CCA would not only be a means by which producers did business, but it, along with other cooperatives, would seek to be the principal spokesman for American agriculture.

The second goal of Project 67 was "operation understanding." Most cooperative leaders admitted that too few people really understood cooperatives and their way of doing business. Despite a good deal of educational effort there was little indication that CCA, or the larger cooperative movement, had succeeded in broadening mass understanding or in winning general adherence to cooperative business principles. As Hamil expressed it: "Many don't listen when we speak; many don't read what we write." He might have added that others did not agree even if they did read and listen. Recognizing this problem, Cowden had pushed to establish a School of Cooperation. In December, 1958, the shareholders voted to set aside one-half of one per cent of the net consolidated savings to accumulate money for the school. Within another year land had been purchased two and one-half miles north of the headquarters building. Modern in every detail, the school was completed in 1961, and the first classes were held in January, 1962. The School of Cooperation was the first of its kind to be built by a cooperative in the United States. It offered short courses, management-training institutes, and other types of education to hundreds of students annually. Expenditures of the division administering the School of Cooperation amounted to $128,361 in 1962–1963.

But CCA officials realized that much more needed to be done to increase cooperative understanding. One problem was getting members of local associations to realize that they actually owned the cooperatives to which they belonged. Thus a critical task was to convince farmers that they owned their cooperatives just as they did their land, machinery, and livestock. Furthermore, farmers must be sold on the desirability of large integrated cooperatives that could control farm supplies from raw materials to finished products. CCA had been preaching this message for years, but officials admitted that they had not been fully successful in getting the idea accepted. Operation understanding, then, must "explain and justify the importance of size in today's competitive environment," CCA executives argued. To achieve a higher degree of understanding among farmers in these areas, CCA committed itself to more and better publicity and advertising, to increasing the efforts of fieldmen, to providing more education in cooperative principles, to assisting leaders of local associations, and to improving cooperative product identification.

Efficiency was the third area of commitment. CCA officials recognized that if cooperatives were to be successful, which meant being competitive, they must be run efficiently. To be efficient demanded more than just careful management of present facilities. It meant handling the right products, introducing new lines and services, and dropping items no longer needed. To improve over-all performance, CCA promised to look at its own corporate organization, expand training programs for local association managers, and provide a wide variety of advisory and consulting services to member cooperatives.

"Operation excellence" was the fourth objective of Project 67. This goal involved producing "top quality in both products and services." Product excellence would be enhanced by the Research and Development Division established in 1963 (which will be discussed later). Accompanying excellent products, CCA officials said, must be good service.

Next, Project 67 called for "operation inspiration." Cowden and other founders of CCA had been inspirational leaders, but as the organization grew, it was more difficult to maintain a high degree of spirit and inspiration among those associated with the organization. For many managers of local cooperatives, running the association was a job not a calling or a cause; cooperative members were mainly interested in quality products, service, and refunds. Even some of CCA's own employees had relatively little appreciation of the distinctiveness of cooperatives. Consequently, Project 67 sought to "find new and better ways. . .to inspire and encourage the people who work in cooperatives." In the years ahead CCA pledged to use incentive programs, the annual meeting, scholarships, camps, and bus tours of cooperative facilities as means to inspire people more effectively than in the past.

Finally, CCA called for "operation teamwork." According to Young, the strength of the cooperative movement was in people working together. The local depended on loyal farmer members and in turn the regional must have the support of strong locals. There was an inter-

dependence that demanded teamwork all up and down the line if
farmers were to find significant economic strength in their cooperatives. Young said that he hoped Project 67 would "inspire new interest in cooperatives and new concern for them." It was a blueprint
for growth, he concluded, and "with the help of many people" it
could bring "economic strength and security" to farmers in the
Midwest.[11]

A great deal of effort had gone into developing and promoting
Project 67. Preparation of position papers, numerous meetings, and
publicity campaigns had required much time and energy by CCA
executives. But they firmly believed that planning and establishment
of objectives were necessary if CCA and its member cooperatives were
to meet their fullest potential. They could leave nothing to chance.
At the annual meeting in December, 1964, shareholders enthusiastically endorsed the plans and urged all cooperatives to accept the new
challenges and opportunities. The annual meeting was designed to
provide some of the inspiration called for in Project 67.[12] The entire
effort had done much to revive and stimulate enthusiasm among member associations throughout the region and to sharpen the over-all
interest in cooperatives.

While Project 67 was under consideration, there was some quiet
in-house discussion of changing the Consumers Cooperative Association's corporate name. In his first draft of material dealing with Project 67, Hamil had written that CCA's membership should consider
"whether the corporate name of the regional organization serves
properly to identify its basic functions and services." He added that
there were "powerful arguments for getting the identification of the
farmer-owner into the name."[13] On November 16, 1964, Hamil sent
a memorandum to Young suggesting a number of new names. Rather
than making any specific recommendation, Hamil explained that he
was only trying to combine a variety of words that would best describe
CCA's business. Most of the thirty-five suggestions did not include
the word *cooperative*.[14]

11 "Project 67, A Plan of Action to Help Farmers, Their Local Cooperatives. . . ."
The final version of "Project 67" was similar in many respects to Hamil's original draft,
but there were some significant differences.
12 Shareholders' meeting, Minutes, December 11, 1964.
13 Hamil, "Project 67, To Open the Doors of the Future . . . ," 1964.
14 Hamil to Young, November 16, 1964. See also Hamil to Young, October 19, 1965,
CCA History Files. Unless otherwise indicated all memoranda and correspondence cited
are in the company's History Files.

While CCA executives discussed this matter over the next several months, they did not bring it officially before the Board until August, 1965. After considering the question, the Board directed management to discuss possible name changes at the fall district meetings. Young insisted that the membership be kept informed of any possible changes. Two months later the Board indicated that it had decided in favor of a name change. Their main concern was over the best procedure to accomplish that goal.

There were two main reasons for adopting a new name. The most important was that "Consumers Cooperative Association" did not adequately identify the company with agriculture. Moreover, the word *consumer* in the name confused some people. CCA was not strictly a consumer company. It was not even any longer just a supplier to farm consumers. CCA had become, among other things, a large complex of manufacturing industries. Company management had concluded by early 1965 that a name more descriptive of the firm's industrial activities and its relationship to agriculture was essential.

At its December, 1965, meeting, just before the annual gathering of shareholders, the Board expressed firm support for a name change. It voted to recommend to the shareholders that the chairman of the Board be authorized to appoint a committee to study and develop a recommendation for a new name. If the Board supported the committee's recommendation, it would then call a special meeting of the shareholders to vote on the issue "with the intent of changing the name effective September 1, 1966."[15]

At the annual meeting on December 10, less than a week later, shareholders approved the appointment of a special twenty-five-man committee that would study the matter and report back to the Board no later than March 1, 1966.[16] The committee urged management to employ a consulting firm to do the basic work. In January CCA employed the firm of Lippincott and Margulies of New York City, which specialized in corporate names. This was approved by the Board at its February meeting.[17] Lippincott and Margulies put together a list of some three hundred names, including those submitted by the special committee. The list was reduced first to thirty, then to ten, and finally to five. Two representatives from the New York office, five members of the special committee, and the CCA Executive Council

15 Board of Directors, Minutes, August 24–25, October 26–27, and December 6–7, 1965.
16 Shareholders' meeting, Minutes, December 10, 1965.
17 Board of Directors, Minutes, February 2–3, 1966.

composed of CCA's leading executives, finally eliminated all but two possibilities—Farmland Industries, Inc. and Farmbest Industries, Inc. The committee finally supported Farmland Industries, Inc. by a vote of 20 to 3.

The Board promptly and unanimously approved the committee's recommendation at a meeting on May 25, 1966.[18] A special meeting of shareholders was then called for July 15 to amend the Articles of Incorporation, and the secretary was instructed to distribute mail ballots to all eligible shareholders.

Management immediately set out to assure a favorable vote on the proposal. Young wrote to all fieldmen and division general managers urging them to work for passage among local cooperative boards. He explained that many local directors were unfamiliar with the name change "and some may be cold to the idea. . .at first."[19] There was some concern that dropping the word *cooperative* would arouse opposition. However, management hoped to overcome that criticism by continuing the double circle CO-OP trademark on all products.

The member associations, each of whom had one vote, overwhelmingly supported the new name by a margin of 906 to 147.[20] On September 1, 1966, the Consumers Cooperative Association, a name carried for thirty-five years, became Farmland Industries, Inc. Before the annual meeting in December the large "CCA" letters over the front door of the headquarters building had been removed and the new name was prominently displayed. Management did not want a name that could be conveniently reduced to initials. In a memorandum to all employees on August 22, Young wrote that "we expect everyone to avoid the use of initials or shabby nicknames." He explained that "Farmland" identified the cooperative's relation to agriculture, and that "Industries" was descriptive of the company's manufacturing services that was the beginning of distribution to local associations and farmers. So use the name Farmland Industries, he strongly advised, and this would contribute to a "quick and easy transition."[21]

A name change required a good many modifications. The newspaper, *The Cooperative Consumer* became *Farmland*, and many

18 *Ibid.*, May 25, 1966. See also *Leadership*, June–July, 1966.
19 Young to Division General Managers and All Fieldmen, May 31, 1966.
20 *Cooperative Consumer*, September 1, 1966, 1. See also the "Special Statement Regarding Name Change," September 1, 1966; W. Gordon Leith, "Notice of Special Shareholders Meeting," June 1, 1966.
21 Young to All CCA Employees, August 22, 1966.

other name changes had to be made official. People had to learn to identify products with Farmland Industries and make other adjustments in their thinking. However, the new name caught on quickly and soon the entire "Farmland family" found pride in the name.

Other changes were also stirring around 3315 North Oak Trafficway in Kansas City. With the increasing size and complexity of the cooperative, Young implemented additional reorganization of his top administrative staff in 1964. As of September 1, Lindsey and Stephenson became senior assistant general managers in charge of operations. Lindsey was given responsibility for oil production, refining and warehousing, transportation, and the planned Florida fertilizer plant. Stephenson would continue to direct matters relating to distribution and in addition manage some of the manufacturing. Two administrators were promoted to assistant general manager. Paris A. Nichols became head of management services that involved working with the member associations, and Warren E. Dewlen assumed responsibility for field services. Ewing, the treasurer, Leith, the secretary, and Hamil, assistant general manager, information and public relations, completed the group that made up the Executive Council, and all reported directly to Young.[22] This could be considered a reasonably lean administration and one where executives were rather poorly paid. Cowden had always kept his own salary low, and the Board continued this pattern with Young. His salary was only $45,000 a year in 1964, and other executives were well below that figure.[23] However unfair the low-salary policy may have been to capable executives, it certainly removed any possibility of patron complaints about waste or extravagance in the central administration.

While CCA emphasized planning and new directions in the mid-1960's, the major thrust of company policy was to enlarge the manufacturing facilities. The reasons for this were clear enough. In so far as possible CCA wanted to reduce its dependence on noncooperative sources of supply. It had made progress in this direction, but as of 1963–1964 only 61 per cent of the commodities it distributed to farmers came from factories owned by CCA and its subsidiaries.[24] Secondly, the returns from manufacturing were much better than from distribution. So long as CCA had remained simply a broker of

22 *Cooperative Consumer*, September 15, 1964, 1; *36th Annual Report*, 1964, 6, 8.
23 CCA, *Prospectus*, December 22, 1964, 22. In addition Young received some special retirement benefits.
24 *Ibid.*, 12.

petroleum products, its margins were small. Only after the cooperative moved into oil refining and fertilizer production did it begin to
show spectacular growth. If CCA was going to generate a good share
of the capital required to expand sales and services to farmers, it must
build more manufacturing plants. By 1963 CCA executives were
determined to move boldly in this direction, especially in the production of fertilizer. As Young said, CCA wanted to "strengthen
farmer ownership in the farm supply business at the manufacturing
level—the level of greatest effectiveness."[25]

The procedure for developing major policy initiatives usually involved a presentation by management to the Board of Directors at
one of the six regular meetings held annually. A position paper would
be presented by the executive responsible for the specific area under
consideration. This usually included a discussion of the need for the
facility, cost, available financing, and the likely payout of the project.
During the period when new policy was being studied, it was also
common for CCA executives to go to the grass roots and seek ideas
and suggestions from the managers and directors of local cooperatives. Once the policy package was in order it would be presented to
the Board that would authorize management to proceed. Only on
rare occasions did the Board reject management's recommendations.
However, management usually did not push a new idea or program
without first getting input from Board members and others who
might be affected by new or different policy.

The need for more fertilizer production became increasingly clear
in the early 1960's. Indeed, fertilizer had become CCA's fastest growing product line. This reflected the move by farmers to increase their
productivity through the use of larger quantities of commercial nutrients. For example, in Missouri, Kansas, Iowa, and Nebraska, where
CCA did a great deal of business, farmers applied about 860,000 more
tons of commercial fertilizer in 1960 than they had in an average year
from 1950 to 1954. CCA more than doubled its sale of fertilizer between 1960 and 1963, rising from 370,469 to 762,524 tons.[26] And every
indication pointed to greater sales in the future. Not only was the
total market growing, but CCA hoped to gain a much larger share of
that market from farmer cooperatives.

Meanwhile, management was studying the feasibility of enlarging

25 *36th Annual Report*, 1964, 6.
26 *Agricultural Statistics*, 1962 (Washington, D.C., 1963), 578; *37th Annual Report*,
1965, 18.

CCA's fertilizer capacity. Controller Jack P. Blair, who came to the company from the Coffeyville refinery, undertook a series of payout studies which showed that investment in fertilizer production would bring handsome returns. Blair's reports over the next few years did a great deal to build Young's confidence in the wisdom of constructing new fertilizer facilities.

Having concluded internally that more fertilizer production would be a good business move for CCA and its patrons, Young took the question to the territory. In March, 1963, CCA officials called a meeting of Iowa shareholders at the Kirkwood Hotel in Des Moines to consider the matter. This meeting was chaired by Kenneth Nielsen, CCA's division general manager in Iowa. There was strong enthusiasm for moving ahead. On February 4–5, 1964, the Board agreed to build a 400-ton per day nitrogen plant near Fort Dodge, Iowa. But before plans were even developed, Young recommended increasing the capacity to 600 tons a day.[27] The reason for the change was that a 600-ton facility was about the minimum size in which the contractor, the Kellogg Company, could install the latest and most efficient equipment. Moreover, it could be done at very little extra cost. The Board readily approved the change. The feasibility study estimated the plant price at $11,700,000 with pre-operating and working capital needs raising the total cost to $14,600,000. September 1, 1965, was the target date for completion.[28]

Meanwhile, discussions had been underway regarding construction of a phosphate plant. At the Des Moines meeting Ralph A. Olsen, manager of the Boone Valley Cooperative Processing Association at Eagle Grove, Iowa, and several managers and board members of local cooperatives, had urged CCA executives not to confine their efforts to nitrogen, but also to arrange as soon as possible for production of phosphate. One Iowa director in particular chided CCA officials for not thinking in larger terms. He challenged management to go to Idaho, Florida, or any other appropriate place and become "basic" in phosphate fertilizer. The term *basic* meant controlling production and distribution from raw material to farmer customer.[29] This was an example of farmers who believed in their local cooperatives pushing CCA to meet crucial agricultural needs.

[27] Board of Directors, Minutes, February 4–5 and May 27–28, 1964.
[28] "Feasibility Report, Iowa Ammonia Plant," February 3, 1964, Secretary's CCA No. 102. All of these reports are located in the files of the corporate secretary.
[29] "Going Basic in Phosphates," typewritten summary.

After further consideration, at its meeting on March 31–April 1, the Board approved construction of a phosphate facility in Polk County near Bartow, Florida, generally known as the Green Bay plant.[30] While the investment was estimated at $27,814,000, studies showed that the payout would be some 23 per cent annually after taxes. It looked like a good business move, and, as CCA management expressed it, this would be another "step in line with CCA's policy of complete integration with a view of becoming 'basic' in the major product lines CCA patrons use."[31] Thanking the Board for expressing confidence in management's decision, Young said he believed that "it was one of the most significant steps ever taken by a cooperative."[32] A 420-acre site was acquired and work began in late 1964 under the general supervision of Miles F. Cowden. Most of the actual construction occurred in 1965.[33]

The two fertilizer projects represented the largest capital outlay ever undertaken by CCA. By the time both plants came on line the investment reached approximately $42 million. A few years earlier, it would have been impossible for the regional cooperative to have undertaken projects requiring such huge capital outlays. However, good savings during the previous years and continued support from the Wichita Bank for Cooperatives made these investments reasonably easy. At its meeting in May, 1964, the Board authorized management to obtain loans of up to $37 million from the Wichita Bank for Cooperatives to help finance the new facilities.[34]

The Florida phosphate plant began production in November, 1965, and was dedicated on January 12, 1966. To expose as many shareholders as possible to the new facilities, arrangements had been made to fly hundreds of managers and board officers of local cooperatives who had met certain business goals to a Florida vacation that would include a visit to the new fertilizer plant. Spouses were also invited but at a cost of $150. About 1,830 farmers and cooperative managers took advantage of the tours. CCA executives and those who made the trips proclaimed the Florida outing a huge success.[35] To

---

30 Board of Directors, Minutes, March 31–April 1 and May 27–28, 1964.
31 "Proposal for Production Facilities . . . in Florida and Warehouse and Terminal Facilities in CCA Territory," March 31, 1964, Secretary's CCA No. 105.
32 Board of Directors, Minutes, March 31–April 1, 1964.
33 *Cooperative Consumer*, February 25, 1965, 3.
34 Board of Directors, Minutes, May 27–28, 1964.
35 *Ibid.*, November 28–29, 1964, and February 2–3, 1966; "Going Basic in Phosphates."

show off CCA facilities was one way to build pride in the regional
and to bind individual members more closely to CCA.

The Iowa nitrogen plant located on 240 acres six miles east of Fort
Dodge was not completed until October, 1966. Operations were delayed because several gas companies brought suit to void CCA's contract for gas with the Northern Natural Gas Company. The contract
was eventually approved but the legal actions caused several months
delay.[36] An open house and dedication attended by some 2,000 visitors took place on October 26. After conducting morning tours
through the facility and enjoying a Farmbest ham luncheon, people
listened to Young explain why farmers should own their own fertilizer plants. It made sense, he said, because they were the main users
of fertilizer.[37] Young told the admiring owners that what they were
seeing represented the third largest investment ever made by CCA
in a single project. Only the Florida and Lawrence fertilizer plants
had cost more. But Young emphasized that the plant was more than
just another modern manufacturing facility. "It symbolized the unity
of agricultural producers," he said. "It is an anchor against the economic storms that could completely destroy our system of family-
owned farms. It symbolizes the modern business-farmer."[38]

At the dedication of the Fort Dodge nitrogen plant, CCA officials
announced that another fertilizer facility would soon be constructed
at some undetermined site in southwestern Kansas to serve that area,
Oklahoma, the Texas Panhandle, and southeastern Colorado. Following meetings with local cooperative leaders in that region, it was
announced in late January, 1967, that an anhydrous ammonia plant
similar to the one at Fort Dodge would be built at Dodge City.[39]
Young told the Board at its March meeting that the added plant
would cost about $19.9 million. The Board authorized him to pro-
ceed with the construction contract. The Dodge City plant came on
line July 17, 1968, under the management of Dwight Anderson.[40]

By 1967 Farmland Industries had manufacturing facilities for various kinds of fertilizer at Lawrence, Kansas; Hastings, Nebraska;
Green Bay, Florida; Fort Dodge, Iowa; Joplin, Missouri; and the

---

36 Typewritten statement by Young, undated.
37 *Farmland*, November 15, 1966, 10; Dedication Program.
38 Young, speech, October 26, 1966, CCA Speech Files.
39 *Farmland*, November 15, 1966, 1, and January 31, 1967, 1.
40 Board of Directors, Minutes, March 28–29, 1967; *Farmland*, August 31, 1968, 1.

plant under construction at Dodge City. The combined production capacity of these facilities available to Farmland customers was about 1,350,000 tons per year. Farmland also owned a number of fertilizer-mixing plants in key locations throughout its patronizing territory. Altogether investment in fertilizer properties, including undeveloped phosphate land, reached $106,096,304 on August 31, 1966. This figure did not include the projected Dodge City plant.[41]

What Farmland lacked for a completely integrated farm fertilizer system was ownership of the basic phosphate rock and natural gas needed in the manufacture of nitrogen. Farmland did purchase 5,100 acres of land in Hillsborough County, Florida, but the mining of phosphate had not proven feasible on that property by the mid-1960's. While the cooperative had some natural gas production, it did not have enough nor was it located in the right place. Consequently, Farmland had to purchase phosphate, sulphur, natural gas, and other raw materials from noncooperative suppliers. Fertilizer operations were managed mainly through Farmland's subsidiaries, the Cooperative Farm Chemicals Association and the Farmers Chemical Company, of which Farmland owned 75 and 77 per cent, respectively.

Farmland also built a number of warehouses that served as distribution centers. Two of the most important were at Council Bluffs, Iowa, on the Missouri River, where a warehouse of 25,000 tons capacity was constructed to receive shipments from Florida by either barge or rail, and one at Muscatine, Iowa, on the Mississippi River.[42]

While the decision to build three large fertilizer plants were the most significant actions taken by CCA in the mid-1960's, other important facilities were constructed or purchased. To house a variety of research and production enterprises, CCA began constructing a large industrial complex on 18 acres in North Kansas City. One of the activities to be housed there was an expanded research and development program. Research and development became a company division in 1963. The establishment of a research and development center represented a growing determination by CCA officials to protect and guarantee the quality of oil, grease, feed, fertilizer, paint, agricultural chemicals, and other products sold to member cooperatives. Late in 1964 a new battery plant with a capacity of 184,000 batteries a year was also opened in this industrial center, giving the

---

41 Farmland Industries, Inc., *Prospectus*, December 27, 1966, 10.
42 *38th Annual Report*, 1966, 14; *Cooperative Consumer*, September 30, 1965, 9.

cooperative production of another item in demand among farmer customers. With gasoline, oil, grease, tires, and batteries, cooperative service stations affiliated with CCA were now in a position to handle products manufactured mainly in cooperative-owned plants.

Also located in this complex were new grease-manufacturing facilities completed in June, 1965, and a new paint plant finished later in the year. Over the next few years the annual capacity for paint production rose from about 350,000 to 1,200,000 gallons per year. The printing plant and warehousing and terminal facilities were also located in the new industrial center that could be seen from the south windows of the headquarters building. CCA also expanded its commercial feed-mixing facilities. In 1964 it had an annual capacity of 238,000 tons in its seven plants, while two years later this had increased to some 348,000 tons in one animal protein plant and eight feed-mixing plants.[43] Plans were underway to expand even more. In addition to constructing a variety of manufacturing facilities during the mid-1960's, Farmland constantly improved and upgraded its older plants. For example, additions to the Lawrence nitrogen plant were nearly continuous as one expansion followed another.

During 1964 CCA also sought to obtain an increasing supply of crude oil from its three refineries at Coffeyville and Phillipsburg, Kansas, and at Scottsbluff, Nebraska. Management's goal was to have enough primary production to provide at least 50 per cent of the daily requirements for CCA refineries. Those units had a daily capacity of about 44,500 barrels. During 1964, however, CRA, Inc. (formerly the Cooperative Refinery Association), CCA's fully owned subsidiary, produced only about 14 per cent of refinery needs. This percentage was a long way from the 50 per cent objective. Actually, CCA had less average daily crude oil production in 1963 and 1964 than in 1960 and 1961. Most CCA crude oil was pumped in Kansas, Oklahoma, and Texas. On August 31, 1964, the cooperative owned 735 net producing oil and gas wells. During the preceding five years, management had budgeted about $4.5 million annually for oil production; but in 1965 this figure jumped to $8.3 million, indicating CCA's desire to gain ownership of more crude oil.

In the early 1960's CCA decided that it should cautiously explore the possibility of obtaining crude oil in North Africa. In December,

[43] Farmland Industries, Inc., *Prospectus*, December 27, 1966, 16–17; *36th Annual Report*, 1964, 25; and *Prospectus*, December 22, 1964, 17.

1960, the Board approved organization of Cracca Libya, Inc., a wholly owned subsidiary, and joined other cooperatives and independents in what became known as the Eastern Hemisphere Group. This organization set out to explore for and to produce foreign crude oil. The managing company was the Kewanee Oil Company of Pennsylvania. CCA protected itself well by signing an agreement that the partners must give unanimous approval to all direct costs and expenses. Once those costs were agreed to, however, Cracca Libya, Inc. had to bear 35 per cent of the expenditures. In January, 1962, partners in the Eastern Hemisphere Group participated in forming the National Oil Company of Libya, a private Libyan Corporation. Cracca Libya, Inc. owned about 10 per cent of the capital stock. This company hoped to acquire oil concessions in Libya and to develop oil production. However, the company was unable to obtain any drilling rights, at least without resorting to unacceptable business practices, and the prospect for CCA to solve its crude oil needs through this international venture failed.[44] Indeed, in July, 1966, CCA liquidated Cracca Libya at a loss of $604,307. Meanwhile, a new subsidiary, CRA International, was organized in 1966 to cooperate with other oil companies to explore for oil and gas in Canada.

While international oil ventures proved unsuccessful in the mid-1960's, Farmland made a major move at home to expand its resources of crude. At the annual meeting in December, 1966, Young announced that Farmland had completed negotiations to purchase the AMAX Petroleum Corporation with headquarters in Tusla, Oklahoma. He said that already Farmland's Phillipsburg and Scottsbluff refineries had been receiving oil from AMAX wells, and he hoped to assure this continued source by buying the properties. The deal was closed on May 1, 1967,[45] at a cost of $28.9 million, the largest single capital expenditure ever undertaken by Farmland up to that time. The properties included 545,000 acres of leases, increasing "wildcat acreage," or undeveloped reserves, from 105,000 to about 650,000 acres. The number of oil and gas wells owned entirely or in part by CRA, Inc. jumped from 586 to 1,261, and daily production rose from 5,991 barrels in 1966 to 16,050 at the end of 1967.[46] Farmland had an interest in even more wells. With the acquisition of AMAX, much of

---

44 Farmland Industries, Inc., *Prospectus*, December 27, 1966, 13.
45 *Farmland*, December 31, 1966, 3, and May 15, 1967, 1.
46 *39th Annual Report*, 1967, 9; *Farmland*, December 15, 1967, 14–15; and Farmland Industries, Inc., *Prospectus*, January 8, 1968, 12.

the company's new oil activity shifted to Wyoming and Montana. But most active production continued to be in Kansas, Texas, and Oklahoma. As of August 31, 1966, Farmland had spent $83,806,000 on refining and oil production, some $23,000,000 less than the investment in fertilizer capacity. The purchase of AMAX raised oil investments to $113,294,184 as of August 31, 1967, some $3 million more than had been spent for fertilizer facilities.[47]

As modern commercial farmers demanded more herbicides, insecticides, and other chemicals, CCA enlarged its program to supply farm chemicals. For several years it had bought large quantities of its chemicals from the Woodbury Chemical Company of St. Joseph, Missouri. Farmland had not moved to establish its own plants. However, to gain greater control over needed farm chemical supplies, CCA arranged to purchase 48 per cent interest in the Woodbury Chemical Company in July, 1966, and later purchased the remaining interest. The total cost for this facility reached $1,555,900.[48]

One of the boldest actions taken in the Young years was the decision to save the Farmers Elevator Mutual Insurance Company. With headquarters in Des Moines, FEMIC's main business was with farmers and farmer cooperatives, especially grain elevators, in the Midwest. It carried insurance for a large number of cooperatives affiliated with Farmland Industries.

In late September, 1966, a member of FEMIC's Board of Directors called Young and reported that the company was in serious financial trouble. Some heavy losses from reinsurance operations and poor management had combined to bring about the crisis. By the end of September the company did not have the necessary $500,000 in surplus required by the Iowa Commissioner of Insurance to do business in the state.

The main questions were clear enough. Would Farmland permit FEMIC to go broke or be absorbed by a noncooperative firm, or would it step in and save the company for the benefit of farmer cooperatives? There was no doubt in Young's mind what must be done, and he moved promptly and decisively to save FEMIC. As he put it, the failure of FEMIC would "permanently damage the image of farmer cooperatives," a most unpleasant development in his thinking.[49]

[47] Farmland Industries, Inc., *Prospectus*, December 27, 1966, 10, and January 8, 1968, 10.
[48] *Ibid.*, 17; *38th Annual Report*, 1966, 14; *Cooperative Consumer*, July 30, 1966, 10; and Young's report to the Board of Directors, May 23, 1967.
[49] Undated statement by Young, March, 1967.

Under Young's prompting, and in cooperation with FEMIC leadership and the Iowa Commissioner of Insurance, an agreement was reached on November 18 that Farmland would advance FEMIC $3,576,895 before January 1, 1967. The contribution to surplus provided sufficient capital to permit the company to continue doing business. Farmland's investment, however, was subordinated to claims by other creditors and policyholders that made it a somewhat risky venture. But, while saving FEMIC, Young was determined to protect Farmland's investment. Therefore, he insisted on controlling and managing the insurance company. Between November, 1966, and January 25, 1967, arrangements were worked out to give Farmland control of the FEMIC board. Young became chairman of a board dominated by Farmland directors and supporters.

Once in control, Young moved quickly to improve the company's financial position. He sold the company plane and automobile fleet for about $140,000 and collected $165,000 of the $190,000 in overdue accounts receivable. He obtained the resignations of some ineffective FEMIC executives and appointed Thomas J. Luck who had been with the State Farm Insurance Company, as a new executive vice-president to manage the company. He cancelled unprofitable reinsurance agreements and made other changes. Within a year the company was well on the road to economic recovery. As will be shown later, this company provided a base on which Farmland built a full insurance program.

The importance of Young's decision to save FEMIC went far beyond just preserving another farmer cooperative enterprise. It greatly enhanced the over-all position of Farmland Industries in Iowa and reduced much of the opposition to Farmland in the rather vigorous competition among regional cooperatives for business in that state. Farmland was the only regional cooperative with sufficient resources at hand to help FEMIC, and by saving and rebuilding the company Farmland improved its image and produced a great deal of good will for the company among Iowa cooperatives.[50]

In the midst of rather feverish company expansion, Young imple-

---

50 For accounts of the acquisition of FEMIC, see Young to S. C. Du Rose, deputy commissioner, Wisconsin Department of Insurance, April 25, 1967; Young to Board of Directors, Farmers Elevator Mutual Insurance Company, January 3, 1967; undated statements by Young, late 1966 and March, 1967; and Board of Directors, Minutes, October 25-26, 1966.

mented a major administrative reorganization. Fry Consultants of Chicago had recommended the basic plan that called for naming ten vice-presidents. However, only one of these, Jack M. Shea, vice-president for marketing, was new to Farmland. Shea had been a vice-president of the American Petrofina Company and more recently he had worked for Fry Consultants. Other executive vice-presidents were Stephenson, distribution, and Lindsey, manufacturing and marketing. Hamil became senior vice-president, information and public relations. These senior executives, along with Ewing, corporate treasurer, and Leith, corporate secretary, made up the Executive Council, or the top management advisory group. Six other vice-presidents directed major company operation: Walter R. Horn, phosphate production; Warren E. Dewlen, fertilizer; Chase C. Wilson, feed; D. Ross Denison, farm supplies; Paris A. Nichols, membership and finance; and Miles F. Cowden, manufacturing operations. Jack P. Blair was controller. For the most part these executives had been with Farmland for many years. They were knowledgeable, competent, and committed to the cooperative philosophy. Young felt comfortable and secure with them. Only the newcomer Shea did not work out.[51] Shea was soon replaced by Guy Williams, division general manager in Kansas and another old-timer.

The strong move by Farmland into manufacturing, and its ability to provide commodities produced in cooperative plants, attracted a good deal of attention in cooperative circles during the mid-1960's. Some of the other regional associations watched Farmland with some apprehension, and even envy. Among the cooperatives that felt the pressure of Farmland's territorial expansion were Midland Cooperatives, Inc., the Farmers Union Central Exchange in Minnesota (later known as CENEX), the FS Services, Inc., the Farm Bureau regional in Illinois, and the Farmers Elevator Service Company in Iowa. While there was a good deal of talk about cooperation among the regional cooperatives serving Midwestern farmers, there was really more competition than positive cooperation.[52]

At the request of many managers and directors of local associations, Farmland officials discussed the prospect of merging with several of the leading Midwestern regionals. In the spring of 1966 Farmland

[51] *Cooperative Consumer*, March 15, 1966, 1.
[52] Board of Directors, Minutes, August 27–29, 1967; Executive Committee, Board of Directors, Minutes, June 20, 1967.

actually made a concrete proposal to consolidate with Midland Cooperatives, but nothing came of the suggestion.[53] However, Farmland's Board did develop a formal policy on mergers. That policy
called for being receptive to any merger "proposals from other regional farm supply cooperatives," but took the position that Farmland must proceed on its own to meet requests for service and
assistance from local associations that had not been patrons of Farmland. Responsibilities to local farmer cooperatives, the Board said,
must take precedence over any possible moves toward merger. The
Board admitted that "duplication of services by regional cooperatives
was costly to the farmer," but at the same time Farmland leaders made
it clear that service to local cooperatives was more important than
working with other regionals.[54] As Young expressed it, Farmland
should not "relax its activities [of getting new member cooperatives]
while we wait for other organizations to decide what they want to
do."[55]

Consequently, Farmland was always alert to the opportunity to expand the number of its affiliated associations. Most of the increase in
local association membership came from cooperatives that had never
affiliated with any regional. Sometimes they were newly organized
associations. But at other times local cooperatives dropped their affiliation with other regionals and joined Farmland.

Speaking to a group of Minnesota cooperators in October, 1965,
Young said that he saw no reason to recognize some imaginary geographical boundary between Farmland and other regional cooperatives in Minnesota. Farmland, he said, should welcome membership
of local associations who wanted the services and products that could
be provided by the Kansas City cooperative. Young added that "the
bulk of Farmland's membership" was not "afraid of getting too big.
It is urging management to grow and expand wherever growth and
expansion can mean more service to farmers and better savings." At
the annual meeting a few weeks later, the delegates approved a principle on bigness that said of CCA: "It must be big enough to be efficient. It must be big enough to attract top-quality technicians and

53 Executive Committee, Minutes, April 15, 1966; Board of Directors, Minutes, May
24–25, 1966.
54 Board of Directors, Minutes, October 26–27, 1965.
55 Talk by Young, October 28, 1965, "CCA's Position in Relation to Consolidations and
Mergers," Farmland Industries, Inc., Merger File.

administrators. It must be strong enough to stand up to special interest groups that would destroy cooperatives if they could."[56]

For some time a few cooperatives in Illinois had considered affiliation with Farmland Industries. In April, 1966, representatives from nine associations in North-Central Illinois traveled to Kansas City to inspect Farmland facilities there and to visit the nitrogen plant at Lawrence, Kansas, with the intent of possible affiliation with Farmland. On May 17, Farmland officials formally invited those nine cooperatives to become members, an invitation that was readily accepted. This was Farmland's first expansion into Illinois, a move that was not welcomed by FS Services, Inc., the Farm Bureau regional.[57]

Other affiliations and mergers came the following year. At Young's last Board of Directors' meeting before his retirement on August 31, 1967, he reported on merger negotiations with the Minnesota Farm Bureau Service Company, a regional cooperative in St. Paul. The arrangements were completed in October when Farmland bought the company's facilities, including the headquarters in St. Paul, a fertilizer plant, a feed mill, and some other property. This was a full merger that absorbed into Farmland some seventy-six people as well as properties of the Farm Bureau Service Company.[58] Fourteen Minnesota cooperatives joined Farmland. Discussions were also carried on with the Southern Farm Supply Association of Amarillo, Texas, during 1966 and 1967. In March, 1968, Farmland purchased this regional, giving Farmland a strong foothold of eighty-three member cooperatives in West Texas.[59]

Steadily increasing sales volume and larger savings demonstrated the economic wisdom of expanding Farmland's manufacturing facilities. Young and other Farmland executives had insisted that simply being a broker or distributor of commodities could not earn the margins generated by manufacturing. This had proved to be a sound position. As the fertilizer plants came on line in the middle 1960's, each year's business topped the one before. At the close of the fiscal

[56] *Ibid.*; *Guidelines For Growth*, December, 10, 1965, pamphlet.

[57] *Cooperative Consumer*, April 30, 1966, 1; memorandum, Vernon Lewis to Young, May 17, 1966; Minutes of meeting on Illinois Accounts; and *Leadership*, June–July, 1966, 14.

[58] *Farmland*, November 15, 1967, 1; *Teammates*, January–February, 1968, 3, Secretary's Farmland No. 135, Office of Corporate Secretary.

[59] Board of Directors, Minutes, April 2–3, 1968; *Farmland*, March 15, 1968, 3.

year on August 31, 1967, a date that coincided with Young's retirement, Farmland's gross sales reached $367 million, nearly double the
figure of 1961 when he assumed the presidency. Savings climbed to
$29.2 million, up from $14.9 million six years earlier. The number
of member associations had grown only modestly, increasing from
1,704 to 1,780 in the same period, but many of them were doing a
great deal more business. By 1967 some 37 of Farmland's affiliated
local associations were doing an annual volume of more than $1
million, with the top association showing sales exceeding $5 million.[60]

While Farmland handled a wide range of products, it concentrated
on petroleum, fertilizer, and commercial feeds. These were commodities that large, efficient farmers were using in ever-increasing quantities. The cost and quality of these products were of utmost importance
to farmers who suffered from a tight cost-price squeeze during the
middle 1960's. In 1966 petroleum, fertilizer, and feeds accounted for
82 per cent of the merchandise furnished patrons, and about the same
percentage of gross margins.[61] While, as will be shown later, Farmland
engaged in some unsuccessful enterprises, it followed the kind of
businesses that would best serve Midwestern farmers and those where
the company had a proven success record.

When the time came for Young to retire, the Board of Directors
had no inclination to extend his tenure as it had done with Cowden.
The Board did permit him to continue to the end of the fiscal year on
August 31, 1967, some three and a half months beyond his sixty-fifth
birthday. But that was all.

Young's retirement ended an era in Farmland's history. He was
the last person to head the company from among those who might be
considered the "founding fathers." Young began working for Cowden
in 1931, and now the only first-generation top executive left was
Treasurer Ewing.

Young made some distinctive contributions during his long years
of service, including his six years as president. Believing strongly in
cooperative principles, Young sold CCA to doubting farmers during
the years of struggle when he had little to offer except an idea. There
were no refineries, fertilizer plants, or oil wells to discuss in those
early days. Yet, through his efforts many local cooperatives joined up
with CCA.

---

60 *39th Annual Report*, 1967, 22.
61 Farmland Industries, Inc., *Prospectus*, December 27, 1966, 10.

His greatest contribution as president was to expand Farmland's manufacturing capabilities. Young was intensely proud of the company's expansion during his presidency. In a summary report to the Board on May 23 prior to his retirement, he pointed out that total volume had increased 92 per cent and savings 102 per cent in the six years he had headed Farmland Industries. He especially emphasized that during his years in office $63 million went to member patrons in cash refunds. While he boasted of company achievements, he never tried to hide Farmland's problems. In his final report to the Board he mentioned five projects "that are not doing so well," but he predicted that "they will all work out in good shape in the future." Time proved him only partly correct.

Young had an innate sense of when to act. His leadership in building three large fertilizer plants in the mid-1960's, and his quick move to rescue FEMIC were excellent examples of his decisiveness. On the other hand, he knew when not to act. His economic research staff once recommended that Farmland build an egg plant at Storm Lake, Iowa. Young, however, concluded on the basis of other information that the egg industry was leaving the Midwest and shifting to the South. In that case the Farmland plant simply could not succeed. After some ballyhoo about the egg facility, Young simply called the whole thing off. He also promptly dismissed Shea, the new vice-president who had come on Board after the Fry Consultants recommended an administrative reorganization. Within a short time Young saw that Shea was not going to fit successfully into the Farmland organization and promptly eased him out.

Young was not an easy executive to work for. He was impatient, somewhat unpredictable, and a driver. As one longtime associate said, "he did not get ulcers, he gave them." Other top Farmland officials learned to appraise his moods carefully. During a meeting held to discuss the corporate name change, Young walked out because he did not believe that the hired professionals were doing their job. It was sometimes tense around the corporate headquarters during the Young years because the president's anger was known to explode on more than one occasion. As one executive remarked, there were times when it was not easy to work for Young, but it was never dull. Near the end of his presidency, some strain existed between Young and a few members of the Board of Directors. Young was at his best in the field conducting local or regional meetings. He had an astonishing ability to control an audience, and anyone who tackled him in a parliamentary maneuver was likely to come out the loser. Young's strengths were especially appropriate for the years he led the company, and his shortcomings were less of a handicap than they might have been in a different period. He was a mover and a shaker at a time when the company needed that kind of leadership.

Chapter 16

The Early Lindsey Years

T HE BOARD OF DIRECTORS did not wait for Homer Young's official retirement before naming his successor. At its January 31, 1967, meeting, the Board appointed a Management Committee consisting of Chairman John L. Schulte, Vice-chairman George Voth, and Byron Torell to screen prospective candidates and make a recommendation to the full Board. Two months later, on March 28, this committee recommended that Ernest T. Lindsey, executive vice-president for manufacturing and production, be named president effective September 1, 1967. The Board enthusiastically approved this recommendation and instructed the Management Committee to work closely with Young and Lindsey to insure a smooth transition of leadership in the months ahead.[1] *Farmland* gave the appointment modest coverage in a short front-page story on April 15. It was clear that no action would be taken to reduce or impair Young's effectiveness before his actual retirement. One of the reasons the Board appointed Lindsey early was to get him fully involved in budget preparation for the following year.

If there had been speculation among members of the "Farmland Family" as to who might succeed Young, the Board never had any doubts—it would be Lindsey. A. H. Stephenson, executive vice-president for distribution, had aspirations for the top post, but he was unable to gain support from more than one or two Board members. Moreover, the Board did not seriously consider going outside the Farmland group for new leadership. As Torell, a member of the

---

[1] Board of Directors, Minutes, January 31–February 2 and March 28–29, 1967.

committee recalled later, "we wanted someone, if possible, from within the organization."[2] Board members had full confidence in Lindsey as an executive and as a person. They saw no need to look further. His experience in production and manufacturing may have been important because this had been Farmland's emphasis and the direction in which the Board wanted to continue.

Lindsey was Farmland's first president who did not have a solid farm background. While he was born on a farm near Canton, Texas, in 1915, he spent his youth in the small towns of East Texas. After graduating from Trinity University with a major in chemistry, he went to work for the Humble Oil Corporation (Exxon). He eventually worked up to manager of a butadiene plant. In 1945 he joined the Celanese Chemical Company in Corpus Christi as a production engineer. By 1957 he became the manager of manufacturing and later vice-president. After seventeen years with Celanese, he accepted Young's offer in 1963 to become assistant general manager of manufacturing. Lindsey's calm, quiet, and effective leadership had impressed Board members from the time he moved to Kansas City. What they really liked was what one Board member called his "solid character." His lack of farm background was soon forgotten as he developed an easy relationship with cooperative leaders and members of local associations throughout Farmland territory.

There was no doubt about his commitment to farmers and to the agricultural industry. Raised in predominantly rural communities, he held many of the ideas adhered to by the most dedicated agricultural fundamentalists. "I have always held a strong belief," he told a Kansas City audience, "that the moral fiber of our nation, from the beginning, has been deeply rooted in the agricultural people. This is so fundamental to our well-being as a country," he continued, "that our efforts to maintain an economically strong farm populace can bring rewards far beyond the material." On another occasion he talked about the family farm being the "bulwark of our nation in these tumultuous times." This kind of rhetoric struck a warm response among Farmland's patrons. However, Lindsey viewed farming as a business, an attitude that was never swayed by any kind of agrarian sentimentality.

The element that distinguished the Lindsey administration was the apparent difference in spirit, tone, and attitude within the co-

2 Byron Torell to author, February 8, 1978.

operative, rather than any major change in corporate organization or policy. He was much more the modern organization-type executive than either Cowden or Young. Lindsey gave people authority and responsibility and expected them to perform. He operated through the organizational chain of command to a much greater extent than his predecessors who were known to ignore vice-presidents and other executives and go directly to a person down the line for information or to get a job done. As one second-level executive said who worked for all three presidents, "Cowden and Young would give you the responsibility but not quite the needed authority to do a job. Lindsey gave you both the responsibility and the authority." People felt at ease with Lindsey. He was even-tempered, democratic, and friendly. He could often be seen eating lunch in the company cafeteria and chatting with any and all levels of employees. As one third-level manager said, "In what other large company could I see and visit with the president at lunch?" Lindsey was a teamman. As he told all employees early after he took office, "we work *with each other* to accomplish great things." He added: "We must work, too, at keeping this a warm and friendly and personal organization."[3]

There were other changes around Farmland headquarters. For years bells signaled the beginning and end of each day. Lindsey viewed this schoolmaster approach as unnecessary and inappropriate. He quietly ordered the bells discontinued. Much more important to company executives was Lindsey's view toward salaries. As mentioned earlier, both Cowden and Young had kept their salaries relatively low, which, in turn, held down the compensation of second- and third-level administrators as well. No top executive in Farmland Industries really made a competitive salary until Lindsey's presidency. While the Board initially paid Lindsey $60,000 annually, plus benefits, the same as Young received in his last year, salaries soon began to rise substantially.

Early in Lindsey's administration the Board, under his careful guidance, recognized the importance of paying competitive salaries. The Board frankly admitted, at least to itself, that "the compensation of top officials has been very modest compared to compensation of top officials in other businesses of comparable size." The Board emphasized that salaries should be determined on the basis of "responsibility, productivity, creativity, performance, potential, and internal

[3] *Teammates*, August–September, 1967, 2.

equity as well as external competitive conditions."[4] Executive salaries soon began to increase. By the fiscal year ending August 31, 1970, Lindsey received $85,000, and Ewing, the treasurer, and Leith, the secretary, earned $40,000 and $37,000, respectively. This was encouraging to younger executives who could see better days ahead as the president's salary was removed as an effective lid on other salaries. By 1976 Lindsey's salary had gone to $195,000, and two top vice-presidents to $103,000 and $100,000.[5] Salaries moved up all along the line. While Farmland still paid its top administrators less than non-cooperative firms of equal size, the salaries were good enough to hold top people. Having adopted a more competitive salary structure, Farmland abolished the policy of paying deferred compensation without any employee contributions. Cowden had received $20,000 a year for four years after retirement at age sixty-eight, and Young got $25,000 annually for ten years following retirement at age sixty-five.[6] Farmland did provide regular retirement and incentive plans, and also a management performance plan and executive deferred compensation plan. These latter benefits were based upon the record of company performance and net savings.

Upon assuming the presidency, Lindsey gave first priority to corporate planning that would involve both Farmland and its affiliated associations. Even before he formally assumed the presidency, he outlined what he hoped to achieve, or what he called "dimensions of growth," at a manager-president conference held in Kansas City on August 24–25. Some 1,800 people from 675 cooperatives attended to honor Young in retirement and to hear the new president state his views. When he would walk out "the front door to retirement" [1980], Lindsey said that he wanted to look back upon a "billion dollar cooperative still dedicated to improving the economic position of farmers." Moreover, he wanted to see a financially sound corporation, a cooperative completely integrated "from production of minerals to manufacturing of consumer food products," and an organization that placed cooperatives on a new footing and "recognized as a basic part of our national agricultural structure." Finally, he hoped to leave a business that distributed agricultural products world wide

---

4 Board of Directors, Minutes, October 27–28, 1968.
5 Farmland Industries, Inc., *Prospectus*, January 11, 1977, 42, and January 14, 1972, 18–19.
6 Board of Directors, Minutes, August 27–28, 1968.

and have Farmland held in "the highest respects by all segments of society." In short, the new president had large and ambitious goals.[7]

On Lindsey's initiative, at its August 29–30 meeting, just two days before he officially became president, the Board devoted extensive discussions to future objectives and planning. Besides passing a resolution supporting long-range planning, the Board directed Lindsey and his management team to draw up a new statement of company objectives. Actually, work had already begun on this. Hamil reported to the Board on plans for a new program entitled "Route 70" to replace the previous goals outlined in "Project 67." *Route 70* was the term to be applied to "a developing program that will point Farmland Industries and its member cooperatives toward opportunities and challenges of the 1970's." The specifics of the program would be worked out after soliciting ideas from the local associations.[8]

Early in September Lindsey appointed a committee consisting of Hamil, Leith, and Williams to update Farmland's objectives. He wanted something to present to the Board of Directors at the October meeting less than two months away. The committee quickly prepared a new statement of objectives that received Board approval at the October 24–25 meeting. The statement began by reemphasizing that the basic goal of Farmland was "to improve the economic position of agricultural producers." Farmland's patron-ownership and "its singular involvement with the welfare of agricultural producers" was, according to the committee, what made the cooperative distinct and different from investor-owned businesses.[9]

The question of how to develop and maintain the concept of Farmland's uniqueness was becoming an increasingly troublesome problem to company officials. To many people Farmland was beginning to look like numerous other large industrial corporations listed in *Fortune*'s 500. In his first annual report Lindsey openly confronted this matter. He admitted that there was much in his presentation that "is quite similar to the contents of the annual reports of conventional businesses of comparable size." But then he proceeded to tell the shareholders that Farmland was much more than a company that made money manufacturing and distributing supplies to farmers.

7 *Farmland*, September 15, 1967, 7.
8 Board of Directors, Minutes, August 28–30, 1967.
9 Memorandum, Ernest T. Lindsey to Hamil, September 8, 1967; Board of Directors, Minutes, October 24–25, 1967.

Farmland was different, he said, because the company dealt with its owners and saved money *"for them."* [10] This message was repeated with increasing frequency, and it was central to planning and to the development of long-range objectives.

After declaring that Farmland was "sensitive to its agricultural origins and support" and to economic conditions that "tend to put the basic agricultural producer at a disadvantage," fifteen basic objectives were outlined for future guidance. These included providing high-quality products and services, assuring member associations a full complement of needed services, maintaining a sound financial structure, encouraging farm marketing cooperatives, and continuous planning for growth "in size and effectiveness." These and other objectives were not new. They simply emphasized and advertised Farmland's current directions. The statements and editorial comment were published in leaflet form and approved by the shareholders at their annual meeting on December 8.[11]

Meanwhile, Farmland officials were considering ideas to be incorporated into the Route 70 program. While continued expansion and efficiency of Farmland facilities was assumed, the immediate problem was to help strengthen the local member associations. As Lindsey stated, Farmland was urging "local boards and managers to look at their organizations in terms of what Farmland Industries could do to meet new and changing conditions." "We are asking," he added, "the locals to join with us in building. . .a new road that they and Farmland Industries can travel together in the 1970's,"—Route 70.[12]

To map out this road, an evaluation committee headed by Leith surveyed local associations in the fall of 1967. While Leith found much to encourage Farmland officials, the survey turned up numerous problems that needed attention. These included better recruitment and training of managers, and over-all management assistance and advice to member associations. Locals also needed help with capital financing, member relations, director-training programs, and merchandising. The survey revealed that many local cooperatives were not being operated as effectively and efficiently as was either possible or desirable, and they were looking to Farmland for advice and help. The Board voted to budget $1 million to assist member

[10] *39th Annual Report*, 1967, 4.
[11] *Statement of Objectives*, leaflet, 1967.
[12] *39th Annual Report*, 1967, 5.

cooperatives in the year ahead.[13] If Farmland was to expand, and if cooperatives were to provide greater service to farmers, they must work closely together and be mutually supportive.

To get firsthand views from the grass roots, Lindsey and other Farmland executives set out on February 26, 1968, to explain the goals of Route 70 in a series of meetings with local cooperative leaders. Starting at Manhattan, Kansas, they ended up with a gathering in St. Paul on March 24. Lindsey talked about purposes "beyond the dollar sign" and argued that strong cooperatives would help preserve the family farm.[14]

As finally developed, the Route 70 program established six major objectives for the local associations. The goals were to increase membership and pride in cooperatives, to achieve better financial standards, to improve educational and communication programs, and to work for increased volume. Farmland set up an awards program to stimulate local associations to meet fixed objectives, especially in membership, education, and sales. For example, to qualify for CO-OP JETAWAY, a trip to Mexico City, a cooperative must increase its purchases from Farmland by 5 per cent, or $100,000 a year, whichever was greater. The program was to extend for two years, from September 1, 1968, to September 1, 1970. This was really the beginning of a planned incentive program by Farmland, which continued in future years on a regular basis. Such programs were part of the total Farmland effort to bring the regional and the member associations into a closer and more effective working relationship.

The goal of increasing total business was achieved rather easily. From sales of $367,091,000 in 1967, volume jumped to $442,279,000 in 1969 and to $629,803,000 in 1970.[15] This record came both from serving larger local associations and adding more members. But the largest gain came from including for the first time in 1970 all income from Farmland food-marketing operations that added $188.9 million to total volume. Nevertheless, the expansion without food marketing was impressive, increasing nearly $75 million in three years.

As mentioned earlier, in 1967 and 1968 groups of cooperatives in Minnesota and Texas became members of Farmland, and individual

13 Memorandum, Route 70 Evaluation Committee to Lindsey, November 29, 1967; Board of Directors, Minutes, December 4–5, 1967.

14 *Farmland*, March 15, 1968, 10.

15 *42nd Annual Report*, 1970, 18.

associations in New Mexico, Kentucky, Louisiana, North Dakota, and elsewhere affiliated with the Kansas City regional. Thus Farmland's service territory gradually expanded from the Canadian border nearly to the Rio Grande, and from the Rocky Mountains to east of the Mississippi. This expansion occurred when Farmland took in cooperatives that had previously done business with other regionals, while in other cases it attracted those with no regional affiliation. In a few instances Farmland helped to form new local associations that became members. The number of member cooperatives remained fairly steady at between 1,700 and 1,800 from 1960 to 1967, but substantial growth occurred in 1968 and 1969. By 1970 some 2,085 local cooperatives were members of Farmland Industries.[16]

The growth in membership did not just happen. It was the result of a basic Farmland policy to expand its services and product sales. As early as May, 1965, Lindsey had sent an interoffice memo to Hamil, saying that Farmland should stake out its geographical territory and work at its development. Personnel at all levels, from fieldmen to president, touted the benefits of membership in Farmland. The main sales pitch was that Farmland could provide more and better services than other regionals. Company spokesmen made much of Farmland's growing fertilizer plants, oil refineries, feed mills, farm chemical facilities, research and development offices, and credit services, all patron owned. They had about $330 million worth of property, plants, and equipment to talk about. The message seemed to be, join Farmland and become a part of a vibrant, growing organization that will save farmers more money and provide better services than other suppliers.

Farmland's burgeoning business was also closely associated with the growing volume handled by many of the local associations. This meant that an increasing number of farmers were turning to cooperatives for their operational supplies, and that larger producers were purchasing bigger quantities. For example, in 1965 only 4 out of 1,788 members purchased in excess of $2 million in products from Farmland, but by 1970 there were 13 in that category. By 1975 all of the member associations in the top 50 exceeded $2 million in wholesale purchases from the regional.[17]

One of the problems of member cooperatives was to get wider participation by farmer members. It was what some cooperative leaders

---

[16] *Ibid.*, 1970, n.p.
[17] See pertinent annual report.

called the 20—80 problem—20 per cent of the members often generated as much as 80 per cent of the volume. Lindsey was much aware of this situation. He repeatedly urged member associations to appeal to all farmers. "The big job," he said, "is to find out what members want and need and what they might want and might need tomorrow." Cooperatives, Farmland officials warned, must be able to service the needs of both big and small farmers, and be able to adjust to the rapidly changing conditions in agriculture.[18]

One of Farmland's advantages over other regionals in the Midwest was the development of a wide variety of services to the member associations, especially in the areas of education, management, and finance. While these services had been provided for several years, the Route 70 program recognized that Farmland must do more to assist the locals. As mentioned elsewhere, historically many local cooperatives had failed because of poor management and lack of capital. Often these two matters were directly related. With poor management capital was hard to acquire, and, if obtained, its unwise use would probably lead to failure. While Farmland had been active in trying to help locals solve these and other problems, most of the effort had been directed toward smaller and weaker associations. After 1967, however, management and financial assistance were offered to the most successful cooperatives as well as those in trouble.

To meet the problem of poor management among local cooperatives, Farmland intensified its educational and management-training programs in the field. The regional employed management specialists who helped locals with credit and marketing policies, consumer relations, product displays, personnel matters, and other problems. In 1969 Farmland added several men to the field force in order to step up training of local employees. Farmland also conducted schools and clinics for managers and directors in its Kansas City School of Cooperation. The over-all aim, according to company officials, was to "improve the professional leadership of member associations."[19]

Local cooperatives also needed financial and credit assistance. The Cooperative Finance Association, a wholly owned subsidiary, provided operating and facility loans to member associations. Beginning modestly, by the late 1960's Farmland had millions of dollars in outstanding loans to local associations. The figure reached $57.2 million in 1969 and continued upward. By year end in 1975, CFA had out-

18 *Farmland*, May 30, 1968, 21.
19 *41st Annual Report*, 1969, 8.

standing loans of $78.5 million. The income from interest on such loans became substantial by the early and middle 1970's, reaching nearly $8 million in 1975.[20] These loans, along with money from the banks for cooperatives, greatly strengthened the credit and financial situation of many local associations. This, of course, was to Farmland's advantage because larger and stronger cooperatives handled more commodities.

One of the most serious problems facing local cooperatives was the lack of loyalty by member patrons. Coming from the noncooperative business sector, this situation puzzled Lindsey. In his first report as president, he declared: "Ever since I came with Farmland Industries, it has been a little hard for me to see why a cooperative should constantly have to be selling itself and its services to the people who own it. But the hard, cold facts are that no cooperative can survive without an active and aggressive program of member relations."[21]

The evidence clearly confirmed Lindsey's observation. Many members of farmer cooperatives were not completely loyal to their association. Late in 1965 Farmland's Planning and Research Division did a study of "Iowa Farmers and Farm Cooperatives" to determine the extent to which farmers in that state depended on their cooperatives. The results were not encouraging for the farmer cooperative movement. The survey found that eight out of ten Iowa farmers belonged to a cooperative and that 90 per cent of them lived within fifteen miles of a local association. But only about 30 per cent reported 100 per cent loyalty to their cooperatives, and a mere 5 per cent bought all of their petroleum, feed, and fertilizer from cooperative sources. The survey also showed that there had been no significant change in farm attitudes between 1957 and 1965 regarding whether or not cooperatives were a real help to farmers. When members were asked why they did not buy 100 per cent from their cooperatives, they gave such replies as, "if I find a better buy somewhere else, I buy from another firm"; "can get them [supplies] as cheap and often quicker elsewhere"; "not if I can buy more competitively from a private firm"; and "I can buy some things of same or as good quality cheaper elsewhere."[22] Such replies indicated that farmers were sensitive to prices, especially during a severe cost-price squeeze.

20 *47th Annual Report*, 1975, 38.
21 *39th Annual Report*, 1967, 6.
22 Planning and Research Division, "Iowa Farmers and Farm Cooperatives," November, 1965.

Somehow farmers had to be convinced that they must buy from their cooperatives, even when they might make a better business deal elsewhere. But it was tempting for members to purchase products from noncooperative sources when they could get a better price or perhaps better service. In the 1960's price wars among marketers of petroleum and fertilizer were fairly common and sometimes gasoline might be bought for a penny or two a gallon less from one of the major oil companies than from the cooperative handling Farmland petroleum products. How could cooperatives meet that kind of situation? One alternative was to join the price cutting, but that would reduce profits and refunds to members. While most cooperatives sought to be competitive, sometimes their prices were slightly higher than that of other dealers. In those cases it took considerable persuasion to convince the farmer of marginal loyalty that he should continue to patronize his cooperative. To deal with this problem, cooperative spokesmen argued that, despite some differentiation in price, members should buy from their own organization. This, they said, would help strengthen the cooperative and in the long run assure farmer members high-quality merchandise at fair prices. They also held out the prospect of always having the kind of services that farmers needed such as supplying equipment to spread fertilizer when the producer needed it. Besides, farmers would earn refunds when they did business with their cooperative.

In the late 1960's Farmland stepped up its advice and assistance to local associations in the area of member relations. Personnel in the member cooperatives were urged to call on local farmers and explain to them the values of membership and loyalty to their association. Farmland provided ideas, publicity materials, and directed fieldmen to help local associations carry out member relations programs.

As a part of developing better service and building stronger member support, Farmland officials urged local cooperatives to build what were called full farm service centers. Such centers envisioned a single place where farmers could go for their petroleum products, tires, batteries, accessories, fertilizer and equipment to spread it, farm chemicals, and other operational needs. In May, 1969, Lindsey presented a special report to the Board on this subject. He argued that Farmland needed to be doing much more to encourage the building and operation of such centers by local cooperatives. The Board of Directors than passed a resolution saying that "modern efficient retail facilities" were essential to strengthen local associations and authorized Farmland officials to work with farmers and member cooperatives to develop such centers by providing financial and management assistance.[23]

During the next few years, an increasing number of cooperatively owned farm service centers sprouted up in towns throughout Farmland's territory. Farmland helped scores of member associations to establish such centers. Cooperatives affiliated with other regionals followed a similar pattern. While farmer patrons took pride in their new service centers, such enterprises were often unwelcome by other businessmen in the community. Anti-cooperative attitudes and comments found expression on many main streets throughout mid-America as old-line establishments felt the competition of the new, efficient, and attractive cooperative farm business centers.

During the late 1960's, Farmland's total volume expanded rapidly, but savings did not grow proportionately. Indeed savings were embarrassingly small in 1968 and 1969. Net savings before income taxes and patronage refunds on a volume of $442,279,000 in 1969 amounted to only $9,254,000, and cash refunds to patrons fell to a mere $2,161,-000.[24] The problem was a weak fertilizer market.

During the 1960's, fertilizer capacity experienced record growth. Oil, gas, chemical, and other companies rushed to increase their facilities to get in on what most authorities agreed would soon be a most profitable enterprise both at home and abroad. Not only were American farmers buying increasing amounts of chemical nutrients, foreign demand and shipments abroad by the Agency for International Development provided a strong market for the industry. United States companies invested some $4 billion in fertilizer production from 1963 to 1968. This expansion, according to one authority, "bordered on the irrational."[25] The effects of such reckless expansion were predictable—price wars, poor profits or none at all, and, in some cases, quitting the business. For example, Armour and Company sold its fertilizer subsidiary early in 1967, and the El Paso Natural Gas Company closed its large Idaho plant at about the same time.

As previously explained, Farmland had been a part of the fertilizer explosion of the 1960's. However, it and other cooperatives were in a better position to meet the price declines than their noncooperative

---

23 Board of Directors, Minutes, May 27–28, 1969.

24 Farmland Industries, Inc., "Consolidated Sales, Savings and Patronage Refunds, 1929–1977," typewritten summary.

25 Thomas O'Hanlon, "All That Fertilizer and No Place to Grow," *Fortune*, LXXVII (June 1, 1968), 92–95.

competitors. Farmland's advantage rested in having a built-in distribution and marketing system—its network of some 2,000 member cooperatives. Since Farmland was owned by the local associations, they had a self-interest in doing business with their own company. Lindsey said that Farmland's "membership market" represented "stability and continuity beyond anything any other manufacturer can claim."[26] But as prices declined—anhydrous ammonia dropped from $100 to $65 a ton between 1967 and 1968—and noncooperative producers offered fertilizers at cut-rate prices to get rid of huge inventories, Farmland and its member associations faced a real problem of holding customer loyalty.

Farmland, of course, cut prices to meet competition. Even then, however, large amounts of fertilizer were offered at figures well below normal competitive rates—termed by Lindsey as the "temporary price temptations." To build support against any threat to the stability of Farmland's $100,000,000-plus fertilizer program, Lindsey wrote a personal letter to all presidents and managers of the member associations on July 30, 1968. His letter stated that local cooperatives and their farmer members should not give up the long-range advantages of a farmer-owned fertilizer industry for temporary price gains. Admitting that there would be "precious little fertilizer refund" returned to local cooperatives and farmers in 1968, he warned that if farmers were to continue as a major factor in the fertilizer business, they must "stand by their cooperatives" and not succumb to cut-rate prices from noncooperative sources. He compared the situation to the gasoline price wars of a few years before when the major oil companies put pressure on the independents. Farmers, he wrote, must trust "their cooperatives to supply fertilizer at the lowest possible cost, while still keeping cooperatives' fertilizer systems strong and vital." With loyal support from member cooperatives and their farmer patrons, Lindsey believed Farmland's fertilizer program would remain strong and competitive.

Lindsey and the Board had no intention of being stampeded into any rash business decisions because of problems in the fertilizer industry. Even though the new Dodge City anhydrous ammonia plant came on stream in August, 1968, right in the middle of large surpluses and sharp price reductions, Farmland officials were determined to build an industry for the long run. They refused to be influenced by

---

26 *40th Annual Report*, 1968, 3.

temporary setbacks. In 1969, according to Lindsey, fertilizer continued to struggle "in a chaotic market." But Farmland did not retrench, even though several other major companies abandoned production. By the spring of 1970 market conditions greatly improved, and Farmland's fertilizer business increased some 20 per cent over the year before.[27] This condition seemed to prove that Farmland had retained the loyalty of its member associations, and that its determination not to be influenced by temporary setbacks was wise.

If fertilizer production and sales had problems in the late 1960's, the move toward a well-integrated food-marketing program gained strong momentum. This was in line with grass-roots demand that Farmland get more heavily involved in the processing and marketing of farm products. Every study of Farmland's future directions indicated that farmers wanted and expected this of their regional cooperative. Farmers were not only concerned about reducing the cost of off-farm inputs through cooperative action; they were equally interested in getting better prices through cooperative marketing. They wanted cooperative action on both sides of the cost-price equation.[28]

As explained earlier, Farmland had become involved in pork-processing at Denison, Iowa, in 1959, and in late 1963 a new hog plant was opened at Iowa Falls. The packing plants at Denison and Iowa Falls had a capacity to kill 30,000 hogs per week by 1964. Between 1962 and 1967 the pork operations were expanded to include sixteen hog-buying stations, slaughtering and chill plants, and cutting facilities at both locations. In addition, Farmbest moved into processing such finished products as bacon and ham. Its brand names included Farm-King, Farmbest, and Country Manor. Farmbest officials concluded early that they should get into the business of marketing finished products. A study prepared in August, 1960, reported that "the greatest returns can be realized if we develop our own brand and create, through effective merchandizing [*sic*] and superior product quality, strong consumer demand for our products. We must recognize that to create consumer demand for a new brand requires time and a substantial investment in advertising."[29]

27 *41st Annual Report*, 1969, 6; *42nd Annual Report*, 1970, 1a.

28 "Special Report to the CCA Board of Directors on an Integrated Pork Program," August 29, 1960, typewritten report.

29 CCA owned six and leased nine buying stations; one was owned by a local cooperative. *This is Farmbest*, 1966; "Report . . . on an Integrated Pork Program."

The study's conclusion had been a correct prediction. It had taken substantial investment by Farmland to acquire or build plants and to provide operating capital. Farmland had bought 4,000 shares of Farmbest common stock at $1 per share to give the regional cooperative control and then loaned its pork subsidiary $863,755 on a promissory note to purchase the Crawford County Packing Company in 1959. Later Farmland acquired additional common stock and by August 31, 1966, owned 7,500 shares, or 40 per cent of the amount outstanding. In 1963 Farmland provided $1.8 million to build the new Iowa Falls plant. Expansion at Denison, completed early in 1966, took another $900,000, and the cutting equipment at Iowa Falls about $350,000 more. Altogether by August, 1965, Farmbest had invested $4,286,403 in plant and equipment for its pork operations. By that time the subsidiary's long-term debt had reached $5,136,825, which was owed to Farmland and to the Omaha Bank for Cooperatives. Total investment by Farmland in Farmbest reached $5.7 million by August, 1966. Furthermore, Farmbest had established National Farm Lines, a cooperative transportation company to haul Farmbest products and eliminate reliance on commercial carriers. Investment in this company reached $1,121,318 by October, 1965.[30]

During the middle 1960's, Farmbest also expanded other aspects of its meat operation. In 1964 Cheraw Turkeys, Inc. was organized in Colorado to handle turkey production. Farmland had feed-supply arrangements with Colorado turkey growers' cooperatives. As these cooperatives faced financial difficulties, Farmland found it necessary to move into the business to protect its feed investments. By 1967 Farmbest had acquired the assets of the Holbrook Turkey Growers Association, the Colorado Turkey Breeders Association, and those of certain individual producers. The properties included a breeding farm, a hatchery, growing houses, and a processing plant. Farmbest's egg division headquartered at Sioux City, Iowa, opened an egg-cartoning plant at Freeman, South Dakota, in 1963, and later established egg operations at Hutchinson, Kansas, and Eagle Grove, Iowa. By 1967 these plants handled 2.9 million dozen eggs. Eggs were purchased only from producers using CO-OP feed. Farmland loaned money to several local cooperatives to finance both turkey and chicken

---

[30] Farmbest, Inc., *Prospectus,* January 4, 1966; Young, "Report of the President, Farmbest, Inc., September 24, 1962"; and Farmland Industries, Inc., *Prospectus,* December 27, 1966, 17.

enterprises,[31] as a part of the nationwide move toward integration in the poultry business in the 1960's.

In 1964, at the urging of cattle feeders in western Kansas, Farmland began plans to organize a cooperative and construct a beef-packing plant near Garden City. Leith said that such a business would be "a milestone in farmers' efforts to improve the marketing of their own products."[32] On October 30, 1965, Farmland officials and some 3,000 local residents were on hand to dedicate the Producers Packing Company plant. The new facility covered some 35,000 square feet and had a slaughter capacity of about 300 head a day. Located in the heart of a major cattle-feeding area, farmers and cattle feeders in the region believed producers would help them to obtain higher prices. Clarence Winger, a cattle feeder and president of the company, said that "it used to be that we loaded up our cattle, shipped them to market and took what we could get for them." But with a cooperative packing plant, Winger believed farmers and feeders would be in a better marketing position. Cooperative leaders from all over western Kansas and nearby states agreed. They stood by proudly as officials mounted a plaque that read: "This plant is dedicated to the building of a strong livestock industry based upon producer and feeder participation in the processing and marketing of meat." Processed meat was to be sold in large wholesale lots under the Farmbest name.[33] After operating for nearly three years as an independent cooperative with $850,000 of Farmland backing, stockholders of the Producers Packing Company voted to merge into Farmland, making it a Farmland Industries subsidiary as of July 1, 1968. By that time the plant had a capacity to kill some 700 cattle daily.[34]

Farmland's meat operations experienced some troublesome times during the 1960's. The optimistic pronouncements from corporate headquarters and the encouraging references in annual reports could not hide some genuine difficulties. Any hope that farmers had about improving the marketing conditions for hogs and cattle in Farmland territory was just that—hope. The Producers Packing Company

31 Board of Directors, Minutes, March 28–29, 1967; Farmland Industries, Inc., *Prospectus*, January 8, 1968, 18; "A History of Farmland Foods, Inc., March, 1977," typewritten; *40th Annual Report*, 1968, 25; and *Cooperative Consumer*, October 31, 1963, 1.

32 See *Cooperative Consumer*, October 15, 1964, 1, and June 29, 1963, 1, for additional background.

33 *Ibid.*, November 15, 1965, 3–5.

34 *Farmland*, June 29, 1968, 2; Board of Directors, Minutes, April 2–3, 1968; and Farmland Industries, Inc., *Prospectus*, January 8, 1968, 18.

suffered yearly losses between 1965, when it opened, and 1968. In 1967 the losses reached $621,655. Farmbest, Inc., which covered the pork operations, also faced serious financial problems. In 1966 and 1967 losses totaled $1,136,170.[35] The turkey and egg business also lost money. Needless to say, in most years producers failed to receive any patronage refunds from their cooperative sale of cattle, hogs, turkey, or eggs.[36]

There were no easy solutions to the problems confronting Farmland's meat-processing business. In the first place, profits in meat packing were historically small. The entire meat industry seldom showed profits above one or two per cent of sales during the 1960's. Furthermore, Farmbest had difficulty establishing an efficient and well-managed operation. While Farmland controlled Farmbest, it was not a wholly owned subsidiary. Its headquarters was in Denison, Iowa, far removed from Kansas City. Moreover, at that time no top-level Farmland executive possessed real expertise in the meat business. Farmland officials soon discovered that slaughtering and wholesaling animal carcasses produced minimal, if any, profits. The only substantial margins in meat came from the sale of finished products such as bacon, ham, weiners, and other ready-to-eat meat. To get into a position to produce finished products and market them took longer and required more capital than most Farmland executives originally realized.

Board members and corporate officials were disappointed over failure of the meat operations to show decent margins. At a meeting in October, 1966, the Board expressed its frustration by passing a motion that said: "Due to inefficiences apparent in the operations of Farmbest, Inc., the Board of Directors of this association hereby instructs the president to use authority in correcting this situation." But to have the authority to act and to know just what to do were two entirely different things. As mentioned above, losses mounted at Farmbest in 1966 and 1967. In 1967 the Board again emphasized the need "to get our present meat operations on an economic [profitable] basis."

The meat operations needed better organization, administration, and management. This included making some hard and painful decisions. For example, the Colorado turkey operations were not profit-

---

[35] Farmland Foods, Inc., historical data. See also *38th Annual Report*, 1966, 16; *39th Annual Report*, 1967, 14.

[36] Board of Directors, Minutes, October 25–26, 1966, and October 24–25, 1967.

able. In the year ending August 31, 1969, Cheraw Turkeys Inc. showed a loss of $84,048. Altogether losses had reached $601,929. Several years of effort had not improved the turkey outlook, and good-business practice dictated that Farmland take its losses and abandon this enterprise. From time to time the Board and management considered doing just that. But it was difficult to pull out and admit failure. Such a move would bring poor publicity to cooperatives in some localities. Moreover, there was always a chance that the operations could be placed on a profitable basis. Consequently, the Cheraw turkey enterprise struggled along. The annual reports either ignored or glossed over the turkey operations. The 1968 annual report announced that the "turkey operations at Cheraw were improved," but it failed to add that they still lost money.[37] One positive aspect of the turkey and egg operations was that they stimulated a demand among various cooperatives for CO-OP feed. Farmbest also lost substantial sums by operating National Farm Lines, its cooperative trucking company.

During the late 1960's, Farmland officials spent a great deal of time studying the food-marketing operations. In August, 1967, the Board directed management to make a thorough investigation of the association's marketing activities. One idea explored was to unify the administration of that phase of Farmland's business.[38] At that time the beef, turkey, and egg businesses were administered directly by divisions of Farmland Industries, but Farmland Industries owned only 40 per cent of Farmbest, which handled the pork processing. Farmbest was not included in the association's consolidated financial statements. Within two months after the Board asked for action, a long-range marketing committee was at work.[39]

But more than two years elapsed before management and the Board were ready to reorganize the food-marketing business. Finally, on April 1, 1970, the Board voted to create Farmland Foods, Inc., a new, almost wholly owned corporation, to handle the association's meat business. This included the pork-packing plants at Denison and Iowa Falls, Iowa, the beef plant at Garden City, Kansas, the turkey-processing plant in Colorado, egg plants at Hutchinson, Kansas, and Eagle Grove, Iowa, and the four-swine testing stations in Iowa and

---

37 Report on Farmland Foods, Inc., March 31, 1970, typewritten statement; *40th Annual Report*, 1968, 25.

38 Board of Directors, Minutes, August 29–30, 1967. A poultry division was organized in 1968. Beef operations were not included in the consolidated statement of Farmland Industries until 1968.

39 Board of Directors, Minutes, October 24–25, 1967.

Nebraska. Through an exchange of marketing facility assets with a book value of $4,893,707 and cash of $1,500,000 in exchange for 6,393,707 shares of Farmland Foods common stock, Farmland Industries gained ownership of 99 per cent of Farmland Foods. Participating livestock producers owned the remaining 1 per cent of the common stock. All of the necessary arrangements were approved by the Farmbest shareholders at a meeting on April 23. The office of Farmland Foods was moved to Kansas City, and Fred R. Clymer became president. Clymer had joined Farmland Industries in 1964 after being with Swift and Company for some twenty-five years.[40] Thomas A. Dempsey, who had been controller of Farmbest, became secretary and assistant treasurer. Lindsey became chairman of the Farmland Foods board of directors, and Leith, Farmland's corporate vice-president and secretary, was named vice-chairman and given over-all operational responsibility.

Farmland Industries also organized Farmland Agriservices as a wholly owned subsidiary in 1970. The main function of Agriservices was to purchase hogs, cattle, and poultry for slaughter and processing by Farmland Foods. Agriservices soon took over the four-swine testing stations and by the mid-1970's owned and operated twenty-one hog-buying stations. This company also administered Farmland's research and demonstration farm located near Trimble, Missouri. Established in 1958, Farmland employees carried on practical research and various experiments to achieve better crop and livestock production. Much of the work involved the more efficient utilization of feeds and fertilizers. The demonstration farm was also a valuable public-relations tool as it attracted thousands of visitors annually.

In 1971 Farmland purchased 260 acres of land in Wyandotte County, Kansas, near Bonner Springs, about twenty miles west of Farmland's headquarters building in Kansas City, for a new demonstration farm. At its March meeting, the Board authorized management to spend up to $500,000 for land and not more than $1.4 million for improvements. Although not entirely completed until 1973, the new research and demonstration farm held an open house for Farmland members who attended the annual meeting on December 5, 1972. The farm included a 60-acre plot to test fertilizers, seeds and agricultural chemicals, and facilities for practical research in dairying, hog

---

[40] Farmland Industries, Inc., *Prospectus*, November 1, 1971, 47; report on Farmland Foods, Inc., March 31, 1970; *42nd Annual Report*, 1970, 7a; and *Farmland*, April 30, 1970, 1.

and poultry raising, and animal-waste disposal.[41] In 1975 the new demonstration farm attracted nearly 16,000 visitors.

Formation of Farmland Foods as a major corporate subsidiary in 1970 represented a strong commitment by Farmland Industries to expand and improve its marketing services to farmers. Lindsey said that "the consolidation of these food operations in one corporate unit will permit new efficiencies that are increasingly important as our activities in these areas expand."[42] More specifically it indicated a strong desire to help Midwestern livestock farmers, especially pork producers, in the marketing aspect of their business. Farmland's entire livestock program involved upgrading the quality of hogs through operation of its swine-testing stations and feed programs, offering competitive market prices for these better hogs, paying patronage refunds to cooperative producers, and finally marketing the processed pork. Farmland officials said thay wanted an integrated swine program that would extend "from testing station to dinner," or as it was expressed, "from first oink to the dining table."[43] By 1973 Farmland Foods processed about 10 per cent of the hogs raised in Iowa.

Fortunately, the organization of Farmland Foods coincided with better general business conditions and improved prospects for the meat industry. In 1971, the first full year of operation, the food-marketing business showed remarkable gains. Farmland Foods slaughtered and processed 2,042,437 hogs at Denison and Iowa Falls, and 242,000 cattle at Garden City. Patronage refunds to hog producers were substantial for the first time, reaching an average of $1.22 per hog. On cattle the patronage refund was $2.48 per head.[44] The low price of hogs in 1971 made the refund most welcome to producers and strengthened the grass-roots support for Farmland Foods' hog-marketing operations.

Even as Farmland Foods was organized, plans for expansion were already being considered. Leith, the "architect" of reorganization, said in April, 1970, that "long-range plans already formulated involve additional facilities and programs to mesh the capabilities of the modern farmer with the needs of a dynamic food industry." Plans to enlarge the so-called red meat operations called for a fixed capital

---

41 Board of Directors, Minutes, March 30–31, 1971; *37th Annual Report*, 1965, 31; *41st Annual Report*, 1969, 10; and *47th Annual Report*, 1975, 20.

42 Farmland Industries, news release, April 23, 1970.

43 *Cooperative Consumer*, February 15, 1962; *Leadership*, February, 1976, 3.

44 Farmland Foods, Inc., historical data.

investment of some $5,300,000 to be completed in several stages. The first move was to acquire a canning plant at Carroll, Iowa, with the idea of ultimately transferring the canning operations from Denison. Farmland Foods purchased a facility from Ocoma Foods that was enlarged and extensively renovated. Canning began on a limited basis at Carroll on September 15, 1972, and full production followed in January. Some 3,500 persons attended the open house on October 21 and observed one of the largest and most modern facilities of its kind in the United States.[45]

Another phase of the food-marketing expansion, which was completed in 1974, was to enlarge the curing, smoking, and slicing facilities, and to alter and expand the hog-cutting operations at Denison. Also during 1974 the Iowa Falls plant was enlarged to include cutting facilities that began operation in October. With improved processing facilities at both Denison and Iowa City, Farmland Foods no longer sold hog carcasses. Another major expansion in 1974 was the beginning of construction of an addition to the Garden City beef plant to provide more processed meat, including boxed beef. This facility was completed in 1975.

But more important was the decision to build another pork-processing plant. On August 29, 1972, the Board decided to construct a slaughtering and processing facility somewhere in eastern Nebraska at a cost of around $12 million. On December 20 Lindsey and Gov. J. J. Exon of Nebraska jointly announced that the new plant would be located near Crete. In July, 1973, the Farmland Industries Board approved expenditures of up to $18,500,000 for construction of the plant and working capital. While officials hoped to complete the facility by mid-1974, it was not ready for operation until about a year later. An estimated 10,000 visitors were on hand to help dedicate the plant on August 24, 1975, and to enjoy a free lunch featuring Farmland ham.[46] Using the latest and most modern meat technology, this plant had a capacity of about 3,600 hogs per day. By the middle 1970's Farmland Foods was selling branded products in forty-two states.

Despite the corporate reorganization and expansion of facilities, problems continued in the food processing and marketing business.

45 *Farmland*, April 30, 1970, 2; Fred R. Clymer, management report for Farmland Foods' Annual Shareholders' Meeting, December, 1972; and *Farmland News*, November 15, 1972, 14.

46 Farmland Industries, Inc., *Prospectus*, January 14, 1972, 16; *Farmland News*, December 30, 1972, 16; Board of Directors, Minutes, August 29–30, 1972; and Farmland Industries, Inc., news release, August 24, 1975.

The good margins of 1971 dropped dramatically the following year. Even though total food-marketing volume increased from $188.3 million in 1971 to $214.7 million in 1972, savings amounted to only $1.8 in 1972 compared to $3.4 million the year before. The refund on hogs averaged $0.80 in contrast to $1.22 a year earlier. No patronage refunds were paid on cattle in 1973 as that part of the business barely broke even. The high cost of live hogs and the narrowing margins for finished products were largely responsible for lower returns in 1972. Income from food operations in 1973 reached $251 million, a rather dramatic increase in volume over the preceding years, but savings were only $1.1 million. Nevertheless, small-cash refunds, which amounted to 35 per cent of the savings, were paid to patrons on both hogs and cattle that year.[47]

Some of the enterprises operated by Farmland Foods were outright money losers. The Colorado turkey business continued unprofitable. Part of the problem was that it was a seasonal operation. The turkey-processing plant at Cheraw usually operated only between twenty and thirty weeks a year. During 1972 and 1973 the Board periodically considered closing out the turkey enterprise, but it took no positive action. However, after several years of reappraisal, on October 25, 1976, the Farmland Foods board decided to quit the turkey operations at the end of the current season. The last turkeys were processed on December 17. Leith explained the decision to quit the turkey business by saying there was insufficient membership interest to provide the kind of year-around business that was necessary to compete successfully in the market. There were many sighs of relief around executive offices that this long overdue action had been taken.[48]

Another failure was National Farm Lines, the cooperative trucking company. In 1970 Farmland Foods discontinued this enterprise and wrote off losses of $1,698,941. In its place, the company organized a small trucking firm to haul meat to major outlets within a radius of approximately 600 miles of its plants. This proved to be a successful move. On the other hand, in October, 1973, Farmland Foods acquired Intercontinental Food Industries, Inc., a modern food plant located near Chicago. This wholly owned subsidiary produced a line of pre-cooked, frozen, and ready-to-eat foods for sale to institutional users

---

[47] *44th Annual Report*, 1972, 11; *45th Annual Report*, 1973, 13; Farmland Foods, Inc., historical data; and Farmland Industries, Inc., *Prospectus*, January 16, 1974, 18–19.

[48] *Farmland News*, November 15, 1976, 21; *Lamar News* (Colorado), November 1, 1976; Board of Directors, Minutes, December 4–5, 1972, and December 3–4, 1973; and interview with Thomas A. Dempsey.

such as hospitals, schools, and airlines.[49] Intercontinental Food Industries, which one member of the Farmland Foods board called "that Chicago monstrosity," lost money from the outset. A change of name to Farmland Food Services, Inc. in 1975 did nothing to help the situation. In his annual report of 1975, Lindsey admitted that the "results have been very disappointing" but added that "losses have trended downward for several months." However, this was small comfort. In eleven months in 1974–1975 Farmland Food Services lost about $3.8 million, and losses continued large in subsequent years. Farmland Foods also organized Porkland, Inc., a New Jersey meat enterprise, that proved to be a financial burden.[50]

Nevertheless, food marketing became a major factor in Farmland's total volume after 1970. In 1971, the first year that Farmland Foods was consolidated into Farmland Industries, sales amounted to $188.2 million out of the company's net volume of about $685 million. This was about 27 per cent of the regional's total business. Food marketing continued to produce about that proportion of Farmland's volume through 1972 and 1973, but thereafter its percentage fell substantially. Even though food-marketing volume reached $355 million in 1976, the last year before Farmland's merger with Far-Mar-Co, the big grain-marketing cooperative, that was only 19 per cent of the business done by Farmland Industries.[51]

While Farmland Foods developed a very large red meat business— it ranked around twelfth in the nation in size by the mid-1970's—the company never produced substantial margins, especially when compared to Farmland's other products. According to Leith, "meat marketing is a tough, competitive business, subject to many ups and downs." For example, in 1975 total gross savings amounted to only $5.5 million on $274 million worth of business. All of this came from the hog operations, as the beef, turkeys, and precooked entrees suffered substantial losses. On the much smaller volume of $159.4 million, the company's feed business earned gross savings of more than $12 million. Farmland Foods margins in 1976 did not justify any patronage cash refund. However, in 1977 it appeared as though the meat operations were beginning to turn around. Cash refunds on hogs amounted

49 Farmland Industries, Inc., *Prospectus*, November 1, 1971, 47; Farmland Foods, Inc., *Prospectus*, January 8, 1975, 25.

50 *47th Annual Report*, 1975, 4; Farmland Foods, Inc., historical data. See *Farmland News*, December 31, 1974, 22, for references to losses by Intercontinental Food Industries, Inc., in 1974. Losses from 1974 to 1977 totaled more than $12 million.

51 See the annual reports for the years 1971 to 1976.

to $2.02 per head, the highest figure ever up to that time.[52] John H. Westerhoff who had been active in the meat business for many years became president of Farmland Foods in 1975. He made every effort to increase margins from food marketing.

Up to 1977, the patronage refunds on hogs and cattle were either nonexistent or too small to make a significant difference in the profits of most farmer members. In three of the seven years, from 1971 to 1977 inclusive, no refunds were paid on cattle. In the four years when the producer did receive a patronage refund, it was less than $1 per head except in 1971. Member hog growers got a refund every year except one in that period, but except in 1971 and 1977 it was usually considerably under $1 per head. Over all, pork-processing activities showed substantial savings in the 1970's, but a considerable portion of the margins were offset by losses in other foods operations.

Farmland's food-marketing program had other than financial values. The breeding and feeding programs made available to producers had definite values as the quality of hogs improved. The long, lean, and meaty animals provided the kind of pork consumers demanded. Secondly, Farmland supplied another marketing outlet for hog growers in those areas where processing plants existed. This increased the competition for hogs and may have had some strengthening effect on the market. Furthermore, by encouraging and increasing the number of hogs in such areas as eastern Nebraska, farmers had a better market for their grain. The livestock-marketing program also expanded the demand for Farmland feeds. But perhaps even more important was the fact that it met part of the growing demand by farmers for Farmland Industries to get more heavily involved in farm marketing. It also stimulated pride in being a member of Farmland and its affiliated cooperatives. That food marketing did not produce greater savings was due more to the nature of the meat business than to any other single factor. However, the pork operations had to carry losses in other aspects of Farmland Foods, which reduced the over-all margins of the company.

While it attracted much less attention than the development of Farmland Foods, Farmland Industries put together a full insurance program during the late 1960's and 1970's, as a part of expanding services to cooperatives, their members, and farmers in general. Farmland had avoided getting into the insurance business until 1967 when

---

[52] *48th Annual Report*, 1976, 5, 29; and 1977, 38.

Young decided to save FEMIC from bankruptcy. An investment of $4,476,896 in FEMIC gave Farmland firm control of a financially troubled but going insurance business that had been serving cooperatives in the Midwest for many years. While it was somewhat accidental that Farmland got into the insurance business, in the decade after 1967 the company organized a full line of insurance services.

After gaining control of FEMIC, the next step was to acquire the Farmers Life Insurance Company. Organized in 1961, Farmers Life was a fully owned subsidiary of FEMIC. In December, 1967, Farmland bought the life company's common stock from FEMIC for $1,053,830, and spent $400,000 additional in January, 1968, to obtain the preferred stock owned by the Farmers Grain Dealers Association's Retirement Plan. This gave Farmland 100 per cent ownership of Farmers Life, a stock company.[53] Farmland officials continued to operate the life company as an integral part of FEMIC. At the time it was acquired by Farmland, Farmers Life was a small company with about $64 million of life insurance in force.

During the next few years Farmland moved vigorously to enlarge the services and improve the financial strength of these companies. In February, 1972, Farmland invested another $2 million in Farmers Life whose name was changed to Farmland Life Insurance Company the next month. The idea was to strengthen the company so that it could offer what officials called "a complete line of life, health and accident insurance coverage" to the farmers and ranchers in Farmland's business territory. The insurance programs were also given new leadership. Thomas J. Luck who had been brought in by Young to manage FEMIC resigned, and William L. Balliu was named executive vice-president and chief operating officer. Balliu had been with FEMIC before Farmland took it over and currently held the top position with Farmland Life. As a part of the efforts to improve the insurance business, Balliu moved the executive offices from Des Moines to Kansas City. From 1972 onward the insurance companies began to make real gains.[54] In 1973, Ewing became vice-chairman of the Board of Farmland's subsidiary insurance companies.

In 1973 FEMIC was in a position to repay $2 million of the more than $4 million that Farmland had advanced in 1966 and 1967. Farmland Life and FEMIC both inaugurated new policies and services and gained admission to do business in additional states. In 1972

---

53 *Farmland*, January 15, 1968, 1; W. L. Balliu to author, February 1, 1978.
54 *44th Annual Report*, 1972, 11, 23; *Farmland News*, October 16, 1972, 10.

the life company could sell insurance in only nine states; by 1975 it was authorized to market policies in seventeen states. FEMIC, which had nearly lost its right to do business anywhere in 1966, was providing coverage to cooperatives in thirteen states by the mid-1970's. In December, 1973, Farmland Industries organized a new insurance firm known simply as Farmland Insurance Company. It was wholly owned by Farmland Life and sold personal, casualty, and fire coverage to cooperative members and employees. It added hail insurance in 1976 by which time it was doing business in eleven states.[55]

In 1974 Farmland Industries grouped its three insurance companies into Farmland Insurance Services. It developed a new logo to identify Farmland insurance operations the following year. It also added to the group the Farmland Insurance Agency that had been a part of Farmland Industries since 1940. This company did not issue policies but functioned as an agent to obtain insurance coverage for Farmland Industries' extensive properties. The over-all goal of the insurance programs, according to Balliu, was to provide "*the* insurance service for farmers and ranchers in our marketing area—just as CO-OP feed and fertilizer and other supplies are *the* products for those same farmers and ranchers."[56]

During the early 1970's, the insurance program made substantial progress as the combined assets of the three policy-issuing companies rose from about $33 million in 1971 to $47 million in 1976. The largest of the three companies was FEMIC, whose name was changed to Farmland Mutual Insurance Company in 1976. Now all of the insurance companies had the Farmland name and identification. The company had assets of $40.2 million in 1976 compared to $22 million for Farmland Life. Its main business was to insure the buildings, elevators, and equipment of farmer cooperative associations.

By the mid-1970's the company faced some serious problems. In 1976 grain-dust explosions and fires in elevators were, according to Balliu, "at a record level." During 1972, 1973, and 1974, elevator and mill losses totaled only $3.5 million. In the first eight months of 1976 losses exceeded that figure. To withdraw from this business was not a viable alternative because the cooperatives who needed protection also owned the company. These member-owners required protection at the least possible cost. Thus Farmland Mutual launched a prevention program that would help elevators avoid grain-dust ex-

---

[55] *44th Annual Report*, 1972, 23; *48th Annual Report*, 1976, 22–23.
[56] *Farmland News*, March 15, 1974, 12.

plosions and reduce company losses. It hired a grain-dust explosion expert and trained representatives who visited cooperative elevators in the Midwest and recommended safety procedures.[57] While the company had shown substantial growth, as of October 31, 1976, it still owed Farmland Industries slightly more than $3 million in principal and interest on the original advance of a decade earlier.

Development of a full line of insurance services gave Farmland Industries another direct tie to its member cooperatives and to thousands of farmers and ranchers in its sixteen-state service territory. It was an additional step in supplying member associations a full range of services and products. Moreover, it was becoming increasingly important for cooperatives to have access to special kinds of insurance, such as product liability coverage, directors' liability, and protection in the use and sale of dangerous agricultural chemicals. Farmland officials considered it important to have a farmer-oriented insurance company that understood the special and unique needs of farmers and ranchers. Although the insurance companies did not provide much in the way of savings, they added to Farmland's presence and image in a most important way. They were, as Balliu said, "an extra voice for cooperatives and for Farmland."

A small but potentially important service activity undertaken by Farmland in 1974 was a program of rural health care. Through the auspices of American Health Profiles of Nashville, Tennessee, Farmland provided well-equipped health-screening vans that traveled to rural communities in the Midwest and offered up to 110 health tests for a set fee. The results of the tests were then sent to the person's physician for any needed treatment. By the end of 1977 some 70,000 people had visited the health vans for tests.

Farmland officials viewed the program favorably, but many local physicians were critical of this approach to health care. They argued that patients came to them feeling that they had already paid for their treatment and that further charges by the doctor were unfair. Doctors also said that they could provide the same tests at about the same price and were in a better position to treat patients after their own testing. While some controversy surrounded the program, support of the testing vans by Farmland was a sincere effort to do something about inadequate health care in the rural Midwest. But how effective or useful the program could be was still uncertain in 1978.

---

[57] Farmland Insurance Services, *Annual Report*, 1976, n.p.; Balliu to author, February 1, 1978.

Chapter 17

Progress and Problems
in the Early 1970's

WHILE FARMLAND INDUSTRIES expanded its services and marketing activities, the main company thrust continued to be in the
direction of building up its petroleum and crop-production resources.
This included obtaining more crude oil for Farmland refineries and
developing greater capacity to manufacture fertilizer and agricultural
chemicals. On February 5, 1970, the Board approved a plan to establish a noncooperative corporation to acquire oil properties and to
explore and drill for oil and gas. The justification for organizing a
regular stock company was the belief that it would attract "risk capital
not available to a cooperative organization" and would provide some
tax advantages. In announcing the organization of Terra Resources,
Inc., Lindsey said that "we hope through a subsidiary corporation,
new sources of capital will be available for expansion of oil production activities faster than possible if tied directly to the rest of the organization."[1] Sale of Terra stock on the open market, it was thought,
would produce an additional supply of funds and free Farmland's
regular sources of capital for other purposes.

On March 1, Farmland transferred assets valued at $31,186,753 to
Terra Resources in exchange for 2,881,000 shares of common stock.
In August additional stock valued at $1,050,000 was purchased, giving
Farmland and its wholly owned subsidiary, CRA, Inc., 100 per cent
ownership of this Tulsa-based company. Terra Resources now became

---

[1] Board of Directors, Minutes, February 4-5, 1970; *Farmland*, April 15, 1970, 2.

Farmland's main enterprise to acquire needed crude oil and natural gas. On the basis of known primary reserves, Terra properties contained 9.5 million barrels of recoverable oil with 11.4 million barrels available through secondary recovery. About 52 per cent of Terra's oil reserves as of August, 1970, were in Wyoming with the rest scattered over Kansas, Texas, and other states. Terra also controlled an estimated 77.8 billion cubic feet of natural gas located mainly along the gulf coast of Texas and Louisiana. To raise needed capital Terra announced in 1971 that it would offer 800,000 shares of common stock to the public. However, it was not until 1972 that Terra actually sold any stock. On February 23, 400,000 shares were sold for $12 a share, netting $4.2 million, after selling costs. About $2.3 million of this income went to reduce bank borrowings and the remainder for the acquisition and development of additional crude oil properties. Farmland and its subsidiaries still owned 88.2 per cent of Terra's common stock.[2]

After operating for six years as a stock company, Terra was merged into Farmland, becoming a full subsidiary effective November 1, 1976. In October CRA bought back the 400,000 shares of common stock for $31 a share, or $19 more than those shares had sold for only four years earlier.[3] The "going public" had not worked out as anticipated by Farmland officials in 1970. As one executive said, it looked wise at the time, but it actually proved to be a costly move. One reason was that changes in the tax laws at about the time Terra was formed reduced some of the advantages of oil investments. Increasing value of the properties between 1972 and 1976 somewhat offset the cash loss.

During the next few years, Farmland intensified its crude oil operations in an effort to own and control a higher percentage of the oil needed for its three refineries and to acquire gas for its ammonia plants. For the first time Farmland and its subsidiaries began to spend relatively large sums to acquire leases and for exploration and production. In 1973 Farmland spent only $6.5 million for properties, exploration, and production of crude oil, but in 1974 the figure jumped to $47.1 million, including $18.8 million for leases offshore Texas and Louisiana. In the past Farmland had relied mainly on the purchase of developed properties to increase its self-reliance in crude oil

2 Farmland Industries, Inc., *Prospectus*, January 15, 1971, 15–17, and January 16, 1974, 14; *42nd Annual Report*, 1970, 1a; and *44th Annual Report*, 1972, 22.

3 *Wall Street Journal*, September 27, 6, and October 29, 1976, 35; Farmland Industries, Inc., *Prospectus*, January 10, 1977, 27; and *Farmland News*, November 15, 1976, 21.

and natural gas. However, after about 1973 this approach became impractical. With rising oil prices it became increasingly expensive to buy developed properties if, indeed, they were available at any price. Consequently, Farmland shifted its emphasis to leasing land with potential oil and gas supplies and expanding exploration and drilling activities. William L. Rader, vice-president for petroleum, exploration, and production, after 1975, organized a leasing and exploration team of more than fifty geologists, geophysicists, and other professionals to develop a basic petroleum-production program.

In addition to Terra Resources, Farmland organized two other non-cooperative companies to expand the oil operations. In 1975 CRA, Inc. purchased 90 per cent of Cayman International, Inc., an oil-exploration firm that had interests in South America. This subsidiary, renamed Farmland International Energy Company, completed producing wells in Colombia, South America, as well as in the United States. A third company, the CRA Exploration Company, also engaged in oil exploration.

By the mid-1970's Farmland was intensely trying to gain control of needed crude oil and natural gas. Without its own supplies, the company feared being cut off or denied needed raw materials for its refineries and fertilizer plants. Expenditures for developed and undeveloped leases reached $85 million in 1976. By that time Farmland had crude oil and natural gas interests in the United States and offshore, in Canada, and several other foreign countries.

Besides investing fairly large sums to build up crude oil supplies, Farmland also enlarged and improved its capacity to produce refined fuels. In 1971 the company's three refineries had a daily capacity to refine 55,000 barrels of crude oil. In 1973 capacity was increased at both Coffeyville and Phillipsburg. The next year capacity at Coffeyville was expanded from 35,000 to 48,000 barrels daily. By 1975 daily refining capacity at the two Kansas refineries and at Scottsbluff had been increased to 78,000 barrels of crude. Farmland also produced propane and butane at its four natural gas plants, the largest being located at Mertzon, Texas.[4]

As foreign crude oil became more important in refining operations in the mid-1970's, the company gained a 12 per cent interest in Seaway Pipeline, Inc. This company had a dock facility at Freeport, Texas,

---

[4] Farmland Industries, Inc., *Prospectus*, January 14, 1972, January 16, 1974, January 8, 1975, January 26, 1976, and January 10, 1977.

and a 510–mile pipeline from there to Cushing, Oklahoma. By 1977 about 50 per cent of the crude refined at Coffeyville went through the Seaway pipeline. O. N. Shoup, executive director of crude purchasing and pipelines for Farmland, said that "there's no other way of being sure of getting foreign crude to our refineries. Before, our hands were tied. Now we shop for foreign crude, exchange it, or bring it home."[5] Farmland continued to maintain about 900 miles of other trunk and gathering pipelines to serve its refineries.

By 1976 Farmland and its subsidiaries had $407 million invested in oil operations. While Farmland had built a well-integrated petroleum business, it did not have the resources to become more than a modest independent. In the late 1960's Treasurer Ewing was visiting with a New York banker when the question arose as to what it would take to make Farmland 50 per cent self-sufficient in crude oil. The banker estimated that it would require a minimum investment of $200 million. At that time all of Farmland's assets only slightly exceeded $300 million. Thus, it was not feasible for Farmland to reach that frequently stated goal of becoming 50 per cent self-sufficient in crude oil. Moreover, it would not have been good business. To do so would have absorbed excessive amounts of capital and denied expansion in other areas of company business. To have withheld capital from fertilizer, feeds, agricultural chemicals, and other products to expand the search for oil would have been detrimental to Farmland's total service to Midwestern farmers. Thus, during the 1970's, Farmland budgeted substantial amounts of capital for oil development, but not so much that it would hurt or restrict other aspects of company business.

While it was not practical for Farmland to achieve a high degree of self-sufficiency in crude oil, plans to produce enough fertilizer to meet the needs of farmer patrons continued without let up. This was a logical area for Farmland to become a large factor in the market. Like oil, fertilizer was a capital intensive industry. But it was unlike oil in that farmer patrons would use practically all of the product. In 1970 Farmland and its subsidiaries produced 1,533,501 tons of fertilizer and sold 1,877,540 tons.[6] Officials expected the market to grow substantially during the next few years. To meet this growing demand

5 *Farmland News*, March 31, 1977, 10.
6 John Sprugel, Farmland Industries' price coordinator for fertilizer sales, to author, January 31, 1978.

and to get into a position to serve its farmer patrons better, Farmland spent millions improving and expanding its old fertilizer plants and constructing new facilities.

Early in 1970 the Board authorized upgrading and expanding the Green Bay phosphate plant in Florida at a cost of more than $19 million, and in August construction began on a new 1,000-ton per day ammonia unit to replace an old, rather inefficient 600-ton facility at Lawrence,[7] thus requiring an outlay of some $18 million. During the next few years additional expansion and improvements were made at those plants. On May 24, 1972, the Board authorized the construction of a new 400,000-ton anhydrous ammonia plant at Enid, Oklahoma, at a cost not to exceed $33 million. The new plant was completed in July, 1974, and dedicated on September 18. These ceremonies coincided with the growing national concern over agricultural shortages and high food prices, a subject that will be discussed later. Lindsey said that "growing food has always been a noble achievement of man, but it is especially important right now."[8] When this plant came on stream, it placed Farmland as the leading producer of ammonia in the United States.

By 1973, at the time of the critical fertilizer shortages, Farmland was producing 1,656,695 tons of chemical nutrients at its major plants, about 123,000 tons over the 1970 figure. Farmland's production was still only about 72 per cent of the total units sold, and demand was skyrocketing. The shortage situation encouraged Farmland more than ever to insure its farmer customers adequate future supplies by building additional capacity. The first Enid plant was scarcely in operation before management began feasibility studies for another anhydrous ammonia facility in Oklahoma and one in Texas.

After further discussions, on January 30, 1975, the Board authorized Lindsey to arrange for another plant at Enid and one in Louisiana, rather than in Texas as had been contemplated several months earlier. The decision to locate a plant in Louisiana was influenced by the prospect of Farmland obtaining its own supply of natural gas needed for nitrogen production. At the same time the Board raised the authorized investment for a second plant at Enid to $39 million. Earlier the Board had acted to assure the necessary natural gas for nitrogen production at Enid when it approved an interest-free loan to the Okla-

[7] Board of Directors, Minutes, February 4–5, 1970; Farmland Industries, Inc., *Prospectus*, January 14, 1972, 15; and *42nd Annual Report*, 1970, 8.
[8] Board of Directors, Minutes, May 24, 1972; *Farmland News*, September 30, 1974, 18.

homa Natural Gas Company not to exceed $3,250,000. In April, 1975, Board members approved a limit of $121,630,000 in capital expenditures for the Louisiana properties. Shortly thereafter, on July 9, Lindsey and Gov. Edwin Edwards of Louisiana publicly announced that Farmland would build a nitrogen plant north of Pollock with an annual capacity of 420,000 tons. Lindsey said that the unique thing about the projected facility was that Farmland would own or control the supply of natural gas used at the plant.[9]

Meanwhile, a new urea ammonia nitrate fertilizer solution plant, begun in 1974, came on stream at Dodge City, Kansas, in February, 1976. In March, 1977, ammonia from the Pollock plant began moving through the Gulf Central pipeline to terminals on its way to Midwestern farmer customers. With the completion of these facilities, and the multimillion-dollar expansions at Green Bay and Lawrence, Farmland was keeping promises made to farmers during the shortages in 1973 and 1974 that "more product is on the way."[10] Expenditures for new fertilizer plants from 1971 to 1975 totaled $122 million. In 1976 Farmland's fertilizer production reached 2,574,026 tons, some 258,000 tons above 1975. In the five years ending August 31, 1976, annual productive capacity increased about 1.2 million tons, or 57 per cent. Fertilizer had become increasingly important in Farmland's business expansion in the 1970's. Sales accounted for 52 per cent of the company's increased volume and 86 per cent of the larger gross savings in 1974 and 1975 over 1973.[11]

The largest fertilizer project considered by Farmland officials was never undertaken. On March 15, 1974, Lindsey announced that Farmland would participate in the construction of a major manufacturing complex for anhydrous ammonia in the Province of Alberta, Canada. The finished product was to be shipped through a planned pipeline from Lethbridge, Canada, to Garner in northern Iowa. A good deal of fanfare surrounded this proposal at Farmland headquarters, and the Calgary *Herald* published several articles on the project in the fall of 1974. However, lack of government support in Canada, increasing cost of natural gas, and other problems caused Farmland to drop the project in 1975.

During the middle 1970's, Farmland also made some progress to-

---

9 Board of Directors, Minutes, July 24, 1974, January 29–30, 1975, October 21–22, 1974, and April 16, 1975. See news release, July 9, 1975.

10 *Farmland News*, June 15, 1976, 3.

11 *47th Annual Report*, 1975, 30; Farmland Industries, Inc., *Prospectus*, January 11, 1977, 21, 32.

ward its goal of obtaining ownership or control of basic raw materials needed in fertilizer production. Although for several years Farmland had owned mineral rights on 6,481 acres in Hillsborough County, Florida, it was not an economically viable unit. Therefore, the property had not been developed. Following Board approval on September 1, 1976, the company acquired mineral rights in December from the Duval Company on 7,000 acres of phosphate reserves in Hardee County, Florida, at a cost of some $38 million. Plans continued to make the company basic in phosphate rock but much remained to be done in the late 1970's. Also, in 1976, after two and a half years of discussions and negotiations, Farmland purchased a sulphur mine from Atlantic Richfield Corporation at Fort Stockton, Texas. This produced about 40 per cent of the sulphur needed at the Green Bay plant.[12]

The expansion of fertilizer capacity required an average yearly investment of nearly $25 million during the first half of the 1970's. By 1976 Farmland had invested $300,326,000 in plant, equipment, and other properties in connection with fertilizer manufacture. As a result of this increasing output, by 1977 Farmland produced a high percentage of fertilizer sold to its member cooperatives. In other words, it had become nearly self-sufficient in that area of company business. Moreover, Farmland had become a strong factor in the total fertilizer market throughout the Midwest. The company was the largest single marketer of fertilizer in its sixteen-state service territory, furnishing nearly 13 per cent of the fertilizer sold in the region.[13]

While Farmland's largest industrial enterprises continued to center in petroleum and fertilizer, its third largest business was processed feeds. In December, 1973, Kenneth Nielsen, vice-president of sales and merchandising, declared: "It's time we concentrate on becoming No. 1 in feed in our area just as we are first in fertilizer and petroleum." Farmland was making rapid progress toward that goal. By 1976 Farmland had seventeen feed-mixing plants and one animal-protein plant scattered from Fruita, Colorado, in the West to Lincoln, Illinois, in the East, and from Huron, South Dakota, in the North to Gatesville, Texas, in the South.[14] In addition, a wholly owned subsidiary, Farmland Soy Processing Company, organized in 1976, oper-

---

12 The Board had authorized purchase of this Atlantic Richfield property on May 30, 1974. See Minutes, May 30–31, 1974, and August 30–September 1, 1976; Farmland Industries, Inc., *Prospectus*, January 10, 1977, 31.
13 Farmland Industries, Inc., *Prospectus*, January 22, 1976, 21.
14 Farmland Industries, Inc., *Prospectus*, January 11, 1977, 34.

ated two soybean-processing plants. The capacity of these mills varied from a modest 24,000 tons a year to 730,000 tons at the large soybean-processing plant near Sioux City, Iowa.

In May, 1973, the Board authorized construction of the $12.5 million Sioux City facility, a figure later increased to $19 million. Lindsey announced plans to proceed on September 15.[15] Some construction difficulties, cost overruns, and other problems delayed opening the soybean plant until July, 1975. One of the largest facilities of its kind in the nation for the production of soybean meal and oil, it could process about 67,000 bushels of soybeans a day. These came from farmers who marketed through their cooperatives located in Iowa, Minnesota, South Dakota, and Nebraska. The meal and oil produced at Sioux City were more than enough to meet the needs of Farmland's string of feed mills and the requirements of member associations and left a substantial amount for export. At the plant dedication on October 16, Dean Lee Kolmer of Iowa State University called the facility a "bench mark in the farmers march to where they will control their own marketing system." This, he added, was vital "to the maintenance of the family farm concept."[16] Investment in feed production reached $26 million by the end of fiscal 1976. In 1969 Farmland led in the sale of commercial formula feed only in Kansas, but by 1976 Farmland livestock feeds had become the leading seller in most of the company's territory. Moreover, feed was a good margin item. On sales of $257.8 million in 1976, gross savings were $18.8 million.

Farmland also moved actively in the early 1970's to expand its output and sale of herbicides, insecticides, and other agricultural chemicals. In 1974 Farmland became full owner of the Missouri Chemical Company of St. Joseph, Missouri, after purchasing the 50 per cent interest owned by the Dow Chemical Company. This permitted Farmland to increase its production and distribution of agricultural chemicals to member cooperatives at a time when severe scarcities existed. The Missouri Chemical Company produced some 200 different products sold under the CO-OP label. On March 1 Lindsey announced that Farmland would build a plant to produce triazine-based products at St. Joseph. With a capacity of 10 million pounds a year, this facility began production in December, 1976. One of the

---

[15] Board of Directors, Minutes, May 23–24, 1973; *Sioux City Journal*, September 16, 1973.

[16] *Farmland News*, September 15, 1, and October 21, 1975, 3; news release, July 18, 1975; *Sioux City Journal*, July 28, 1974, and April 16, 1977.

popular chemicals was atrazine, an important corn herbicide. Farm-land's production and sales of agricultural chemicals rose rapidly, increasing from $37 million in 1971 to $152 million in 1977 when seed was added.[17]

Farmland also continued to expand output and distribution of its other farm supplies. CO-OP tires, batteries, and accessories, better known as TBA, and paint found increasing acceptance among farm-ers. Another growing business line included fabricated steel buildings and equipment. The company's plant for production of steel build-ings was located at Hutchinson, Kansas. In August, 1971, much of this facility was unfortunately destroyed by fire. It was quickly rebuilt, however, with increased capacity, and in the 1970's sales of steel build-ings, grain bins, hog troughs, and other products mounted rapidly. By 1975 Farmland's Equipment and Supplies Division had sales of $99 million.[18] This was more than double that of only five years before.

Farmland's unprecedented expansion in manufacturing during the early 1970's required tremendous amounts of capital. Indeed, no farm cooperative had ever expended such huge sums for industrial facilities. In 1970 Farmland's annual capital outlays were about $20.2 million; in 1972 they increased to $37.2 million, and in 1973 to about $46.8 million. These were fairly large amounts compared to earlier capital expenditures, but they were modest, even small, in relation to the years ahead. In 1974 the company invested $189.5 million and in 1975 an additional $140.7 million. The largest capital expenditures were for oil and fertilizer plants and properties, with food marketing and other aspects of company business getting lesser amounts. For example, in 1975 some $60.6 million was allocated to oil and gas properties, $19.6 million to fertilizer facilities, $14.2 million to food marketing, $13.6 million to storage facilities, and smaller expendi-tures for equipment and supplies.[19]

How were these large sums obtained? The traditional sources of long-term capital had been savings, depreciation, depletion, and loans from the Banks for Cooperatives. Commercial banks provided some credit for seasonal operations, but relatively modest amounts. One of the major sources of capital came from retained savings. Since this was the case, it was important that savings be strong and that they

---

17 *46th Annual Report*, 1974, 10; *47th Annual Report*, 1975, 17; Farmland Industries, Inc., *Prospectus*, January 22, 1975, 20; *Farmland News*, January 15, 1977, 1; and *St. Joseph News-Press*, March 11, 1975.

18 *47th Annual Report*, 1975, 15.

19 See the annual reports for the appropriate years.

not fluctuate too much from year to year. It would be especially difficult to plan future capital expenditures if savings dropped drastically after being at a more favorable level. In other words, healthy savings
were a crucially important ingredient in Farmland's ability to expand
its facilities and improve its products and services. Lindsey constantly
reminded farmers and their cooperative leaders of this fact. "A strong
savings performance is important," he wrote, "because it measures
Farmland's ability to grow." [20]

As previously mentioned, it had been Farmland's policy since 1963
to return 50 per cent of the net savings as cash patronage refunds. The
savings remaining after distribution of these cash refunds and income-
tax payments were retained as members' ownership in Farmland. Thus
as net savings increased, Farmland had larger amounts for reinvestment. Net savings before income taxes and patronage refunds went
from $21.1 million in 1971 to $31.2 million in 1973. Then in 1974
and 1975 these savings shot up to $98.2 and $196.8 million, respectively. In 1974 the retained surplus available for investment reached
$50.3 million and in 1975 it nearly doubled to $96.5 million. Capital
generated by depreciation and depletion were related to the amount
and kind of property held by the company, but in 1975 it reached
$35.7 million. [21]

By 1967 it was becoming clear that Farmland's need for capital
exceeded what could be generated from the usual sources. Treasurer
Ewing told a planning conference in September, 1967, that he "could
see the day, . . . that our need for borrowed funds will exceed the
capacity of the Farm Credit System." But he expressed confidence
that Farmland could "go to the public money market on a sound
cost basis." [22] Discussing this matter at a Board of Directors' meeting
in August, 1968, Ewing recommended greater reliance on commercial
banks for needed credit. James R. Williams of the Wichita Bank for
Cooperatives, who attended that meeting, agreed with Ewing and
told the Board that Farmland's capital requirements "were outgrow-
ing the Farm Credit System." At that time Farmland's mortgage debt
to commercial banks was only $1,632,623. The Board then directed
management to negotiate a $3 million loan from the Bank of the
Southwest Association in Houston. Two months later the Board
authorized Lindsey to borrow up to $25 million from the Bankers

[20] *49th Annual Report*, 1977, 2.
[21] *47th Annual Report*, 1975, 35.
[22] *Teammates*, August-September, 1967, 7.

Trust Company in New York. Officials from the Banks for Cooperatives favored Farmland's arranging for private bank credit and even
accompanied Farmland executives on some of their visits to commercial bankers.[23]

At the next annual meeting in December, Lindsey informed the
membership that Farmland officials had discussed the company's capital requirements with "several large private banks and financial
houses" and added that Farmland would be using more noncooperative institutions "for some of our capital needs in the future."[24] Not
all company officials were enthusiastic about turning to private financial institutions for funds, but Farmland had no alternative if it
hoped to expand the construction of manufacturing facilities and
undertake huge capital outlays.

From 1968 onward Farmland sharply increased its borrowings from
commercial banks, as well as from the Banks for Cooperatives. In the
1970 annual report, Lindsey said that Farmland was willing "to borrow as much as it needs—without endangering liquidity." He added
that the "creative use of borrowed capital has been a hallmark of
American business." However, he continued, cooperatives had tra-
ditionally been hesitant "to employ financial leverage." Lindsey made
it clear that Farmland had not been "hesitant" in the past, nor would
it be in the future.[25]

By August 31, 1973, Farmland Industries and its consolidated subsidiaries owed commercial banks $6,015,000. However, this was still
a small figure compared to the $60,315,000 in notes and long-term
debt owed to Banks for Cooperatives. By 1976, short- and long-term
debt to commercial banks rose to $31,917,000. Also in 1976 Farmland
began borrowing large sums from insurance companies, and as of
August 31 owed them $68.4 million.[26]

Another source of capital came from the sale of Farmland's own
certificates of indebtedness and other securities. While the company
had been selling such certificates since 1949, as of August 31, 1969,
only about $48.9 million was outstanding. Beginning in 1969–1970,
the company presented a new package of securities that became popular with investors. In January, 1971, Farmland offered $30 million of
subordinated certificates of investment carrying interest rates from

---

23 Board of Directors, Minutes, August 29 and October 24–25, 1968; Farmland Industries, Inc., *Prospectus*, January 29, 1969, 44.
24 *40th Annual Report*, 1968, 4.
25 *Ibid.*, 1970, 4.
26 *Ibid.*, 1976, 33, 40.

7½ to 10 per cent. During the next few years millions more were marketed. In September 1974, Treasurer Ewing announced a securities program designed to raise $150 million over the next three years. This, he said, would be a key part of the $1.1 billion of capital needed by 1980 for additional productive facilities. In 1977 sales of long-term corporate securities amounted to $92 million, and Farmland's total long-term liabilities represented by subordinated debt certificates reached a total of $315,714,000.[27] Besides raising capital funds, the sale of certificates provided investment opportunities for member cooperatives, farmer members, employees, and others. A great many farmers found Farmland securities an attractive investment and the interest went back to actual farm operators.

Beginning with the first Enid fertilizer plant in 1974, Farmland turned to a method of financing known as leveraged leasing. In May, 1973, the Board authorized management to negotiate with the First Chicago Leasing Corporation to finance this new facility.[28] Under this arrangement a private leasing firm, usually a subsidiary of a large bank or other financial institution, would agree to finance the plant and lease it back to Farmland for twenty years at so much per year. At the end of the twenty-year period, Farmland had the opportunity to buy the plant back at fair market value. The funding institution realized such benefits as investment tax credits and depreciation, in addition to the annual lease payment, while Farmland benefited by not having to raise such large amounts of investment capital. This arrangement considerably lowered the cost of capital financing.

Farmland Industries turned to leveraged leasing to finance both of the Enid, Oklahoma, and the Pollock, Louisiana, fertilizer plants, and the soybean-processing facility at Sioux City. Commitments under the leveraged lease program amounted to a little more than $13 million annually for the five years beginning in 1978, and a total of about $169.6 million after 1983.[29] Over all, the profitability of Farmland's manufacturing facilities kept the company in a fairly strong capital position.

One of the factors in company success was the growing commitment to research and development. B. W. Beadle, a chemist who became executive director of that division in 1963, and vice-president in De-

27 *49th Annual Report*, 1977, 19, 35; *Farmland News*, September 30, 1974, 2; and Farmland Industries, Inc., *Prospectus*, January 15, 1971, 6.

28 Board of Directors, Minutes, May 23–24, 1973.

29 *49th Annual Report*, 1977, 45.

cember, 1968, had an extensive background in both government and private industry. For several years he had served as director of the chemical and biological sciences at the Midwest Research Institute, a highly respected organization in Kansas City. Beadle's goal was to maintain quality control over all products sold by Farmland and to develop new product lines. Within a short time he put together a program that he called "applied research, quality assurance and technical services." The "services" involved helping farmers to understand how best to use CO-OP products and advising Farmland officials in areas where technical expertise was needed. For example, studies done in research and development resulted in a design for a new farm chemical plant built by the Woodbury Chemical Company, a Farmland subsidiary. Also, research done in 1975 established the feasibility of building an atrazine plant in St. Joseph.[30]

In 1969 Farmland introduced Ruff-Tabs, a polyethylene product, fed to cattle as a substitute for roughage. It was reported that 100,000 cattle in Western feedlots were eating this plastic product instead of natural roughage such as hay by late 1969. However, the initial enthusiasm for Ruff-Tabs soon disappeared as the product failed to gain acceptance. The Research and Development Division also did applied research to improve CO-OP paint, oil, gasoline, feed, fertilizer, herbicides, pesticides, and other products. To meet the growing requirements for research and development, Farmland doubled the size of its laboratory in the North Kansas City Industrial complex in 1974–1975 at a cost of about $1.3 million. Operating expenditures rose rapidly. In 1972 Farmland spent $716,000 for R and D; by 1976 the figure had shot up to $2,015,000, an increase of nearly 300 per cent. The number of division employees rose to ninety by 1976, more than double the number four years earlier.[31]

As Farmland's operations became larger and more complicated, economic research joined product research to help determine company business decisions. Leith first headed this activity, which remained small until the late 1960's. In 1968 Bernard Sanders was hired to manage the division of economic and market research, an area that continued under Leith's general administration. At that time there were only two professionals in the division. The growing need for a

30 B. W. Beadle to author, December, undated, 1977.

31 *39th Annual Report*, 1967, 25; Farmland Industries, Inc., *Prospectus*, January 16, 1974, 19, January 8, 1975, 26, January 22, 1976, 24, and January 10, 1977, 36. The annual report figures differed from those found in the *Prospectuses* for some years. The 1977 *Annual Report*, 46, gave the expenditures for 1976 as $2,962,000 and $4,350,000 for 1977.

wide variety of marketing and economic studies required additional personnel. By 1977 there were fifteen professional researchers doing studies on market shares, forward pricing of fertilizer, production needs, and other important topics.

Farmland's business expansion in the early 1970's occurred in a difficult and rapidly changing economic environment that challenged both the cooperative and its member associations. The energy shortages, the scarcity and rising cost of raw materials, the need to allocate supplies of fertilizer and fuel to member cooperatives, and fluctuating profits combined to test management's skill and dedication. Farmers, on the other hand, faced scarcities of fuel and fertilizer, sharply rising production costs, and criticism from consumers for rising food prices. The world wide demand for American farm products, however, caused some agricultural prices to advance to unprecedented levels. In 1973 and 1974 American farmers experienced the most profitable years in all of American history. It was an abnormal boom period that led to a bust in 1977. But the boom years were full of problems, as well as profits.

Trouble began mounting for Midwestern farmers in the fall of 1972. It was a wet harvest season and snow came early. Some corn and soybeans remained in the fields, and that harvested had a high moisture content. By December propane, the most common fuel used to dry grain, was in short supply. Some grain elevators actually closed down for a time.[32]

Responding to this situation, Farmland sought to increase its output of fuel oil and propane to meet the needs of its cooperative members. However, scarcity of crude oil and rising prices made it impossible for Farmland to operate its three refineries at capacity. Also the federal government placed price controls on refined products, creating a cost-price squeeze in Farmland's petroleum operations. Farmland, like other small independents, was especially hard hit because it owned and controlled less than 20 per cent of the crude oil needed by its refineries. The company had to rely heavily on outside suppliers.

Until the fall of 1972, Farmland's refineries and the National Cooperative Refinery Association of which Farmland owned 30 per cent, had produced more refined fuel than was needed by the member associations. The surplus had been sold to independent marketers in

---

[32] "It's a Tough Winter for Crops and Fuel," *U.S. News and World Report,* December 25, 1972, 23.

Farmland's trade area. But seeing the shortage coming in the latter part of 1972, Farmland cut off sales to nonmember accounts early in 1973 in order to provide as much fuel as possible to member cooperatives and their farmer patrons. The company also developed an allocation system to assure equitable distribution of distillate and propane in the winter of 1972–1973, and for gasoline in the summer of 1973.[33] Despite some problems in late 1972, Farmland's petroleum business hit a new high that year.

The problems experienced during the winter of 1972–1973 were only a prelude to much more serious difficulties in 1973 and 1974. Shortages of fuel that developed in the spring of 1973 prompted the federal government to implement a policy of voluntary allocations in May. A scarcity of fertilizer began to show up in the spring, but by August and September when farmers on the Southern Plains were ready to plant wheat the situation had become critical. Sen. Dewey Bartlett of Oklahoma declared in August that high export prices were attracting fertilizer into overseas markets, leaving domestic consumers without needed supplies. Since price controls existed on fertilizers sold domestically, Bartlett, along with industry spokesmen, urged a restoration of the free market. At that time diammonium phosphate brought about $75 a ton in Iowa compared to an export price of $115.[34]

Meanwhile, farmers were in a fighting mood. Everywhere they turned they faced scarcities and higher prices for fuel and fertilizer. A Kansas farm wife wrote to the *New York Times* in September saying that the local fertilizer dealer had gone to Houston for a truck load of fertilizer only to return empty-handed. However, the truck driver had reported seeing fertilizer being loaded on ships for export.[35] As the weeks passed, fertilizer manufacturers who sought the higher foreign prices and ignored domestic customers were bitterly criticized by farmers.

The situation became even more complicated because during the shortages of farm inputs, the government was urging farmers to increase production in order to slow down skyrocketing food prices. During 1973 consumer food prices rose about 15 per cent, stimulating

---

33 "A Statement on Crude Oil, Propane and Middle Distillate Supplies for Midwestern Agriculture," November 12, 1973, typed report. A special issue of *Leadership*, July, 1973, deals with the shortages of fuel and fertilizer.

34 *New York Times*, August 24, 1973, 42; *Wallace's Farmer*, XCVIII (September 22, 1973), 18–19.

35 *New York Times*, September 15, 1973, 35.

meat boycotts by housewives and bringing sharp criticism to farmers. On October 25 the Cost of Living Council exempted the fertilizer industry from wage and price controls with the hope that anticipated higher prices would encourage production, keep more of the product at home, and put "a brake on food price increases."[36]

Meanwhile, the Arab oil embargo announced on October 21, 1973, intensified the national fuel crisis. Within a few days the federal government adopted a national mandatory allocation system to replace the voluntary allocation program that had been in effect since May. Farmland officials had been urging mandatory allocation because they believed it would improve the situation at their refineries and make more refined fuels available for farmers. Under the mandatory allocation program, agriculture received a high priority for gasoline, diesel, and propane. Although farmers were to get all of the fuel they needed in the spring of 1973, in many cases the supplies were simply not available. They had to settle for 80 to 90 per cent of what they had used in 1972.[37] Farmland executives believed that supply could be greatly increased for farmers if the federal government would assure their refineries, and those of other small independents, enough crude oil to keep them running at capacity. In 1973 Farmland's three refineries operated at about 75 per cent of capacity.

For several years Farmland had traded foreign crude oil import rights, known as trade or import tickets, to major oil companies for domestic crude. This permitted the major companies to import cheaper foreign oil to their coastal refineries, while smaller independents like Farmland received domestic crude. However, by January, 1973, after foreign oil prices rose sharply, Farmland could not trade these tickets for domestic crude. Unable to import crude oil directly from abroad, Farmland's refineries ran thousands of barrels below capacity in 1973 and early 1974. In this situation Farmland executives pleaded with federal officials throughout 1973 to move to mandatory allocations that would assure Farmland refineries enough crude oil to operate at full capacity. Only in this way, they said, could Farmland's member associations and farmer patrons be provided enough fuel to increase agricultural production.

It took the Arab embargo, however, to bring about mandatory allocations, which became effective January 15, 1974. Despite the fact that farmers were to receive 100 per cent of their needs under the new

---

[36] *Ibid.*, October 26, 1973, 22.
[37] *Wallace's Farmer*, XCVIII (January 26, 1974), 19.

energy program, Farmland could not obtain enough crude oil to operate its refineries at capacity. On March 25 and 26 Vice-president Nielsen and George Statham, vice-president for petroleum, testified before the Senate Agriculture Committee and outlined their problems with the Federal Energy Office. They received a sympathetic hearing from Sens. George McGovern and Robert Dole.[38] Finally, beginning April 15, 1974, Farmland was allocated enough crude oil to operate its refineries at 100 per cent capacity, at least through June 30. This outcome resulted from innumerable telephone calls, many meetings, trips to Washington, and insistence by Farmland spokesmen that granting their requests would be beneficial to Midwestern farmers.[39]

By the spring of 1974 shortages of fertilizer were even more serious than the scarcity of fuel. Following the removal of price controls in October, 1973, prices moved dramatically upward. Within less than a week Allied Chemical raised its prices 30 per cent for some fertilizers, and W. R. Grace, another major manufacturer, increased prices between 20 and 40 per cent. But this was just the beginning. By the spring of 1974 anhydrous ammonia brought as much as $300 to $350 a ton, compared to about $70 in 1972; and there were reports of black market nitrogen bringing as much as $400 a ton.[40] Farmers were angry but were willing to pay most any price. Agricultural prices were high, and producers wanted fertilizer to assure maximum production on their expanding acreages. Occasionally farmers expressed their rage at high prices by trying to block supply facilities as they did at Denison, Kansas, in April 1974, but such opposition was sporadic and infrequent.[41]

Farmland officials sought to solve the problems of scarcities and high prices by increasing production in their own facilities, allocating the available supplies equitably among their own member cooperatives, and using whatever influence they had to get government agencies to modify federal rules and regulations in favor of farmers. Since Farmland's welfare and that of its farmer customers was directly re-

38 U.S., Senate, Committee on Agriculture and Forestry, Subcommittee on Agricultural Credit and Rural Electrification, *Farm Fuel Situation*, 93 Cong., 2nd sess., March 25, 26, 1974, 53–72.

39 "A Statement on Crude Oil, Propane . . . "; *Leadership*, July, 1974.

40 *Wall Street Journal*, February 20, 1974, 2; *Wallace's Farmer*, XCIX (April 27, 1974), 1; *Wallace's Farmer*, C (February 8, 1975), 13; *Business Week*, June 8, 1974, 53–58; and *Kansas City Star*, October 5, 1975.

41 *Topeka Daily Capital*, April 11, 1974.

lated, it made good economic sense for the company to do everything possible to see that supplies were available to farmers through their member associations.

As the shortages grew, Farmland exerted every effort to increase production at the company's fertilizer plants. Output was pushed to rated capacity, and on occasion even beyond. In 1973 Farmland's production of fertilizer reached 1,656,695 tons, about 60,000 tons above that produced in 1972. In 1974 production rose by nearly an additional 175,000 tons. The first Enid nitrogen plant came on stream in July, 1974, but that was too late to help meet peak demand during the spring. Farmland also stepped up its purchases of fertilizer from regular commercial sources in 1974 for resale to member cooperatives. Much of this business represented service to local associations rather than profit as Farmland resold a good deal of the product at cost.

But even the best efforts at production and acquisition could not supply all of the fertilizer needed by cooperative patrons. Therefore, Farmland allocated supplies to member associations on the basis of average purchases over the previous three years. Also the company made sales only to cooperatives with whom it had done business in the past. Noncooperative farmers pleaded for fertilizer, but Farmland officials and most managers of member associations took the position that available product should be sold only to those cooperatives and their customers who had helped build the regional's manufacturing capacity through previous support and loyalty. Sometimes nonmember farmers placed considerable pressure on cooperatives to supply their needs, but usually without success. Joe Roth, the manager of the Fertilizer Department of Cooperative Equity Exchange, in Garden City, Kansas, expressed the general view when he said in May, 1974: "We are not taking on any new customers at this time. Our belief is that all available fertilizer should go to the people who have used co-op products and programs in the past."[42]

It was a hectic time in Farmland's fertilizer division during the late winter and spring of 1974. Executives at headquarters and fertilizer specialists in the field worked tirelessly to obtain needed supplies and see that it was delivered equitably throughout the company's trade area. In January fertilizer managers and division sales managers were informed on all phases of the allocation program at a training

---

[42] *Farmland News*, April 30, 6, and May 31, 1974, 6.

session in Kansas City. Reporting on conditions in Kansas in March, 1974, Gerald Brown, division director of fertilizer, wrote that he was greatly impressed "with the efforts that all of the personnel in Kansas are putting forth to make the allocation program work."

But however hard company representatives worked, not all customers were satisfied. Brown wrote that Farmland's image was down "with the large farmers" in one area of Kansas because of dissatisfaction with some phases of the allocation program. To explain Farmland's distribution policies, three Farmland vice-presidents, Kenneth Nielsen, George Statham, and Warren Dewlen, vice-president for fertilizer, made a flying trip through five Midwestern states to meet with cooperative managers in May, 1974. They answered questions and reviewed Farmland's policies for meeting customers' needs. One of the distinctive things about Farmland management was the personal contact between high company officials and their customers in the field.[43]

Over all, however, Farmland's allocation program worked well, and most customers received from 80 to 90 per cent of needed fertilizer in 1974, the worst shortage year. To achieve this record some member cooperatives had to rely on noncooperative sources to meet the requirements of members. They balanced the price of the more expensive fertilizer from outside the cooperative system with the cheaper Farmland product and arrived at a compromise figure. Farmland received some criticism for not being more aggressive in obtaining product from outside suppliers, but Nielsen argued that it would have been poor business for both Farmland and its customers to pay the outrageously high prices demanded by some suppliers. While spotty shortages continued into the 1974–1975 season, and Farmland administered another allocation program, by 1975 the worst was over. There was some drop in fertilizer prices in 1975 and supplies were generally adequate.[44]

Farmland and many of its member cooperatives came out of the period of shortages with a greatly enhanced image. Thousands of Midwest farmers realized, perhaps for the first time, that Farmland existed to serve them and their local associations. When they saw Farmland doing everything possible to provide members with fertil-

---

[43] *Ibid.*, May 31, 1974, 1; Gerald Brown to Warren Dewlen, March 4, 1974; Dewlen to Don Bergman and others, January 8, 1974; and Dewlen to Dear Co-op Managers, January 26, 1974.

[44] *Leadership*, July, 1974, 3–5; *Topeka Daily Capital*, April 11, 1974.

izer, while some other companies were making extra profits by selling outside their usual domestic markets, or abroad, farmers became more convinced than ever of the advantages offered by cooperatives. Elroy Odland, manager of the Brown County Cooperative Association, wrote to Norbert Faulstich, Farmland's district manager in North Dakota, on January 17, 1973: "Quite often in the past I have called or wrote [sic] to someone complaining about a product or service. Now I feel it is time to compliment you in the petroleum department. First providing us with such a good supply, keeping us informed on fuel situation, and delivering the product to our facility." "We sincerely thank you all," he concluded. The president of the Joice Cooperative Elevator Company in Iowa told members in his annual report in late 1974 that Farmland had provided them "with product in the vacuum that was left when the private companies left you high and dry taking more profitable markets overseas."

Some farmers who had been opposed or indifferent to cooperatives now joined their local associations. Others united to form new cooperatives and to join the "Farmland family." For example, a group of farmers around Perkins, Oklahoma, formed the Cimarron Valley Cooperative after their local dealer had shipped fertilizer outside the community at higher prices rather than selling it to longtime customers. The Cimarron Valley Cooperative became a member of Farmland Industries, sent their new manager to a training school at Farmland, and within two years had a well-established cooperative business.[45]

Furthermore, Farmland strengthened its position as a spokesman for agriculture during those crucial years. Company officials spent a great deal of time in Washington trying to convince Congress and federal agencies that farmers' needs must be met. During the arguments over mandatory allocation of fuel in 1973, Farmland officials insisted that the rules and regulations must permit farmers to obtain maximum quantities of fuel and fertilizer. On one occasion a Farmland spokesman argued that the early allocation program had been drafted "to satisfy the needs of urban areas and the major oil companies," while ignoring the requirements of farmers. Farmland also joined other farmer cooperatives in an effort to exert economic and political pressure on Washington decisionmakers. In April of 1974, Lindsey and Leith attended White House conferences and spoke

---

[45] *Leadership*, April 1975, 3–5.

vigorously for the needs of cooperatives and their farmer patrons. Vice-president Leith served as chairman of the National Council of Farmer Cooperatives in 1973, giving Farmland a strong voice in pushing cooperative demands.[46]

Farmland's enhanced image of service to farmers and the company's aggressive marketing resulted in huge increases in unit sales and profits in 1974 and 1975. In those years the company sold 2,655,039 and 2,766,049 tons of fertilizer, respectively. In 1975 sales were up nearly a half million tons over 1972. Because of higher prices, dollar volume increased from about $201 million in 1973 to $517 million in 1975. The volume in other lines also rose in those years, giving Farmland its first billion dollar-plus sales year in 1974. The next year sales reached $1.5 billion. Net savings before income taxes and patronage refunds went up from only $31.2 million in 1973 to $98.2 in 1974, and the figure doubled again in 1975 when it rose to $196.8 million.[47]

Margins on fertilizer accounted for most of the increase in net savings. Although total petroleum sales exceeded that of fertilizer by some $60 million in 1974, fertilizer produced more than twice as much profit. In 1976 fertilizer sales simply "exploded," jumping more than one million tons in a single year to a total of 3,835,468 tons. President Lindsey attributed the remarkable expansion in volume to what he called a "carryover of confidence" from the shortage years.[48] However, prices dropped sharply and margins declined accordingly. The decrease of about $41 a ton for fertilizer between 1975 and 1976 substantially benefited farmers, but it was responsible for a rather drastic drop in the company's net margins. In any event, by mid-1970's Farmland had established itself as a major supplier of fertilizer in the Midwest, a phase of its business vitally important to farmers and also to company margins.

While Farmland Industries came through the period of farm supply shortages stronger than ever, the company faced a growing number of problems. Many of these were endemic to business as a whole in the United States. They included labor relations, law suits, tax controversies, industrial accidents, inflation, environmental concerns, and, in Farmland's case, attacks on the cooperative way of doing business.

By the 1960's Americans were becoming keenly aware of the de-

---

46 "A Statement on Crude oil, Propane . . . "; *Farmland News*, April 15, 1974, 1.
47 *47th Annual Report*, 1975, 29.
48 *Ibid.*, 1976, 4.

clining quality of the nation's environment. Public opinion demanded that the water and air pollution caused by industrial firms be eliminated. Federal and state laws were passed, and administrative agencies were given the responsibility for enforcement. For industry the new environmental requirements meant expenditures of capital on which there would be no monetary return. Farmland's oil refineries, fertilizer plants, and meat-packing establishments had a relatively high potential for pollution. Consequently, beginning in the late 1960's, Farmland spent millions for pollution abatement.

At its meeting in May, 1967, Farmland's Board of Directors passed a series of policy resolutions dealing with pollution and the environment. Stating that an agriculturally oriented company such as Farmland was "especially conscious of the need for pure air and uncontaminated water," the Board resolved to assist and cooperate with "governmental bodies in the drafting and enforcement of rules and regulations for pollution control." The Board said that Farmland favored standards "that protect the public but are also reasonable to industry." Then the Board moved to insure that existing plants were operated within prescribed standards and pledged to meet pollution-control requirements in any new facilities.[49] While Farmland's management supported the national move toward a cleaner environment, it opposed unrealistically high standards and unreasonable timetables for achieving those standards.

During the early 1970's, Farmland engineers and technicians worked constantly to reduce pollution around the company's fertilizer plants. At the Cooperative Farm Chemicals Association plant at Lawrence, Farmland faced difficult technical problems, as well as some hostile local public opinion. Entitling his editorial, "The Co-op Cloud," the editor of the Lawrence *Journal-World*, wrote on January 18, 1971, that the fertilizer plant left a "permanent gray cloud" that at times stretched for miles. While admitting that the "former heavy yellow color" had been removed, too many solid substances, he said, were still filling the air and sprinkling the countryside. In August, 1972, Farmland installed a pollution-control device on the prilling tower at a cost of some $300,000, but it failed to be as effective as desired.

Farmland continued to receive local criticism. The editor of the Lawrence newspaper wrote on January 3, 1973, that the community

---

[49] Board of Directors, Minutes, May 23–24, 1967.

suffered from "a form of pollution never before experienced or anticipated" and accused CFCA's management of not taking the problem seriously. This, however, was not the case. Much of the difficulty stemmed from the fact that no fundamental data or technology existed to assure pollution control on ammonium nitrate prill towers. Lacking workable existing technology, CFCA engineers under the direction of Hays Mayo set out to develop new pollution-control devices. By June, 1974, Farmland had installed a new system on the small prilling tower that met the standards of the Department of Health in Kansas. The same system was added at the larger tower by 1976. So successful was Farmland's environmental work at Lawrence, that in 1976 Cooperative Farm Chemicals Association was named air conservationist of the year by the Kansas Wildlife Federation.[50]

Also during the early 1970's Farmland committed millions for clean air and water at its other plants. In 1974–1975 the company spent $6 million for sulphur dioxide-control equipment at the Green Bay, Florida, facility.[51] Improvements in waste control at the Denison and Iowa Falls meat-processing plants continued steadily in the 1970's. In November, 1968, Farmbest announced that the company would receive a $289,790 federal grant to help develop a pollution-control system at its Denison plant that might serve as a model for disposing of industrial waste.[52]

However, one incident occurred at the Iowa Falls packing plant in December, 1969, that brought Farmland some embarrassment and considerable unfavorable publicity. Over a period of about four hours pollutants ran through an outlet that should have been plugged, bypassed the waste-treatment system, and flowed into School Creek and the Iowa River. This was quickly corrected, but several months later on May 5, 1970, the *Des Moines Register* announced that the state's pollution laws had been violated. The editor also charged that Iowa authorities had failed to investigate or take appropriate action. The *Register's* headlines on May 29 announced: "State to Sue on Pollution." The newspaper publicity undoubtedly prompted legal action. Meanwhile, Farmland officials in Kansas City expressed concern about

50 *Teammates*, September and December, 1976; *Chemical Processing*, mid-November, 1975, 88; Lawrence *Journal World* (Kansas), January 18, 1971, July 7, 1972, January 3 and November 13, 1973, and February 6, 1976.
51 Board of Directors, Minutes, February 5–6, 1974; *47th Annual Report*, 1975, 28.
52 *45th Annual Report*, 1973, 27; *Farmland*, November 15, 1968, 15.

what Robert L. Beasley, executive director of communication services, called the "possible erosion of member confidence in Iowa" as a result of any lawsuit.

The only practical alternative was to plead guilty. Robert L. Gowdy, Farmland's general counsel, so advised, but he also urged the company's attorney in Des Moines who was handling the case to seek something less than the maximum fine of $1,000. As it turned out, Farmbest pleaded guilty at the June 29 hearing and was fined $300, along with court costs. The amount of pollution had not been significant and the fine was miniscule. However, the case received much more attention than the offense warranted because it was the first prosecution under the Iowa water pollution law.[53]

There were also other kinds of environmental problems. By the 1970's the demand to reduce pollution required that numerous studies and investigations be conducted before building permits would be issued. A good example of this was the extensive environmental investigations undertaken before the construction of the Pollock nitrogen plant in Louisiana. The Louisiana Stream Control Commission, the Wildlife and Fisheries Commission, the State Parks and Recreation Commission, the Governor's Council on Environmental Quality, and the Environmental Protection Agency were all involved at some stage in reviewing Farmland's construction application and determining whether the projected nitrogen plant would have any adverse effect on the environment.[54] In addition to the extra cost of pollution-control equipment, the delays in construction caused by waiting on decisions by state and federal agencies, especially in a period of inflation, greatly added to capital outlays. These indirect expenses may have been even more than the actual cost of antipollution equipment. Nevertheless, Farmland met these added expenditures in a cooperative spirit, recognizing this as a part of the growing popular climate demanding greater social responsibility by industry.

While Farmland maintained generally good labor relations, occasional strikes led to temporary production losses. As the company built more manufacturing facilities in the 1960's and 1970's, the number of industrial employees increased rapidly. On August 31, 1965,

---

[53] See Memorandum, Fred Clymer to Leith, May 25, 1970; Robert L. Beasley's report, June 17, 1970; Robert L. Gowdy to Harris M. Coggeshall, June 22, 1970; Farmland's copy of the court file; and *Hardin County Times* (Iowa Falls), June 30, 1970.
[54] *Red River Journal* (Pineville, La.), June 25, 1975.

Farmland and its subsidiaries employed 2,466 people of whom 689
were at the Kansas City headquarters. A decade later the total employees numbered 6,159 with 1,151 at the central office.[55] Of the industrial workers at Farmland plants and factories in 1970, about 30
per cent were unionized. Most of the organized workers were members
of the Oil, Chemical and Atomic Workers International Union
(OCAW), and the Amalgamated Meat Cutters and Butchers of North
America. Both were tough unions.

One of the longest strikes against Farmland began at the Fort
Dodge, Iowa, nitrogen plant on October 19, 1967. The previous May
the workers had decided to affiliate with the OCAW, but after several
months of bargaining the two sides had failed to negotiate a contract.
The main conflict was not over wages but over control of work schedules. As the strike continued and Farmland tried to continue some
work in the plant with supervisory personnel the situation became
rather tense. Some plant windows were broken, automobiles were
struck with ball bats, and tires were slashed. Nevertheless, it appeared
as though the strike had ended on December 12 when the union
representative advised that the men "are returning to work uncondi-
tionally." While workers did enter the plant on December 18, it was
more to harass people inside than to work. At the close of the day,
after some minor violence, the employees left not to return.

Meanwhile, Farmland carried on a publicity campaign against the
union. On December 22, it ran a full-page advertisement in the *Fort
Dodge Messenger* giving the company side of the dispute. Then on
January 4, 1968, Lindsey wrote to Gov. Harold E. Hughes that Farmland had a responsibility to its farmer-owners and planned to get the
"plant back into production." He informed the governor that Farmland would not be intimidated, and he wanted Hughes to know that
in situations of that type "breaches of conduct and violation of law"
were possible.

By February, Farmland had cleaned and repaired the equipment
and moved to get production underway with supervisory and other
personnel. Production was beginning to get back to near normal when
the union agreed to a new contract and called off the strike, effective
February 26. The settlement was little different than that offered by
the company before the work stoppage began. The four-month strike
had been costly for both sides. The thirty-seven workers lost about

55 Farmland Personnel Records.

$75,000 in wages and Farmland lost the production of about 70,000 tons of fertilizer.[56]

Another lengthy strike began at the Carroll, Iowa, canning plant in April, 1976. Wage rates and the union's demand for a cost-of-living escalator clause in the contract were the main issues in dispute. It was not until late August, four and one-half months later, that the strike ended after the two sides had compromised the major questions. In 1976 the OCAW struck the Farmers Chemical Company at Joplin, Missouri, but the strike did not last long.[57]

The longest work stoppage in Farmland's history took place at the Iowa Falls pork-processing plant. Beginning in May, 1977, the union charged Farmland with wanting the plant closed down until a new sewage facility was installed. The local union president said that rather than "being honorable and paying us unemployment while they close down until the new sewage plant is done, they've forced a labor dispute on us." However, Farmland officials blamed excessive economic demands by the union for the strike. In any event, negotiations proved fruitless for more than five months. Early in December a contract was signed that carried about the same terms Farmland had offered back in May. The major issue was not money, but management rights and control of work schedules.[58]

Farmland's management accepted collective bargaining as a part of modern business life, but officials jealously guarded such management rights as job classifications and work schedules. Some of the sharpest disputes between Farmland negotiators and union leaders centered around the company's determination not to compromise management prerogatives. Part of the reason that Farmland enjoyed fairly good labor relations was the fact that most plants were located in small or moderate size towns where labor unions had not been strong. Many of the workers came from the surrounding farms and villages and did not have a strong industrial consciousness. Also Farmland had a good health and benefit package and always paid competitive wages.

Over all, compared to similar firms Farmland Industries and its consolidated subsidiaries had an excellent record for industrial safety, but occasional accidents caused some substantial property losses. An

---

56 *Farmland*, January 15 and February 29, 1968; *Teammates*, April, 1968; Lindsey to Hughes, January 4, 1968; Lawrence E. Hunter, OCAW representative, to Merle Blue, plant manager, December 12, 1967.

57 *Carroll Times-Herald* (Iowa), April 15, 19, 1976; *Sioux City Journal*, August 27, 1976; *Iola Register* (Kansas), June 1, 1976; and *Joplin Globe*, June 2, 1976.

58 *Marshalltown Times-Republican* (Iowa), May 25, 1977.

industrial accident that caused personal injury or death was very rare, but did occur. For example, on October 17, 1967, an explosion at the Phillipsburg refinery caused the death of a truck driver and hurt two other workmen. Early the following year a large storage tank ruptured at the Lawrence fertilizer plant, causing several hundred thousand dollars worth of damage. Nitrate solution swept one worker fifty yards and caught another even further from the tank. While no one was severely hurt, the plant superintendent, John Anderson, said: "We're fortunate no one was killed."[59] In 1971 the steel plant at Hutchinson, Kansas, burned, requiring new construction at the cost of nearly a million dollars. While such incidents were bothersome, they were not of sufficient magnitude to adversely affect company progress.

As the company became larger and more complex, various kinds of litigation kept Farmland attorneys busy. Robert L. Gowdy replaced F. R. Olmsted who retired in 1970 as general counsel, and by 1977 he headed up a staff of six attorneys. As Farmland's legal problems became more difficult and complicated, including the increase in all kinds of government regulations, management employed more and more outside legal help. To be sure, Farmland's legal division handled court cases, but its main effort was directed toward solving issues before they became problems requiring litigation. For example, this might involve getting the proper permit from the Environmental Protection Agency in order to build a certain facility, making certain that contracts were in order, advising Farmland executives on government rules and regulations, and a host of other matters.

Nevertheless, from time to time Farmland faced some tough legal problems. One of the most serious matters was a series of court cases brought against several oil companies including Farmland Industries, in Kansas, Iowa, and Oklahoma, regarding the sale of asphalt. In 1966 the State of Kansas filed a suit against twelve oil companies seeking damages of more than $12 million because of an alleged price-fixing conspiracy in connection with the sale of liquid asphalt to the state. The complaint sought $2,398,815 in damages from Farmland Industries.[60] Iowa brought a similar suit in which Farmland was involved.

In 1970 all of the defendants in the Kansas case except Farmland settled out of court. Farmland officials insisted that their employees had not engaged in any wrong doing. It appeared as though the case

---

59 *Farmland*, October 31, 1967, 1, and February 29, 1968, 2.
60 Farmland Industries, Inc., *Prospectus*, January 30, 1970, 20.

was headed for trial. However, in May, 1971, Farmland officials agreed to a settlement that involved payment of $420,812.27. But the agreement expressly provided that the settlement "shall not be construed as an admission of liability or guilt for any purpose whatsoever but is wholly a compromise of a disputed claim." Meanwhile, a class action suit had been filed against Farmland Industries and other oil companies on behalf of the seventy-three counties in Kansas who charged that a pricing conspiracy had existed on asphalt between 1958 and 1968. The plaintiffs alleged that Farmland's share of this claim was $166,275. In 1972 Farmland also settled this case out of court for slightly more than $18,000. The Iowa case was concluded by a payment of $4,500. In October, 1971, Oklahoma officials filed another case against Farmland and other oil companies in connection with alleged price conspiracies. This case lingered in the courts for several years without ever coming to trial. Finally, Farmland agreed to pay $45,000 in an out-of-court settlement in 1975.

The amount of Farmland's income-tax liability was another problem that required almost constant attention in the 1960's and 1970's as the company grew and prospered. The Internal Revenue Service regularly audited Farmland's tax records and more often than not insisted that the company owed additional income taxes. Farmland had to pay federal income taxes on net margins or profits that were not returned to patrons in the form of refunds. After examining Farmland's returns for the three years ending August 31, 1967, the IRS proposed that CRA, Inc. owed an additional $3,170,721.[61] Farmland management denied any such tax obligation, hired outside attorneys, and appealed to the Appellate Division of the IRS. In this appeal Farmland won most of the issues in dispute but, finally, paid a small amount to clear its tax record up to the end of that examination period.

In succeeding years differences continued from time to time between Farmland and IRS examiners. The IRS representatives held that Farmland had underpaid, and company officials maintained that their tax filings were accurate and complete under the law. Most of the differences arose over conflicting interpretations of how such things as depreciation, operating losses, deductible patronage refunds,

---

[61] Interview with Gowdy, December 7, 1977. See sections on litigation in the *Prospectuses*, 1970 to 1975; see especially January 30, 1970, 46; Board of Directors, Minutes, March 25–26, 1969.

trading operations in oil, and other matters should be handled. Some of the questions that came about were new and no precedent existed for their determination. In any event, Farmland managed to settle the issues through administrative procedures and never took an income-tax case to court. Farmland paid the regular federal and state income-tax rates on all earnings, except the savings distributed to members. Whatever differences did exist between Farmland and the IRS over tax liability, the company paid substantial amounts of income tax in the late 1960's and 1970's. On a taxable income of $4.2 million in 1968, for example, Farmland paid $1,348,200. In 1975 Farmland and its consolidated subsidiaries paid $9,463,000 in current and deferred federal and state income taxes.[62]

As mentioned above, income taxes paid by cooperatives such as Farmland were based on the statute that permitted cooperatives to exclude patronage refunds from their taxable income. However, some private interests continued to argue that this gave cooperatives an unfair advantage over other corporations. The National Tax Equality Association, which had been so active against cooperatives in the 1940's, never ceased working to revise the tax laws as they applied to cooperatives.

The question of taxation also got confused with the belief by some congressmen and senators that cooperatives were becoming too big. During the debate over tax reform in 1969 and 1970, the anti-cooperative forces argued that cooperatives no longer needed special tax treatment. Sen. Abraham Ribicoff said that some cooperative giants "had invaded the commercial marketplace with the aid of their special tax status to become aggressive and formidable competitors."

During the congressional attempts to reform the tax code, several amendments were introduced that would have been harmful to co-operatives. For example, one provision would have forced the associa-tions to pay out 50 per cent of their patronage refunds in cash the first year, and the remainder within fifteen years. Cooperative spokesmen, including Farmland officials, argued that this would deny coopera-tives the ability to earn and retain capital. Such a law would have been most harmful to Farmland because much of its capital was generated from retained earnings. In any event, intensive lobbying by the National Council of Farmer Cooperatives, and support from farm state congressmen and senators, was too much for the Ribicoffs

---

62 Farmland Industries, Inc., *Propectus*, January 15, 1971, 43, and January 22, 1976, 61.

and the NTEA. The so-called tax reform act of 1970 did not change the law for taxing cooperatives.[63]

While the problems of operating a large and varied manufacturing, distribution, and service cooperative increased as the company became larger, they did not slow Farmland's growth. Indeed, most of its problems were relatively small. To be sure, they demanded a certain amount of management's time, and in some cases substantial amounts of money, but the company's record was not adversely affected.

---

[63] *Farm Journal*, XCIV (March 1, 1970), 50d; *New York Times*, July 24, 1, and October 18, 1969, 15.

Chapter 18

The Nation's Largest
Farmer Cooperative

$\mathbf{D}$URING HIS FIRST few years as president, Lindsey kept most members of the administrative team who were on hand when Young retired. As a result of retirements and other changes, however, he was able to appoint several new people to top posts by the early 1970's. The two veterans, Ewing and Leith, continued in their important positions of financial vice-president and treasurer and corporate vice-president and secretary, but gradually changes occurred in the other vice-presidencies. All of the new top vice-presidential appointments came from within the Farmland organization.

One of Lindsey's first appointments was his own replacement as vice-president for manufacturing and production. Effective September 1, 1967, this position went to Miles F. Cowden. Miles F. Cowden had been with Farmland in a variety of capacities since 1929. He had held some top positions in the company but had been demoted under Young because of some differences between the two men. Lindsey, however, had been impressed with Cowden's work in supervising the construction of the Green Bay fertilizer plant in the middle 1960's. He believed in Cowden's abilities to manage the company's important manufacturing functions.

Cowden held this important executive vice-presidency until his retirement in 1974. At that time he was replaced by John F. Anderson, a graduate of the University of Missouri in chemical engineering, who began working at the Coffeyville refinery in 1949. Anderson became plant superintendent at the Lawrence fertilizer facility in 1962 and moved up to vice-president and general manager of the Cooperative Farm Chemicals Association six years later. In 1972 he transferred to the headquarters office as vice-president for fertilizer before being appointed to the top post in manufacturing and production.

Ray J. Barry, another longtime employee, was senior vice-president for membership services and distribution. He began to work for Farmland in the early 1950's as manager of the wholesale-grocery department that eventually had been eliminated. During his twenty-four years with Farmland, Barry held various important posts. Most of his functions were taken over by Robert E. Johanson who became senior vice-president for membership services and personnel in 1976. Johanson had worked for local cooperatives in Iowa before joining Farmland in 1961. He became executive director of Farmland's member management development in 1969 and held other key positions before becoming senior vice-president.

A. H. Stephenson who had shown a keen interest in the presidency at the time of Lindsey's appointment served as executive director for distribution until June 1970, when he was shifted to a less responsible post as vice-president of Farmland Foods, Inc., where he served until his retirement in 1972. He was replaced by Nielsen whose new title was executive vice-president for sales and merchandising. Nielsen started with Farmland as a feed salesman in Iowa and in 1954 was promoted to general manager of the Iowa sales division. After serving only about a year as vice-president and general manager for feed sales at company headquarters, he was named executive vice-president in the important merchandising area.

For two decades Harold Hamil had handled the responsibilities for information and public relations. During that time he had directed a rather low key but effective public-relations program. His idea was to communicate effectively with member associations and farmers, but to discourage local publicity of company matters. For example, when Young fired Shea, there was scarcely a notice of it in the Kansas City press. Hamil retired in September, 1971, and Robert L. Beasley became vice-president for information and public relations. A graduate of the University of Missouri's School of Journalism, Beasley wrote for several newspapers before joining Farmland in 1957. He worked with publications and in 1968 became executive director of communications, an area under Hamil's jurisdiction.

Ewing, Leith, Beasley, Anderson, Nielsen, and Johanson made up Lindsey's Executive Council. After the merger with Far-Mar-Co in

1977, George Voth, president and chief executive officer of the subsidiary, was added to this group. These executives had all come up through the ranks and were thoroughly committed to cooperative enterprise. Lindsey gave them broad authority to act in their areas of responsibility. It was an effective administrative team that worked well internally and outside of the headquarters as well. Every fall these executives traveled throughout Farmland's service territory to explain company programs and objectives and to answer questions. They visited with cooperative managers, board members, and ordinary farmers in district, and other meetings. There was no company jet airplane to whisk them from place to place; a jet could not land at many of the towns they visited. As mentioned earlier, it is doubtful if there was any other large company in the United States where the top executives spent as much time with the firm's customers.

Farmland's Board of Directors was also unusually close to the membership. By long precedent a majority of the twenty-two members of the Board had been farmers. Later bylaws specified that at least half of the board members must be farmers. Lindsey was director-at-large, and the others were generally managers of member cooperatives. The leadership of Farmland's Board was remarkably stable over the years. Chairman John L. Schulte, manager of the Farmway Co-op, Inc. at Beloit, Kansas, was elected to the Board in 1939 and became chairman in 1961. After thirty-three years on the Board, and eleven as chairman, Schulte retired in December, 1972. The Board then named Roy F. Chelf, manager of the Panhandle Cooperative Association of Scottsbluff, Nebraska, as chairman.

For general administrative and business purposes, Farmland's service territory that covered all or parts of sixteen Midwestern states was divided into sales divisions. Each had a division general manager. In the early 1960's there were seven divisions, but the number was raised to nine when expansion occurred in Minnesota and Texas after 1967. Subsequently, a tenth division, Illinois, was added. As of 1977, division one included Colorado, Wyoming, and small parts of Nebraska, and South Dakota; division two consisted of Iowa; three, North Dakota and most of South Dakota; four, most of Nebraska; five, Kansas; six, most of Oklahoma and part of northwest Arkansas; seven, Missouri and extreme western Kentucky; eight, Texas, eastern New Mexico, and the Oklahoma Panhandle; nine, Minnesota and part of Wisconsin; and ten, Illinois.

Directors were elected from director districts that were not the same as the sales divisions. The number of directors from each district was determined by the volume of wholesale business done with Farmland. As some districts increased their business they were entitled to more directors, while those that expanded less rapidly lost representation.

At the annual meeting in 1970, delegates passed a resolution calling for a special committee to study the method of nominating, apportioning, and electing directors. The delegates approved revised procedures at the annual meeting in 1971. These included appointment of a nominating committee for each district where a vacancy existed by the chairman of the Board. The nominating committees presented their nominees to a caucus of delegates from the respective districts at the annual meeting. The function of these caucuses was to vote on committee's nominees or on others nominated from the floor. The names of those nominated in the district caucuses were then placed before the delegates of the annual meeting for election. To be elected, a person must receive a majority vote of the convention's delegates. This system permits a great deal of grass-roots participation in the nomination and the election of Board members. Unlike many large corporations where the board is for all practical purposes self-perpetuating, Farmland's Board represents the majority will of the member-owners.[1]

The question was often asked how a Board of Directors half made up of farmers could determine policy for a multimillion- or billion-dollar corporation. The answer was not hard to find. While farmer directors were not versed in high finance or the techniques of industrial production and distribution, they knew the needs of modern and progressive agriculture better than anyone. Indeed, they were usually personally on the cutting edge of change on American farms. The farmer directors knew firsthand the direction in which agriculture was moving, and they helped to keep Farmland in tune with the rapid changes in Midwestern agriculture in the post-World War II years. Likewise, the directors who managed local member cooperatives had a close contact with the farmers who were Farmland's ultimate customers. In other words, Farmland's Board of Directors all had a direct tie to farmers, the main consumer of company products and services. Such a board, if only for self-interest, would not often

---

[1] "The Nomination and Election of Directors of Farmland Industries, Inc.," a pamphlet; *Farmland*, December 31, 1970, 3; and *44th Annual Report*, 1972, 3.

permit management to undertake projects that did not directly help farmers.

As head of what was rapidly becoming the nation's biggest farmer cooperative, Lindsey believed that Farmland Industries had a major responsibility to speak up for farmers. When complaints by housewives over rising food prices occurred in 1969, Farmland set out to counter the view that producers were responsible for the increases and to dispell the idea that consumers were paying too much for food. Hamil developed an advertising and publicity campaign that Lindsey unveiled at the annual meeting in December, 1969. He told the delegates that Farmland was "going to bat" for the half-million farmers in the company's trade territory and would explain to consumers that "food today is a bigger bargain, a bigger value, and takes a smaller bite out of the family's spendable income than ever before."

The "Speaking Out For Agriculture" campaign took the form of running full-page color advertisements in the Sunday magazine sections of six leading metropolitan newspapers in Farmland's area. According to Lindsey, such a program was justified because Farmland "wanted to tell the agricultural producer's story." "The rather frail structure of our agricultural economy," he wrote, "could be seriously damaged by a wave of public sentiment against our basic producers." The reaction to Farmland's advertising campaign was most positive. Hundreds of letters poured into headquarters complimenting the company for "speaking out." Farmers, especially, reacted favorably as they saw a major company defending them when they were under attack for high food prices. Partly because of the demand for copies of the advertisements, they were reproduced, along with an explanation of the campaign, and published in pamphlet form. Lindsey said that he hoped other organizations would join Farmland "in defending agriculture from the hurlers of false charges."[2]

This was the beginning of a consistent effort by Farmland to enhance the image of farmers in a growing urban society. In 1970 the company also ran a series of advertisements under the slogan: "The Farmer Is Doing His Part to Keep America Beautiful." Captions beside nostalgic rural scenes in full color declared that people in agriculture had "done more than any other segment of our society to improve our environment." The common slogan was: "The Ameri-

2 Memorandum, Hamil to Lindsey, April 13, 1970; news release, December 3, 1969; and *Leadership*, August, 1970, 8.

can Farmer, Creating A More Livable Environment for All."

As inflation gained momentum in the early 1970's, Farmland intensified its efforts to remove the onus of higher consumer prices from farmers. On April 12, 1972, a full-page advertisement appeared in the *Washington Post* that carried large headlines reading, "Midwestern Farmers Ask to Be Heard." The text explained that farmers were not responsible for high beef and other food prices. This same advertisement ran in the *New York Times* and other metropolitan newspapers throughout the country.

In July and August, 1972, the company published another series of advertisements directed toward counteracting growing criticism of rising food costs. One advertisement showed a farmer feeding cattle with the caption, "He Raises Food. Not Prices." As food prices climbed even more sharply in 1973, Farmland stepped up its advertising program on behalf of farmers and the agricultural industry. Another series of full-color advertisements was published in 1973 with the theme that agriculture was highly important to the total economy. One picture showed a farmer on his tractor in the field with the accompanying caption: "When he breaks ground, he plants billion-dollar payrolls."

Farmland continued its "speaking out for farmers" campaign and in 1976 turned to nationwide television to tell the farm and cooperative story. On July 1, Lindsey announced to company officials that later in the year Farmland would telecast a John Denver special on the ABC network. This project would be the first national television program sponsored by a farmer cooperative, Lindsey wrote, and "is an exciting venture for all of us." Beasley, the vice-president for information and public relations, headed up the effort. The programs were shown on November 17 and December 14. "America and American Farmers—We Need Each Other" was the theme developed in the commercial messages.[3]

While many listeners congratulated Farmland for sponsoring these programs, some raised questions about both their effect and cost. One Minnesota cooperative member said he believed that Farmland could have used "our money better." Another writer called the program a "rip-off," while the manager of a member cooperative in Oklahoma said that the true image of the farmer did not come through and "the

---

[3] Copies of the advertisements are in the Farmland Industries Historical Files; John Carroll to Dear Co-op Managers, September, undated, 1972; and Lindsey to Management Council and others, July 1, 1976.

coop message fell flat."[4] There could be honest disagreement over whether this $1 million extravaganza achieved any measurable public-relations benefits for agriculture among urban consumers. It is definite, however, that many farmers felt frustrated because of their inability to get consumers to understand that producers also had problems. They deeply resented the image portrayed by some city writers that farmers were waxing rich off the poor urban housewife. Thus, many farmers expressed appreciation that someone was speaking for them. One farm wife typified a common attitude in the agricultural sector when she wrote: "We get tired of feeling we always must defend ourselves and our products to people who think meat or milk is too high. . . . So . . . a big thank you for spending a large sum of your advertising budget in this manner."[5]

But, really, how useful were the John Denver programs in helping urban residents to better understand agriculture and farm problems? Farmland officials were uncertain. Beasley pondered this question but came to no definite conclusions. Beasley wrote that he was glad Farmland had sponsored the shows but admitted that no one knew whether the broad commercial messages did much good. He answered his own rhetorical question "Would we do it again?" with "I don't know." As a specialist in communications, however, Beasley said his preference was to stress programs "crafted especially by and for us."[6] That was undoubtedly a sound judgment. The John Denver shows were costly and really represented more symbol than substance in the area of effective public relations for agriculture.

Another aspect of Farmland's public-relations activities was the move to increase the company's political influence on behalf of farmers. The program, however, avoided partisan politics. Farmland supported the National Council of Farmer Cooperatives in Washington, worked with congressmen on specific issues, designated officials to testify before congressional committees, and assigned a person within the organization to coordinate governmental matters. Also Farmland kept consulting firms on retainer in Washington to help "keep on top of political affairs."[7] On some issues that affected the company or the welfare of farmers, Lindsey might write directly to the president

---

[4] A. L. S. to Beasley, November 18, 1976; R. B. B. to Lindsey, November 19, 1976; and J. W. S. to Lindsey, November 23, 1976.

[5] G. and J. T. to Farmland Industries, January 6, 1977.

[6] Beasley to S. S., March 28, 1977.

[7] *Farmland News*, January 31, 1976, 4–5.

of the United States, to the secretary of agriculture, or other high government officials. While the company maintained a low political profile, it had the muscle to generate considerable political pressure by working with its member cooperatives who in turn could encourage local farmers to express their views to congressmen and senators through letters and telegrams.

In October, 1972, Lindsey told the Board that Farmland must develop "an accelerated public affairs program," because of state and federal activities that affected cooperatives. After some discussion, Board members authorized a stepped up program but insisted that it must be completely nonpartisan. "All activities conducted herein," the resolution read, "shall strictly avoid participation in partisan politics," and work was to be "directed to areas of specific concern to Farmland, to cooperatives and cooperative activity." Furthermore, the Board required that "high standards of ethics" be followed at all times.[8]

Soon the program was in place. A Government Affairs Committee of Farmland executives determined and implemented basic policies and specific activities. These included contacting legislators on key issues, supplying information, and supporting the larger cooperative movement. If an issue had no evident effect on farmers or member cooperatives, the guidelines said that "Farmland will not express a position on it." While Farmland officials could engage in politics as individual citizens, they were strictly forbidden to involve the company in partisan political activity. Farmland had no political arm or agency through which contributions could be made. This nonpartisan policy seemed to make good sense because Farmland's agricultural constituents represented all aspects of the political spectrum. A position on a partisan question would be sure to alienate some customers. The main objective of Farmland officials was to improve the economic position of farmers and they believed this could best be done by non-partisan action.[9]

Farmland directors as individuals sometimes contributed to the political arm of the National Council for Farmer Cooperatives known as the Political Action for Cooperative Effectiveness, or PACE. However, some directors were slow to contribute even small amounts. When the Agricultural Council of America was formed in 1973 to

---

[8] Board of Directors, Minutes, October 24–25, 1972.
[9] Farmland Industries, Inc., "Corporate Government Affairs Policy," September, undated, typed.

conduct public-relations activities on behalf of farmers, Farmland made a corporate contribution of $10,000 to assist the organization.[10]

Most of Farmland's public-relations activities were directed toward improving communications with local cooperatives and their farmer members. Basic to this effort was the *Farmland News*,[11] formerly the *Cooperative Consumer* and *Farmland*, which was mailed to some 400,000 farmers and ranchers twice monthly. Member cooperatives provided the subscription lists and paid for the publications through deductions from their cash patronage refunds. This tabloid carried a great deal of information on cooperatives—local, regional, and national—including summaries of business by member associations. But it also served as a general farm paper. Editor Frank Whitsitt and members of his staff published excellent articles in the *Farmland News* on broad economic problems, food, inflation, international agricultural issues, new developments in farming, and other subjects.

In addition to *Farmland News*, Communication Services, headed by Bill Matteson who joined Farmland in 1971, put out many other publications and advertising pieces. *Leadership*, started in 1959, went to cooperative managers, Board members, and other cooperative leaders, and carried articles on such practical matters as marketing, management, finance, and member relations. Other publications included the manager's *Newsletter*, *Teammates*, and the *Annual Report*. In addition there was a steady flow of press releases, booklets, brochures, and leaflets emanating from the modern Farmland printing plant in the North Kansas City industrial complex. According to one report, these publications were all designed "to create greater membership understanding and participation and a positive general attitude toward Farmland and cooperatives."[12]

Farmland Industries also carried on a great variety of other public-relations activities. Beginning in 1962, the company established a scholarship program at Iowa State University, the University of Nebraska, and at Kansas State University. Four students at each of these institutions received grants of $400 each. Subsequently, two $400 scholarships were established at the other land-grant universities in Farmland's service territory. A $1,500 Homer Young Scholarship was

---

[10] Board of Directors, Minutes, October 26–27, 1971, February 8–9 and October 24–25, 1972, and October 23–24, 1973.

[11] The newspaper took the title *Farmland News* beginning with its September 30, 1971 issue.

[12] "Report on Communications and Public and Member Relations," November 22, 1975.

started at the University of Missouri in 1968 to honor Young and to help needy students. To be eligible for a Farmland scholarship, a student must have a farm background, and his parents must be members of an agricultural cooperative. Farmland also gave small amounts to several junior colleges in the Midwest. By 1977 the company was spending $16,050 annually on its scholarship program.[13]

Quite a number of top executives and high-level employees were graduates of the region's land-grant universities. As a source of farm-oriented employees, these institutions were important to Farmland and its programs. Consequently, the company worked to develop close relations with these universities. Starting in the mid-1960's, the Board of Directors arranged to hold at least one meeting a year on a land-grant university campus. Farmland executives also worked closely with the deans of the colleges of agriculture on those campuses. They often involved the deans in company educational programs, plant dedications, and other affairs.[14]

Corporate donations also helped to establish good will for Farmland Industries. While the company probably did not spend as much on contributions to education, charitable and cultural causes as other firms of equal size and income, Farmland did donate thousands of dollars each year. In fiscal 1977 general contributions by the company totaled $146,545.[15] If contributions were a little on the light side, Lindsey and other executives justified it on the basis that every dollar they gave away was a dollar not available to pay out in patronage refunds. In other words, they followed a careful policy when it came to giving away other people's money.

The Board's policy on contributions provided that the directors must approve any donation over $10,000. For many years gifts were given on a kind of ad-hoc basis, but by the 1970's contributions were budgeted in the same way as other aspects of company business. Farmland's donations varied widely in amount and purpose. For example, the company gave $100,000 during a four-year period to assist the development of cooperative fertilizer plants in India. Over a two-year period the Agricultural Hall of Fame, originally promoted by Howard A. Cowden and supported by Farmland, received an additional $10,000. There was some disappointment that the company did not

---

[13] *Farmland*, January 31, 1968, 7, and March 31, 1970, 23; Board of Directors, Minutes, August 29–30, 1967; Farmland Industries, Inc., records of scholarship grants.
[14] Board of Directors, Minutes, October 27–28, 1970.
[15] Company figures.

contribute more liberally to that institution. In Kansas City the Nelson Art Gallery, the American Royal, the United Way, the Philharmonic Orchestra, and the North Kansas City Hospital were among the recipients of one-time or regular contributions from Farmland. Worthy causes in communities where the company had industrial facilities received donations from Farmland headquarters or the subsidiary located there.[16] Over all, Farmland sought to be a good corporate citizen, but, as already mentioned, in the area of gifts and contributions it operated on the conservative side.

Farmland sponsored various other programs to keep members informed and aware of company activities. These included bus tours to the headquarters building and trips to corporate industrial facilities. In 1973 some 11,291 people made such visits.[17] Often these would be scheduled in connection with a baseball or football game, or some major entertainment event in Kansas City. Other specialized tours were conducted for managers of member associations. Hundreds of Farmland customers also attended the CO-OP Family Conference held at Estes Park, Colorado, each summer. There were other special conferences for youth. At most of the meetings and conferences sponsored or arranged by Farmland, those attending received a good dose of cooperative philosophy and principles. Farmland and member associations employed many people with no background in, or understanding of, cooperative business. Therefore, the company constantly preached and taught cooperative ideals and practice.

One of Farmland's most successful public-relations programs continued to be the annual meeting held each December in Kansas City. As member cooperatives moved into a position to pay delegate expenses and as farmers had more money to spend, the attendance climbed. In the 1960's from 8,000 to 12,000 farmers and cooperative leaders generally attended. By the mid-1970's a crowd of more than 15,000 was common. The Farmland annual meeting became the largest gathering of farmers in the United States, and it far outstripped the yearly conventions of such farm organizations as the American Farm Bureau Federation or the Farmers Union.

In earlier years the delegates passed resolutions on important questions and handled other business, but after about 1970 the programs were largely educational and social. As early as 1967, a headline in

---

16 Board of Directors, Minutes, August 26, 1968, May 26–27, 1970, January 28–29, 1971, and May 23–24, 1973; *Farmland*, August 15, 1967, 8, and January 31, 1968, 7.

17 *45th Annual Report*, 1973, 15.

Farmland announced: "Annual Meeting Is Time to Come to Kansas City for Fun—and Refunds." The whole affair stressed inspiration, entertainment, and just plain fun. Keynote speakers included such nationally known figures as George McGovern, John B. Connally, and Secretary of Agriculture Earl L. Butz, while the top entertainers varied from Floyd Cramer and Brenda Lee to Fred Waring and the Kansas City Philharmonic Orchestra. Much emphasis was placed on the idea of the "Farmland family" at these meetings, and they also offered an excellent opportunity to state and restate the company's major theme—Farmland existed to improve the economic position of farmers. Lindsey always gave an over-all summary of the previous year's business and other Farmland executives reviewed special aspects of company affairs. The highlight of every annual meeting was the distribution of millions of dollars in patronage refund checks. In 1975 this amounted to $90.4 million.

Some aspects of Farmland's public relations were closely integrated with its ongoing educational programs. By the 1970's the company had developed an effective and sophisticated group of educational activities. Some of these were located at the School of Cooperation, named the Farmland Training Center in 1975, while others were carried on in the field. The center provided housing, food, and classrooms for a host of conferences, seminars, short courses, and workshops. By 1977 the center had eighteen professional instructors on the staff. Besides conducting programs in Kansas City, members of the staff traveled throughout Farmland's sixteen-state territory, taking seminars and workshops to where the people lived. There were training programs for cooperative managers, board members, salesmen, cooperative accountants, those handling special products such as petroleum and chemicals, and many others. For example, in 1973 Farmland hosted 500 cooperative managers at a special seminar that coincided with the All Star baseball game in Kansas City.[18] Farmland also worked constantly to upgrade and professionalize its field representatives because they were an important and direct link between the company and member associations. In September, 1976, the Training Center established a program with Park College whereby an employee of a member cooperative could earn an Associate of Arts or Bachelor of Arts degrees in management/agribusiness. Part of the work could be taken at the center, some by correspondence, and other courses at Park College. Hundreds of students were enrolled in cor-

---

18 *Ibid.*

respondence courses administered out of the Training Center.

In the 1970's the number of people participating in Farmland educational programs rose rapidly. In 1974–1975 some 4,000 students enrolled; two years later the figure had jumped to 10,000. The company kept costs low to encourage participation. For example, a four-day senior petroleum clinic at the center only cost $100, which included food, lodging, materials, and one night out for recreation. This entire program was what Thomas J. Stevenin, executive director of the Cooperative Training Division, called "emphasis on people development." Many early cooperatives had failed because of inefficient and untrained personnel. Farmland was determined not to let this happen either within its own corporate organization or its member cooperatives.[19]

When Farmland moved into the meat-processing business in the late 1950's, it was in response to farmer demand for greater control over the marketing of their hogs and cattle. However, this action did not quell the strong undercurrent among many of Farmland's members who wanted the company to get much more involved in the marketing of other commodities, especially grain. Cooperative grain elevators were old and established institutions in the Midwest, but they had never become united or large enough to have any significant influence on the grain market or farm profits. More than 90 per cent of the grain export trade was in the hands of seven or eight major firms.

Farmland officials were well acquainted with cooperative elevator companies in the Midwest. Most of them handled fertilizer and other farm supplies, as well as grain, and many joined Farmland to purchase these supplies. During the 1960's, representatives of some member associations urged Farmland to get into the grain business as a means of extending another service to farmers. Company officials, however, were cautious. They knew the problems of operating a successful grain cooperative and realized that profits were small, especially when compared to the margins on petroleum and fertilizer. Besides, at that time Farmland was doing about all that its resources permitted. There was some interest in cooperative grain marketing around headquarters offices, but it was submerged below other company priorities.

Meanwhile, officials of several Midwestern regional grain cooperatives were discussing some kind of a merger that would give greater strength to farmer-owned grain marketing. After considerable dis-

19 Thomas J. Stevenin to author, January 9, 1978; *Leadership*, April, 1977, 3–5.

cussion, in the late spring of 1968 four regional grain cooperatives agreed to consolidate their businesses into a single association to be known as Far-Mar-Co, Inc., effective June 1. The associations that formed Far-Mar-Co were the Equity Union Grain Exchange of Lincoln, Nebraska; the Farmers Cooperative Commission Company of Hutchinson, Kansas; the Cooperative Marketing Association of Kansas City; and the Westcentral Cooperative Grain Company of Omaha. James H. (Jimmie) Dean who had been general manager of the Farmers Cooperative Commission Company became executive vice-president and general manager. The headquarters office was located in Hutchinson.

During the next few years Far-Mar-Co added member associations to its organization, began to manufacture a number of grain-based food products, such as soy flour, and greatly expanded the amount of grain handled. In 1971, the company marketed 217.4 million bushels of grain, and by 1974 the total volume had jumped to 335.6 million bushels. About 57 per cent of this was wheat. Far-Mar-Co was also a member of the Farmers Export Company that had an export terminal at Ama, Louisiana. Farmers Export had been formed in January, 1967, by eight regional grain cooperatives, four of which later formed Far-Mar-Co. This represented an effort by grain-marketing cooperatives to engage directly in the export business so that farmers would not have to rely exclusively on Cargill, the Continental Grain Company, Cook Industries, and other major exporters.[20]

Farmland officials watched this development with interest. Here was an important marketing cooperative operating right in the heart of Farmland territory. The development of Far-Mar-Co was of even greater interest to some of Farmland's member cooperatives who had dreamed of the day when Farmland would add grain marketing to its activities. In the summer of 1971, three local associations urged Farmland's management to consider a merger with Far-Mar-Co. After discussing this matter at a meeting on August 24 and 25, the Board of Directors passed a resolution stating that, "such a step appears to be in the best interest of both associations, their respective member associations, and farmers and ranchers." Chairman Schulte was directed to appoint a committee of three directors to meet with a similar group from Far-Mar-Co "to pursue this matter further."[21]

During the next several months Lindsey, Ted P. Sutter, and Roger

20 Far-Mar-Co, Inc., *Annual Report*, 1974.
21 Board of Directors, Minutes, August 24–25, 1971.

R. Clark met with Far-Mar-Co officials to explore some kind of "joint relationship." Lindsey reported to the Board on May 24, 1972, that the most recent discussions had gone very well, but he explained that much more discussion would be necessary, especially in regard to "corporate structure." In August, a year after the Board resolved to investigate some kind of merger, discussions were still in the preliminary stage. Nevertheless, the Board passed a resolution thanking the Far-Mar-Co directors for the progress made during the previous year in bringing the organizations closer together. Then the Board went on record as officially favoring a merger with Far-Mar-Co.[22]

Some consideration of merger continued during 1973 and 1974, but neither regional took any concrete actions to achieve what seemed to be a mutually desired goal. Lack of progress may have been partly due to rising grain prices that reduced grass-roots demand for cooperative grain marketing. Also during that time, Far-Mar-Co suspended discussions with Farmland as it explored the possibility of merging with the Union Equity Cooperative Exchange of Enid, Oklahoma, and the Producers Grain Corporation of Amarillo, Texas. These talks were discontinued in 1974 as being what Voth called "unfruitful." On the other hand, Farmland officials were harried by shortages and other challenges that occupied their time and attention. In other words, a merger between the two regionals was not a top priority in either headquarters office.[23]

At the very time Farmland and Far-Mar-Co representatives were discussing the problems and opportunities of some type of merger, the growing size of farm cooperatives came under increasing attack. Much of the earlier criticism leveled at agricultural associations had centered around their alleged tax breaks, but by 1974 so-called bigness and lack of responsiveness to members' needs became the most serious public-relations problem facing large regional and interregional cooperatives.

In early April, 1974, a publication appeared in Washington, D.C., entitled, "Who's Minding the Co-op? A Report on Farmer Control of Farmer Cooperatives." Written by Linda Kravitz and supported by several private foundations, this so-called Agribusiness Accountability Project aroused a flurry of reaction in cooperative circles. The report's general theme argued that farmer cooperatives were becoming too big, that farmer members had lost control of their associations

---

22 *Ibid.*, May 24 and August 29–30, 1972.
23 *Farmland News*, January 15 and February 15, 1977, 1.

to a "management elite," and that the large associations were becoming no different from huge private agribusiness. In a section, "Who's In Charge Here," Kravitz declared that hired managers had taken over the farmer cooperatives and were pursuing their own interests that were not "necessarily the same as the membership's." When cooperative leaders "speak on what is good for cooperatives," Kravitz wrote, "the speaker is not a farmer but a manager."[24]

When the report was issued, the Agribusiness Accountability Project distributed a news release summarizing its findings. On April 8 scores of the nation's newspapers carried all or part of the prepared message. Such headlines as "Co-ops Hurting Farmers, Study Says," and "Co-op Exploitation Reported in Study" could only serve to arouse cooperative spokesmen. *Newsweek* and *Business Week* carried similar stories on April 22 and June 8, respectively.[25]

Farmland officials reacted quickly and strongly to the study's charges. They were especially sensitive because Farmland was one of the large cooperatives frequently mentioned in the report. Also a summary of the company's recent business was included in an appendix, which implied that Farmland was typical of those large, unresponsive cooperatives described in the study. To make matters worse, the AAP publication appeared while the illegal political contributions to the 1972 Nixon campaign by certain milk cooperatives were being publicized. Such activities had prompted closer scrutiny and a good deal of criticism of all cooperatives.

Vice-president Beasley moved quickly to discount the report and its charges against large cooperatives. In the next issue of the *Farmland News* he deplored the study's one-sided approach and denied that professional management was removing control from farmer members. He argued that management worked hard to keep control among farmer-owners and charged that the report greatly harmed thousands of cooperative directors and managers by implying that purposely or inadvertently they were wresting control away from farmers. He also accused AAP of giving the public media only the most uncomplimentary and critical parts of the report. In another article Jay Richter, the *Farmland News'* Washington correspondent, questioned Kravitz's qualifications for writing a story about cooperatives.[26]

---

[24] Linda Kravitz, "Who's Minding the Co-op? A Report on Farmer Control of Farmer Cooperatives" (Washington, D.C., April, 1974), 81.

[25] *New York Times*, April 8, 1974, 31; *Kansas City Times*, April 18, 1974; and *Wichita Eagle*, April 8, 1974.

[26] *Farmland News*, April 30, 1974, 1.

Stimulated by some recent examples of cooperative illegalities and irresponsibilities as well as by the AAP report, the *Farm Journal* carried two articles on cooperatives and their public-image problems in October and November, 1974. Much of the material was based on interviews with farmer members of cooperatives. The *Farm Journal* writers found that very few farmers had read the AAP study, but that many of them were concerned about some of the problems raised in the report. The question of how to maintain farmer control, they found, was of major concern. However, the great majority of those queried believed that cooperatives must get bigger if they were to be competitive in the marketplace and be of maximum benefit to producers.[27]

While *Farm Journal* subscribers were reading a review of farmer cooperative problems, in October urban businessmen could get their impression of cooperatives from *Forbes* magazine. The text was not particularly critical of farmer cooperatives, but the headlines gave a most unfavorable impression. The title "Speaking of Bigness" was followed by a subtitle: "What kind of business is exempt from income tax and most antitrust laws and grossed $44 billion last year? Read on."[28]

Farmland officials believed that offense was the best defense against the growing bad publicity for cooperatives. Leith was then ending his second year as chairman of the board of the National Council of Farmer Cooperatives, and he used Farmland's annual meeting in December, 1974, to praise the work of cooperatives and to urge members of associations to work together to improve both the business operations and public image of their associations. He entitled his address: "Needed—More Cooperative Clout." Others at the annual meeting also outlined the positive contributions of Farmland and explained the plans for even greater production and distribution of products manufactured by cooperatives.[29] Several months earlier, Beasley had been quoted in *Business Week* as saying: "To be in competition with big corporations, we have to act like big corporations."[30] Obviously, the criticism of bigness had made no impression on Farmland officials or its farmer-owners. Leith also wrote an article for the March, 1975,

---

27 "What Went Wrong with These Co-ops?," *Farm Journal*, October, 1974, 20; "Who's Minding Your Co-op?," *Farm Journal*, November, 1974, 26.

28 *Forbes*, October 15, 1974, 57.

29 Leith, speech, December 12, 1974; *Farmland News*, December 31, 1974.

30 *Business Week*, June 8, 1974, 54.

issue of *Farm Journal* entitled, "Members Are Minding The Co-ops—That's Who," which answered many criticisms of farmer cooperatives.

Meanwhile, discussions regarding merger continued. Finally on June 3, 1976, the two boards of directors met at Hutchinson, Kansas, and adopted identical resolutions "authorizing study and consideration of possible merger or consolidation of the two organizations."[31] A Far-Mar-Co-Farmland coordination committee of three persons from each regional cooperative was appointed to review the entire matter and develop recommendations on "the most practical manner of bringing the two cooperatives together." This committee, consisting of Voth, executive vice-president and general manager, Paul Sherard, financial vice-president, and Gary Mundhenke, director of management services of Far-Mar-Co, and Lindsey, Leith, and Ewing of Farmland, was directed to study the question and report by September 1. This meeting was widely publicized. On June 4, the *Kansas City Star* carried a headline, "Regional Co-ops Open Merger Talks," and other newspapers gave the prospective merger prominent attention.

The Coordination Committee held meetings on June 17, July 1, July 19, and August 12, and had its report ready for the two boards to consider on September 1. It was an enthusiastic endorsement of merger. The main reason to merge the two large cooperatives was to give farmers some meaningful control over the export market. If producer associations were to compete in the same league with the agribusiness giants, the report said, "it calls for large, diversified, hard-hitting cooperatives to act as a farmer-owned countervailing force." The committee believed that a large cooperative agribusiness firm "embracing an integrated farm supply activity, plus grain and meat marketing, would be of great value to farmers." Referring to the fact that only five firms exported most of the nation's grain, the committee predicted that "American farmers will continue to be at the mercy of this oligopoly" unless they developed a cooperative with competitive power. In short, the fundamental reason for merger was to increase the bargaining power of farmers in the marketplace.[32]

A condition that favored merger was the fact that about 95 per cent of Far-Mar-Co's 604 members were also affiliated with Farmland In-

---

[31] "Report to the Boards of Directors of Far-Mar-Co, Inc., and Farmland Industries, Inc., by the Far-Mar-Co-Farmland Consolidation Committee," September 1, 1976; Board of Directors, Minutes of a special meeting, June 3, 1976; and press release, June 4, 1976.
[32] "Report of the Boards of Directors . . ."; Consolidation Committee, Minutes, June 17, July 19, August 12, October 21, and November 18, 1976.

dustries, while 26 per cent of Farmland member associations were members of Far-Mar-Co. This meant that there already was an overlapping of ownership and interest at the grass roots. There were also some administrative and organizational advantages in a merger. For example, Far-Mar-Co had developed an excellent data-processing system for its associations that could be rather easily expanded to all of Farmland's members. Also such functions as public relations could be unified. Not to be overlooked, of course, was the fact that a merger with Farmland would add financial strength to Far-Mar-Co's grain-marketing activities.

Farmland's and Far-Mar-Co's directors gathered in Kansas City on September 1 to consider the report of their joint committee. Agreement was soon reached that Far-Mar-Co would be merged into Farmland and operate as a subsidiary corporation controlled by Farmland. The Coordination Committee was instructed to prepare the articles of incorporation, bylaws, and any other necessary legal documents for consideration by the boards on November 30.[33]

During the next few weeks officials from both cooperatives worked out the details of the merger. At the same time the whole question was discussed at Farmland's district meetings. Board members reported that most reaction from members "was positive and constructive," although this was not a unanimous opinion. Farmland also had to prepare a registration statement for filing with the Securities and Exchange Commission, file a prenotification statement with the Federal Trade Commission, and make other notifications and reports to government agencies. On November 29, with everything in order, the two boards of directors approved the "plan and agreement of merger."[34]

The two remaining actions taken to fully complete the merger were approval by Farmland's shareholders and a favorable vote by Far-Mar-Co's members. Farmland officials presented the proposal to their shareholders at the annual meeting on December 3, only four days after the Board meeting. No formal vote was required under Farmland's bylaws, but officials wanted "a vote of confidence." A few delegates raised questions and suggested that the proceedings were moving too fast, but a motion to approve the merger passed over-

[33] Board of Directors, Minutes, September 1, 1976.
[34] *Ibid.*, November 29, 1976. See also the informal notes on the joint meeting of the Far-Mar-Co and Farmland boards on November 29. This account reported some opposition.

whelmingly. Walter W. Peterson, a Nebraska farmer who had been president of Far-Mar-Co since 1968, addressed the Farmland convention and declared that farmers must organize strong cooperatives so they could improve their income from marketing. "Only so much water can be squeezed out of the input side," he said, or, to put it another way, farmers could not save themselves into prosperity. He went on to explain that cooperatives were only exporting about 7 per cent of the grains, and if they were going to become a major factor in overseas markets they must control export elevators, shipping facilities, and other properties. This would take enormous amounts of capital. He implied that Farmland and Far-Mar-Co together could meet the challenge.[35]

The last step was for the Far-Mar-Co stockholders to approve the merger. As the Far-Mar-Co meeting to be held in Denver on February 10, 1977, approached, some grumbling and opposition surfaced among a few cooperative leaders. William Daniels, president of the Kansas Cimarron Cooperative Equity Exchange, declared that the two companies would be incompatible and that merger would not help get better prices for grain.[36] But the delegates voted 462 to 44 to become a subsidiary of Farmland Industries. Peterson became chairman of the new Far-Mar-Co board of directors that consisted of twelve members of the old board and thirteen persons from Farmland's Board and management team. Voth was named president of the new subsidiary. Voth had spent most of his life working for cooperatives and had served on Farmland's Board of Directors from 1959 to 1968. Since 1972 he had been executive vice-president and general manager of Far-Mar-Co.[37]

The merger brought together the largest farm supply cooperative and the biggest grain-marketing cooperative in the United States. As Peterson said, this was neither "a shotgun wedding nor an elopement," but a marriage of two strong associations. Their combined sales volume in the fiscal year ending August 31, 1977, amounted to $3,039,611,000. This figure placed Farmland among the nation's largest industrial corporations. It ranked 78 among *Fortune's* largest 500 industrials, moving up from 123 in 1976 before the merger. By the merger Farmland greatly expanded its marketing service to farmer

[35] *Farmland News,* January 15, 1977.
[36] *Hutchinson News* (Kansas), January 13, 1977.
[37] *Farmland News,* February 15, 1977, 1. Leith gave details of the merger process in a speech before the National Society of Accountants for Cooperatives on August 18, 1977.

members. Far-Mar-Co handled about 350 million bushels of grain, owned sixteen terminal elevators, controlled a part of the Farmers Export Company and the export terminal at Ama, Louisiana, owned or leased about 1,000 jumbo hopper railroad cars for grain transport, and manufactured some food products. In 1975–1976, the company had inaugurated a grain program known as the Producers Marketing System, or Promark. This was a wheat-pooling plan whereby farmers would commit a percentage of their production to the pool and receive the average price obtained by the centralized selling agency, less expenses. In fiscal 1977, Far-Mar-Co's grain sales and operating revenue amounted to $690 million, down considerably from 1975. Unit sales were also down. Farmland's food-marketing subsidiary had sales of $436,911,000, giving a total marketing volume of $1,127,295,000.[38] This was a little more than one-third of Farmland's total business.

From the summer of 1976 when serious merger talks began, until the spring of 1977 following the agreement, the move toward consolidation received rather widespread press attention. Some of the headlines and the prospective size of Farmland after the merger helped to revive the bigness controversy that had raged in 1974. For example, the *Wichita Eagle* (Kansas) headlined its story on June 5, 1976: "Co-op Giants Study Merger." On November 22, however, *Business Week* carried an article entitled: "Hatching a New Giant Down on the Farm," that aroused renewed controversy over the size of cooperatives. This story told of the possible merger of Farmland and Far-Mar-Co and quoted critical remarks by representatives of the fertilizer industry who accused large cooperatives of "abusing their position by virtue of legal privilege." Except for the headline, the article was only moderately anti-cooperative as the author also quoted at least one strong cooperative supporter.

But this was just the beginning of *Business Week*'s critical attitude toward cooperatives. On February 7, 1977, just a few days before Far-Mar-Co members voted on merger, the magazine published a long account of cooperatives under the heading: "The Billion-Dollar Farm Co-ops Nobody Knows," plus a critical editorial. The writer mentioned *Farmland* in the first sentence and said that when President Lindsey "talks about the record of his diversified merchandising and manufacturing operation, he sounds like the proud top officer of any

---

[38] *49th Annual Report,* 1977, 33.

big, successful corporation." Referring to Farmland as a "giant" and the "most aggressive co-op" in the United States, the writer said that the growth of large cooperatives had been one "of the best kept secrets" in American business. According to the author, these huge enterprises provided unfair competition to noncooperative business because of tax breaks and exemption from the antitrust laws. He pictured cooperatives as having "forced independent farm suppliers out of business in droves" and quoted a representative of W. R. Grace and Company who feared that if cooperatives were permitted to grow and merge "private enterprise will be squeezed out of agribusiness." Considerable attention was given to the alleged tax advantages of cooperatives. In conclusion, the author said that the "surprising growth" of cooperatives and their competitive strength would "force them to a higher level of visibility" that could "prove to be their biggest problem in the next decade." The accompanying editorial urged Congress to take a hard look at some of the privileges enjoyed by cooperatives such as the "tax exemptions and special status under the antitrust laws." These, the writer said, might have been justified for small cooperatives, but not for the big agribusiness associations.

Material in the *Business Week* story was picked up by newspapers and other magazines around the country, keeping the bigness controversy alive into the early summer. Writing in *Food Engineering* in April, Mel Seligsohn said that the size of the Farmland merger was "stunning." "Those accustomed to viewing co-ops as plodding, quaint relics of the era when farmers banded together for mutual protection to combat hard times of one sort or another," he continued, had no concept of reality. Other publications echoed the idea that huge cooperatives were a danger to noncooperative business. Some competitors began labelling the large associations "mega-cooperatives."

Farmland officials admitted that the *Business Week* article "contained a lot of truth and some flattering assessments of cooperatives" but vigorously objected to what they considered inaccuracies and inflammatory language.[39] Also they did not appreciate the effect it had in reviving the bigness controversy. Bill Matteson, executive director of communication services, called John Love, the article's author, expressing disappointment that the account had been so heavily weighted against cooperatives. It was not an objective piece, Matteson contended. He especially disliked what he called the "highhanded

---

[39] Leith, speech, August 18, 1977.

editorial treatment." But a rather extended telephone conversation did not convince Love that his article was inaccurate or unfair.[40]

While Farmland executives did not like the anti-cooperative publicity generated by the *Business Week* article, they were not unduly alarmed by it. They knew that President Jimmy Carter and Secretary of Agriculture Robert Bergland had expressed strong support for farm cooperatives. Moreover, Congress had refused to take any action on several proposals that would have limited the size of cooperatives or restricted them in other ways. Their position was not to try to hide Farmland's size, but to capitalize on it; not to cover up criticism but to deal with it openly. Consequently, *Farmland News* carried the entire *Business Week* article in its February 28 issue, making it available to some 400,000 Midwestern farmers and cooperative leaders. Vice-president Beasley wrote an editorial for the same issue of *Farmland News*, calling for greater understanding of the "fundamental differences" in both purpose and ownership between cooperatives and regular corporate business.

The controversy over bigness did not deter Farmland officials from moving ahead to work out the final details of merger that became legally effective May 2, 1977. However, there were many problems to be addressed before the merger could work smoothly and efficiently. A merger coordinating committee was appointed on April 7 and it had the over-all responsibility for coordinating special committees and task groups that dealt with specific policies and administrative matters. The work included eliminating overlapping programs, coordinating certain company functions, and long-range planning. An example of removing duplication was the decision to discontinue publication of *The Marketer*, Far-Mar-Co's magazine, and add a new marketing page in *Farmland News*.[41]

The Farmland-Far-Mar-Co merger was hailed by cooperative enthusiasts as one of the most significant events in the history of farmer cooperatives. Farmers and ranchers finally had "a fully integrated supply and marketing cooperative," Lindsey wrote in the 1977 *Annual Report*. Lindsey was proud of Farmland's size and had no fear of the cooperative becoming too big. On numerous occasions, he approvingly quoted Cowden, who had told delegates during the annual meeting

40 Bill Matteson to Beasley, Lindsey, and Leith, February 2, 1977.
41 "Plan for Effectuating the Merger," undated; Report of the Merger Policy Committee to the Board of Directors of Far-Mar-Co, Inc., August 24, 1977.

in 1959: "I urge upon farmers that they think about their regional cooperative in terms of bigness and be proud of the bigness it has attained. We must be big to be effective. We must be big to protect farmers. We must be big to survive." No one could have expressed the philosophy of Farmland's leadership in 1977 more accurately. But Lindsey would add one further idea. Farmland must use its size "to do the job our farmer-owners expect of us."[42]

The merger had scarcely been completed before Farmland's new subsidiary faced what might have been a serious legal challenge. In August, 1977, Secretary of Agriculture Bergland ruled that cooperatives holding pooled grain for their members could obtain Commodity Credit Corporation price support loans for their members on wheat and feed grains in storage. This was highly important to the success of Far-Mar-Co's Promark system. A grain company in Kansas filed a class action suit against the secretary of the U.S. Department of Agriculture, arguing that this action gave cooperatives an unfair advantage over private grain dealers. Farmland worked hard to win this case, and on January 18, 1978, the U.S. District Court in Topeka, Kansas, upheld the secretary's decision. Far-Mar-Co was now in a stronger position to achieve its goal of controlling grain marketing at every stage between the original producer and the foreign consumer. To strengthen its export activities, Far-Mar-Co purchased a large elevator at Fort Worth, Texas, in June, 1977, and joined six other cooperatives and two interregional associations in the Farmers Export Company to purchase grain storage and shipping facilities in Galveston from Cook Industries, Inc.[43]

Despite the controversy over bigness that was stimulated by the merger, Lindsey could report to delegates at the annual meeting in December, 1977, that "the public image of farm cooperatives is generally favorable." He added, however, that as cooperatives became "a larger and more potent force in the marketplace, we can expect more and harsher challenges from non-cooperative competitors and from some segments of the government." That seemed to be an accurate assessment. So long as farmer cooperatives had been small and inefficient, they attracted little attention from either business or gov-

---

[42] *Leadership*, March, 1977, 2.
[43] *Farmland News*, June 15, 1977, 1; *Kansas City Star*, November 7, 1976, and July 10, 1977; Lindsey to All Member Associations, August 19, 1977; and *Farmland News*, January 31, 1978.

ernment. As they became larger, however, and begun to get a substantial share of the market in some areas, they came under sharper attack.

But Lindsey stood solidly behind size and efficiency. In his ten years as president, he said, nothing had caused as much excitement "in the cooperative family as the merger of Farmland and Far-Mar-Co." However, a subtle danger existed. Would farmers have unrealistic expectations in regard to Farmland's ability to improve their grain-marketing business? Lindsey warned repeatedly that, despite the historic merger action, farmers might expect "too much too soon." Only time could determine whether Farmland would be able to benefit grain farmers by gaining control of a larger share of export markets.[44]

---

44 *Leadership*, March, 1977, 2.

Chapter 19

What of the Future?

IT WAS A HUGE and enthusiastic crowd of 20,679 Farmland supporters who gathered in Kansas City for the annual meeting on December 3, 1977. They nearly inundated the Midwest's old cow town. There was plenty of fun as Erma Bombeck combined wit and wisdom in her remarks, and Hee-Haw star Roy Clark entertained more than 15,000 at Kemper Arena. Farmers and their wives from all over the Midwest enjoyed the performances, but they also listened attentively as Congresswoman Virginia Smith of Nebraska lambasted America's growing bureaucracy. They hoped that Marshall Loeb, national editor of *Time* magazine, was correct when he said that farmers rated high in public esteem. The highlight of the meeting was an address by Secretary of Agriculture Robert Bergland, who reviewed the difficult position of farmers and pledged to do everything he could to expand exports.

But it was the "home folks" who got down to practical matters. Lindsey proudly reported a sales volume for the fiscal year ending August 31 of $3,039,611,000. This was the first annual meeting since the merger with Far-Mar-Co, but even without the grain volume Farmland's sales would have been about $2.3 billion. While net savings before income taxes and patronage refunds were down some $32 million from 1976, member cooperatives still received $78 million in refunds of which $38.3 million was in cash. Considering the depressed condition of agriculture in 1977, it had been a good year for Farmland Industries.

Moreover, those attending the annual meeting in 1977 had an opportunity to visit the greatly enlarged headquarters building that had been completed just a few weeks before. This was the fourth major addition to the office building, which had been finished in October, 1956, just twenty-one years earlier. The total cost of this fine, modern office complex, and six-story garage, now reached about $12.5 million. The headquarters building, covering 231,000 square feet, plus some satellite office space in Kansas City, housed 1,284 employees out of a total company work force of 9,264. All of the qualified employees enjoyed retirement, insurance, health, and disability benefits. Farmland had realized for many years that if the company were to attract loyal and capable employees it must provide a competitive package of benefits.

Despite a $3 billion sales year in fiscal 1977, Lindsey told the "Farmland family" that the company could look forward to even a better future. He predicted that Farmland would spend some $3 billion during the next decade to get more basic in petroleum and fertilizer and to expand the output of farm supplies, feed, and other products and services. The dream held by many farmers that Farmland would become a major exporter of grain, he said, would surely come true in the next ten years. While he recognized such problems as diminishing energy supplies, he talked about growth, size, and greater services to farmers and ranchers.[1]

Lindsey had every reason to be optimistic about the future as Farmland approached the end of its first half century of business. When the books were closed in 1929 the little Union Oil Company reported a first year volume of only $309,891. Sales increased nearly 10,000 times during the next forty-nine years. No longer was the company simply a broker of petroleum products. Farmland Industries, Inc., was a huge cooperative conglomerate engaged in providing a wide variety of products and services to Midwestern farmers whose off-farm inputs needed for production had risen dramatically during the preceding half century. By 1977 Farmland had $1.1 billion invested in property, plants, and equipment for the production and distribution of petroleum products, fertilizer, agricultural chemicals, feed, meat, grain, and such farm supplies as metal buildings, paint, and batteries. The company also provided a wide range of services, including education, management advice, financial aid to member associations, and insurance for both cooperatives and individuals. Farmland's enterprises were all geared toward the specific objective of supplying products

---

1 *Farmland News,* December 21, 1977, 1.

and services to farmers and ranchers through their 2,260 member co-operatives in the company's sixteen-state service territory. While the company had many facets, it had the single purpose of trying to serve farmers. There had been no change in that goal since Cowden organized the Union Oil Company.

Most of Farmland's growth occurred after the middle 1960's when the company entered the fertilizer business in a major way. In 1963 Farmland's assets amounted to only $167 million and its total volume reached $242 million. By 1977 assets were valued at $1,490 million and sales exceeded $3 billion. While all aspects of the business had contributed to this growth, fertilizer was a vital key in the over-all picture of company expansion. It was fertilizer more than anything else that provided the margins necessary for much of the company's growth. The savings generated by fertilizer and agricultural chemicals classified in reports as crop production far exceeded those earned by petroleum and other major company activities. For example, in the five years, 1972–1976 inclusive, gross savings from crop-production sales amounted to about $507 million compared to only $214 million for petroleum products. Or to put it another way, in those five years fertilizer produced just about 50 per cent of the company's gross margins from all products handled.

By most any business standards Farmland Industries had been a marked success. But what factors were responsible for its growth? What accounted for the transformation of a small brokerage firm to the nation's largest farmer cooperative in less than a half century? The answers to these questions are fairly clear. Probably the most important factor was Cowden's early decision to achieve a high degree of vertical integration and the subsequent actions taken to implement that objective. As mentioned earlier, savings that could be realized from distribution alone were severely limited in the farm supply field. The margins generated from manufacturing provided much of the funds for capital expansion. By getting into oil production and also the mining of sulphur, Farmland also benefited from depletion allowances. Thus, the company came to produce profits all the way through the production and distribution process from raw material to the sale of finished products. Farmland has gone further than any other farmer cooperative in the country to achieve vertical integration.

Secondly, Farmland, for most part, confined its business activities to products that were important to the Midwest's progressive and productive farmers. It purposely placed itself in league with modern

agriculture by concentrating on the production and distribution of
petroleum products, fertilizer and agricultural chemicals, feed and
farm supplies that became so important in farm production. While
farmers required these products, most of the time they also produced
good margins for the company. It was a mutually beneficial relationship. The programs to market meat and grain may pay off for both
producers and Farmland some time in the future, but so far the positive results have been limited. Indeed, it was Farmland's concentration on petroleum, fertilizer, and feed that produced the margins to
undergird the marketing operations. As Farmland officials repeat
time after time, the company must make money if it is to continue
serving farmers by providing a steady supply of good products at fair
prices. Those profits will continue to come in the foreseeable future
from oil, fertilizer, and feed.

Farmland, of course, was not always successful in its endeavors.
The grocery business, lumber mill, National Farm Lines, the turkey
operations, and Farmland Food Services were among a rather substantial string of failures. Some of these enterprises failed because of
special business conditions, but more often than not they were outside
the area that was directly related to the welfare of modern farmers.
Farmland had an enviable record of success when it stuck to the things
it knew and did best, namely, produce and distribute products needed
by the expanding and efficient Midwest farmer. In any event, the
failures were not really significant because they were too small to
affect over-all company business. They were irritants, rather than
threatening problems.

A third source of Farmland's strength has been its system of marketing products through member cooperatives. Over the years it
built a strong federated system where farmers own the member associations that in turn own Farmland. Farmers, the ultimate customers
of Farmland's products, are, through their local associations, also
the owners of the company facilities that make and distribute commodities and provide services. Since Farmland cannot force local
associations to do business with the regional, it must win support by
providing good service and quality products at reasonable prices. As
part of its program, Farmland has worked hard to make the local
cooperatives successful. The company probably has provided a larger
group of services to member associations than any other regional. It
supplies credit, management training, advice on sales and member
relations, and all kinds of education on the philosophical and practi-

cal aspects of farmer cooperatives. Farmland has spent millions nourishing the federated system on which it depends for support. The company has developed a definite constituency that is interested in its prosperity because that prosperity funnels money back to the member-owners.

As a result of having a strong built-in market, Farmland has been more willing to take business risks and to launch out boldly on new projects. It has been a doer and an innovator. Farmland has been more aggressive in using credit to build facilities than most other cooperatives because it had confidence in the support of member associations.

Farmland greatly improved the image of cooperatives among members at the grass roots when it inaugurated the Ownership Retirement Program in 1971. This program assisted local cooperatives to pay in cash the deferred refunds of members who retired. When local associations received cash refunds from Farmland, they returned part of that refund to farmer members and retained the remainder for use in the business. For example, if a farmer had a refund coming of $500 on the basis of business with his local association, he would receive $250, or some set percentage of the $500, in cash, and the remainder in equities in his cooperative. Previously, individual members of cooperatives complained that they had to die to collect these equities, which were being held by their locals. Lindsey admitted that "in too many cases" this complaint was valid. Some cooperatives could not even pay off the equities of deceased members.

Under the new plan, Farmland redeemed in cash a part of the member cooperative's equity in the regional to assist the local association with its cash flow needed to redeem equities of retired farmer members. In 1972 Farmland paid $290,350 to 88 cooperatives, and in 1973 the company expended $519,825 to 288 locals. By 1977 this amount had increased to $4.2 million to 750 local cooperatives. This policy proved to be popular. It gave farmers who had been members of cooperatives for many years what amounted to an added retirement fund. In October, 1974, three Minnesota farmers ran an advertisement in the Worthington newspaper in which they pictured themselves with their retirement checks. To receive cash for their deferred refunds, they said, proved that they had been "right in supporting the cooperative philosophy over the years."[2]

Furthermore, business success at Farmland bred further success.

---

[2] Board of Directors, Minutes, August 24–25, 1971, and April 4–5, 1972; *Farmland News,* October 31, 1974; and *Leadership,* January, 1976, 5.

Many farmer patrons took great pride as Farmland expanded and diversified its business. Farmer members of cooperatives believed that they were a part of a growing, vibrant, successful organization, and it gave them a good feeling. Farmland's development, along with the progressive member cooperatives, were in sharp contrast to the small, inefficient associations that many farmers had known in earlier years. Cooperators at the grass roots began to feel that at last they were part of an organization that could compete successfully with the big corporations and monopolies. It was somewhat contradictory, but farmer patrons did not look upon Farmland Industries as being unduly large even after it became a $3 billion corporation. Many farmers said it should become bigger if it were to be an effective countervailing power on behalf of producers. Of forty-four farmers and managers in Farmland territory who answered a questionnaire on bigness, only two thought that Farmland was getting too big. A majority of those queried believed that even greater size was necessary to provide farmers with more clout in the marketplace.

What farmers had been demanding for years was some means of strengthening competition among those who bought farm products and sold them supplies. Agriculture was a highly competitive industry, but in dealing with other segments of the economy farmers often ran into monopoly and administered prices. They wanted a strong competitive force in the market and viewed Farmland as a source of additional competition. While some cooperators believed that their associations should bring direct benefits to members through lower prices for supplies, Farmland officials and most cooperative members held that this policy would be unwise. They argued that charging competitive prices and returning refunds to members was the best policy for two reasons; first, because it would generate enough income to help Farmland expand; secondly, because, at the same time, it would provide savings that could be returned to members in cash. Most Farmland constituents favored making the company strong enough so that it could be a major competitive force in the market. They viewed Farmland competition as one of the company's major values to farmers.

Despite its growing size, Farmland managed to retain some of the characteristics of a smaller company. While employees around the headquarters work hard, they appear satisfied and relaxed. Interviews with employees indicate that they consider Farmland a good place to work. Visiting farmers and cooperative officials from Farmland territory constantly tour the headquarters building. Not until 1978 was uniformed security provided. Earlier the head custodian was responsible for security and safety. Farmland succeeded to a large extent in meeting the challenge of what Randall Torgerson, head of the Farmer Cooperative Service (named Economics, Statistics and Cooperatives Service, ESCS, in December, 1977), referred to as "growing big, but seeming to stay small to the membership."[3] The image Farmland portrayed to many was "the giant with the personal touch."

Farmland's success was also closely tied to good management and effective corporate planning. While the principle of planning was not unusual, the end toward which planning was directed was unique. The plans for company growth were not designed for the sake of size and profits but "to improve the economic position of agricultural producers." This would be achieved by furnishing supplies, marketing, and other services to farmers. A high level of savings was always a part of any Farmland plan, but the purpose of good margins was to achieve the larger objectives of serving agriculture. Savings were the means to help farmers, not an end in themselves. The degree to which Farmland helped farmers might be debated, but that was the basis of corporate strategy.

Planning at Farmland Industries was done mostly on an ad-hoc basis until the late 1960's. There had been such programs as Project 67 and Route 70, but these efforts were not very sophisticated or formalized. In 1970, however, Leith, who chaired the long-range planning committee, presented the first "comprehensive, detailed, all-embracing long range plan" to the Board of Directors.[4] From that time onward, planning became a major function in corporate administration. The plans were developed by planning task groups designated for each major division of the company. Bulky planning documents began to appear annually in 1973-1974, and in some cases they carried projections for a decade ahead. While Farmland officials recognized that their plans might be thwarted by fluctuations in farmer income, they based their projections on the assumption that agriculture would continue to be a growth industry.[5]

There was a remarkable stability and commitment to cooperative principles among Farmland's top management. Unlike many other corporations where executives flitted in and out in the 1960's and

---

[3] *Farmland News*, February 15, 1977, 1.
[4] Board of Directors, Minutes, March 31–April 1, 1970.
[5] Farmland Industries, Inc., "Long Range Plan, 1976–77," March, 1977.

1970's, the people who held the reins at Farmland were tried and trusted in company affairs. By 1978 the eight top officials, including Lindsey and his Executive Council, had all been at Farmland fifteen years or more—most of them much more. Only Voth was a newcomer. He joined the Executive Council in 1977 as head of Far-Mar-Co, but even Voth had been connected with Farmland earlier as a member of the Board of Directors. Treasurer Ewing had been with the company for forty-five years, Leith and Anderson twenty-nine years, Nielsen twenty-seven years, Beasley twenty-one years, and Johanson seventeen years. Of this group, Lindsey had the shortest tenure with fifteen years. As Farmland expanded in the 1960's and 1970's, the company employed many professional and technical people who did research, managed plants, ran computers, and performed a host of other jobs. Many of these individuals had no farm or cooperative background. They viewed their employment much as they would a position with any large corporation. However, Farmland's top executives were deeply committed both to cooperative enterprise and to farmers. They believed in what they were doing. Most of them had come from farms or from rural settings, and they exhibited a little of the missionary spirit as they worked to help agriculture. They liked farmers and associated with them in a free and easy manner. In short, there was a friendly relationship between Farmland's top management and the company's customers.

The personal leadership of Farmland's presidents has been extremely important to company success. Cowden, who died in December, 1972, provided the imagination, initiative, and practical guidance that the company needed from its founding in 1929 through the 1950's. For thirty years he was an inspirational leader at a time when inspiration was important in building the farmer cooperative movement in the Midwest. Cowden combined the ideal and the practical in a remarkable way. Young assumed the presidency in the 1960's and pushed hard for greater growth. He improved the company's organization and administration but still relied on strong personal leadership. Lindsey's leadership was firm, but somewhat less visible as he installed a broad corporate administration more in keeping with the size and complexity of Farmland Industries. He worked through effective subordinates. It was Lindsey's management style to decentralize control of the firm's growing subsidiaries. In addition to Ewing and Leith who assumed responsibility for insurance and food, respectively, John Anderson administered the fertilizer subsidiaries, soy processing was delegated to Nielsen, and William L. Rader became chairman of the board of Terra Resources, Inc. All of Farmland's presidents provided strong personal leadership and direction for the company, but they implemented that leadership in different ways. As John Schulte, chairman of the Board of Directors, said in his farewell address in 1972: "Howard Cowden, Homer Young and Ernest Lindsey are different kinds of men, but each [was] right for Farmland at the time he conducted its business." [6]

There were other sources of Farmland strength. The decision to avoid identification with any farm organization or special farm group proved to be wise. Maintaining neutrality in regard to the established farm organizations meant that the company could seek business from farmers and local cooperatives without regard to their organizational connections.

Also the timing of certain projects was most fortunate. Perhaps this was luck as much as anything else. For example, if the Phillipsburg refinery had been built in 1932 instead of 1939, the story of that enterprise, and perhaps of the company, might have been different. Heavy oil surpluses and low oil prices in the early 1930's could have created grave problems as they did for numerous independents. As it was, the refinery was built when prices of construction were low and just before wartime needs had a favorable effect on demand and on prices for petroleum products. While construction of the Lawrence nitrogen plant created a company crisis, its completion came at a time when farmers were rapidly expanding their use of commercial fertilizer. Savings from that plant provided much of the capital needed for further expansion of industrial facilities.

Farmland, like other cooperatives, was encouraged by the federal government. This included the policies of not taxing allocated, undistributed patronage refunds and permitting those earnings to be held for capital expansion. Moreover, relatively low-cost credit from the Banks for Cooperatives was helpful. Without this source of capital, expansion would have been much more difficult and perhaps even impossible. The regional cooperative, as well as many other companies, also benefited from the acquisition of some surplus government property after World War II. It acquired the high-octane

---

[6] *Farmland News*, December 20, 1972, 4.

refinery at Coffeyville from the War Assets Administration for about one-fourth of its original cost. Thus Farmland owes some of its success to a friendly government.

Finally, one of the most significant reasons for Farmland's growth has been that the company is located in the heart of one of the world's most productive agricultural regions. The sixteen states in which Farmland does most of its business normally produces some 70 per cent of corn, 74 per cent of the wheat, 60 per cent of the soybeans, 67 per cent of the hogs, and 62 per cent of the cattle produced in the United States. Iowa is the leading corn state and Kansas excels in wheat. Both are strong Farmland states. Many of Farmland's ultimate customers are large, efficient, business-oriented farmers whose operations have been expanding rapidly. In other words, Farmland operates in a wealthy agricultural region where much of farming has become relatively big business. These farmer consumers do not use hundreds of gallons of fuel, but thousands; they do not buy sacks of fertilizer, but tons. The number of farmers in the region is declining, but more and more of the nearly one million who remain are big consumers of products supplied by Farmland.

Despite a remarkable business history, Farmland Industries faces problems in the years ahead. Since its strength rests on the vigor of the member cooperatives, which, in turn, rely on the farmer members, the welfare of both Farmland and the locals depend on the loyalty of farmer patrons. Studies and surveys have shown that the loyalty of many farmers to cooperatives is weak. A poll by the Gallup organization in 1976 showed that only about half of the people living on farms claimed to be reasonably well informed about farmer cooperatives. Thus, while cooperatives did a considerably greater share of the farm supply business in the Midwest in 1977 compared to the 1950's or 1960's, it is a fact that most farmers are not fully committed to cooperative business enterprise. The major challenge facing Farmland and its member cooperatives in the late 1970's is to sell the idea of cooperative business to more farmer customers.

It is absolutely essential in the years ahead that Farmland maintain a close relationship with the member associations and build an even stronger federated system. The communications developed over the years between Farmland and the member cooperatives have been good, but they must not be allowed to decline. Of equal importance is the need for the local cooperatives to keep in close touch with individual members. As local associations become multimillion-dollar businesses, they must have programs that keep individual farmers feeling that they are a part of the enterprise and, indeed, really own it. The local patron must not be permitted to be a member in absentia.

Farmland also faces the challenge of maintaining a sound financial structure. In the late 1960's and 1970's Farmland turned to an extensive use of credit to build productive facilities. Farmland's huge borrowings for capital outlays set the company apart from other regionals. The expansion of business based on credit permitted the company to gain access to raw materials and to build manufacturing and distribution facilities far beyond anything that could have been undertaken in any other way.

By 1977 Farmland carried nearly $572 million in long-term debt, and slightly over $1 billion in total debt. The relationship between debt and assets was about 1 to 1.4. Looking at the situation another way, the company's equity was only about 27.5 per cent of total assets as of August 31, 1977. This figure is slightly below the 30 per cent that Farmland's management believes is desirable to maintain. The company's debt position is such that future growth will probably be paced more closely to cash flow with less reliance on long-term credit. In any event, it is essential that earnings continue high in order to carry the debt and provide additional funds for further expansion. The facilities built with credit in the past will be important in keeping earnings at a good level in the years ahead.

One of Farmland's aims from the late 1950's onward was to keep savings consistently strong. However, during the 1960's and 1970's, net savings fluctuated from as little as $10 million to as much as $200 million a year. This instability was associated with product price changes, and sharp variations in farmer income. The problem in the late 1970's and 1980's will be to assure good savings that can help carry the company debt and provide for the expanding needs of farmer members. Being highly leveraged, Farmland will need to protect itself as much as possible from the dangers of agricultural price cycles.

A major problem facing Farmland and all cooperatives is their public image. During the 1970's a series of events occurred that brought cooperatives under sharp public scrutiny and criticism. The illegal political contributions by the Associated Milk Producers, Inc., and subsequent court fines, received widespread publicity in 1974. The embarrassment to cooperatives over that affair had hardly died down before other scandals arose. In 1976 and 1977 investigations revealed that the Progressive Farmers Association of Springfield, Missouri, had sold more than $12 million worth of securities only to have most of the money lost in poor investments or siphoned off by the promoters. These so-called pseudo-cooperatives, such as PFA, gave the anti-cooperative interests an excuse to attack the legitimate business cooperatives.[7] Because of Farmland's size and influence in the Midwest, it is in a position through it own actions and publicity to counteract much of the unfavorable image.

So what of the future? There is little doubt but that Farmland Industries will continue to grow. The long-range plan developed in 1976–1977 projected more than the doubling of sales by 1986. In light of past projections that seems entirely reasonable. When Lindsey became president in 1967, he expressed the hope that when he retired in 1980 Farmland would be a billion-dollar company. It exceeded that by three times long before that date. So long as the cost-price squeeze pressures farmers, they are likely to turn more and more to companies that they believe will reduce their costs and improve income from marketing. Farmland, located in the heartland of America, is in a strong position to become the agency through which farmers will work to solve some of their economic problems. It is important to note that from 1929 to 1977, Farmland earned savings of $809.5 million and returned $321,650,000 in cash funds to member cooperatives. Tens of millions of this amount was then refunded in cash to farmer members.

With few exceptions, company management so far has been in the hands of executives who have had long association with farmer cooperatives. These officials have remained close to farmers and believe deeply in the importance of agriculture. The number-one question facing Farmland will be the kind of leadership that replaces the present generation of executives. Will the future leaders have the same commitment to cooperatives and service to farmers as Cowden, Young, Lindsey, and their top associates; or will they think mainly in terms of business success for its own sake and assume attitudes similar to those of noncooperative corporate executives? Can the purpose and spirit of Farmland's founders be maintained in the second half-century of company history? These are questions that can only be answered by the Board of Directors and Farmland's management team. If the company departs from its commitment to cooperative business and from the objective of serving farmers it has no reason to exist.

7 *Kansas City Star*, October 17, 1976, and August 28, 1977.

In one of his inspirational moments in 1954, Cowden told delegates at the annual meeting:

> CCA is an ideal enshrined in the hearts of the people. It is not the externals that give the organization stature—not the oil wells, the pipelines, the refineries, the buildings of steel, brick, and mortar. These are but outward tokens of inner strength. These are but the symbols of power; the power itself is in the people who nourish the cooperative idea with patronage and who otherwise give devoted loyalty to it. It is recognition that wealth is produced not by individuals, but by fellowship.

Nearly a quarter of a century later, Lindsey spoke in similar terms. He declared that the challenge to cooperatives was "to continue to stress the cooperative principles that make us more than just another business group." Since many young farmers did not know what conditions were like without a cooperative or did not understand how cooperatives worked, he continued, "we must become champions, advocates for cooperation." Besides promoting cooperative business, Farmland in its own self-interest, needs to become an even stronger spokesman for farmers who have become such a small minority of the nation's population.

There is no evidence that any kind of cooperative commonwealth is approaching in the United States. However, to the extent that people work together as they do through Farmland to solve some of their own problems, they promote a degree of economic democracy greatly needed in twentieth-century America.

Appendix

ACKLEY, R. J., GARDEN CITY, KANSAS, 1931–1956.

ANDERSON, JOSEPH A., SALT LAKE CITY, UTAH, 1934–1936.

BACKUS, E. A., WRAY, COLORADO, 1931–1937.

BALL, RALPH, STERLING, KANSAS, 1972–.

BEALS, C. E., CRETE, NEBRASKA, 1935–1937.

BURNS, IRA A., GRANT, NEBRASKA, 1947–1950.

BYERS, WILLIAM A., FRUITA, COLORADO, 1949–1965.

CHELF, ROY, SCOTTSBLUFF, NEBRASKA, 1966–.

CLARK, ROGER R., BRADY, NEBRASKA, 1965–.

CLINE, B. F., MEDFORD, OKLAHOMA, 1937–1958.

CLUTTER, HERBERT W., HOLCOMB, KANSAS, 1956–1959.

COGSWELL, C. C., TOPEKA, KANSAS, 1932–1939.

COOPER, J. B., JR., ROSCOE, TEXAS, 1968–1971.

CORY, F. BYRON B., COLORADO SPRINGS, COLORADO, 1955–1959.

COWDEN, HOWARD A., KANSAS CITY, MISSOURI, 1929–1963.

CRAWFORD, AL J., ATLANTA, MISSOURI, 1936–1939.

DEAN, R. E., SR., WESSINGTON SPRINGS, SOUTH DAKOTA, 1943–1948.

DETMER, W. R., PARSONS, KANSAS, 1929.

DEWITT, THOMAS H., MILAN, MISSOURI, 1929–1960.

DILLINGER, TROY T., BREWSTER, KANSAS, 1958–1972.

DREYER, FRANK, BRIGHTON, COLORADO, 1944–1956.

DUERR, FRED, SEWARD, NEBRASKA, 1936–1937.

EBBERT, S. S., QUINTER, KANSAS, 1931–1946.

ENSIGN, CHARLES H., SCRANTON, NORTH DAKOTA, 1943–1955.

ERREBO, CARL F., DODGE CITY, KANSAS, 1946–1948.

EVELO, FRANCIS J., ABERDEEN, SOUTH DAKOTA, 1955–1958.

FITZGERALD, J. E., GRANT, NEBRASKA, 1937–1946.

FUSER, J. M., JR., AFTON, OKLAHOMA, 1956–1975.

GALE, A. W., CHILLICOTHE, MISSOURI, 1930–1934.

GARRETSON, LOREN N. (PAT), HAXTUN, COLORADO, 1968–1974.

GEDDES, DR. JOSEPH A., LOGAN, UTAH, 1937–1948.

GELBACH, STANLEY, EDINA, MISSOURI, 1977–.

GWIN, FRANCIS B. (FRITZ), BELOIT, KANSAS, 1972–.

HAND, PHILIP, CENTER POINT, IOWA, 1972–.

HAPPEL, MAURICE L., PALMYRA, MISSOURI, 1963–1975.

HEATH, FRANK F., MONTROSE, COLORADO, 1946–1949.

HEDDING, R. A., BURLINGTON, COLORADO, 1929–1936.

HOUSTON, A. F., GROVE, OKLAHOMA, 1948–1956.

HOVEY, EDGAR C., BADGER, IOWA, 1945–1966.

JOHNSON, A. E., MARCUS, IOWA, 1939–1948.

JOHNSON, J. ELMER, LONGMONT, COLORADO, 1965–1968.

JOHNSON, L. T., MARQUETTE, NEBRASKA, 1937–1940.

JOHNSON, NORRIS C., HOLDREGE, NEBRASKA, 1960–1968.

JOHNSON, WESLEY C., LARAMIE, WYOMING, 1941–1959.

JORGENSEN, ARCH, FARNAM, NEBRASKA, 1950–1965.

KEARNS, W. A., KAHOKA, MISSOURI, 1929–1935.

KESTER, E. B., CAMBRIDGE, NEBRASKA, 1935–1937.

KIRBY, DON T., LAMONT, OKLAHOMA, 1975–.

KIRCHNER, JOE J., ALLIANCE, NEBRASKA, 1951–1966.

KRAMER, GEORGE, WAUKEE, IOWA, 1959–1968.

KUEHL, CLAUS C., SELBY, SOUTH DAKOTA, 1958–1970.

LIGHTNER, FRANK W., GARDEN CITY, KANSAS, 1974–.

LINDSEY, ERNEST T., LIBERTY, MISSOURI, 1967–.

LULL, DR. H. G., EMPORIA, KANSAS, 1937–1947.

MCCRACKEN, VERNER, HOLLY, COLORADO, 1962–1965.

MCGOHAN, LES N., MT. PLEASANT, IOWA, 1964–1970.

MCGOUGH, EDMUND, ACKLEY, IOWA, 1966–1972.

MCNICKLE, DAN, FARNAM, NEBRASKA, 1942–1945.

MILLER, CLIFFORD, BREWSTER, KANSAS, 1935–1965.

MILLER, DORANCE L., CAMBRIDGE, NEBRASKA, 1937–1942.

MILLER, KENNETH, SHENANDOAH, IOWA, 1948–1952.

MILLER, OSCAR J., CARROLLTON, MISSOURI, 1960–1970.

MOEN, JAMES M., KINDRED, NORTH DAKOTA, 1975–.

MONTGOMERY, GEORGE, MANHATTAN, KANSAS, 1952–1958.

MUSGRAVE, B. E., KANSAS CITY, MISSOURI, 1929.

NEWCOMB, ED M., WOONSOCKET, SOUTH DAKOTA, 1931.

NICHOLL, J. E., HITCHCOCK, SOUTH DAKOTA, 1931–1943.

NICKEL, H. R., HILLSBORO, KANSAS, 1947–1952.

NIMMO, RAY B., HAXTUN, COLORADO, 1937–1944.

NOREM, HOMER J., NEWARK, ILLINOIS, 1970–.

OSTERMANN, HAROLD, OCHEYEDAN, IOWA, 1966–1975.

PETERSON, ALBERT, MARCUS, IOWA, 1948–1966.

PETTY, EDGAR N., KEARNEY, MISSOURI, 1970–.

QUIGLEY, DAN, SPRINGLAKE, TEXAS, 1974–.

RAMAN, WILLIAM, HULL, IOWA, 1933–1934.

RICE, WILLIAM E., BALDWIN, KANSAS, 1974–.

RISE, J. E., SCRANTON, NORTH DAKOTA, 1931–1943.

SALLEE, EMMETT, BETHANY, MISSOURI, 1929.

SAUDER, W. O., CENTER, COLORADO, 1937–1946.

SCHAKEL, REUBEN H., PELLA, IOWA, 1942–1955.

SCHEELE, GUS, DIX, NEBRASKA, 1946–1947.

SCHLADWEILER, GREGOR J., PARKSTON, SOUTH DAKOTA, 1963–1967.

SCHMIDT, JOHN O., WAHOO, NEBRASKA, 1955–1958.

SCHMITZ, N. B., ANDALE, KANSAS, 1959–1970.

SCHRAMM, ALBERT, WINNER, SOUTH DAKOTA, 1967–.

SCHROEDER, ALLEN, LEIGH, NEBRASKA, 1973–.

SCHULTE, JOHN L., BELOIT, KANSAS, 1939–1972.

SCOTT, IVAN J., WINFIELD, KANSAS, 1941–1955.

SERVIS, O. C., WINFIELD, KANSAS, 1931–1941.

SHULTZ, REYNOLDS, LAWRENCE, KANSAS, 1965–1968.

SIGWING, A., MCCOOK, NEBRASKA, 1932–1935.

SINCLAIR, VAUGHN O., ST. JAMES, MINNESOTA, 1968–.

SKOOG, C. A., HOLDREGE, NEBRASKA, 1931.

SMITH, DOYLE N., FRUITA, COLORADO, 1974–.

SMITH, ROBERT C., YUMA, COLORADO, 1956–1962.

SNYDER, RALPH, MANHATTAN, KANSAS, 1932–1934.

SOLTER, W. J., LA GRANGE, MISSOURI, 1929–1930.

STEELE, C. G., BARNES, KANSAS, 1934–1937.

STRATTON, J. G., SR., CLINTON, OKLAHOMA, 1958–1970.

SUTTER, TED P., EATON, COLORADO, 1965–1977.

TE SELLE, RAYMOND E., FIRTH, NEBRASKA, 1945–1951.

THARP, E. G., PROTECTION, KANSAS, 1932–1945.

TOWNSEND, DWIGHT D., BADGER, IOWA, 1936–1942.

TORELL, BYRON, GRESHAM, NEBRASKA, 1958–1973.

TREMBLAY, PHIL A., SIOUX FALLS, SOUTH DAKOTA, 1954–1963.

TRIBBETT, CLAUDE, YUMA, COLORADO, 1936–1938.

UEHLING, ERNEST H., OAKLAND, NEBRASKA, 1940–1955.

VERT, D. E., MARYVILLE, MISSOURI, 1934–1936.

VOIGT, KEITH M., EAGLE GROVE, IOWA, 1970–.

VOTH, GEORGE, GARDEN CITY, KANSAS, 1959–1968.

WAUGH, ED M., CHEYENNE, WYOMING, 1938–1941.

WELCH, RICHARD, PARKSTON, SOUTH DAKOTA, 1954.

WELTY, GEORGE K., ESSEX, IOWA, 1952–1964.

WEST, JERE O., CRESCENT, OKLAHOMA, 1970–.

WHITE, ROLAND R., AURORA, NEBRASKA, 1968–1977.

WILHELM, ROY C., REDFIELD, SOUTH DAKOTA, 1948–1954.

WILLIAMS, DAVID L., VILLISCA, IOWA, 1975–.

WILLIAMS, GUY O., PEETZ, COLORADO, 1936.

WINTER, CLEM C., ANDALE, KANSAS, 1955–1959.
WITHAM, HARRY E., KANSAS CITY, MISSOURI, 1930–1935.
WRIGHT, WINTON W., BENEDICT, NEBRASKA, 1977–.
YEAGER, ARTHUR J., BRYAN, TEXAS, 1971–1974.
YOUNG, HOMER, LIBERTY, MISSOURI, 1961–1967.
YOUNG, HOWARD, DODGE CITY, KANSAS, 1968–1974.

FARMLAND INDUSTRIES, INC. CORPORATE FAMILY

Consolidated Subsidiaries*

CRA, Inc., Kansas City, Missouri. Petroleum refining, crude purchasing, pipeline operation.
CRA Oil Exploration Co. Oil, gas exploration, production.
Terra Resources, Inc., Tulsa, Oklahoma. Oil, gas exploration, production.
Northern Terra Resources, Inc. Canadian oil exploration.
Farmland International Energy Co., Houston, Texas. Oil, gas exploration and production.
Farmland Soy Processing, Inc. Soybean processing.
Far-Mar-Co, Inc., Hutchinson, Kansas. Grain marketing.
Farmland Foods, Inc., Kansas City, Missouri. Beef and pork processing, food marketing.
Porkland, Inc., Kansas City, Missouri. Real estate.
Farmland Food Services, Inc., Franklin Park, Illinois. Institutional food processing.
Farmland Agriservices, Inc., Kansas City, Missouri. Livestock, poultry purchasing.
Cooperative Farm Chemicals Association, Lawrence, Kansas. Nitrogen fertilizer manufacturing.
Farmers Chemical Company, Joplin, Missouri. Ammonium phosphate fertilizer production.
Farmland Insurance Agency, Inc., Kansas City, Missouri. Insurance for Farmland Industries, Inc., facilities.
Farmland Service Company, St. Paul, Minnesota. Auditing for local cooperatives in Minnesota.
Techne Corporation, Kansas City, Missouri. Nitrogen fertilizer storage, ag chemical sales.
Ceres Development Corporation, Kansas City, Missouri. Real estate.
Missouri Chemical Company, St. Joseph, Missouri. Formulator, distributor of ag chemical products.

* The consolidated subsidiaries are those whose business record is included in the annual report of Farmland Industries, Inc.

Farmland Securities Company, Kansas City, Missouri. Broker-Dealer.
Cooperative Service Company, Lincoln, Nebraska. Auditing, insurance, management service for local cooperatives.

Other Farmland Affiliations

CRA International, Ltd., Tulsa, Oklahoma. Oil, gas exploration, production.

The Cooperative Finance Assn., Inc., Kansas City, Missouri. Commodity, operating, facility loans for local co-ops.

Farmland Mutual Insurance Co., Des Moines, Iowa. Casualty, surety, liability, hospitalization insurance.

Farmland Life Insurance Company, Executive Offices, Kansas City, Missouri. Life insurance.

Farmland Insurance Company, Executive Offices, Kansas City, Missouri. Casualty insurance.

National Cooperative Refinery Assn., McPherson, Kansas. Petroleum refining, production, exploration.

Universal Cooperatives, Inc., Alliance, Ohio. Cooperative distribution of farm, home, automobile equipment.

Boone Valley Cooperative Processing Association, Eagle Grove, Iowa. Soybean, feed processing.

CF Industries, Inc., Chicago, Illinois. Cooperative fertilizer manufacturing.

Seaway Pipeline, Inc., Bartlesville, Oklahoma. Crude oil pipeline.

International Energy Cooperative, Inc., Washington, D.C. Oil exploration.

Kansas City Terminal Elevator Company, Kansas City, Missouri. Grain marketing.

Kansas Farmers Service Association, Hutchinson, Kansas. Auditing, insurance, management service for local cooperatives.

Farmers Export Company, Overland Park, Kansas. Export grain marketing.

FARMLAND INDUSTRIES, INC., AND CONSOLIDATED SUBSIDIARIES
CONSOLIDATED SALES AND SAVINGS
FOR THE FORTY-NINE YEARS ENDED AUGUST 31, 1977

Years	Farm Supplies	Consolidated Sales Grain Marketing	Food Marketing	Total	Consolidated Savings after Incentive and Minority Interest and before Income Taxes
		(amounts in thousands)			
1929	$ 310			$ 310	$ 5
1930	890			890	26
1931	981			981	46
1932	1,340			1,340	26

Years	Consolidated Sales				Consolidated Savings after Incentive and Minority Interest and before Income Taxes
	Farm Supplies	Grain Marketing	Food Marketing	Total	
	(amounts in thousands)				
1933	1,433			1,433	37
1934	2,019			2,019	51
1935	2,995			2,995	94
1936	3,756			3,756	60
1937	3,090 (eight months)			3,090	101
1938	4,285			4,285	88
1939	4,425			4,425	112
1940	6,211			6,211	152
1941	10,081			10,081	431
1942	14,427			14,427	695
1943	15,248			15,248	870
1944	16,388			16,388	1,980
1945	26,560			26,560	2,430
1946	26,244			26,244	2,112
1947	38,419			38,419	4,752
1948	54,071			54,071	8,386
1949	55,368			55,368	494
1950	62,428			62,428	511
1951	74,886			74,886	6,747
1952	82,442			82,442	2,837
1953	83,950			83,950	1,256
1954	85,740			85,740	318
1955	90,553			90,553	2,534
1956	97,622			97,622	5,819
1957	113,349			113,349	7,565
1958	129,280			129,280	5,226
1959	153,844			153,844	10,270
1960	168,006			168,006	8,869
1961	193,676			193,676	14,889
1962	215,490			215,490	13,492
1963	242,067			242,067	18,709
1964	249,157		484	249,641	16,782
1965	276,969		991	277,960	21,049
1966	329,383		748	330,131	23,123
1967	366,071		1,020	367,091	29,201
1968	375,759		14,902	390,661	16,161
1969	375,793		66,486	442,279	9,254
1970	440,212		189,591	629,803	19,719

Consolidated Sales and Savings (continued)

Years	Consolidated Sales				Consolidated Savings after Incentive and Minority Interest and before Income Taxes
	Farm Supplies	Grain Marketing	Food Marketing	Total	
	(amounts in thousands)				
1971	497,370		188,304	685,674	21,040
1972	537,797		214,768	752,565	19,800
1973	671,663		249,547	921,210	31,238
1974	974,797		277,460	1,252,257	98,260
1975	1,254,854		273,950	1,528,804	196,865
1976	1,507,429		355,077	1,862,506	105,980
1977	1,912,316	690,384	436,911	3,039,611	79,013
49-Year Total	$11,851,444	$690,384	$2,270,239	$14,812,067	$809,475

FARMLAND INDUSTRIES, INC., AND CONSOLIDATED SUBSIDIARIES
PATRONAGE REFUNDS PAID IN CASH
FOR THE FORTY-NINE YEARS ENDED AUGUST 31, 1977

Patronage Refunds Paid in Cash First Year:	Farm Supplies	Grain Marketing	Food Marketing	Total
		(amounts in thousands)		
1929	$ 0	$	$	$ 0
1930	7			7
1931	18			18
1932	17			17
1933	12			12
1934	15			15
1935	15			15
1936	18			18
1937	14			14
1938	17			17
1939	18			18
1940	17			17
1941	29			29
1942	19			19
1943	28			28
1944	30			30
1945	37			37
1946	31			31
1947	103			103
1948	62			62
1949	22			22

Patronage Refunds Paid in Cash (continued)

Patronage Refunds Paid in Cash First Year:	Farm Supplies	Grain Marketing	Food Marketing	Total
		(amounts in thousands)		
1950	0			0
1951	143			143
1952	75			75
1953	0			0
1954	203			203
1955	362			362
1956	639			639
1957	782			782
1958	488			488
1959	1,369			1,369
1960	1,302			1,302
1961	2,404			2,404
1962	2,095			2,095
1963	7,678			7,678
1964	6,162			6,162
1965	8,177			8,177
1966	9,798			9,798
1967	13,621			13,621
1968	6,070			6,070
1969	2,161			2,161
1970	7,024			7,024
1971	7,488		477	7,965
1972	7,386		347	7,733
1973	13,375		197	13,572
1974	43,942			43,942
1975	90,273		209	90,482
1976	48,567			48,567
1977	35,602	1,552	1,153	38,307
Total through 1977	$317,715	$1,552	$2,383	$321,650
Patronage Refunds Paid in Equities and Redeemed for Cash Through August 31, 1977	53,452	0	0	53,452
49-Year Total	$371,167	$1,552	$2,383	$375,102

Bibliographical Note

The history of Farmland Industries, Inc. is based mainly upon the company records. These materials include minutes of the meetings of the Board of Directors, minutes of shareholder meetings, annual reports, office memoranda, general correspondence, audits, the printed prospectuses filed with the Securities and Exchange Commission after 1949, pamphlets, speeches by company executives, and other kinds of material. The biweekly company newspaper also carried a wide variety of information on company activities. Beginning as the *Cooperative Consumer* in December, 1933, the newspaper later took the title of *Farmland*, and in 1971 it became *Farmland News*.

For the early history of Farmland Industries, the reports, speeches, and memoranda of Howard A. Cowden are most valuable. The company public-relations office also developed two large scrapbooks that contain many important printed and unprinted historical documents that relate to early company history. There is a large collection of photographs that reveal much about Farmland's historical growth and development. Besides examining a wide variety of records, numerous individuals connected with Farmland Industries during much of its history shared their ideas and experiences in personal interviews.

Scholarly literature on farmer cooperative developments is more limited than might be expected. Every reader, however, should begin with the works of Joseph G. Knapp who over the years has probably been the country's foremost authority on farmer cooperatives. His books include: *Farmers In Business* (Washington, 1963); *The Rise of American Cooperative Enterprise, 1620–1920* (Danville, Ill., 1969); *The Advance of American Cooperative Enterprise, 1920–1945* (Danville, Ill., 1973); and *Seeds That Grew: A History of the Cooperative Grange League Federation Exchange* (Hinsdale, New York, 1960), which is one of the better cooperative business histories.

Martin A. Abrahamsen's *Cooperative Business Enterprise* (New York, 1976) is a valuable study that shows very well how farmer cooperatives operate. *Agricultural Cooperation: Selected Readings* by Martin A. Abrahamsen and Claud L. Scroggs (Minneapolis, 1957) also contains much useful material. Florence E. Parker has written an excellent book on cooperative developments in her book, *The First 125 Years: A History of Distributive and Service Cooperation in the United States, 1829–1954* (Superior, Wis., 1956). Other helpful studies include Roland S. Vaile, editor, *Consumers' Cooperatives in the North Central States* (Minneapolis, 1941); Joseph G. Knapp and John H. Lister, *Cooperative Purchasing of Farm Supplies*, Farm Credit Administration Bulletin No. 1 (Washington, 1935); and Harlan J. Randall and Clay J. Daggett, *Consumers' Cooperative Adventures: Case Studies* (Whitewater, Wis., 1936). Every student of cooperation will want to consult "The Cooperative League of the United States of America, 1916–1961: A Study of Social Theory and Social Action," by Clarke A. Chambers in *Agricultural History*, XXXVI (April, 1962), 59–81.

The history of another regional cooperative wholesale has been studied by Norman Eugene Taylor in "The Midland Cooperative Wholesale, Inc.: Its History and Analysis," a doctoral dissertation done at the University of Minnesota in 1955. Finally, a great variety of materials on cooperative activities and ideas can be found in *American Cooperation*, a volume published annually by the American Institute of Cooperation since 1925.

Index